AMERICAN ENLIGHTENMENTS

The Lewis Walpole Series in Eighteenth-Century Culture and History

The Lewis Walpole Series, published by Yale University Press with the aid of the Annie Burr Lewis Fund, is dedicated to the culture and history of the long eighteenth century (from the Glorious Revolution to the accession of Queen Victoria). It welcomes work in a variety of fields, including literature and history, the visual arts, political philosophy, music, legal history, and the history of science. In addition to original scholarly work, the series publishes new editions and translations of writing from the period, as well as reprints of major books that are currently unavailable. Though the majority of books in the series will probably concentrate on Great Britain and the Continent, the range of our geographical interests is as wide as Horace Walpole's.

AMERICAN ENLIGHTENMENTS

Pursuing Happiness in the Age of Reason

CAROLINE WINTERER

Yale

UNIVERSITY PRESS

New Haven and London

Published with assistance from the Annie Burr Lewis Fund.

Published with assistance from the foundation established in memory
of Calvin Chapin of the Class of 1788, Yale College.

Yale University Press books may be purchased in quantity for educational,
business, or promotional use. For information, please e-mail
sales.press@yale.edu (U.S. office) or sales@yaleup.co.uk (U.K. office).

Set in Janson type by IDS Infotech Ltd., Chandigarh, India.
Printed in the United States of America.

Library of Congress Control Number: 2016937262
ISBN 978-0-300-19257-5 (hardcover: alk. paper)

A catalogue record for this book is available from the British Library.

This paper meets the requirements of ANSI/NISO Z39.48-1992
(Permanence of Paper).

10 9 8 7 6 5 4 3 2 1

For Kurt, Julia, and Nicholas
with love

Contents

Acknowledgments

It is a pleasure to thank the many friends and colleagues who gave their time and energy over the years as I worked on this book.

I owe an enormous debt of gratitude to Mark Peterson and James Turner. Both read and made extensive comments on each chapter as I finished it. Their suggestions have improved the book immeasurably. Thanks to Jennifer Ratner-Rosenhagen, Daniel Rodgers, Mark Peterson, and Jonathan Gienapp for reading the whole manuscript and then participating in a three-hour seminar at Stanford University in September 2015 dedicated to analyzing the book's central claims and improving the argument. All entered cheerfully into the spirit of what I was trying to do and gave me many superb suggestions for revision.

A number of other colleagues commented on individual chapters or in some way entered substantively into the conceptual architecture of the book. Many thanks to Keith Baker, Mary Elizabeth Berry, Jennifer Burns, Leslie Butler, Giovanna Ceserani, Francis Cogliano, John Dixon, Dan Edelstein, Paula Findlen, Estelle Freedman, Nils Gilman, David Hollinger, Sarah Igo, Joel Isaac, James Kloppenberg, Christopher Krebs, Emily Levine, Suzanne Marchand, Carol McKibben, the late Michael O'Brien, Jessica Riskin, Daniel Rosenberg, Dorothy Ross, James Sheehan, David Grant Smith, Amy Dru Stanley, Richard White, and Kären Wigen. Two of the anonymous readers for Yale University Press provided extremely helpful suggestions for revision. I thank my editor at Yale,

Steve Wasserman, for ably shepherding the manuscript through its final stages. Susan Laity of Yale copyedited the manuscript with magnificent skill and sound judgment.

Over the years I have presented aspects of this book in various settings, and I thank the many participants who improved the manuscript with their ideas and suggestions: the Department of History at the University of California, Berkeley; the Representing Time workshop at the Stanford Humanities Center; the Futures of Atlantic Intellectual History conference at Harvard University; the Republic of Letters in North America conference at the Huntington Library; the Let There Be Enlightenment conference at Stanford University; the Department of History at Stanford; the Bay Area Seminar in Early American History and Culture; and the Humanities Center at the University of Rochester.

Colleagues at the Stanford University Library are a constant source of help on research matters large and small. I am especially grateful to Becky Fischbach, John Mustain, and Benjamin Stone for their expertise and kindness over the years. Scott Spillman, who is completing his dissertation in the Department of History at Stanford, secured the illustrations and permissions; I thank him for going about these tasks with his usual superhuman efficiency and competence. My wonderful colleagues at the Stanford Humanities Center make coming to work each day a pleasure. Special thanks to Susan Sebbard for daily doses of good cheer.

Barrett Moore and Sherril Green listened to my various ideas on long hikes among the redwoods and banana slugs of the Santa Cruz mountains; they are partially responsible for maintaining my optimism and sanity as I directed a large research institute and wrote a book. My family is an endless source of encouragement. I especially thank my parents, Jacqueline Mammerickx Winterer and Edward L. Winterer; my sister, Juliette Winterer; and my nieces, Amelia and Linnea Wright. My love for the three delightful people who lived with this book and its author every day is reflected on the dedication page.

AMERICAN ENLIGHTENMENTS

Introduction: American Enlightenments

URING THE SECOND HALF of the eighteenth century, some of the most articulate and reflective inhabitants of British America began to think of themselves as *enlightened* and of their era as an *enlightened age*. To these people, becoming enlightened meant using reason and empirical data as their guides rather than inherited tradition or biblical revelation. Yearning for a day when humanity would be happier than it was now or had ever been in the past, they hoped that through sheer human effort tomorrow's sun would rise over a more just, prosperous, and peaceful earth. They now turned to an array of long-standing interests—in nature, history, population, farming, society, religion, political economy, and government—and set about trying to approach them in ways they called enlightened. To be enlightened was to be filled with hope. This book is about those hopeful people in British America and what became the new United States.

Today, we do not necessarily agree that these self-anointed enlightened people made the world a better place. We wonder how they dared call themselves enlightened when they left so much misery and injustice in the world, and when some of the projects they put into motion appear to us to have yielded such ambiguous or even tragic results. We consider them hypocritical, pompous, or self-deluded because they did not deliver on their promises. But our duty to the past is not to judge it; our duty is to understand it. In this book I neither celebrate nor condemn these first prophets of tomorrow. Instead, I reconstruct the world as they saw it, showing how enlightenment was felt, perceived, and lived during the moment when the idea first captured the imaginations of a motley group of people living on the fringes of the British Empire, people who communicated intensively and feverishly with interested others scattered across the Americas and Europe.

Nowhere was enlightenment a formal political program, nor were the enlightened a sharply defined group. Rather, enlightenment was a process of becoming, a way of imagining the relationship of the present to the past. According to people who imagined themselves to be enlightened, the present should be better than the past and the future better than the present. They now routinely began to say that they lived in an enlightened age, in which the light of reason and science would free humanity from the darkness of the Middle Ages, when popes and kings had shackled humanity to ignorance and bigotry. Around Europe, in many languages, others found similar terms to describe the sense that a new dawn was breaking, filling the world with the light that would show humankind the way forward to a happier future. The enlightened age formed the pinnacle of a homogeneous chronology of historical time stretching from the very deepest human antiquity to the present. This secular, historical time became the new framework in which human society and action were contained and understood. Other chronologies, such as the cosmic eternity described in the Bible, now receded in importance without ever being entirely displaced. People who thought themselves enlightened were acutely self-conscious of their era and their own self-imposed duty to promote the improvement of future ages. What good was the enlightenment of the eighteenth century, asked J. Hector St. Jean de Crèvecoeur in his salute to the American potato, if it did not help us see and adopt everything the genius of man had invented for the happiness of humanity?[1]

The happiness of humanity. Crèvecoeur's words—and Thomas Jefferson's far more famous ones in the Declaration of Independence, "Life, Liberty, and the pursuit of Happiness"—remind us that the pursuit of happiness was one of the principal quests of enlightened people. But happiness meant something different in the eighteenth century from its meaning today. In our era, an industry of self-help books reminds us that modern happiness is an emotional state of self-fulfillment and personal well-being. Eighteenth-century people would have been puzzled by our narrow definition. For them, happiness first of all had expansive, public meanings. People at that time often spoke of a happy people and a happy society. A society was happy when its people enjoyed the security, stability, and peace that allowed them to prosper. The purpose of government was to create public or social happiness by shielding the state from foreign enemies and internal threats. The opposite of public happiness was not sorrow but anarchy or tyranny. Educated leaders would be the architects of the good government that led to a happy society. But since it was never known which data would become most relevant to what John Adams called "the science of social happiness," many realms of knowledge—nature, religion, art, literature, and politics—awaited exploration.[2] Once achieved, social happiness freed people to go about seeking private happiness, a way of life that serenely balanced the intellectual and moral faculties. Private happiness might include the opportunity for advancement in the earthly realm, harmony around the family hearth, and perhaps even a glimpse of the eternal happiness of heaven. The people I discuss in this book hoped that enlightenment would yield both kinds of happiness, public and private.

Could anything be more exhilarating than the new idea of enlightenment? People now felt free to build the world anew, as though endowed with the power of creation itself. Precisely for this reason, enlightenment was also frightening. The past had always been a source of wisdom and comfort, for there lay the great civilizations of Egypt, Greece, and Rome, the patriarchs and mighty kings of the Bible, and before all these God himself conjuring the earth from nothing. But now a new idea emerged, that people might improve on that past, on what God had given and what kings and popes had decreed. Wielding the gleaming razor of human reason, sharpened by empirical evidence, common sense, and withering sarcasm, they would slash away at traditions that rested on nothing but the dust of convention and privilege. Staking

claim to the existing term *enlightened* and deploying it for new purposes, forward-looking people in the eighteenth century imagined
that it was their particular duty to apply reason to the continual
improvement of human society. This was a daunting task, placing a
new responsibility for social transformation on the shoulders of
human beings who, like Atlas, sometimes staggered under the
weight of it all. Thus the people who called themselves enlightened
were restless rather than calm, doubtful rather than self-assured.
They squabbled endlessly about everything, especially about what
enlightenment was and how to achieve it.

This was not just a clash of titans, a war waged in canonical
texts and solemn founding documents. Nor was it only the disputation of philosophers, floating elegantly in an ether of abstractions.
To be sure, enlightenment did not involve, let alone acknowledge,
everyone. But what is astonishing is the sheer variety of people
who began to insist that things might be seen or done differently:
mapmakers, artists, farmers, physicians, ministers, astronomers, poets, diplomats, novelists, and many others joined in the large, baggy
conversation of enlightenment. In scrawled marginalia and hasty
sketches as much as in somber tomes and blistering pamphlets,
Americans from many quarters poured out their excitement, their
awe, their wonder at the possibility that they might set the world
on fire. That they pinned their hopes to endeavors that in some
cases seem strangely unexalted or obscure to us today—the origin
of fossil shells, the meaning of Aztec temples, the proper manure
ratios for planting turnips—reminds us that the great undertaking
of enlightenment in eighteenth-century America that seems so familiar to us today has in many ways slipped from our fingers.

In this book I restore what eighteenth-century Americans themselves meant by enlightenment. Doing so requires that we scrape
away the many barnacles that have glued themselves to the idea of
enlightenment in the past two centuries so that we can actually see
and hear what eighteenth-century people are telling us.

Nowhere is this more difficult than in the United States, where
the idea of the *American Enlightenment* enjoys a quasi-mythical
status. We are accustomed to speaking of a phenomenon called
the American Enlightenment as though it were a concrete event.

But the term did not exist in the eighteenth century; it was invented in the United States immediately after World War II to sooth Americans' fears about the rise of totalitarian regimes abroad. A kind of historical containment doctrine, the idea of an American Enlightenment proposed the founding moment of the United States as the cradle of an ideological heritage of freedom and democracy that would shield the modern nation from the looming ideological threats most menacingly embodied by the Soviet Union.[3]

The first to popularize this idea was the historian Adrienne Koch, who singled out what she called the Big Five founders—John Adams, Benjamin Franklin, Thomas Jefferson, Alexander Hamilton, and James Madison—as representatives of the "vision" and "spirit" that underlay the "free society" and "democratic civilization" of modern America. In Koch's view, the political drama of the American Revolution formed the center of the American Enlightenment, and she argued publicly that Enlightenment ideals remained of the utmost relevance in the twentieth century. "Although some radicals today shout obscenities at the great American revolutionary states-men," she wrote in the *New York Times* in 1970, during the height of American protests against the Vietnam War, "they count on the protection of the principles of free speech, equal opportunity and individual liberty the revolutionary leaders bequeathed to us."[4] We should appreciate our American Enlightenment, she seemed to say, the way we appreciate vaccines and other modern wonders that protect us from threats to the American way.

The idea of an American Enlightenment remains enormously powerful, appealing, and influential to Americans today. What a contrast to Europe, where ambivalence reigns about the historical era the twentieth century christened "the Enlightenment." With one world war behind them and more ominous clouds gathering, Europeans of the 1930s—and American scholars of Europe—drew a straight line from the Enlightenment to the horrors of commu-nism and totalitarianism, now seen as the bitter harvest of eighteenth-century rationalism and scientism. In *The Heavenly City of the Eighteenth-Century Philosophers* (1932), Carl Becker invoked the contemporary relevance of the Russian Revolution and the menacing advance of communism abroad. From the bleak preci-pice of early 1930s Germany, Ernst Cassirer too sent out a distress signal, calling on the Enlightenment to save modernity from itself. "More than ever before, it seems to me," wrote Cassirer in *The Philosophy of the Enlightenment* (1932), "the time is again ripe for applying such self-criticism to the present age, for holding up to it that bright clear mirror fashioned by the Enlightenment." Since that moment, Europeans have had a combative relationship with their Enlightenment, one that nurtures a flourishing industry of bracing reinterpretations that are often as critical of the present as they are of the past.[5]

By contrast, the American Enlightenment is foundational to modern Americans' sense of themselves as a people of progress. Foundational arguments assume a solid base on which to support their conclusions, and Americans have chosen to ground their Enlightenment in the patriotic pride of the founding moment of the republic. Americans generally greet their Enlightenment with sunny enthusiasm as the nursery of American freedom. Since the post–World War II era, they have diagnosed modern problems as deviations from the upward trajectory of enlightenment rather than predictable eruptions of its latent hypocrisies and ironies. The sociologist Robert Bellah, who in 1967 popularized the idea of civil religion, invoked the secular saints Benjamin Franklin, George Washington, and Thomas Jefferson as embodiments of an enduring and particularly American mix of Protestantism and enlightenment. "The words and acts of the founding fathers," he argued, "especially the first few presidents, shaped the form and tone of the civil religion as it has been maintained ever since." For historians of the Civil Rights era such as David Brion Davis, American slavery fundamentally contradicted the so-called "meaning of America" as a promised land of freedom and hope. Tacking American slavery onto the grand historical canvas of Western Civilization itself, Davis maintained that an alleged "problem of slavery" had afflicted the West from the ancient Greeks on, a problem that the morally charged climate of the Enlightenment had raised into high relief. In 1995, the philosopher John Gray singled out the United States as the exception to his otherwise depressing assessment of the legacies of the Enlightenment "project" (a term invented in the 1980s by Jürgen Habermas and Alasdair MacIntyre to take stock of the Enlightenment's unsettling moral consequences). "In the late modern period in which we live," wrote Gray, "the Enlightenment project is affirmed chiefly for fear of the consequences of abandoning it. Except in the United States, where it has the status of a civil religion, it carries little positive conviction."[6]

Today, many Americans proudly call themselves enlightened in their attitudes toward everything from race to government to God. Like the French economist writing to Thomas Jefferson, they hold themselves to a high standard of laborious national progress rooted in an unwavering faith in the timeless nobility of the American Enlightenment. "My friend," wrote Pierre Samuel du Pont de Nemours to Jefferson, "we are snails and we have a mountain range to climb. By God, we must climb it!"[7]

But do the little snails now scale the mountain range for the same reasons their eighteenth-century ancestors did? The trouble with a label such as "the American Enlightenment" is that it determines in advance—and according to our modern preferences—which ideas qualify as enlightened rather than using the vocabulary of the eighteenth-century actors themselves. The term throws a screen of modern expectation onto the eighteenth century that clouds our ability to see the complex and contradictory processes of enlightenment that were in fact at work. While the idea of a unitary American Enlightenment remains powerfully appealing today, in fact it is American *enlightenments* that more accurately reflect the multiple strands of conversation that cohered around the conviction that human reason might be applied to better the human condition.

For this reason, I do not use the terms *the Enlightenment* and *the American Enlightenment* (capitalized) except when discussing them as twentieth-century concepts. Nor do the words *radical, conservative, moderate, democratic,* and *revolutionary* appear in this book to describe the process of becoming enlightened since they were not used in this way during the eighteenth century. Modern terms such as *radical enlightenment* risk putting eighteenth-century actors into categories that they themselves would not have recognized, smothering the past with our modern hopes and dreams. The word *radical* in the eighteenth century, for example, usually meant fundamental rather than extreme; nor did it refer to a person holding politically or religiously polarizing views.[8]

This charged vocabulary also concocts genealogies between the present and the past that are not supported by the historical evidence. Even if the word *enlightened* has persisted today, the lineages connecting the eighteenth-century people who called their initiatives and themselves enlightened are not always clearly connected to the projects and attitudes we call enlightened today. The surest link between the two eras is the genealogical impulse itself. Like self-described enlightened people two centuries ago, we insist on our own modernity by pointing to our emancipation from the barbaric practices that allegedly tarnished earlier epochs. We define and celebrate our modernity in similar terms to those first invented in the eighteenth century, the first in human history to call itself enlightened.

We should also avoid the term *counter-Enlightenment*, another twentieth-century coinage, because it suggests a unified and coherent bloc of opposition to those who hoped for enlightenment.[9] Self-described enlightened people in the eighteenth century spied enemies around every corner: papal and monarchical absolutism, superstition and fanaticism, religious violence, and an array of human behaviors they deemed barbarous and backward. But for whatever reason, people at the time never called the totality of these alleged evils a counter-Enlightenment, though on rare occasions they called people who held such views unenlightened, a rather less ominous formulation. And part of the hopeful goal of enlightenment was to imagine that anything and anyone could be improved: monarchs could be reformed to become *enlightened despots*, a term that was in fact coined and broadly current in the eighteenth century; barbarians could be schooled to join the ranks of the *civilized*, a term that also flourished from the eighteenth century on.

Our best guide to what enlightenment meant in the eighteenth century is the word used by people at that time: *enlightened*. Something remarkable happened to this word in the middle of the eighteenth century. For centuries, it had described the religious experience of the soul being illuminated by the grace of God. This older, religious meaning of enlightenment stretched back into antiquity, when the sun was an object of worship and a metaphor for truth, as in Plato's parable of the cave. Christianity had joined this to the belief that the human soul was filled with light by God through the act of salvation, and many people, from ministers to pamphleteers, from the seventeenth century through the nineteenth continued to understand enlightenment in this way.

But suddenly in the second half of the eighteenth century English speakers invented a battery of new uses for the words *enlightened* and, to a lesser extent, *enlightenment*. Every conceivable facet of life—from politics to society to science to religion itself—seemed ripe for improvement through the process of becoming enlightened. Now, the older meaning of *enlightened* as an awakening of the soul to the light of salvation was joined to a more corporeal, empirical meaning—of light as illuminating the natural world so that humans could perceive it with their senses and thereby gain knowledge of an external world whose authority was grounded in God but also in the new, primal truths of the laws of nature and society. Isaac Newton's *Opticks* (1704) explained the general physical properties of light and then applied these insights to the human realm by focusing on the eye. Newton's physics could literally light the way: after Newton, exclaimed the poet Alexander Pope, "all was light." Moral philosophers soon declared sight to be chief among the five senses because it illuminated—or enlightened—the human experience by giving people direct access to knowledge of the outside world. Thomas Reid's widely admired *An Inquiry into the Human Mind, on the Principles of Common Sense* (1764) called the human eye "a masterpiece of nature's work," and sight the "noblest" of the five senses. In league with the other four senses, sight helped human beings gain experience of the world around them and thereby understand it. Reid called the process of acquiring knowledge "experience enlightened by the inductive principle."[10]

Now perceived by newly enlightened eyes, projects that had lain inchoate over the previous decades seemed to demand immediate reform through political, scientific, economic, or social change. Armed with the new idea of enlightenment—that purposeful human effort and reason could yield positive good in this world—Americans set about changing their world. The constant lexical companion of the new idea of enlightenment was not *radical* or *revolutionary* or *democratic*, but instead the urgent *now* that fills the era's pamphlets and manifestos, spurring whole peoples to throw off the habits of mind that seemed to shackle them to a dark, oppressive past.

The "enlightened now" played out differently in every realm of thought, however, and the chapters in this book reflect my desire to give these different chronologies free rein. Instead of starting with what we today think enlightened thinking should have been, I probe the topics people in eighteenth-century British America corresponded most intensively and passionately about when they talked about becoming enlightened. The chapters are representative rather than comprehensive: they are core samples of eighteenth-century conversations about matters considered particularly enlightened at the time. The chapters appear in an order that would have made sense to a person living in the eighteenth century who was influenced both by the Bible and new, secular theories of social development. Beginning with ideas about the creation of the earth and the growth of human societies, I go on to consider the rival concepts of religion, political economy, and government that gripped those who yearned for enlightenment.

I also depart from conventional understandings of American enlightenment by rejecting the idea that enlightenment was hatched in Europe and then traveled to the Americas. The diffusionist theory of the American Enlightenment flourished during the bicentennial of the American Revolution. Twentieth-century European historians had by now anointed the Enlightenment as a Europe-centered phenomenon in magisterial syntheses such as Peter Gay's two-volume *The Enlightenment: An Interpretation* (1966, 1969), which announced the dependence of the American revolutionaries on Europe: "The substance of their ideas came from a handful of European thinkers." Even historians who took a dim view of the legacies of enlightenment, particularly Max Horkheimer and Theodor Adorno in the wake of the calamities of World War II, accepted that its origins and career lay primarily in Europe. In these tellings, Americans were relegated to the role of latecomers, rustic savants who received the airy ideas of the Europe-based Enlightenment and then pragmatically put them to work, like blacksmiths hammering rugged tools from the golden filaments of the gods. These scholars saw the Europe-based ideas of enlightenment most dramatically realized in the American Revolution, an event they celebrated as the great achievement of the bustling Americans. As Peter Gay put it, the United States saw "the program of enlightenment in practice" and thereafter became an "exporter" of ideas to Europe. The three major works on the American Enlightenment to emerge from the 1970s reinforced the diffusionist paradigm: Donald Meyer's *The Democratic Enlightenment* (1976), Henry May's *The Enlightenment in America* (1976), and Henry Steele Commager's *The Empire of Reason* (1977). As Commager put it, the Old World "imagined, invented, and formulated" the Enlightenment; the Anglo-American New World "realized it and fulfilled it."[11]

Two major problems bedevil the diffusionist theory of enlightenment from European center to American periphery. First, it neglects the links that tied Europe and the Americas together from the late fifteenth century on. In an age when the letter was the only readily available technology for distance communication, thousands of correspondence chains connected people around the Atlantic, allowing for deep intellectual and emotional relationships to form among learned people across large distances. The open-ended, inquisitive, and doubting spirit of enlightened people was born in part from the letter form itself. In letters, people could venture new ideas, ponder strange possibilities, and juggle uncertainties more freely than in publications. With letters arrived other things: boxes of caterpillars, military intelligence, careful instructions for the circulation of the letter to a learned society, perhaps a squirrel, sometimes a microscope, often a young person needing an introduction in either Europe or America. These correspondence chains record every human emotion and ambition imaginable: they are by turns charismatic and scheming, selfless and vindictive, informative and tight-lipped. Yet across many decades, these distant people developed projects of mutual illumination and clarification, such that between the first moment of contact in 1492 and the eighteenth century many people knew much more about one another than they ever had before in the history of the world.

In the English-speaking world, this traffic of things, ideas, and people gave rise to the new vocabulary of enlightenment that saturates the written record of the period after 1760. But never did enlightened ideas cross the Atlantic just once: instead, books, magazines, letters, people, and a variety of objects from mosses to moose antlers crossed that ocean numerous times, small scraps of larger conversations among a great variety of people on a great variety of topics that developed and changed over time. Always the process of becoming enlightened was a confusing tangle of influences rather than the realization of European ideals in the drama of the American Revolution. Downgrading the American Revolution as the core of Americans' enlightenment also requires that we decenter pragmatism and practicality as singularly American achievements. But as Benjamin Franklin realized when he donned a beaver-skin cap in France, the idea of rustic American practicality was primarily a front to serve Europeans' self-perceptions as exalted philosophes rather than a self-evident truth about Americans.

More fundamentally, the diffusionist theory neglects the essential role the Americas played in the rise of the idea of enlightenment in the first place. It was in part through contact with the Americas that Europeans first began to grope toward the idea that alternatives to their long-held political and religious convictions were possible. Enlightenment was a phenomenon of the age of empires: imperialism was the constant companion of the idea of enlightenment, not incidental to it. The European colonies in the Americas were vast, transforming peoples, states, and tribes. At the most basic level, empires needed to be understood by their builders, and by the seventeenth century states had found new ways of measuring and assessing them. These bore spectacular fruit in the eighteenth century as self-styled enlightened programs of governance. Eventually the first sustained criticisms of the imperial mission itself emerged from the rising chorus of enlightenment, the snake gobbling up its own tail.[12] Thus enlightenment by the eighteenth century had become thoroughly bound up in questions of state power.

But the web of empire also captured imaginations, those capricious sallies of the human heart and mind. The expanded world of trade, of material comfort and wealth, of ethnographic, botanical, and zoological diversity—all these factors redefined the way Europeans experienced the local situation of Europe. Their Atlantic port cities now swollen with the traffic in slaves and sugar, their cabinets and museums stuffed with American curiosities, seventeenth- and eighteenth-century Europeans awoke each day to the different possibilities opened by two centuries of colonization and exploration, of novelty and transformation, of accumulating wonders that stirred their hearts and fired their imaginations.

Developments that so often seem peripheral to accounts of enlightenment in Europe in fact deeply preoccupied European thinkers, who grappled with their philosophical, moral, political, and economic implications. The Americas changed many things for Europeans, even their sense of where they stood in time. "Thus in the beginning all the World was *America*, and more so than that is now," John Locke wrote in his *Second Treatise*, a text whose vision of the first, primordial human societies was dependent on Locke's secondhand knowledge of the American setting.[13] Yet these concerns have tended to remain marginal in many accounts of enlightenment in Europe, as though it can continue to be understood as a self-contained, autonomous process, with non-European regions tacked on as afterthoughts.

What then was American about enlightenment? For the American historians writing at the bicentennial in 1976, the most important feature of what they called the American Enlightenment was its overwhelmingly religious and specifically Protestant quality. Their reasoning went something like this: Unlike France, where godless revolutionaries dedicated to the austere Cult of Reason had converted cathedrals into Temples of Reason, in British America Protestant ministers had cheerfully climbed onto their wooden pulpits to broadcast their moral and political opposition to Britain. These ministers invoked what they called the sacred cause of liberty, weaving revelation and reason together to endorse political revolution based on ideals they called enlightened. Armed with the definition of religion set forth by the anthropologist Clifford Geertz—that religion was not a strongbox of specific creeds but a set of symbols endowed with supreme authority and motivating power—American historians such as Henry May envisioned the American Enlightenment not as anti-religion but instead "*as* religion."[14] Thus whatever gray, soulless regimes of centralized control the Kremlin might be plotting, mid-century Americans could take comfort in their American antidote, the national legacy of mixing Protestant religion and enlightened rationalism.

It is certainly true that Protestants formed an overwhelming majority of European colonists in British America. Of the roughly thirty-two hundred communities of worship in the British American colonies in 1775, only about sixty were Catholic churches, and five were Jewish synagogues.[15] But other local factors also shaped the career of ideas considered enlightened in the eighteenth century.

First, although Europeans participated actively in the slave trade, plantation slavery itself was a phenomenon of the Americas, where it was lived, felt, and experienced on a daily basis by millions of people. On the eve of the American Revolution, approximately one in every five people living in British North America was a slave; in the British Caribbean, slaves formed a substantial majority of the population. What to do about slaves and slavery in an era that promised human progress remained one of the central preoccupations of Americans who considered themselves enlightened.

The presence and pressure of American Indians also deeply influenced enlightened trains of thought. In the eighteenth century, Indians still far outnumbered any European population in the Americas, and still formed a substantial population within British America and the early United States even as their numbers were plummeting from disease and warfare. Their religions and languages formed a patchwork of diversity rivaled nowhere in Europe. Information about Indians in North and South America profoundly shaped the new theories of social evolution undergirding the thought of people who considered themselves enlightened. Based in part on data culled from the Americas, these new theories were developed not just in Europe (particularly among the Scots), but among intellectuals in eighteenth-century British and Spanish America, who now for the first time opened direct north-south lines of communication with one another and founded the first archives of manuscripts and books by and about the indigenous peoples of the New World.

Similarly, New World animals and plants both as commodities and curiosities transformed transatlantic conversations about the nature of life. Was America really a fetid swamp crawling with colossal insects and reptiles, as some European scientists declared? Did an elephant-like creature, its fearsome bones wrested from North American mud, still stalk the land? While these debates raged among natural philosophers, American commodities quietly revolutionized daily life around the Atlantic. The Americas pumped the Old World full of sugar, chocolate, coffee, and tobacco, luxuries that became necessities, ensuring that oceanic trade and its protection rose to the forefront of every national agenda from Britain to France to Spain to Russia as political economy developed as a major strand of enlightened thought.

And whereas the cushioned courts of Europe buzzed with princes and courtiers, not a single royal foot stepped onto American soil before the nineteenth century. "Kings We never had among Us, Nobles We never had," John Adams correctly observed of a land bereft of the many institutions of aristocratic patronage that had nurtured European political and intellectual life since the Renaissance.[16] The experience of long-lasting, distant colonization by monarch-led empires forced a raft of new ideas onto the agendas of colonists in the Americas and interested observers back in Europe. What was this new species, the globe-spanning commercial empire, and was the venerable institution of monarchy the best vehicle for delivering political and intellectual enlightenment to large numbers of people?

Confronted with a flood of novelties from the Americas and elsewhere, minds around the Atlantic searched for solid ground. They found it in nature. Nature was everywhere at this time, both as a stand-alone word and as part of a new or revitalized compound such as human nature, Nature's God, natural man, natural rights, natural religion, and the state of nature. But though they sometimes seemed to use *nature* to mean anything and everything, people at this time in fact shared some common presuppositions about what the word meant, meanings that are different enough from our own that it is worth recapturing them with some precision.

In this pre-Darwinian era, commentators especially emphasized the teleology of nature. Like God, nature wanted certain things: it was a transcendent, inexorable, and active force that operated from the creation of the universe to the present. Nature existed outside of human beings as ultimate creator, value giver, and moral arbiter of the universe, but it also dwelled within every person as the essential, shared quality that both granted and demarcated his or her humanity. These three realms—the human, the divine, and the earthly/cosmological—were not strictly differentiated in these understandings of nature, and thinkers constantly mixed metaphors from all three domains. Natural law, for example, which was inherited from the ancient world and rose to new prominence in the seventeenth and eighteenth centuries, mixed the ideas of human law as socially created, divine law as given, and the nonhuman, transcendent world of nature.[17]

Coping with an avalanche of the new, British Americans leaped headfirst into transatlantic debates about nature as a guide, arbiter, and helpmeet for changing the world. They pondered the essential qualities that made up the new, precultural entity they were calling human nature; helped shape the new science of political economy, which promised to illuminate the ostensibly natural laws governing commerce and statecraft; contributed essential data about the origins of the earth in nature and humanity's staircase-like progression upon it from a state of nature to a state of civilization; and wrote feverishly about how certain natural rights were essential for achieving a full humanity within the context of society. Finally, they worried about God's place in a natural world in which happiness increasingly seemed attainable in the short span of a human life rather than in the eternity beyond the portal of death.[18]

The unsparing sunrise of enlightened reason left few corners untouched. The imagery of light, ascent, and order filled the textual and pictorial archive of the era. There would be tables and pie charts, clean lines scrubbed of despotic ornamentation, words and images married in new ways to spur urgent programs of action. Electricity, candles, glowing orbs, piercing shafts of sunlight, golden silks and wallpapers: the empire of the color yellow knew few frontiers in the eighteenth century. As darkness became a sign of social and natural disorder as much as a moral failing, invisibility became the only refuge from the enlightened eye. To be uncounted, untabulated, uncharted, unnamed, unseen, or unnoticed could be a curse but also a blessing for those who lived at the edges of enlightenment.

Thus the projects of enlightened Americans were not just hopeful but also human: flawed, limited, and blinkered by time and place. Doubt rather than certainty was the constant companion of enlightened hope. Seventeenth-century Calvinists had doubted whether the feeble efforts of human beings could ever result in salvation in the world beyond. In the late eighteenth century, enlightened Americans doubted whether humans could create perfect societies and human happiness in this world. They struggled when the evidence of their senses and experience betrayed them or failed to point to a clear answer. Regularly sensing the limits of their evidence and their abilities, they just as regularly wrote about their failure to know. They were not the last Americans to ponder the phenomenon of known unknowns, but they were surely some of its earliest and most eloquent witnesses. In essay 37 of *The Federalist*, James Madison despaired of humans ever fully grasping the truths of nature or the institutions created by man, considering the "imperfection of the eye which surveys them" and the "imperfection of the human faculties" more generally. Even God's words, luminously arrayed in the Bible, were likely to be distorted by the "cloudy medium" of the book form, vague vocabulary, and shoddy human reason. We should be modest about what was possible for human beings to accomplish on this earth, moderating "our expectations and hopes from the efforts of human sagacity."[19]

If the enlightened did not realize all their dreams during their lifetimes, they took comfort in the certainty that future generations would also put their shoulders to the wheel. Human time was nothing to God, who would watch patiently as his children eventually covered the earth, becoming as happy as human nature permitted. The French economist who had invoked the mountain-climbing snails turned once again to the tiniest of creatures to remind Jefferson to take the long view of enlightenment. It was our childish impatience that demanded that tomorrow's happiness arrive today, wrote Du Pont de Nemours when both men were in their sixties. "We are but poor ants, so let us content ourselves with having carried our kernel of millet to the nest, and die while fetching the next one."[20]

It is easy to condemn the first generation of Americans who called themselves enlightened, to mock their extravagant optimism, their paradoxes and contradictions, their blindness to what they refused to see or failed to foresee, the heartbreaking quantum of misery and injustice they left in the world as they went to their graves. Yet they too saw the size of the task before them and quietly went to fetch the next kernel.

CHAPTER ONE

The American Setting

"HOW CAN I WRITE a journal in the complete absence of everything that could make it interesting?" a French visitor wondered as he visited revolutionary America, a land bereft of palaces, temples, classical ruins, and notable artists and musicians.[1] Not everyone would have agreed that America lacked everything interesting, but the French visitor was correct in identifying North America as a land that was utterly different from Europe in the realm of intellectual and artistic life. The American setting for the ideas that became known as enlightened helped determine what could be imagined, articulated, and realized there.

By the middle of the eighteenth century, British America was a conglomeration of over twenty mainland and island colonies stretching more than three thousand miles from Canada to the Caribbean, all subject to a British monarch enthroned in a palace over a month's sail away. Thirteen of those colonies revolted against British rule in 1776 and established the first long-lasting modern kingless republic, the United States of America. Many other British colonies, such as Canada and the Caribbean islands, did not revolt and remained under British control. Thus the geographical area under discussion here was for over two centuries a colonial one, and then for decades afterward partly a newly independent, sovereign nation and partly the ragged edge of the growing British Empire. The French, the Spanish, and American Indians speaking hundreds of different languages continued to vie for control in the Floridas and west beyond the Appalachian Mountains.

What to call this region could drive a lexicographer to despair. For many people at this time it was simply "America" (a term also, confusingly, applied to the whole of the New World), though in this age of difficult travel and local sympathies people often talked about their own small corner, be it Barbados or Boston. For clarity, I will use "British America" when I mean the territory claimed by Great Britain before 1776, and "the United States" to discuss the states that declared independence that year. But it would be a mistake to try to impose too much order on a time and a place in which national borders and political identities were porous, mutable, disputed, and in many cases nonexistent.

In short, the setting for American enlightenment was a rapidly shifting imperial periphery in a new age of global rivalry, the local American context always experienced on a vastly broader stage of ideas, politics, and demography. Over the seventeenth and eighteenth centuries, the population of Europeans on the eastern seaboard of what became the United States grew to about three million and the number of African slaves to over half a million.[2] During the same time the number of Indians living east of the Appalachians declined precipitously, although they still formed a significant presence there. By the middle of the eighteenth century, a series of navigation laws had lashed the American colonies to Britain's economy by controlling the goods the colonists could import and export from Britain and elsewhere.

The single constant in this world of change was distance. The three thousand miles of ocean separating the imperial capital of London from the American colonies ensured that Europeans were often months or even years behind in their understanding of rapidly changing American realities. European images of American Indians and American cities often remained frozen in time even as the military and political situation shifted abruptly on the ground. The concept of the noble savage—the American Indian who allegedly embodied a primordial human perfection—thrived in part because of this time lag, filling the void between the lived reality in the Americas and Europeans' quest for fixed ideals of human possibility. Thus enlightenment in America involved reminding Europeans that locals often had more reliable empirical evidence about certain realms of knowledge than did Europeans trumpeting universal accounts of seemingly everything. In the first decades of U.S. independence, educated people in Britain's former North American colonies reshaped these old reminders into a new and often sarcastic language of U.S. nationalism. "We are flattered with the idea of seeing ourselves vindicated from those despicable aspersions which have long been thrown upon us and echoed from one ignorant Scribbler to another in all the languages of Europe," the poet Joel Barlow wrote to Thomas Jefferson in 1787.[3]

At the same time, the ideas that Europeans called enlightened drew in part from what they learned by listening to people in the Americas and by carefully studying the rocks, insects, bones, pelts, antlers, plants, Indian artifacts, codices, letters, and reports that arrived from the New World. For Europe too was in flux, its land and peoples being reshaped politically, demographically, and environmentally: Europeans in search of enlightenment needed knowledge of the rest of the world just as Americans did.[4] The American Revolution caused Europeans to sit up and take notice because it successfully put into practice some of the new ideals of popular sovereignty and religious toleration that had been bandied about in European circles for decades. But republican government was not the only enlightened intellectual export from America that Europeans found valuable; it was rather one of many stretching over the course of the long eighteenth century.

The colonial status of British America helped determine the structures of intellectual life there. First, because a major reason for colonizing America had been to supply Europe with agricultural products, the growth of cities was severely limited in favor of farms, whether the smaller family farms that characterized the New England and middle colonies or the large plantations that carpeted Maryland, Virginia, the Carolinas, and the Caribbean. The largest cities in the New World—such as Mexico City, the former Tenochtitlán—were large because they combined the pre-existing cities of American Indians such as the Aztecs with a superstructure of European building. In British America, this kind of overbuilding on native urban cores did not occur, and the largest cities remained mere towns by European measures. In around 1750 the two largest British American cities—Boston and Philadelphia— had populations respectively of approximately 16,000 and 13,000. Contrast this with Spanish America, where by the middle of the eighteenth century Mexico City had a population of 112,000 and Lima 52,000. Most of the first colleges founded in British America—Harvard (1636), William and Mary (1693), Yale (1701), and the College of New Jersey (later Princeton; 1746)—sprouted in such comparatively small towns as to make the idea of rustication seem redundant. British Caribbean planters, lacking almost all educational infrastructure, sent their children to Britain for education in far larger numbers than did planters from the British American mainland colonies.[5]

For British Americans throughout the colonial period and well into the era of U.S. independence, the most important city was London, which grew dramatically in size, population, and cultural and intellectual brilliance during the eighteenth century. London now joined Paris as a real megalopolis, the bustling political, financial, and intellectual nerve center of a global empire. Paris in 1750 had a population of around 570,000, London of 750,000. These magnificent cities could collect on an unprecedented scale many building blocks of intellectual life: publishers, scholars, museums, cabinets, salons, gardens, learned societies, and princely patrons. London's intellectual and cultural supremacy was especially pronounced in book publishing, which over the course of the seventeenth and eighteenth centuries emerged as an ever more important river of information dissemination, supplementing other formats such as letter writing. Even though Edinburgh, Dublin, and Glasgow all became important book export centers, London remained the major exporter of print material to the provinces of Britain and its far-flung world colonies. Despite stereotypes of the Caribbean as an intellectual backwater, the British West Indies in the eighteenth century received a quarter of all North American book imports from London booksellers. The Jamaican planter Thomas Thistlewood's library in the late 1770s may have included over a thousand books, most bought from London suppliers.[6]

In growing numbers over the course of the eighteenth century, American colonists flocked to London, mostly for diplomatic, commercial, cultural, or educational reasons. Southern mainland colonists were especially well represented: 45 percent of Americans in London in the years just before the Revolution were from Georgia and South Carolina alone. Notorious among the locals for their decadence—they could be seen trailing a retinue of slaves, giving rise to the impression that most American colonists were either wealthy planters or African slaves—scions of southern and Caribbean planter families embarked for London chiefly as leisure travelers, American versions of the haughty English milords who gadded about the Continent on the Grand Tour. Elite colonists from the North American mainland and British Caribbean sent their sons for legal training to the Inns of Court in London, where nearly two hundred Americans had enrolled before the Revolution. Talented colonial painters such as John Singleton Copley and Benjamin West capped their careers by moving to London. Conversely, middling British talents such as John Smibert decamped to the colonies to be "lookt on as at the top."[7]

Because so many intellectual functions of American colonists centered on England, British Americans only slowly developed an intercolonial rather than colony-to-Britain intellectual life. Among the first publications with an intercolonial imprint was the *American Magazine and Historical Chronicle* (1743–46), which was sold in Boston, Philadelphia, New York, New Haven, and Newport. The first sustained intercolonial correspondence among men of science such as Benjamin Franklin and Alexander Garden did not emerge until the 1740s. Although the royal postal service ensured that letters and books were traveling with some frequency among the principal American port cities by the middle of the eighteenth century, intellectual life tended to thrive especially in local pockets, such as the dense knot of Boston-Cambridge, with its tangled religious, intellectual, and family trees. At the middle of the eighteenth century, Philadelphia supported the densest and most varied institutional infrastructure in the British colonies: here were the Library Company of Philadelphia, the American Philosophical Society, the Junto, and other venues for civic and intellectual improvement. Even a planter's mansion in rural Virginia could become a tiny

Parnassus, as Philip Vickers Fithian discovered when he spent a year in 1773–74 as a tutor at Nomini Hall, the secluded plantation house of Robert Carter on the Northern Neck of Virginia. Fithian marveled at the library filled with the works of "mighty-Men" such as John Locke, Joseph Addison, John Dryden, and Jonathan Swift.[8]

London was not the only magnet for Americans. In the late seventeenth and early eighteenth centuries, the transnational Protestant confessional community that one historian has called the "Protestant international" stretched from Boston through London and into the Low Countries and Germany. As the eighteenth century passed, the publications of Scottish thinkers such as Adam Smith, Thomas Reid, William Robertson, Lord Kames, and David Hume radiated outward from Glasgow, Aberdeen, and especially Edinburgh. The Scots had lost their Parliament in the Union of 1707 with England and now lacked a muscular political center, so social and intellectual leadership fell to the professional classes—especially lawyers, since Scotland retained its own legal system. As Scottish thinkers retreated into less overtly political discussions than those of their counterparts on the Continent, they poured their energies into moral philosophy, social theory, and political economy. It was for these subjects that they became especially known and admired in British America, another cultural province of London whose intellectual leadership gradually shifted over the course of the eighteenth century from ministers to lawyers. After 1750, learned Scots migrated to various parts of British America, settling in most prominently as leaders in American colleges who were able to influence generations of American statesmen and ministers: John Witherspoon as president of the College of New Jersey, William Smith as provost of the College of Philadelphia (later the University of Pennsylvania), and the naturalist William Small—who was elected to England's Lunar Society, an informal club of naturalists and industrialists—at the College of William and Mary. The current ran the other way as well, however; by 1761, so many Virginians were enrolled at Edinburgh's renowned medical school that they formed their own club.[9]

Moored on the western fringe of the Atlantic Ocean, learned Americans desperately hoped to cultivate a presence in the international learned community known as the republic of letters. This was an informal network of erudite people that had begun to take shape in the Renaissance and thrived before modern academic disciplines and more nationally bound scholarly institutional practices triumphed in the later nineteenth century. In an age of rigid social hierarchies, deadly wars of religion, and emerging state censorship, early modern scholars invoked the idea of a republic to engage one another on terms of relative equality and freedom. This was the great age of the generalist, the polymath, the *polyhistor*, adept in multiple fields of learning, when one could still aspire to know everything. Participants imagined the republic of letters to be universal in scope, extending beyond political frontiers to form a global literary utopia. Governed by etiquette rather than ideology, this imagined intellectual community operated through informal conventions of reciprocity, exchange, and mentoring.[10]

By the eighteenth century, the republic of letters stretched across the globe as European empires and religious organizations such as the Society of Jesus (Jesuits) sent learned merchants, ministers, scholars, and priests into Asia, Africa, and the Americas. Ships became the great ferries of this republic, carrying people, books, letters, and everything from giant butterflies to telescopes from imperial centers to colonial fringes and back again. They did not ply the oceans alone: in the same Atlantic sailed the slave ships bearing millions of Africans to the New World plantations. That intersection of the traffic in human bodies with a central highway of the republic of letters generated one of the great debates among people who strove for enlightenment: What should be done with slaves and slavery?

Several factors made British America distinctive in the republic of letters. One was religion. Not only did Protestants form an overwhelming majority of European settlers in British America, Catholicism remained peripheral to intellectual inquiry there, unlike in the rest of Spanish, Portuguese, and French America. Catholics, for example, dominated the colonies of Canada, Louisiana, Acadia, and Florida. The Society of Jesus provides the most striking example of a rich intellectual network that was barely represented in British America. From its foundation in 1540 to its dissolution in 1773, the Society of Jesus functioned as the chief global intellectual arm of the early modern Catholic church. By 1600, the Jesuits' network of educational institutions and erudite priests had spread Catholic theology and European learning to Asia and the New World. Communiqués transmitted back to Europe by the Jesuits and other Catholic orders greatly increased the knowledge available about the world and its peoples. The Spanish missionary José de Acosta spent fifteen years in Spanish America and in 1590 published one of the first books about the New World Indians. The extravagantly erudite German scholar Athanasius Kircher published over forty books on everything from China to volcanoes to contagion to Egyptian hieroglyphics; his letters reached across the globe to New Spain. These letters helped to link the diverse citizens of the republic of letters at a time when no one drew lines between religious and secular knowledge.[11]

In British America, the Jesuits played a much smaller role. The publications of Jesuits were certainly known there. Acosta was widely consulted as a source of knowledge about Spanish America, and the Jesuit missionary Joseph-François Lafitau's *Moeurs des sauvages amériquains* (1724) was cited as a source of knowledge about the Iroquois, among whom Lafitau had lived for several years. But Catholics were mostly known at a distance: it is estimated that on the eve of American independence, papists (as they were often called) made up only 1 percent of the population in the thirteen colonies. Rumors of papist plots trickled through the British American press amid mounting fears of an imperializing Louis XIV and Catholicizing Stuarts. And although British colonists in America made some efforts to convert the Indians to Christianity— Dartmouth College began life as an Indian school—these paled in comparison to the Catholic conversion programs under way in Spanish and French America.[12]

By far the greatest religious imprint in British America and the early United States was left by Protestantism. But this too was a reality in flux. So many new Protestant denominations found a footing in British America that by the late eighteenth century more religious pluralism existed among Christians in British America than anywhere in Europe. Before 1680, Congregationalists in New England and the Church of England in the southern colonies formed 90 percent of all Christian congregations on the mainland. Over the next century, the Protestant denominations swelled in size and number, and the mid-Atlantic colonies of Pennsylvania, New York, and New Jersey emerged to challenge Boston as the head-quarters of Protestantism in British America. A number of dissenting Protestants—Quakers, Presbyterians, Lutherans, Amish, Mennonites, Moravians, and Baptists—founded churches and created institutions that organized religious life among believers, authorizing which ministers could preach publicly and what kinds of charities would be organized, and settling disputes among parishioners. Strong religious ties connected the colonies to the Continent and especially to England and Scotland throughout the seventeenth and eighteenth centuries. Some were institutional: the Society for the Propagation of the Gospel in Foreign Parts (founded 1701) sent Anglican clergymen to the American colonies as a counterweight to Catholic missionary activities, though the Anglican church was never able to establish a bishop in North America. But many connections were also personal. The colony-wide revival movement today known as the First Great Awakening grew from networks of personal and institutional association across the Atlantic. Within two years of the revival preacher George Whitefield's death in 1770, a collection of his transatlantic correspondence had appeared in print.[13]

Another distinctive feature of British Americans was their unshakable conviction that Europeans regarded them disdainfully as marginal figures in the republic of letters. Not only did British Americans live far from Europe, but as colonists of Britain they linked with some difficulty to intellectual circles thriving on the Continent. Thus, early on, British Americans learned to cultivate London patrons who could act as intermediaries to Continental scholars. The coveted place in what the Harvard tutor Thomas Brattle called "ye Learned World" spurred the young provincial to spend the years 1682–89 in London, where he formed personal relationships with many of the scientific revolution's leading lights: Robert Boyle, Isaac Newton, the royal astronomer John Flamsteed, and Christopher Wren. Newton received Brattle's writings on comets, and Brattle's essays on lunar and solar eclipses were published in the *Philosophical Transactions* of London's Royal Society. A half century later, patronage connections were still important for Continental exposure. With the help of Peter Collinson in London and the

Dutch botanist Johann Friedrich Gronovius, the Philadelphia savant James Logan managed to publish his experiments on maize fertilization with a Leiden publisher. Although by now most British works were being published in English, Continental scholars still communicated largely in Latin, so Logan's work appeared first in Latin in 1739. Hoping for an Anglophone readership, Collinson asked his friend John Fothergill to translate Logan's work into English, and the book appeared in English translation in 1747.[14]

One strategy of connection in the republic of letters was to write letters, and Americans did so in ever increasing numbers over the course of the eighteenth century, when the size of letter networks expanded dramatically. While we often think of the eighteenth century as the great age of print, it was also the great age of the letter. These were the ligaments of empire, connecting minds and hearts over vast distances. Although learned correspondents had been exchanging letters for over two thousand years, the new era of global empires expanded the geographical reach of ordinary people's emotional, intellectual, mercantile, and political attachments through the medium of the letter, the only widespread technology for distance communication at this time. Rising literacy rates and regular packet service between Britain and its American colonies meant that more and more people experienced letters as a feature of everyday life. In city and hamlet alike, the lived environment now began to fill with the technologies and service economies associated with the letter: desks, quills, print and paper shops, bookstores, scriveners' offices, paper mills, and of course the postal system. Taught in a growing number of letter-writing manuals, the epistolary genre migrated rapidly into print. Many influential scientific, literary, and political publications took the form of a letter in the eighteenth century, with a real or imagined author and recipient.[15]

Letters also helped transform the interior landscape. Intimate, handwritten, dialogic rather than authoritarian, the letter could plumb new depths of emotional intimacy on the page, a boon in an age that stressed sensibility and sociability as key attributes of civility and indeed of civilization itself. One historian has argued that the new ideal of the affectionate family emerged in part as a product of transatlantic travel, which separated families and prompted them to pour out their yearning in letters.[16]

A comparison of two correspondence networks in the seventeenth and eighteenth centuries can illustrate the growth in size. John Winthrop, Jr. (1606–76)—the son of the Massachusetts Bay Colony founder John Winthrop—was governor of Connecticut as well as a leading alchemist at a time when alchemy loomed as the scientific-religious key to unlocking the mineral wealth of the New World. In approximately five thousand letters written and received in his lifetime, Winthrop forged a network that extended to England, the Continent (where Winthrop traveled, making connections with scholars in alchemical centers such as Hamburg), the Caribbean, and even the Middle East, where Winthrop met the scholar of Arabic texts Jacob Golius. Winthrop became the first colonial American member of the Royal Society at a time when it formed an interlocking directorate with Whitehall, part of King Charles II's colonial consolidation campaign that also included the new Navigation Acts of 1660 and the founding of the Board of Trade and the Council for Foreign Plantations.[17]

Just a century later, the average size of a letter network had grown enormously in size and complexity; Benjamin Franklin's provides an illuminating example. Born a century after John Winthrop, Jr., Franklin probably sent and received somewhere on the order of fifteen thousand letters during his lifetime, a similar number to that of other contemporary greats in the republic of letters such as Voltaire. Yet in contrast to Voltaire, whose correspondence was almost entirely confined to Europe, Franklin's letter network formed a triangle stretching across Philadelphia, London, and Paris, the result of his numerous voyages across the Atlantic and the great number of individuals—over a thousand—whom he counted among his correspondents. Although many of Franklin's correspondents had been born in either England or British America, Franklin gradually added correspondents from Scotland, France, the Low Countries, Germany, and Italy as his travels allowed him to meet foreigners face-to-face and establish intellectual, political, and personal relationships with them.[18]

Franklin's role in his letter network was just as important as its size, for he became one of the great nodes of the republic of letters, connecting ambitious young people with patrons and linking aspiring American intellectuals with their counterparts in Europe and

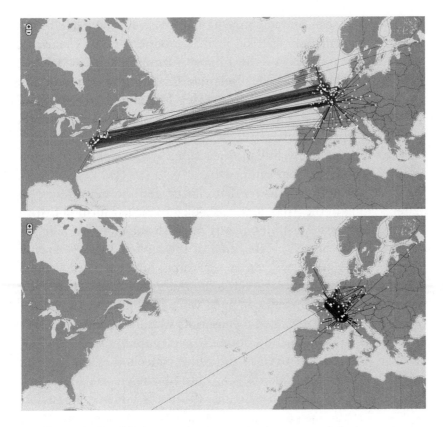

Benjamin Franklin's transatlantic correspondence network (top) contrasts with the Europe-bound network of Voltaire.

Britain. Like David Hume and Thomas Jefferson, Franklin enjoyed writing letters, raising the mere act of writing to a friend into an art form that mixed erudition, wit, and affection in equal measure. Some of Franklin's letters became internationally celebrated in a way that shows the continuing overlap in this era between the world of handwritten letters and the world of printed publication. His letters on his electrical experiments to his London patron Peter Collinson were published as *Experiments and Observations on Electricity* (1751), the tract that made Franklin internationally famous. Franklin and Collinson also traded objects. Franklin sent Collinson his almanacs, colonial curiosities, and political news of the colonies. In return, Collinson sent electrical tubes and other finely crafted scientific instruments that could not be made in the colonies, information on Continental experiments on electricity, books and magazines for the Library Company of Philadelphia, and silks for Franklin's wife, Deborah. Collinson also greased the wheels of London patronage, conveying Franklin's letters on electricity to the Royal Society and ultimately supporting Franklin's election to that organization. The Franklin-Collinson connection was just one of many linking the center and periphery that had grown over the previous century.[19]

The rising literacy levels that encouraged the new culture of letter writing in the Atlantic world took a particular form in British America. Protestantism's emphasis on each individual's ability to read the Bible helped create some of the highest literacy rates in the world for white women at that time. Some learned women formed informal networks through which they exchanged their writings. Since custom discouraged women from publishing their work, they often exchanged manuscripts within a group of friends, part of a flourishing manuscript exchange culture especially in belletristic works that thrived in the clubs, coffeehouses, and taverns of prerevolutionary America. One prominent coterie of learned women in the mid-Atlantic region—Elizabeth Graeme Fergusson, Milcah Martha Moore, Hannah Griffitts, and Annis Boudinot Stockton—exchanged poems and essays. Women's partial exclusion from the public realm of print led to the formation of a female world of writing, reading, and material culture. The subject matter of the female learned world was greatly influenced by classical and biblical subject matter, which women came to know through the increasing numbers of books and magazines in British America, in addition to more traditional sources such as the Bible. Women fashioned objects considered appropriate to their sex, such as small shell grottoes inspired by the story of Calypso in Homer's *Odyssey* and needlework based upon magazine prints of well-known parables of virtuous women from the classical world.[20]

During the revolutionary era, high white female literacy rates in British America in turn nurtured American women's first demands for political involvement based on the doctrine of natural rights. The application of the idea of natural rights to women was increasingly viewed as a sign of enlightenment, of the upward trajectory of civilization. Both in original versions and in American editions that were then excerpted in magazines, women in British America and the new United States became great readers of Scottish theories of social evolution, which posited humanity's progression from savagery through barbarity and thence to civilization. These Scottish stadial theories, along with a raft of new histories of women (or to use the eighteenth century's terminology, histories of "woman"), identified women as major actors in a society's ascent toward an enlightened age. Asserting that women were not inherently inferior to men in mental and moral endowments, they touted the importance of acquired characteristics such as education and social customs in improving the lot of women and cultivating their reason. "There is no truth more generally admitted," argued the American theologian Samuel Miller in 1803, "than that every step in the progress of civilization brings new honour to the female sex, and increases their importance in society."[21]

Gilbert Stuart's unfinished portrait of the published American poet Sarah Wentworth Morton captured the new faith in the powers of female reason. In an age that still idealized the formal portrait of a stiffly seated subject (apparently Stuart's first intention in this painting, since ghostly arms are still visible at Morton's waist), Morton is all pink-cheeked energy as she raises her arms to cope with a billowing veil. " 'Twas heaven itself that blended in thy face / The lines of Reason with the lines of Grace," Stuart wrote to Morton of the painting.[22]

The spread of the idea of natural rights as something possessed by all human beings allowed American women during and after the Revolution to participate—albeit informally—in electoral politics and in the expanded print culture that supported it. Some of the first American women to publish their own writings, such as Judith Sargent Murray and Mercy Otis Warren, extended the idea of the rights of man to the new idea of the "rights of woman," a term popularized by the British writer Mary Wollstonecraft in *A Vindication of the Rights of Woman* (1792). Murray and Wollstonecraft assured their readers that the rights of woman would expand during "this enlightened age." American women learned from these kinds of writing that they could play an important role in the realization of future social and political happiness. "I expect to see our young

Gilbert Stuart, Sarah Wentworth Apthorp, Mrs. Perez Morton, *c. 1802.*
(Worcester Art Museum, Worcester, Massachusetts, Gift of the grandchildren
of Joseph Tuckerman, 1899.2. Image © Worcester Art Museum.)

women forming a new era in female history," Judith Sargent
Murray declared in *The Gleaner* (1798).[23]

Fueled by rising literacy levels, American libraries also grew in
size and number, although they never came close to matching the
great monastic and royal libraries of Europe. The largest libraries,

such as the Wolfenbüttel in Germany, numbered in the hundreds of thousands of texts, inspiring a genre of library travel writing (including a category of worst library, for the most disorganized and worm-eaten). Many a colonial American diary recorded the traveler's slack-jawed disbelief upon beholding a great European library, as when young Jonathan Belcher of Massachusetts spied a tiny Bible once owned by the Stuart king Charles I in the library of the electress Sophia of Hanover. But over time Americans began to create significant private libraries: James Logan of Philadelphia, William Byrd of Westover, and Thomas Jefferson all acquired extensive private libraries numbering in the thousands of volumes. Given the dismal state of American college libraries and the difficulty of ordering books from abroad, these private libraries often became de facto lending libraries for the owner's family and friends. A sampling of these private libraries shows that North American colonists kept abreast of the latest works being read by Europeans: John Locke, Isaac Newton, Joseph Addison, the baron de Montesquieu, Francis Hutcheson, Jean-Jacques Burlamaqui, David Hume, Jean le Rond d'Alembert, Lord Chesterfield, Edward Gibbon, Jean-Jacques Rousseau, the abbé Raynal, the marquis de Condorcet, Lord Kames, Edmund Burke, Voltaire, and Thomas Reid.[24]

Privately organized circulating libraries swelled in number and membership, especially in the port cities that would remain the centers of American intellectual life into the nineteenth century: the Redwood Library Company in Newport, Rhode Island; the Tuesday Club of Annapolis, Maryland; the Library Company and Union Library Company of Philadelphia; and the Charleston Library Society in South Carolina. All relied on agents in England to ship them books, another feature that distinguished American libraries from those in Europe, where many books had been acquired as booty during the seventeenth-century wars of religion. American libraries, by contrast, epitomized the increasing role played by commerce in the intellectual life of the eighteenth century.[25]

American colleges also received books from private donors in Britain. A single gift could be transformative. In the early eighteenth century, Yale College caught up with some of the discoveries of the scientific revolution thanks to a generous gift of books by Jeremiah Dummer, the London agent for the colony of Connecticut. In 1714,

Dummer sent around four hundred books to Yale, including works by Isaac Newton, John Locke, Robert Boyle, Robert Hooke, John Ray, Thomas Burnet, John Woodward, Edmond Halley, and William Whiston. A few years later, the merchant Elihu Yale sent a parcel containing the *Philosophical Transactions* of the Royal Society. The young Jonathan Edwards may have used the copy of Newton's *Opticks* (1704) in Yale's library to write a letter in which he drew the path of an American "flying" spider swinging through the trees. Edwards explained by reference to Newton that the sun's rays magnified the size of the spider's anchoring threads so that they appeared "several thousands of times as big as they ought."[26]

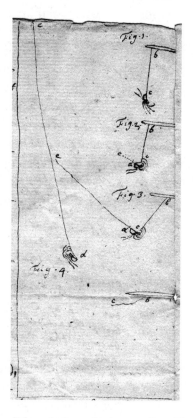

The young Jonathan Edwards drew this image of a spider swinging through the air according to Newtonian principles in a letter dated October 31, 1723.
(Collection of The New-York Historical Society)

In the hopes of catching the eye of London's scientific community, Edwards sent his spider letter to Paul Dudley, associate justice of the Superior Court of Massachusetts and more importantly a fellow of London's Royal Society. But unbeknownst to Edwards, Dudley tucked the letter among his personal papers and never mentioned it to the Royal Society.[27] Edwards's youthful spider letter is significant nonetheless for showing the many ways in which ideas crossed—and failed to cross—the eighteenth-century Atlantic.

Enlightenment involved using human reason to understand the world, a concept that fueled the development of scientific instruments for perceiving and measuring that world. Most scientific instruments had to be imported from Britain and Europe, where skilled craftsmen produced finely wrought telescopes, microscopes, compasses, and other complex devices. Harvard did not receive its first microscope until 1732, but much earlier than that books such as Cotton Mather's *The Christian Philosopher* (1721), which discussed the publications and instruments of dozens of European scientists, had helped popularize the results of European microscopic investigation. These books opened to American eyes the strange world of insects blown up to the size of house cats, as revealed in works such as Robert Hooke's illustrated *Micrographia* (1665). In the late 1760s the Philadelphia clockmaker and astronomer David Rittenhouse built an orrery, or mechanical model of the solar system, which was purchased by the College of New Jersey. These new instruments of perception and measurement aided in the new interest in using empirical evidence to understand the world. But reason never displaced wonder and awe, the sense that God's hand lay behind every natural phenomenon, from the giant planet Jupiter to the tiniest ant. "Behold a sufficient END, as well for a *World* as for a *Worm*," wrote Cotton Mather in *The Christian Philosopher*. "*O infinitely Great GOD, I am astonished! I am astonished!*"[28]

The sheer distance of America from Europe could also work to the advantage of the emerging international scientific community. The efforts to view the transits of Venus in 1761 and 1769 show how global empires could begin to work in concert to gather empirical evidence deemed important for enlightenment. The most significant astronomical events of the eighteenth century, the transits of the planet Venus over the face of the sun promised to help astronomers assign precise distances to the heliocentric solar system proposed by Copernicus two centuries earlier. The events captivated learned people everywhere; Captain James Cook launched his expedition to the Pacific Ocean in part to see the transit of 1769 in Tahiti. Boston also mobilized its political and scientific community for a transit viewing. Funded by the Massachusetts Assembly with the encouragement of Governor Francis Bernard, Harvard's astronomer John Winthrop, Jr., packed his astronomical instruments and gathered two students for a journey to a hill near St. John's, Newfoundland. There, on June 6, 1761, they squinted in awe as the black dot of Venus slid across the brilliant sun. The American painter John Singleton Copley captured the moment in his portrait of John Winthrop. Seated next to his English-made telescope, with the Newfoundland landscape visible through the window, Winthrop points to a diagram of the transit. His hand casts a semicircular shadow on the page, a copy of the circles and semi-circles bedecking the many engravings made of the transit of Venus in Europe and America. Venus had sailed by "the Earth's enlighten'd disk," Winthrop wrote in a neat encapsulation of the many possibilities for enlightenment in eighteenth-century America.[29]

This was also the great age of the collection. Since the Renaissance, Europeans had been collecting and categorizing nature in cabinets, museums, and botanical gardens. Far from imperial centers, British Americans had little in the way of such collections. In fact it was easier to see collections of American birds, insects, reptiles, and Indian manufactures in Europe than in the New World, and Americans eagerly shipped local specimens to London in the hopes that they would enjoy greater visibility there. In Britain, the cabinets of John Tradescant (both father and son) and Hans Sloane became major depositories of Americana. So great was the European demand for American Indian artifacts such as birch-bark boxes and moccasins that a small trade in purpose-made Indian commodities had emerged by the middle of the eighteenth century; these rapidly found their way into cherished family collections in Britain and the Continent.[30]

But objects and ideas did not cross the Atlantic in a single, unidirectional flow; many traveled back and forth numerous times, mutating unpredictably. The thick, creamy pages of Mark

John Singleton Copley, John Winthrop (1714–1779), *c. 1773.*
Oil on canvas, 127.5 × 102.1 cm. (50 ³/₁₆ × 40 ³/₁₆ in.). (Harvard Art
Museums/Fogg Museum, Harvard University Portrait Collection, Gift to
Harvard College by the executors of the estate of John Winthrop and heirs of
Mrs. Andrews, 1894, H113. Photo: Imaging Department, © President
and Fellows of Harvard College.)

Catesby's *The Natural History of Carolina, Florida, and the Bahama Islands* (1731, 1743) illustrate the untidy transnational flow of ideas and objects. The first color-plate book about a North American subject, Catesby's *Natural History* is a brilliantly watercolored carnival of animal energy, with snakes, birds, turtles, and mammals lovingly described in parallel columns of French and English text.

Catesby's *Natural History* revealed how much was already known in Europe of the allegedly new world by the early eighteenth century. He drew comparatively few uniquely American animals such as the opossum because these had already been described by earlier authors. Even his print of the American bison was not based on his own empirical observation but on the drawing of a Dutch artist in the London collection of Hans Sloane.[31]

Eighteenth-century Americans coped with the lack of museums and cabinets in America by visiting those in Europe whenever possible. John Adams took time off from his diplomatic duties in The Hague in 1782 to visit the famous museum of the Dutch collector Pierre Lyonnet, stuffed chock-a-block with insects, shells, and other natural remains. Lyonnet's cabinet stunned Adams in part because opportunities to see natural history specimens in North America before the late eighteenth century were still limited. Adams was so smitten with Lyonnet's insects that he asked Abigail Adams whether she too wanted "to read and inspect Cutts of the Anatomy of Caterpillars—their Nerves, Blood, Juices, Bones, Hair, Senses, Intellects &c. &c.—Their moral Sense, their Laws, Government, Manners and Customs." The royal gardens and cabinets of Paris made him wonder, "When shall We have in America, such Collections?" Traveling to the first Continental Congress in 1774, Adams had gone out of his way to see one of the only collections of "American Curiosities": the cabinet of Edward Arnold in Norwalk, Connecticut, which included birds and insects. The visit had convinced Adams that "our Country affords as ample materials, for Collections of this nature as any part of the World." The fate of Arnold's collection shows the limits of what could be seen on the imperial periphery in the late eighteenth century. Edward Arnold sold the insect and bird collection to New York governor William Tryon, who then handed it off to Sir Ashton Lever, creator of the Leverian Museum in London. In 1783, Adams visited the Leverian, noting in his diary that here "I saw again that collection of American birds, insects and other rarities, which I had so often seen before at Norwalk, in Connecticut."[32]

The founding of Charles Willson Peale's natural history museum in Philadelphia in 1784 thus marked a watershed in

Charles Willson Peale, The Artist in His Museum, *1822. Oil on canvas,
103 ¾ × 79 ⅞ in. (263.5 × 202.9 cm.), 1878.1.2 (Courtesy of the Pennsylvania
Academy of the Fine Arts, Philadelphia. Gift of Mrs. Sarah Harrison
[The Joseph Harrison, Jr. Collection].)*

Americans' ability to see the natural world of America collected and displayed in America. Peale intended his Philadelphia Museum, which he carefully filled over the next decades, to create a book of nature in which people could read the orderly array of God's handiwork. It would also assemble exempla of the greatness of the United States. A particular regret was that the distinguished patriot Benjamin Franklin had not been taxidermied for display in Peale's museum.[33]

In his 1822 self-portrait, Peale lifts a plush red curtain to reveal the Great Hall of his museum, where American nature was arrayed in Linnaean order. On the left, arranged in the hierarchical sequence of the Great Chain of Being, stand the cases Peale designed to display zoological specimens against painted landscapes intended to resemble their American habitats. In the foreground, a dead American turkey sags atop a taxidermist's box, ready for preparation as a museum specimen. Partly shrouded by the red curtain stands the giant mastodon skeleton that Peale had helped exhume decades earlier. The enormous jaw of the mastodon sits in a pool of sunlight, while against the table leans one of the giant's long bones, displayed to compare favorably in height to Peale's own muscular left leg (unfashionably dressed in tightfitting knee breeches and silk stockings at a time when men's legwear had moved to trousers that concealed the precise outline of the leg). Here were Americans—both man and beast—as big as or bigger than European creatures, basking in the orderly splendor of the sunlit museum. God had clearly smiled as much on this new world as he had on the old.[34]

This was the setting for enlightenment in America, a place far from Europe yet connected to it by the many ligaments of intellect and empire. A patchwork of peoples, languages, polities, and religions, British America and the early United States developed some strands of enlightenment with particular intensity. These are the subjects of the chapters that follow. They do not reveal a single, unified "American Enlightenment," an idea that eighteenth-century Americans would have found strange, even implausible. For though enlightenment was a condition that many sought, all searched for it in their own particular ways, just as we do today.

CHAPTER TWO

Seashells in the Appalachians

Hᴵɢʜ ɪɴ ᴛʜᴇ ꜰᴏʀᴇꜱᴛᴇᴅ peaks of the Appalachian Mountains lie seashells entombed in rocks. How those shells got there—so high in the mountains and so far from the sea—became a subject of intense fascination and debate in Europe and the Americas from the late seventeenth century through the early nineteenth. In the age of blue-water empires people circled the globe to lands never mentioned in the Bible, where they discovered marine shells in unlikely places: not just on mountaintops but in mines, inland cliffs, and gravel pits. Some of these shells had no known living analogues.

Mountaintop seashells and other oddities challenged eighteenth-century Europeans and Americans to imagine the history of the earth in new ways, beyond the limits of the Bible and the six- to ten-thousand-year age for the earth that biblical research seemed to suggest. From an early focus on the great flood described in Genesis as the most significant earth-shaping force, Americans and their European correspondents over the course of the eighteenth century moved toward less overtly biblical explanatory schemes. They did not eliminate the biblical deluge as a force but rather diminished its historical and scientific importance as they searched for regular principles of causality in a natural world designed by God.

In short, they began to study the earth and its history in ways they called enlightened. In his *Brief Retrospect of the Eighteenth Century* (1803), the American theologian Samuel Miller explained what that term meant. He praised the rise of "Enlightened mineralogists, practical miners, and patient chemical experimenters" who had "all tended to throw light on the origin and history of our planet," moving away from the "speculations which have *darkened counsel.*" A quarter-century later, by which time the term *geology* had been coined to describe this new field of study, the future looked even brighter. "At this enlightened day," wrote one American surveyor in 1826, the "science" of geology would flourish along with the vast new areas of the nation that had been opened for the collection of "facts."[1]

Enlightened geologists never set out to eradicate God from the story of the earth's formation. Rather, they searched for the regular natural laws that God had set in motion at the beginning of time. Yet by the mid-nineteenth century, geology was posing a greater challenge than biology to the Genesis narrative of creation by vastly expanding the presumed age of the earth and proposing an empirically verifiable series of earthly revolutions rather than special creative acts of God as the chief engines of geological change. In his *Origin of Species* (1859), Charles Darwin built upon the geological enlightenment introduced decades earlier to craft a new story about the development of life on earth. Darwinian processes propelled by natural laws suggested to some the disturbing possibility that the natural world had no moral intentionality: no telos, no purpose. When God had opened the windows of heaven to unleash the mighty flood that washed away his sinful children, the moral purpose of earth's history had been abundantly clear. By contrast, the emerging enlightened idea that the gradual erosion of cliff sediments over millions of years explained the earth's present shape seemed to send much more nebulous messages to humanity about God's intentions. It was the loss of the purposeful universe that was perhaps the most unsettling legacy of the enlightened science of geology.

The development of that enlightened science over the course of the long eighteenth century occurred on many fronts. While enormous fossil bones and teeth riveted the general public, it was the

millions of tiny marine shells lodged in surprising and unlikely locations that set the terms of the international learned community's
debate about the origins of the earth. These shells were so numerous and so widely scattered that it was possible to amass evidence in
this category as in no other. Comparing shells from around the
world, naturalists searched for answers to questions of causation
and chronology. They labored in the twilight of the Renaissance,
when ingenious theories had abounded about strangely located
shells, such as those cemented into solid rock. Perhaps the shells
had sprung spontaneously from those rocks, or maybe they were
jokes of nature (lusus naturae), impishly sprinkled by nature itself to
test even the nimblest minds. The rocky shells made learned
eighteenth-century Americans and Europeans strain against the
maddeningly undetailed account of the flood and other earth-
shaping events described in the Bible. As Moses had hiked down
from Mount Sinai, he had failed to take note of any fossil marine
shells at its peak. "Moses does not particularly mention shell-fish, or
when the sea produced them," complained the eighteenth-century
American naturalist John Bartram.[2]

The Appalachian seashells, then, were not a distinctly American
problem during the long eighteenth century, but were rather an international problem with a local American dimension. The importance of North America to enlightened Europeans and Americans
was not that American mountains or fossils were exceptional,
somehow bigger or better than mountains and fossils elsewhere. It
was rather that the local conditions of North America generated
new information about the earth's workings, just as the local conditions of Peru, the East Indies, and Europe itself generated new information. And this new information suggested that the biblical
narrative of the mighty flood could no longer alone account for the
cataclysms that had disturbed the earth in the past, traumas whose
scars were visible in such oddities as the shells cemented into
the Appalachian rocks. Enlightened Americans began to search for
explanatory schemes that would be unmoored from fanciful, superstitious, or supernatural scenarios. But always what counted was
nature in America, not "American Nature," the bombastic, nationalistic celebration of the unique and God-given beauties of the
United States that emerged during the middle of the nineteenth

century. By then, American geologists and landscape painters had
begun to advertise the United States as the site of God's most ma-
jestic geological confections, signs of the special virtue and mission
of the American people. Americans should no longer even tolerate
the designation "New World," announced the scientist Louis
Agassiz after the Civil War, given that America might be "first-born
among the Continents."[3]

Thus it was not nationalism but increasing international communication and mutual recognition that characterized the enlightened
science of geology as it emerged in the eighteenth century.
Americans and Europeans began to link increasingly detailed studies
of local terrains to a new, planet-wide story of the earth's formation
that rested more and more on empirical data and less and less on
special interventions of the deity. Europeans began to work American
rocks and American knowledge into their views of the formation of
the earth. Similarly, the local American learned community gradually
integrated itself into the international one, which had before been
largely confined to Europe. By the nineteenth century, Americans
and Europeans had together crafted a new story of their earth,
distanced from God and the Bible but closer to the earth itself.

But what remained persistently out of reach of the enlightened
geologists was a new, overarching, explanatory scheme: the earth had
changed, but why? Since antiquity, people had infused nature with
transcendent meaning and purpose, or telos. Christianity reinforced
the teleological reading of nature by emphasizing that God had created the earth and the creatures upon it for a great cosmic purpose.
The search for facts about nature had contributed to the glorifica-
tion of God by revealing the intricacies and wonders of his plan to
his children. Yet as the enlightened study of the earth unfolded during the eighteenth and early nineteenth centuries, the search for
facts gradually began to supersede the search for God's purpose.
The accumulation of geological facts quickly outstripped the number of details about earth-shaping forces relayed in the Bible, and
the assertions of geology gradually moved out of step with holy
writ. Having rejected overtly supernatural and miraculous explanations for earth-shaping processes, Americans and their European
counterparts found themselves groping for a new, overarching,
purposeful narrative to undergird their growing compendium of

empirical facts. This they failed to find. Collected, studied, and understood in greater and greater detail, shells and other pieces of data pointed less and less clearly to any larger purpose for nature and humanity.

Getting to Know the Appalachians

Perched on the edge of an empire, British Americans struggled through the late seventeenth and eighteenth centuries to establish their credentials as legitimate scientific contributors to the republic of letters. Compared to their colleagues in Europe, they had fewer observers on the ground and fewer educated people to collect and spread information about rocks, minerals, and mountains. "I know no body here capable of making very great discoveryes," complained the Virginia planter William Byrd II to the English collector Hans Sloane in the early eighteenth century. "So that Nature has thrown away a vast deal of her bounty upon Us to no purpose."[4] Nonetheless, it was increasingly recognized around the republic of letters that local data—from Europe and the imperial peripheries— contributed material evidence and intellectual insights about the history of the earth. The colonists in North America stood ready to supply their own data for the grand questions of how the earth had formed and when its modern features had emerged.

Among the many problems the New World presented was how it fit into the Genesis story of the earth's formation. Nowhere was America mentioned in the Bible. Learned people in the seventeenth century wondered whether the biblical flood had extended to the Americas, on what moral grounds God might have flooded the American Indians, and whether Indian legends contained evidence of the flood.[5] They wondered whether the strata and shells of American mountains might mark the height of the flood that had swallowed even the highest peaks and drowned every creature except the huddled few carried to safety in Noah's ark.

By "American mountains," people at this time meant the Appalachians and the Andes, which remained the only significantly studied mountains of the Americas until scientists in the nineteenth century added the Rockies and the Sierra Nevada to the roster. The Andes and Appalachians were often compared and sometimes even linked as the great knobby backbone of America.[6] We know today that they have always been distinct ranges, formed by different convulsions at different times. Spanning over four thousand miles from north to south, the volcanic Andes form the largest continental mountain range in the world, as well as one of the highest. At over twenty thousand feet, the glacier-covered peaks of the Andes defied climbers dating back to the precontact Inca, who suffered from the vomiting and pounding headaches that we today would call altitude sickness. By contrast, the Appalachians stand among the most ancient mountains in the world, first lifted up nearly 500 million years ago and gradually worn to nubs by rain, wind, and snow. Unlike the icy needles of the Andes, these low, lushly forested mountains could be crossed with relative ease.

And so they were. The Appalachian Mountains as a specific geographical feature emerged with greater detail in maps and reports over the course of the seventeenth century. Defense and economics drove much of the early exploration, for early modern science was firmly tied to imperial objectives. Colonists were eager to establish boundaries between British America and the French and Indian groups to the west through increasingly meticulous maps and charts. The search for mines to rival the lucrative silver discovered at Potosí in Spanish America yielded significant information about surface rocks and outcroppings. Cartographic refinements were added over the course of the seventeenth century by a series of expeditions, mostly in Virginia, that first approached and then summited the Appalachian range. The first European to crest what he called the "barren rocks" of the "Apalatean" mountains was the German explorer John Lederer in 1669. Augustin Herrman's 1670 map of Virginia and Maryland took note of "These mighty High and great Mountaines," which he surmised formed "the very middle Ridg of Northern America," its western slopes possibly draining into the Gulf of Mexico or the Pacific Ocean.[7]

Just as they did about mysterious European land features, these early explorers in eastern North America occasionally speculated about the processes that had formed the land. At some undetermined point before the recorded memory of humankind, the oceans appeared to have receded, leaving seashells on dry land or deep underground. Lederer argued that "North, as well as

South-America, may be divided into three regions: the flats, the highlands, and the mountains." Noting the "daily discoveries of fish-shells three fathom deep in the earth" in the flatlands, Lederer concluded that "these parts are supposed some ages past to have lain under the sea." John Banister, a naturalist who sent numerous samples to London, observed the "multitudes of Cockles, Scallops, & other sea-shells mixed with the Earth," surmising that the sea "in former Ages came farther up in the Country." Others were less inclined to find an ancient meaning for the stony shells. The minister John Clayton, who had spent the late 1680s in Virginia, reported to the Royal Society that in Virginia "nothing is more common than petrify'd Shells, unless you would determine that they are Parts of natural Rock shot in those Figures, which indeed I rather think."[8]

Alongside this accumulating local data about North America and the Appalachian Mountains stood another, more theoretical body of knowledge about the earth itself. None of these Europe-based theorizers had been to North America. Often well traveled within Europe itself, they based their ideas on eyewitness knowledge of European rocks, on reports culled from other areas of the world, and on armchair conjecture arising from a deep knowledge of the Bible. Because they aspired to universal explanations of the causes of the earth's formation within a history of the cosmos, they hoped to gain knowledge of the Americas generally so as to knit the region into a grand cosmological history. In English this scholarship was called a theory of the earth, in French, *théorie de la terre*. In his *Protogaea* (1696), one of the numerous seventeenth-century works to offer a conjectural history of the earth, the philosopher Gottfried Wilhelm Leibniz mentioned America and emphasized the importance of compiling local knowledge to build a universal theory: "When everyone contributes curiosity locally, it will be easier to recognize universal origins."[9] The idea was not that each locality was exceptional or unique, but that each locality contributed a piece to a universal puzzle.

Three works written by Englishmen were especially influential for British Americans in the first two-thirds of the eighteenth century: Thomas Burnet's *Telluris Theoria Sacra* (1681; first published in English as *The Theory of the Earth* in 1684, and often later titled *The Sacred Theory of the Earth*); John Woodward's *An Essay Toward a*

Natural History of the Earth (1695); and William Whiston's *A New Theory of the Earth* (1696).[10] All three authors fit the natural processes of earth formation into a biblical framework, showing how miraculous events such as Noah's flood could account for the past and present state of the planet.

Even in the earliest of these English works, Burnet's *Sacred Theory*, information from America and other parts of the world had begun to enlarge the geographical limits implied by the Bible. Burnet believed that the present earth was a ruined world, crumpled and wrinkled from its first perfectly smooth, sinless state. This first, preflood earth was literally a *"Mundane Egg"*: oval in shape and made of four layers from an outer shell to a middle abyss that led finally to a soft inner yolk. By the command of a God angered by his sinful children, the shell of the earth had suddenly collapsed into the abyss below, unleashing a great flood that rumpled the original perfection of the earth to create the crags and cliffs that people beheld today. This flood had engulfed not only the eastern Mediterranean but the whole world. Humanity now lived among these sin-generated mountains and valleys, ugly scars that bore witness to "the ruines of a broken World." Burnet called on geographers to replace their smooth globes—which perpetuated the myth of earth's goodness and regularity—with bumpy globes that plainly showed "what a rude Lump our World is."[11]

Burnet had read about America but never been there. Still, his travel to the European Continent, where he had beheld the mighty Alps and Apennines, convinced him of the dangers of parochialism. Plowing flat lands, their eyes glued to the ground, most people took mountains for granted rather than wondering how and why they had formed. "You may tell them that Mountains grow out of the Earth like Fuzz-balls" and they would be entirely convinced, he complained. Invoking the Andes in America, Burnet declared that mountains were everywhere, "in the New World as well as the Old," even on the moon.[12]

Not everyone agreed that the New World had fundamentally changed the reading of the Genesis flood narrative. John Ray's *Miscellaneous Discourses Concerning the Dissolution and Changes of the World* (1692) argued contra Burnet for a local flood only, insisting on the "Unnecessariness of drowning *America*" since the New

World was probably unpeopled at the time of the biblical flood. But Burnet had made a powerful case for the importance of the Americas in providing information critical for a new theory of the earth. The New World had enormous ranges, such as the Andes, "a ridge of Mountains ... reported to be higher than any we have, reaching above a thousand Leagues in length, and twenty in breadth, where they are the narrowest." To illustrate his thesis, Burnet included a map of the youthful, mist-shrouded Americas rising from the sea, like Venus from the foam. The image trails a series of earlier earths, each depicting the planet's transformation over time; one shows Noah's tiny ark guarded by angels, floating in a world of waves. Burnet's map of American mountains conveyed a theological truth rather than a geographical reality (much more

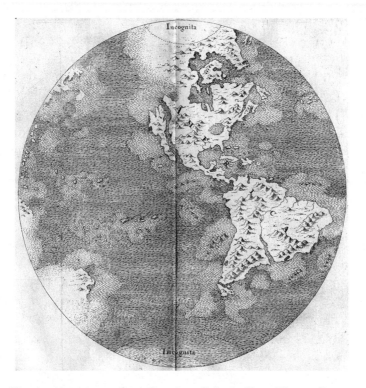

The Americas emerge from the primordial seas. From Thomas Burnet,
The Theory of the Earth *(1697), 101. (Courtesy Department of Special*
Collections, Stanford University Libraries)

topographically accurate maps existed by this time), unveiling the story of creation itself as it had unfolded deep in the earth's past, a past that now included the birth of America.[13]

How was Burnet's *Sacred Theory* received in America itself? One response comes from the wealthy Virginia planter William Byrd II. Possessed of a playfully omnivorous mind, Byrd combined the strongly practical interests of a tobacco planter and politician with more theoretical interests in botany, zoology, and ethnology. His Georgian mansion, Westover, housed one of the major private libraries of colonial America, numbering approximately four thousand books—including Burnet's *Sacred Theory*, requested by Byrd's father from London in 1689, and Woodward's *Essay Toward a Natural History of the Earth*.[14] Educated in Britain, William Byrd II established a dense correspondence network among London scientists. He was admitted to the Royal Society in 1696, one of only two Virginians in the colonial period to be so honored.

William Byrd II can be ranked among the greatest geographical narrators of early Virginia and the Appalachians. His journeys to survey the boundaries of Virginia and search for gold and silver mines yielded detailed descriptions of Virginia's topography and the Appalachian range that blocked British access to the West. Byrd's interest in the Appalachians was also guided by practical concerns of surveying for defense reasons. He despaired of the slow pace at which knowledge of the local terrain accumulated even as the French and the Indians continually challenged British land claims. The English had settled in America for over a century "and still we hardly know any thing of the Appallachian Mountains." He wrote frequently about rocks and ores in his expeditions to survey Virginia lands in the late 1720s, a journey that took his small group from the Atlantic coast nearly 250 miles inland to the foot of the seemingly endless Appalachian range, a piece of "Conjectural Geography" desperately needing an "accurate Survey."[15]

Showing how closely linked science and imperial statecraft had become by this era, William Byrd's descriptions of America lacked any sense of chronology beyond the century of British occupation.[16] His many geographically detailed writings fail to mention puzzling geological features such as fossil shells. Even as he shipped ore samples to his colleagues in London, he remained silent about how such specimens fit into a theological story of the creation of the earth. If he read the edition of Burnet's *Sacred Theory* that lay in Westover's library, he did not apply its time dimension to the rocks and ores and mountains he saw around him. Byrd's silence about the earth's chronology reveals how the local intellectual needs of the British colony of Virginia—for profitable exports and defense—could shape the early understanding of earth theory in America and the kinds of material information British Americans sent back to London.

By contrast, a much more deeply rooted sense of earth's history in America emerged from Byrd's contemporary, the Boston minister Cotton Mather. Unlike the well-traveled Byrd, Mather never left New England; it is doubtful that he ever even climbed a mountain.[17] Yet he was utterly engaged in the latest international debates about the earth's formation, seeing these processes entirely in theological terms. From his Boston base, he cultivated a rich network of transatlantic correspondents who fed his fascination with the great theological question of where American specimens fit into a story of the earth. Although fewer than six hundred of Mather's letters have been located, he may have written and received more than eight thousand during his lifetime. Connected by letters, rock and plant samples, and publications to colleagues in Britain and the Continent, Mather also cultivated a local, New England–centered intellectual network, a miniature republic of letters within the global one. He became a human clearinghouse for regional discoveries and speculations about various curious objects exhumed from the ground, from giant bones to fossil shells. Thanks in part to Cotton Mather, these two networks—the local and the transatlantic— operated together, like cogs in a machine. When Dutch settlers in Claverack, New York, unearthed a giant tooth in 1705, Mather immediately alerted his London network, while the royal governor of New York sent the tooth itself to Britain. The American tooth probably belonged to the early race of giants mentioned in the Bible, Mather asserted, integrating the Americas into the biblical story of creation.[18]

Mather's major London correspondent for scientific matters was the English antiquarian and naturalist John Woodward, one of the leading earth theorists of his era. In his early twenties

Woodward had traveled to Gloucestershire, a region west of London. There, in a small town perched above a stream, Woodward had stumbled upon shells lodged directly in the rock, as well as beds of shells lying in plowed fields nearby. Woodward's youthful puzzlement at how the shells had come to rest in these unlikely locations launched a career in which he attempted to explain the origin and meaning of fossils. (The term *fossil* at this time did not necessarily imply antiquity: it retained its older, Latinate meaning of something that was dug up from the earth.) Over time anxieties about the antiquity of fossils tugged on more and more minds.[19]

Woodward's shells formed part of a much larger early modern world of shell collecting that thrived in Europe's growing empires. With no barrier separating the realms of art, science, and collecting, shells captivated a wide and diverse audience; a subgenre of Dutch still life painting cast shells both local and exotic as symbols of earthly vanity. In Britain a cadre of collector-naturalists—Hans Sloane, John Ray, James Petiver, Martin Lister—filled their cabinets and illustrated compendia with shells, many from North America and the Caribbean. The British shell collector Martin Lister, in his gloriously illustrated *Historia sive Synopsis Methodica Conchyliorum* (1685–92), catalogued many shells, including the first North American fossil shell to be described in scientific literature. At the time of the American shell's first appearance in a publication, however, it was not clear to Lister that this "fossil" shell— fossil because it was found in the ground—might be very ancient. It was commonly accepted at this time that the earth was around six thousand years old, as some readings of the Bible would indicate and as Archbishop James Ussher had influentially maintained a few decades earlier. Lister was puzzled by fossil shells that had no apparently living analogue; while he recognized the similarity of fossil shells to currently living forms, he regarded them as inorganic imitations produced in the rocks. Perhaps, suggested Lister, these were jokes, modern shells placed in mountains by nature for the sheer fun of it.[20]

By contrast, Woodward denied the modernity of the rocky shells, insisting instead that they dated from the biblical flood and so must be several thousand years old. His wide-ranging fossil observations led him to conclude that there had been a worldwide—

not just local—flood that had submerged even the highest mountains. The antediluvian earth had been completely "dissolved, and afterwards framed a-new." Rejecting the idea that nature played jokes or that shells had appeared preformed in mountains and cliffs, Woodward argued that biblical floodwaters had carried marine bodies around the entire earth before retreating into the present-day ocean beds; the heaviest animals sank first, the lightest last.[21]

American information was critical for Woodward's global flood theory. He believed that fossil shells could be found "in all Parts of the known World, as well in Europe, Africa, and America, as in Asia, and this even to the very tops of the highest Mountains." Such fossils would be found to be "exactly conformable to that of *ours* here," proving that "they were all put into this *Condition* by the very *same means*." He cultivated numerous British American informants—including Cotton Mather and William Byrd II—to uncover living analogues to these fossils, basic information about local mountains and rock formations, and, most important, those possibly ancient fossils, or "*Subterraneous Curiosities*," as Mather called them, that would confirm the reality of Noah's flood. These various personal connections within the British Empire also suggested new links among the landmasses of the modern world. Irish correspondents had informed Woodward, for example, that huge antlers from Ireland that resembled those from America implied that some American animals such as the moose had been carried by the Genesis flood from America to Ireland.[22]

Woodward's most devoted correspondent in British America was Mather. From a young age, Mather had been gripped by the same concerns that fired Woodward and other early modern scientists such as Robert Boyle and John Ray: how to reconcile the idea of God's omnipotence with the new quest to discover regular laws in nature's operations. Shipping American specimens to Europe could enable this provincial American to cement reciprocal relationships with glittering but distant eminences of the republic of letters. In 1712, Mather began shipping a steady stream of natural specimens to Woodward that he called his "*Curiosa Americana*." Over twelve years he shipped at least eighty-two papers, including one on "fossils."[23]

Mather also rounded up a local group of helpers to find suitable American fossil shells to ship to London, such as his friend, the wealthy if unfocused John Winthrop, grandson of the governor of the Connecticut colony. Mather lent Winthrop a copy of Woodward's *Natural History of the Earth*, asking asked him to make "as full a Collection as may be of the Fossils; (the Names written on each little Bundle:) to be in *Your Name*, transmitted unto him!" Eager to please Mather and the English scientific elite in the Royal Society, but also to remind Mather of his illustrious pedigree, Winthrop agreed to go fossil hunting: "I shall doe my indeavor to answer both yors & Dr Woodwards requests in making a collection of ye fossils of or country for Gresham Colledge; to wch Society methinks we have some relation, considering my granfather had ye honor to be among the first promoters of it." Winthrop dutifully sent shells to Woodward, only to be reminded that it was not modern shells but American "Remains of ye Deluge" that Woodward wanted for his natural history of the earth. Woodward became Mather's chief link to London's Royal Society, smoothing Mather's election to that body.[24]

It was because of far-flung correspondents like Cotton Mather that Woodward at his death had accumulated an extraordinary collection of fossils from around the world. The bulk came from England and from Continental mines, but the collection also included specimens from Jamaica, Barbados, Newfoundland, Virginia, Carolina, New England, and Spanish America.[25]

Cotton Mather eventually brought together his many observations on earth theory and fossils in *The Christian Philosopher* (1721), which combined the new empirical studies of the earth with the truths relayed in the Bible. Drawing on local American fossil data as well as from the latest Continental and English science, Mather argued that "Philosophy is no Enemy, but a mighty and wondrous Incentive to Religion." As though handing the mystery of the mountaintop shells to the next generation, Mather directed his readers' attention to the layers of the earth and the fossils that lay in them. "The *Strata* of the Earth, its *Lays* and *Beds*, afford surprizing Matters of Observation," he urged."[26]

Appalachian Shells Take Center Stage, 1730–1770

Between 1730 and 1770, Europeans and Americans added much greater detail to their understandings of the seashells embedded in such unlikely places as mountains. More intensive exploration of

the Appalachians, a result partly of the region's geopolitical importance in the struggle for possession of the North American continent, added immensely to transatlantic debates about how the
earth had formed and changed over time. British Americans now
began to contribute more vocally to this international conversation
about earth-shaping forces, drawing on their experience of the
Appalachians to speculate, sometimes quite grandly, about the early
shape and character of the continents: whether America had once
been joined to Ireland, whether islands were seafloor mountains
poking up through the waves, whether the sea had once blanketed
the sandy deserts of Arabia. Still hewing to the Genesis narrative of
Noah's flood, they gradually relaxed their chronologies, allowing
what the American naturalist John Bartram called "a long process
of time" for the unfolding of earth-shaping processes. As the
Dutch naturalist Jan Frederik Gronovius confided to Bartram, the
timing of earthly processes not mentioned in the Bible was difficult
to determine: "What time it was so, no body can say," he despaired
from Leiden.[27]

Philadelphia now became the headquarters of a new generation
of America-based earth theorizers that included John Bartram,
Benjamin Franklin, the Swedish explorer Pehr (aka Peter) Kalm,
and the surveyor Lewis Evans. With its ever denser carpet of
learned institutions, Philadelphia rivaled Boston as North America's
capital of learning. The Library Company of Philadelphia, the largest lending library in eighteenth-century America, continued to import the latest earth theories from Europe, such as Burnet's *Sacred
Theory*. Writing to Jared Eliot of Connecticut in 1747, Franklin explained the topography of "the great Apalachian Mountains" in precisely the terms relayed by Burnet half a century earlier. Springs in
mountaintops had leaked from an "Abyss" below the earth's crust;
the mountaintop shells bore witness to "the *Wreck* of a World we
live on!" The Library Company also amassed a collection of natural
specimens from America. In 1747, Benjamin Franklin noted with
approval that the Library Company had acquired some of the
Appalachian seashells. Philadelphia was also home to the American
Philosophical Society (APS), modeled on the Royal Society, which
began to publish its own learned journal in 1771. Benjamin
Franklin had specifically listed under the goals of the APS that it

collect correspondence about "new-discovered Fossils in different Countries."[28]

Franklin, Bartram, Kalm, and Evans together represented the emerging possibilities of the North American fringe of the republic of letters. Compared to even a half century earlier, the British American learned community had become more tightly integrated as new institutions were founded and intercolonial correspondence networks grew. Still, Americans remained far from the courtly patronage, cabinets, and scholarly connections that Europeans enjoyed. Americans continued to see Britain and Europe as the center of their scientific world. John Bartram, whose botanical discoveries eventually earned him the coveted title of Royal Botanist, became famous in America, Britain, and the Netherlands for his boundless energy in shipping American plant and rock samples to Europe in what became known as "Bartram's boxes." Yet Bartram's provincialism never ceased to embarrass him: possessing no formal education, he never left the American colonies, and he was perpetually undone by the basic protocols of the republic of letters. "Ye lattin pusels mee," he confessed to the Edinburgh University–educated botanist Cadwallader Colden of New York after receiving a translation of the Latin letters of the Dutch botanist Gronovius. Bartram pleaded with Gronovius to write "in English which I can understand much better than Latin." He had never seen a copy of his correspondent Hans Sloane's *A Voyage to the Islands Madera, Barbados, Nieves, S. Christophers and Jamaica* (1707) until shown one by New Jersey's royal governor Lewis Morris.[29] By contrast, the Swedish scientist Pehr Kalm arrived in America in 1748 covered in scholarly glory: a student of the naturalist Carolus Linnaeus and armed with a university degree, Kalm had been charged with the important task of finding American plants and seeds to aid Swedish agriculture. Across the chasm of education, Kalm and Bartram became friends; with Benjamin Franklin, they also became partners in the great mountain shell debate of the eighteenth century.

Even while remaining abreast of European earth theory, British Americans now embarked on the most extensive exploration to date of the curious shells of the Appalachians. Two mid-eighteenth-century expeditions contributed a great deal to new understandings of fossils and the place of America in earth history:

the journey undertaken by John Bartram and Welsh surveyor Lewis Evans in 1743 and the expedition of Pehr Kalm in 1748. These expeditions yielded influential narratives as well as maps that specifically pointed out the locations of fossil shells in the Appalachian mountaintops.

The first voyage took Bartram and Evans from western Pennsylvania to Lake Ontario in Canada. Bartram described the craggy peaks of the Appalachians, the Great Lakes, and the mountaintop fossil shells as products of the great deluge described in the Bible and refined for the modern era by Thomas Burnet. Stones turned on their sides "reminded me of *Dr. Burnets Theory*, and his ingenious *Hypothesis*, to account for the formation of mountains," wrote Bartram.[30]

Inspired by Burnet, Bartram sketched an extraordinary map of three distinct Appalachian sites, each marked with a label such as "limestone & sea shels in it." This empirical evidence added to the "Curious stones figured with sea shells" that Bartram had already been shipping to his correspondent in London, Hans Sloane. After the 1743 expedition, Bartram continued his earlier practice of shipping American fossil shells across the Atlantic both to his London network (Sloane, John Fothergill, and Peter Collinson), and to Gronovius in Leiden. Thanking Bartram for the latest shipment of fossil shells, Fothergill explained their utility in forming a "general Idea" of "the nature of things."[31]

Lewis Evans's map of these travels, produced in 1749, likewise sprang from the great debate about the origin of the American mountaintop shells. Plastered with direct rebuttals to European theories, the map illustrates how local knowledge of American mountains and shells could challenge the earth theories of eminent European scholars such as John Woodward who had no direct knowledge of the American scene. Perhaps, speculated Evans in a long paragraph printed on the map itself, the Appalachians had formed not *during* the biblical deluge as Woodward had proposed but *before* it, at the moment of creation itself. Confined to his British armchair, Woodward had no concept of the American setting, Evans declared, and so reached too much for miracles to explain the local topography. Evans's rebuttal took direct aim at Woodward and his theories:

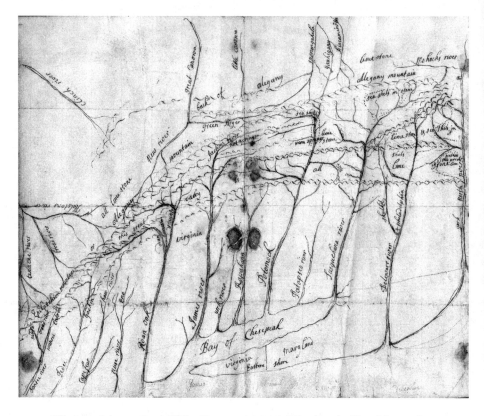

The top right portion of John Bartram's map of the Appalachian Mountains indicates the sites where he found seashells. John Bartram, [Middle Atlantic States . . .], 1750s. (Individually Catalogued Manuscript Maps no. 32 [3]. 650: [c. 1750s]: At61mvc Small. American Philosophical Society.)

They [the Appalachians] furnish endless Funds for Systems and Theories of the World, but the most obvious to me was, That this Earth was made of the Ruins of another; at the Creation. Bones and Shells which escaped the Fate of Softer animal Substances, we find mixt with the old Materials and elegantly preserved in the loose Stones and rocky Bases of the highest of these Hills. These Mountains existed in their present elevated Height before the Deluge, but not so bare of Soil as now. . . . Dr. Woodward from infinite Examples discover'd, that this World had been in a State of Dissolution. But the Power he ascribes to the

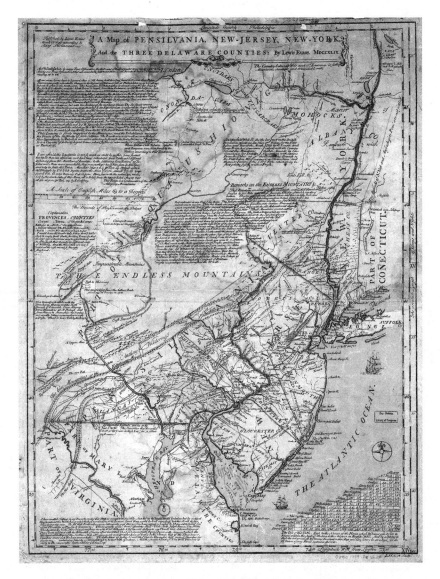

Arguing for the importance of New World evidence in discussions of earth theories, the surveyor Lewis Evans draped his rebuttal to the English naturalist John Woodward directly over the Appalachians in this mid-eighteenth-century map. Lewis Evans, A Map of Pensilvania, New-Jersey, New-York, and the Three Delaware Counties: by Lewis Evans *(1749). (Geography and Map Division, Library of Congress)*

Water of Deluge is too much a Miracle to obtain Belief.
We have here glaring Marks of a Deluge of far more recent
Date, which the Compass of Britain might not perhaps
have furnished the Dr. with.[32]

Other expeditions likewise suggested that New World
rocks might be very old. Stumbling upon unlikely shells in the
Appalachians and in Philadelphia, Pehr Kalm asked Franklin whether
"places which were now a part of the continent had formerly been
covered with water." Kalm noted the presence of "immense quanti-
ties" of oyster and mussel shells in mountain valleys, and deep wells
containing stones that were presumably "made round by the rolling
of the waves." These curious findings prompted Kalm to propose an
early version of a process that would be christened uniformitarianism
a century later: that the same slow, gradual earth-shaping processes
that operated in the present also operated in the past. "Are not these
reasons sufficient to make one suppose that those places in
Philadelphia which are at present fourteen feet and more under
ground were formerly the bottom of the sea, and that by several violent changes, sand, earth, and other things were carried upon them?
or, that the Delaware formerly was broader than it is at present? or
that it has changed its course? This last still happens at present, the
river tearing off material from the bank on one side, and depositing it
on the other." At the same time, Kalm conceded that other scenarios
could also explain the shells in the Appalachians. Noting the important trade in wampum, he proposed that the shells might have been
brought to the mountaintops by the Indians.[33]

Their imaginations freed by this new empirical evidence, British
Americans and their London correspondents now extended their
speculations to the mysterious world that lay hidden under the
oceans. They openly considered the possibility that mountain
chains ringed the seafloor under what Peter Collinson called the
"fathomless depths of the Ocean." Bartram too pondered what
might lie at the bottom of the deepest sea. "I doubt not but there is
a great variety of animals in the deep seas, both swimming and
creeping; and many species of shell-fish on shoals very remote from
the shores, never yet exposed to our sight of knowledge," he wrote
to Collinson. "Sub-marine ridges" and "deep sub-marine valleys"

might extend hundreds of miles under the ocean, generating the great sea currents reported by mariners.[34]

All over Europe and its empires, mid-eighteenth-century observers coped with an ever growing quantity of fossil evidence from around the world. In response, they crafted new scenarios about earth-shaping forces that challenged without entirely displacing biblical narratives of the creation of the earth. By the 1760s, Appalachian evidence had helped incorporate American naturalists and the Appalachians firmly into European earth theories. John Bartram, Pehr Kalm, and Lewis Evans debated Britain's major earth theorists, Thomas Burnet and John Woodward, citing American evidence that contradicted European scenarios. More and more American shells appeared in English and Continental treatises on earth theory, as in the London naturalist and Royal Society member Emanuel Mendes da Costa's *A Natural History of Fossils* (1757), which alluded many times to American data. Attempting to reduce the study of fossils to what he called "a regular science," Mendes da Costa catalogued an array of American rock and shell specimens in a work bought by learned Americans eager to stay abreast of earth theory and America's place in it.[35]

Awash in data, the next generation to plumb the depths of earth history would discover that more information yielded not answers but, rather, more questions. The greatest problem was yet to come: too many answers, with an ever receding consensus on what the big question really was.

Enlightenment, Revolution, Geology, 1776–1820

A new Franco-American intellectual community emerged from the crucible of the American and French Revolutions. The diplomatic channels that first opened between the United States and France after 1775 enabled French and American intellectuals eager to exchange theories about the history of the earth to correspond freely. Until this time, British scholars had dominated the British American conversation about earth theory, but now French scholars and French geography rose to importance.[36] Benefiting from shared details about American and French geological formations, learned people in France and the United States toyed with new, increasingly nonbiblical and fact-driven narratives about the history of the earth. Called enlightened because they were based on observation rather than speculation, these narratives described changes so cataclysmic that they were called "revolutions," the same term being applied to the tumultuous political upheavals around the Atlantic world. The enlightened study of both kinds of revolution required factual evidence, either written documents made by humans or the rocky documents generated by the earth. The age of political revolutions, in short, was tightly linked to the age of geological revolutions. Both required evidence to be sifted and collected, and non-miraculous causes and consequences weighed.

This new community included both Americans in France and French people in the United States. Benjamin Franklin and Thomas Jefferson, for example, traveled to France as part of the American treaty negotiations with the French government. There they joined French colleagues in lively debates about earth theory. They also studied French geological formations in Paris, the Alps, and the dramatically vulcanized Massif Central. Later, the French Revolution and its disruptions brought a cadre of erudite Frenchmen to eastern North America, where they inspected local geological features (including the shells in the Appalachians) and reported on them to their colleagues back home. This group included the political firebrand and friend of Jefferson Constantin-François de Chasseboeuf, comte de Volney, whose backcountry tour of the Appalachians in 1796 yielded his influential *Tableau du climat et du sol des Etats-Unis d'Amérique* (1803), published in English translation the following year as *View of the Climate and Soil of the United States of America;* and the royalist French social reformer the duc de La Rochefoucauld, who fled to America in 1794 and made extensive studies of the eastern United States and Canada that were published as *Travels Through the United States of North America* (1799). These French *érudits* were convinced of the importance of bringing American geological features and specimens to the attention of the learned community in Europe. "To conceive properly the general construction of this vast country," Volney remarked as he shipped American shell specimens to the eminent scientist Jean-Baptiste Lamarck in Paris, "we must acquire a more particular knowledge of the chain of mountains, that forms it's predominant feature."[37]

Americans and Europeans began groping for increasingly secular, time-specific narratives about earth-shaping processes. Borrowing concepts and methods from human historiography— such as the idea of revolutions and distinct ages (*époques*) rather than the vague days mentioned in the Genesis story of creation—natural historians now claimed that they could view the earth historically. Like human history, earth history rested on empirical evidence, they maintained. Earth's documents were shells, rock strata, and volcanoes, which because sturdy formed a more reliable archive than the papery ephemera of human history, argued the French naturalist Barthélemy Faujas de Saint Fond. Educated people also insisted that the ages of the earth advanced through regular, secular chronologies instead of sudden, cataclysmic, and divinely ordained transformations. "The planetary system," argued James Madison in an essay on the natural order, was "regulated by fixed laws, and presents most demonstrably, a scene of order and proportion." Any kind of "revolution on the face of the globe" would have occurred in an empirically plausible rather than a miraculous fashion. Specimens such as fossil shells, which had previously been merely supplementary to speculative earth theory, now became integral to the study of the earth's past, in the way that written documents and archaeological samples were now believed essential to the modern practice of history writing and classical scholarship. What the English historian Edward Gibbon had accomplished for human history in his laboriously documented and footnoted *History of the Decline and Fall of the Roman Empire* (1776–88) was also attempted by the earth's historians, who presented geological samples as evidence of epochs now believed significantly to predate human habitation of the earth.[38]

These inquiries involved a dramatic lengthening of the time span for the operation of geological processes, a recognition that the short age of political revolutions had been dwarfed by the extremely long ages of geological revolution. A number of eighteenth-century naturalists—including James Hutton in Scotland, Abraham Werner in Germany, the comte de Buffon in France, and William Smith in Britain—were concluding that the earth might be hundreds of thousands, perhaps even millions of years old. Each ventured his own time frame. By the end of the eighteenth century, deep time—a time that stretched far beyond Ussher's short, biblically bound chronology—had become a plausible though still controversial and unsettling scenario for learned people. Eventually, these Europeans were joined by Americans such as Thomas Jefferson, who proposed with some anxiety that certain fossil remains might be over 250,000 years old. The intellectual transition to a much longer time span was gradual rather than sudden, and biblical scenarios continued to thrive. In the midst of the American Revolution, in December 1778, the seniors at Yale College held a syllogistic disputation on the subject of whether the biblical deluge had been universal or local in origin.[39]

The American Revolution brought provincial Americans into contact with French naturalists at the very moment when France had emerged as a major center of earth theorizing and exploration. The comte de Buffon, among the most influential natural philosophers of the eighteenth century, proposed that the earth was about seventy-five thousand years old, an idea that earned him condemnation from the church. Dividing earth's history into "époques," Buffon gave shells a starring role in the third age, when water had covered the whole earth, a time so long ago that many of its fossil remains possessed no living analogues. Buffon concluded that these ancient shells were so widely scattered in so many different terrains that "they were not transported there by a flood." He compared his work of natural history to the work of civil historians, except that his own inquiries reached back into the darkest abyss of time. "As in civil History written documents are consulted, medals sought, ancient inscriptions deciphered . . . so in Natural History it is necessary to rummage through the archives of the world, to draw from the bowels of the earth old monuments [and] collect their debris."[40]

Captivated by his literary style and scientific relevance, revolutionary Americans read and admired Buffon as a kind of Gibbon of the natural world, even though they vocally rejected his theory of a degenerate American continent. John Quincy Adams recorded in his diary in the late 1780s that he was "exceedingly pleased" with the style of Buffon in his "theory of the earth." Adams liked that Buffon's "facts"—the widely dispersed seashells—told a magnificent story about the past and future of mountain ranges in Europe and the Americas. "He supposes that the continents and islands which are now inhabited, were covered by the waters of the ocean, and that they will be so again: that at some future period the Alps, the Pyrenees, and the Andes, will be at the bottom of the sea, and that the earth now beneath the atlantic, and pacific oceans, will be the abodes of men, adorned, with splendid cities, and crowned with venerable forests." Adams's father scribbled marginalia in his copy of Buffon, particularly in the section titled "Sur les coquilles" (On Shells), which probed the mystery of mountaintop shells around the world, including the Americas.[41]

Farther to the south, James Madison took copious notes in the volumes of Buffon's work that Jefferson sent him from Paris. Madison called Buffon "the best informed of any naturalist who has ever written" and asked Jefferson the cost of framed color prints of Buffon's birds and quadrupeds to adorn the walls of his plantation home, Montpelier. Buffon especially captured the attention of Americans hoping to make sense of local shells. In Williamsburg, Virginia, the Reverend James Madison (cousin of the future president) collected local tidewater shells, marveling that "Monsr. Buffon in his celebrated Epoques speaks of Shells found in the highest Parts of this Country."[42]

More overtly anticlerical than Buffon and his long chronology was Voltaire, whose sarcastic attack on what he called "shells and systems built on shells" appeared in his *Questions sur l'encyclopédie* (1770–74). Outraged that many recent geological discoveries continued to be deployed as proof of the great deluge, Voltaire argued that "shell systems"—elaborate scenarios concocted to defend the Bible—in fact led straight to ridiculous implausibilities. If the sea had once covered the whole earth, wrote Voltaire, then there must have been a time when only fish lived on earth; the presence of humans could be explained only if those fish had sprouted arms and legs and become men. Hoping to vex the short chronologists, Voltaire pointed out that shells lodged deep in mines implied an earth of unimaginable antiquity, the shells being vestiges not of a single God-directed flood but of the many "revolutions of our planet." Further casting doubt on the biblical flood thesis, Voltaire reminded readers of the allegations of the French antiquarian and seigneur Félix François de la Sauvagère, who claimed that the soil near his château in the Loire Valley had spontaneously generated shells not once but twice. Should not such phenomena raise doubts about whether a biblical deluge had dropped shells in inland strata?[43]

Alongside these anti-biblical French fireworks quietly stood a much more empirical series of works that rested on careful local studies of French terrain. These works influenced not just French intellectuals but scholars in the larger republic of letters. The authors included the Genevan Jean-André Deluc, so widely known that he became reader to Queen Charlotte of England. Deluc was among the first to use the term *géologie*, which he proposed in his *Lettres physiques et morales sur les montagnes et sur l'histoire de la Terre et de l'Homme* (Physical and Moral Letters on Mountains and on the History of the Earth and of Man, 1778), a work addressed to the queen. He hoped the term would help distinguish the study of the earth specifically from the larger study of the cosmos. Referring to the earth's cycles rather than the unpleasantness with her American colonies, Deluc told Queen Charlotte that earth's history could be divided into two distinct periods separated by "the great Revolution."[44]

Other French naturalists also influenced the international conversation about earth's history. Jean-Louis Giraud Soulavie's *Histoire naturelle de la France méridionale* (Natural History of Southern France, 1780–84) emerged from the young abbé's wide-ranging exploration of the volcanic Auvergne region of south-central France. A correspondent of Franklin, who owned Soulavie's book, Soulavie argued that the age of volcanic eruptions could be calculated by measuring erosion times.[45] Indicating the frequency with which these earth theorists also ran in revolutionary political circles, Soulavie later became an early member of the Jacobin club and published a history of the reign of Louis XVI. All these publications found their enthusiasts in the new United States.

In the 1780s, Thomas Jefferson became the first American to engage deeply with French earth theory. With his expansive interests and wide network of correspondents, Jefferson established himself as the major American hub of a worldwide communication network regarding geological formations and fossils. He could glimpse the Appalachian range through the haze of his hilltop home, Monticello, in the foothills of western Virginia. What force, he wondered, had molded the nearby Natural Bridge in Virginia, "the most sublime of nature's works"? To what animals belonged the teeth and bones unearthed around the world, such as the monstrous sea creature recently pulled from the limestone quarries of Maastricht, and the fearsome elephant-like teeth and tusks dug up in Kentucky and Ohio?[46]

The American Revolution gave Jefferson his first opportunity to write publicly about these interests. In 1780, François Barbé-Marbois, the head of the French legation to America, invited Jefferson as governor of Virginia to comment on the specifics of his state. Jefferson's answer appeared in the form of Query VI of the *Notes on the State of Virginia*—which concerned mines, ores, and plants. The essay revealed his already significant knowledge about earth theory, with references to influential works on South America, Russia, and France.[47]

In Query VI, Jefferson immediately launched into the now famous problem of explaining shells in American mountaintops. The Appalachians contained "impressions of shells in a variety of forms"; he had also "received petrified shells of very different kinds from the first sources of the Kentucky, which bear no resemblance to any I have ever seen on the tide-waters." Many thought these mountaintop shells were proof of a "universal deluge."[48]

Allergic to the idea of the deluge, Jefferson ventured a trio of explanations for the mysterious seashells in mountaintops, rejecting each in turn and concluding that "this great phaenomenon is as yet unsolved." He first discarded the idea of a global flood high enough to leave shells on mountain peaks. Such a flood would have reached only about fifty feet high, so this scenario failed to explain shells lodged at fifteen thousand feet in the Andes. Besides, a universal flood seemed "out of the laws of nature"; experience suggested that even the greatest flood of the Virginia tidewater would not reach Kentucky. Although classical and biblical history supplied examples of "a partial deluge" in the Mediterranean, these events "will not account for the shells found in the higher lands."[49]

Jefferson then rejected a second idea, that some "great convulsion of nature" long ago had heaved the ocean bed—"the principal residence of the shelled tribe"—to the great heights in which these shells were now found. But since neither history nor the present furnished examples of any "natural agents" that could hoist mountains from the depths of the ocean floor to the clouds, he rejected this no-tion in turn.[50]

He then showcased Voltaire's dangerously unorthodox view of the shells, bringing the philosophe's searing critique of the Genesis flood narrative to a wider American public. As he so often did, Jefferson concluded that ignorance was preferable to error, and he left the shell problem in this open-ended, unsettled state.[51]

Jefferson's stay in France between 1784 and 1789 gave him a chance to test his shell theories in person. He joined the small U.S. diplomatic community in Paris, a city whose own geology was be-coming the subject of increasing scrutiny by none other than Benjamin Franklin, stationed there since the outbreak of the American Revolution. Not only had Franklin immersed himself in the local discussions about earth theory in the salons and acade-mies, the aging statesman had trudged breathlessly uphill enough times to his lodgings at Passy to think of the hill as nothing short of a mountain. Like the aptly named Montmartre, Passy, located northwest of the center of Paris, stood atop calcium-rich mounds that had formed millions of years before by the receding sea; quar-rying these areas yielded the gypsum for the famous plaster of Paris. In one of the eight letters he exchanged with the French ge-ologist Jean-Louis Giraud Soulavie, Franklin described the shells lodged in the rocks of "this Mountain of Passy on which I live."[52]

Like Franklin, Jefferson soon became immersed in the geologi-cal conversation in Paris. Virginians kept shipping tidewater shells to Jefferson, pestering him for explanations about their origins. He was soon infected by the same volcano bug that had bitten Franklin, splurging on the lavish books about Sir William Hamilton's spectac-ular hikes to see the steaming crater of Mount Vesuvius. In 1795, Jefferson used the term *geology* for the first time in a letter to a French scientist praising the advantages of intellectual interchange about the history of the earth. "Our geology is untouched, and would have been a precious mine for you, as your views of it would have been precious to us."[53]

Armed with this new knowledge of geology, Jefferson em-barked in 1787 on a three-month tour through France and Italy, a journey that also became a kind of geological field trip. Nearing Paris in June 1787 at the close of his tour, Jefferson arrived at the

Loire Valley château of Félix François de la Sauvagère, whose mysterious, spontaneously generating shells Jefferson had read about in Voltaire's essay and had cited in the *Notes on the State of Virginia*.

Alighting from his carriage, Jefferson hoped at last to behold "these shells unconnected with animal bodies" that by spontaneously generating from the rock might cast further doubt on the reality of the biblical flood. Jefferson's inspection of the shells led him to conclude that Sauvagère was correct: these shells really did spontaneously generate, though by what precise means remained baffling. Sauvagère insisted that their spontaneous generation implied that the shells had not emerged from the flood. Triumphant, Jefferson dashed off a letter to his shell-collecting friend in Virginia, the Reverend James Madison, telling him that Sauvagère was correct. The strange shell formations were "so little like any known operation of nature, that it throws the mind under absolute suspense."[54]

Wandering amid the curious shells of the Loire Valley, Jefferson returned to his customary agnosticism about natural processes. He believed that the shells in France, like those in America's mountains and cliffs, could not have been deposited by the biblical flood. But just what forces had put them in these unlikely places remained a mystery.

Outcomes: The Problem of Causality

Jefferson emerged as one of his era's leading advocates of a nonbiblical origin of geological features. Yet though he promoted the study of the specifics of American geology for the remainder of his life, he despaired at ever finding the true cause of the revolutions in the earth. He urged that geology be given "the least possible time" at the University of Virginia because it remained so speculative. He explained his reasoning two months before his death, in 1826. "To learn, as far as observation has informed us, the ordinary arrangement of the different strata of minerals in the earth ... is useful. But the dreams about the modes of creation, inquiries whether our globe has been formed by the agency of fire or water, how many years it cost Vulcan or Neptune to produce what the fiat of the Creator would effect by a single act of will, is too idle to be worth a single hour of any man's life."[55]

Even among those of a more orthodox bent, the biblical story of a mighty flood had receded as an explanatory device for geological changes. The Genesis story was not so much explicitly rejected as quietly shelved in favor of more naturalistic explanations—or no explanation at all. The most eminent geologist in early national America, William Maclure, confessed to being stumped by the causal forces that had shaped the earth despite decades of field research in Europe and the Americas. "I have always thought that the changes on our globe depend more on the coincidence of a great many partial causes and changes rather than on any one great sweeping agent which would have wrought up the whole in seven days, as Moses made the creation," he asserted. Three decades later, in 1832, with even more field research in America and Europe under his belt, Maclure had not changed his mind, and continued to stress the need for closer research into the features of the earth, whose crust was still barely known. "Nothing within our observation proves the priority of one mode of formation over the other," he concluded.[56]

The long quest to discover the origin of shells in American mountaintops had two important outcomes. The first was structural: the integration of the Americas into the international learned community's understanding of earth-shaping forces. Around the republic of letters, increasing numbers of regional studies were gradually incorporated into a wholly new story of the earth, a story whose beginning and end was less and less wedded to the Genesis narrative in part because of the intrusion of so much local data. One achievement of the age of political revolution, in short, was the geological revolution integrating the Americas and Americans into the new, more empirically based international understanding of the earth's structure and formation. From a seventeenth-century world in which the precise role of the New World in the Genesis flood narrative had been baffling at best, there emerged by the early nineteenth century a conviction that natural rather than miraculous earth-shaping forces operated in the same way everywhere, whether in the New World or the Old. Two centuries of data gathering in the Americas—in the form of shells, fossils, and ores—pushed European scientists to fold knowledge from the former periphery of the learned world into their accounts. Reading these European studies, Americans could more easily link distant geologies to local ones. The "Swiss & American Alps," as James Madison called them, were mutually reinforcing.[57]

As they became more self-confident about the importance of their continent, geologists in the United States gradually began to make exceptionalist arguments, moving incrementally toward the moment in the later nineteenth century when they would celebrate the geology of the United States as evidence that God had spread his special grace on America. The American geologist and dentist Horace H. Hayden's *Geological Essays* (1820) pronounced the alluvial deposits of American rivers and coasts important because of "the particular knowledge, that ought to be obtained of all local facts." Hayden argued that "enlightened" people who knew geological formations elsewhere in the world should nonetheless admire the particularity of certain American features, such as the difficulty in gaining "a correct knowledge of facts" about the Mississippi River, since unlike the Nile, the Po, the Indus, and the Ganges, it lacked ancient human monuments suitable for dating fossil features.[58]

The second outcome was epistemological: the quest for enlightenment yielded not just new data but also new uncertainty. By the late eighteenth century, unknown causality had become preferable to divine causality as an explanation for the forces that had molded the planet. This was not necessarily an antireligious or anticlerical stance, since it left open the question of how and especially why strata had formed over time rather than assigning the process to a divine agent. The writer Temple Henry Croker advised Benjamin Franklin in 1787 that the unknown cause of magnetism awaited "Facts" and "real Experiments" rather than "artfully devised Systems." Nearly half a century later, in 1832, the Philadelphia scientist Jacob Green reaffirmed the new message in his study of trilobites in North America. The search for shells had evolved from a "simple amusement" into "the study of scientific men" who based their conclusions on "*geological fact.*" Yet given how big the earth was, how much remained "unexplored by its enlightened and civilized inhabitants," no one could be truly sure about anything.[59]

Not only were the causes of earth-shaping forces debatable now that the Genesis flood thesis seemed less convincing as an explanatory device, but the ultimate purpose of all these geological changes likewise receded from human grasp. Geologists coped with the problem of what we might call causal agnosticism in part by assigning more importance to empirical data gathered through fieldwork. As the teleology embedded in the eighteenth-century concept of nature became muted with God's retreat from direct intervention in earthly processes, geologists too retreated from the effort to find a moral reason for earth-shaping forces. The whole earth, from the highest mountain to the deepest sea, had to be explored before definitive conclusions could be reached about how and why it changed. This was a project of such tiring magnitude that its completion surely lay in the distant future, a future that must be more enlightened and therefore more capable of the reasoned accumulation and interpretation of geological facts.

The legacy of the great Appalachian shell debate was that the biblical flood—and the tiny sea creatures it may have swept high into the American mountains—was not so much attacked as ignored, awaiting a presumably more enlightened future age that would perhaps bring greater knowledge and with it greater understanding of nature's purposes for humanity. Thus the optimistic quest for enlightenment had brought with it an unexpected and unsettling outcome, with more geological facts but less certainty about their larger moral purpose. Nineteenth-century Americans muddled through in various ways. Some moved farther from biblical explanations, while others (such as the Hudson River School painters) infused American rocks with a hyper-nationalistic religiosity. The era of Darwin pushed anxieties about God's purpose for the earth into even shriller directions. Over time everyone gradually forgot about the creatures that had raised these troubling questions in the first place: the tiny seashells lying silently in their Appalachian tombs.

CHAPTER THREE

The Civilization of the Aztecs

W HEN THE BRITISH PAINTER Robert Burford unveiled his panorama of modern Mexico City in the
late 1820s, he declared that the Mexicans at the time
of the sixteenth-century Spanish conquest had been
"the most enlightened nation of the American continent."[1] Many
citizens of the new United States would have agreed. Despite finding little to praise in the modern North American Indians and
Mexicans, they readily affirmed that the pre-Hispanic Mexicans—
first called "ancient Mexicans," then christened "Aztecs" around
1800—had been the most civilized, enlightened people of the
Americas.

Had the indigenous peoples of the Americas ever been enlightened? Or was the New World climate so hostile to civilization (as
many European theorists held) that all life—including newly transplanted Europeans—degenerated into debased forms? These two
questions were vigorously debated in the long eighteenth century on
both sides of the Atlantic. One highly attractive answer came in the
form of the pre-Hispanic peoples of Mesoamerica. Builders of magnificent cities crowned by enormous stone pyramids and fed by aq-
ueducts, the peoples of ancient Mexico left evidence suggesting that
a kind of civilization had once flourished in the Americas, a place
whose climate was routinely condemned by European philosophers

as damaging to humanity's progression up the ladder of social evolution from savagery through barbarity and thence to enlightened civilization. Newly liberated from British rule, people in the United States seized upon the pre-Hispanic Mexicans as a way of demonstrating to skeptical Europeans that civilization was indeed possible in the Americas and that the United States would surely rise to become the mightiest nation of the hemisphere, if not the world. Although the modern Indians of North America might be savages (in the terminology of the eighteenth century), the urban, empire-building Aztecs proved that the New World could be a source of civilization and enlightenment.

To redeem New World civilization in the postrevolutionary era, learned people in the early national United States looked to a group of thinkers in Spanish America who were beginning to piece together historical and archaeological remains to trace the origin and progress of a mighty precontact Mexican people they called the Aztecs. Once largely closed off to British America by linguistic, religious, and imperial barriers, these Spanish American intellectuals suddenly became relevant to educated people in the early United States eager to justify their westward expansion across a continent still largely controlled by Spain and American Indian groups. U.S. intellectuals learned from their counterparts in Spanish America that the ancestors of the indigenous peoples of Mexico had once populated North America, leaving behind the curious earthen mounds in the Midwest that were clearly "the *relics* of a once powerful and enlightened people," as one American author put it. They theorized that these early, mound-building people had then migrated south to central Mexico, where they had continued to climb up the ladder of civilization, building an empire and becoming what one English writer called "the most enlightened nation of the American continent, and considerably advanced in certain arts and manufactures." U.S. intellectuals believed that these allegedly civilized, enlightened Aztecs bore no relationship to the modern Indians currently living in North America, who appeared to build no cities, to possess no writing, and to have lost all memory of the mound-building people. Clearly lacking the markers of civilization, modern North American Indians would surely shrink before the march of U.S. civilization westward over the continent.[2]

To establish the Aztecs as a representative civilization of the Americas, thinkers in the eighteenth and early nineteenth centuries latched onto three particular artifacts. The first was a series of brilliantly colored book-like manuscripts (called Aztec codices today) created by indigenous Mexicans before and after the Spanish conquest. The codices seemed to be both painting and writing, possible evidence of the ancient Mexicans' capacity for art and literacy, some of the major building blocks of what in the eighteenth century was considered civilization. Interest clustered especially around the magnificent Codex Mendoza, a manuscript created jointly by Spaniards and indigenous Mexicans in the years shortly after the Spanish conquest of the capital city of Tenochtitlán in 1521. Shipped to Europe soon after its creation and partially published in a variety of European-language books, the Codex Mendoza became the most widely circulated of the Mexican codices and a staple of transatlantic theorizing about the capacity of the indigenous Mesoamericans for civilization.

Second, thinkers in the new United States turned to the influential history of ancient Mexico published in 1780 by the Mexican-born Jesuit historian Francesco Saverio Clavigero. His *Storia antica del Messico* (Ancient History of Mexico, 1780–81), which was soon translated into English, rescued the indigenous peoples of the Americas from the gloomy verdict of inferiority rendered by eighteenth-century European theorists such as the comte de Buffon, the abbé Raynal, and the Dutch geographer and philosopher Cornelius Pauw. Clavigero's history popularized the theory that the mysterious mound builders of North America had been the ancestors of the civilized Aztecs. For over sixty years after its publication, Clavigero's history influenced thinkers in the United States eager to establish the legitimacy of their new republic. It formed part of a collective, pan-American rebuke to European degeneracy theories during the age of domino-like anti-colonization movements throughout the Americas.

The third important source to rivet citizens of the early United States was the so-called Calendar Stone, an enormous basalt sculpture unearthed in Mexico City, the former Tenochtitlán, in 1790. Dating from some unknown earlier era, the Calendar Stone seemed to be an astronomical instrument, suggesting to Europeans and

North Americans that the ancient Mexicans had had the capacity to perform sophisticated mathematical calculations. They might, in short, have possessed reason, that essential building block of civilization. News of the discovery of the Calendar Stone quickly traveled around the Atlantic, inspiring a wide-ranging conversation about the place of enlightened reason in the history and progress of the Americas.

Together, these three sources, one painted, one printed, one sculptural, promised to answer the critical question of whether enlightened civilization had once flourished—and could flourish again—in the New World. They also inspired the formation of the first truly hemispheric dialogue within the Americas among intellectuals in the United States and Mexico.

The Codex Mendoza

Before they were reimagined as enlightened Aztecs in the late eighteenth century, the indigenous people of Mexico had been known to Europeans for over two centuries through widely circulated texts and images. Among the best known was the Codex Mendoza, one of the hundreds of pictorial manuscripts produced in Mexico before and immediately after the Spanish conquest. These codices (which at the time were called "Mexican paintings" by English speakers) made them particularly attractive to European sovereigns and scholars, who prized them for their great beauty and the light they promised to throw on the aboriginals of the Americas.

Composed by trained indigenous painters, the codices were produced in large numbers throughout pre-Hispanic Mexico. Seeing them as signs of pagan idolatry, the Spanish burned many codices in the century after the conquest; roughly five hundred are thought to survive today. But some codices—such as the Codex Mendoza—were produced after the conquest, during a moment of simultaneous destruction and creativity, as one people encountered another and produced a synthetic culture. Some codices were commissioned for European use as accounts of Mexican society. The Spaniards shipped many pre- and postconquest codices to Europe, where they were received with wonder and safeguarded in princely cabinets and libraries. Today many are known by the names of those European repositories, or the noble families or religious figures who enabled their acquisition and preservation: the Florentine Codex, the Codex Borgia, the Dresden Codex, and so on.[3]

Of these many codices, by far the best known to European audiences from the seventeenth century on was the Codex Mendoza, a manuscript that became central to the eventual transformation of ancient Mexicans into the eighteenth-century idea of enlightened Aztecs. The Codex Mendoza remains famous even today: its image of an eagle alighting on a cactus—the symbol of the founding of Tenochtitlán—has bedecked Mexico's national flag since independence in 1821. The manuscript appears to have acquired the name Mendoza from the man who probably commissioned it: the first viceroy of New Spain, Antonio de Mendoza.

Completed about twenty years after the conquest of Tenochtitlán, the Codex Mendoza is the most comprehensive of the Mesoamerican codices. Divided into three parts, it is the only Mesoamerican codex to combine a record of pre-Hispanic Mexican conquests, tribute demands, and finally—in a third part that charmed European and British American viewers—an ethnographic account of ancient Mexican life from cradle to grave. The codex was made of European paper painted by Indian scribes under the supervision of Spanish priests, who added annotations and commentaries in Spanish. Modern scholars believe that while the whole document was prepared for the Spanish crown, parts 1 and 2 were probably copied from earlier, preconquest pictorials. Part 3, the ethnographic account, has no known indigenous analogue and was probably composed specifically for inclusion in the document. Created in the crucible of immediate postconquest Mexico, the Codex Mendoza is a highly synthetic document, combining indigenous, pre-Hispanic motifs with European ones.[4]

Just as complex as its creation was how the Codex Mendoza crossed the Atlantic, eventually making its way to the Bodleian Library at Oxford, where it remains today. At some point, probably in the 1540s or early 1550s, the codex left the New World, probably bound for the king of Spain. The ship bearing the codex appears to have been captured by French privateers, and its next certain location is in the hands of the controversial French cleric André Thevet, who had it by 1553 and scribbled his name and the date on the document. By 1587, Richard Hakluyt, the English editor of collections of world voyages and travels, had acquired the codex. Hakluyt's great popularizer Samuel Purchas gained access to the Codex Mendoza when it was in Hakluyt's possession, and published a notice of what he called the "Mexican historie" in his *Purchas His Pilgrimage* (1614). Purchas eventually acquired the Codex Mendoza itself sometime after 1616, the year of Hakluyt's death. In the meantime, Purchas somehow obtained fuller and more accurate information about the history of the Codex Mendoza, which he included in his magnum opus, *Purchas His Pilgrimes* (1625). This much-expanded discussion included numerous woodcuts of the codex images, with the original's Spanish-language annotations replaced by English-language explanations. After Purchas's death the manuscript was acquired by the English jurist and antiquarian John Selden, who deposited it in the Bodleian, where it was soon forgotten. However, images of the Codex Mendoza continued to circulate widely, not just in Purchas's illustrations but in books published in the Netherlands, France, and Germany.[5]

It was thanks to Purchas's books that British and American audiences from the early seventeenth century on became aware that the indigenous peoples of Mesoamerica had a complex culture and history. The ethnographic third part of the Codex Mendoza, which Purchas discussed briefly in his 1614 book and then reproduced with elaborate explanation in his 1625 book, opened a window onto some of the most intimate, day-to-day activities of the ancient Mexicans, what Purchas called "their policie and customes." Purchas was not certain whether these Mexican "pictures" constituted writing. Sometimes he explained them as writing: "Their writings were not as ours from the left hand to the right . . .: but beginning below did mount upwards." At other times he searched for different explanations, suggesting that the "figures and Hieroglyphickes represented things after their manner. Such as had forme or figure, were represented by their proper Images, other things were represented by Characters." But whether or not they had writing, the ancient Mexicans—as presented by Purchas—clearly were fully human, endowed with a private life, or what he called *"priuate behauiour."*[6]

The images and explanations of the Codex Mendoza reproduced in *Purchas His Pilgrimes* showed what Purchas called "the

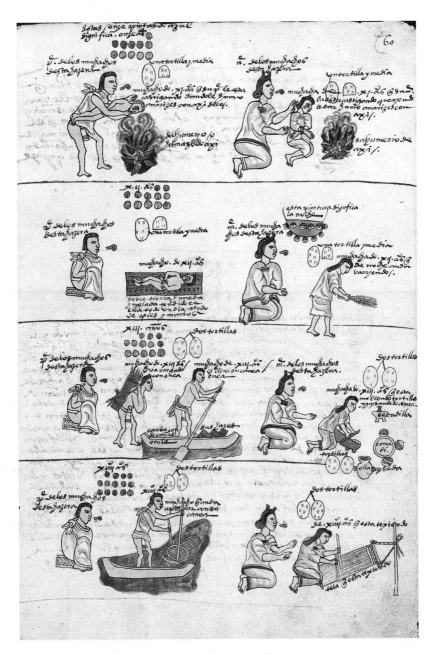

This leaf from the Codex Mendoza shows the "ancient Mexicans" (later called Aztecs) teaching their children various tasks such as fishing and weaving. (The Bodleian Libraries, The University of Oxford, MS. Arch. Seldon. A. 1, fol. 60r)

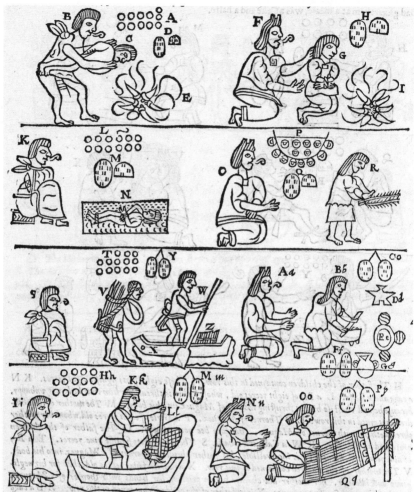

A *These eleuen spots of blue fignifie eleuen yeeres.* B *The father of the children.* C *a Boy of eleuen yeeres old, whofe father is chaftifing him, fmoking him at the Nofe with Axi dried.* D *a Cake and a halfe.* E *a fume or fmoke of Axi or Pepper,* which the Cutter hath not fo well expreffed. F *The mother of the children.* G *a Girle of eleuen yeeres old, whofe mother is chaftifing her fmoking her at the Nofe with Axi.* H *a Cake and a halfe.* I *a perfume of Axi.* K *The father of the children.* L *twelue yeeres.* M *a Cake and a halfe.* N *a Boy of twelue yeeres old, tyed hand and foot and laid a whole day on the wet and moift ground.* O *The mother of the children.* P *This picture fignifieth the night.* Q *a Cake and a halfe.* R *a Girle of twelue yeeres old that is fweeping in the night time.* S *The father of the children.* T *Thirteene yeeres.* V *a Boy of thirteene yeeres old laden with Sedges.* W *a Boy of thirteene yeeres which carrieth Sedges in his Canoa.* X *a Canoa with burdens of Z Canes or Tule.* Y *Two cakes.* A a *The mother of the children.* B b *a Girle of thirteene yeeres, which is grinding and making of Cakes, and dreffing meat.* C c *Two Cakes.* D d *a Porenger.* E e *Comaly* F f *Two Cakes.* G g *a pot of boyled meat.* H h *Fourteene yeeres.* I i *The father of the children.* K k L l *a Boy of fourteene yeeres which goeth a fiſhing with his Canoa.* M m *Two Cakes.* N n *The mother.* O o *a Girle of fourteene yeeres weauing.* P p *Two Cakes.* Q q *The cloth that fhee weaueth.*

I *That*

A page from the Codex Mendoza is here reproduced in the widely circulating book that brought knowledge of the "ancient Mexicans" to an English-speaking audience: Samuel Purchas's Purchas His Pilgrimes (1625). (Huntington Library) naturall *Mexicans*" in activities familiar to everyone: naming their newborns, teaching the girls to weave and the boys to fish, punishing their children for misbehavior, cooking, preparing for war.⁷ Purchas too seems to have been captivated by these images of daily Mexican life, describing each one at length and attempting to decode some of the curious symbols for his readers. By removing the Spanish-language text and replacing it with an English-language key, Purchas reinvented the Codex Mendoza for the audiences of the British Empire.

In the English-speaking world, the Codex Mendoza, or "Mexican historie," as Purchas called it, became one of the first well-known artifacts of the indigenous Mexicans, supplementing

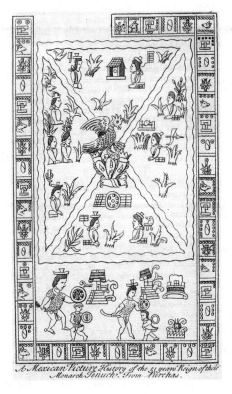

This leaf from the Codex Mendoza was reproduced in William Warburton's The Divine Legation of Moses Demonstrated *(1738–41), an indication of the broad circulation of Aztec imagery in English-language publications.* (Huntington Library)

knowledge about this people from other sources such as travel narratives and widely circulated accounts including José de Acosta's
natural history and the account of the conquest by Hernán Cortés.
Over the course of the eighteenth century, British Americans continued to add Purchas's histories to their libraries: both John
Adams and Thomas Jefferson, for example, owned the 1614 edition
and so would have been able read about the codex. The images of
the Codex Mendoza also continued to be reprinted in eighteenth-
century English-language books, ensuring that it remained current
in debates. William Warburton's anti-deist tract *The Divine
Legation of Moses Demonstrated* (1738–41) reproduced the first plate
of the Codex Mendoza from Purchas to argue that writing began
among the Mexicans in "the most simple way," which was as "a
mere PICTURE." In the hands of the Egyptians, writing improved
to become both a "Picture" and a "Character." Warburton's illustration of the Codex Mendoza—what he called "A Mexican Picture
History"—clearly announced that it was pulled from Purchas.[8]

Interest in the Codex Mendoza increased during the eighteenth
century, when the early Mexicans became a cause célèbre among
philosophers in France, the Netherlands, and Scotland. These
Europeans, none of whom had traveled to America but all of whom
were eager to formulate universal theories of social evolution that
would apply to all the peoples of the globe both past and present,
introduced the indigenous peoples of Mexico as a halfway point between the savage, nomadic tribes of North America and the civilized nations of Europe. The pre-Hispanic peoples of Mesoamerica
offered mountains of intriguing evidence about how to measure the
ineffable but desirable quality of civilization. Voltaire declared the
Mexicans to be a semi-civilized, polite, and sophisticated people,
"prudent and humane," well advanced beyond the nomadic tribes of
America. And what if they practiced human sacrifice? So had the
Jews and the Carthaginians; besides, the Mexicans tore the beating
hearts from the breasts of their enemies, not their own citizens.[9]

In the view of these armchair philosophes, Tenochtitlán offered
some of the clearest evidence of Mexican semi-civilization.
Working from some of the many images of Spanish New World
cities such as Cuzco that had circulated in Europe since the
sixteenth century, philosophers asserted that Mexicans had the

capacity for building magnificent physical sites that were recognizable to Europeans as cities. These city views were rendered to suit European ideals of what a true city should look like and had a tendency to remain frozen in time, seldom being updated to reflect new realities, such as the fact that the Spanish had attempted to eradicate vestiges of Mexican paganism by filling Mexico City with Catholic churches. Yet these were the images that set the debate about the capacities of the indigenous peoples of America. Following Voltaire, the author of the entry on Mexico City for Denis Diderot and Jean Le Rond d'Alembert's *Encyclopédie* called it "the most beautiful monument of American industriousness." Still, despite Voltaire's optimism, it was never entirely clear if these cities—where human blood gushed down the temple stairs and skull racks marked the gruesome tally of the sacrificed—had made the crucial jump from *urbs* to *civitas*, from the city as a place to the city as the incubator of the corporate spirit that encouraged "civilization." European philosophers also debated whether the manuscripts they called "Mexican paintings" (the codices) were writing or art. If they were writing, where on the ascending scale of civilization did they figure: as equivalents to ancient Egyptian hieroglyphics, or as something more primitive? And if the Mexican paintings were art, by what aesthetic standard should they be judged?[10]

Two withering criticisms of the ancient Mexicans appeared in 1768 and 1770 as part of the larger philosophical dispute concerning whether the American climate—cold, damp, and hostile to life—caused plants, animals, and peoples to shrivel into degenerate forms of their vigorous European counterparts. In his *Recherches philosophiques sur les Américains* (1768), Cornelius Pauw heaped particular scorn on the Codex Mendoza, which he had seen reproduced in Melchisédec Thévenot's *Histoire de l'Empire mexicain* (1696) and claimed to have scrutinized with great care. "It would be impossible to draw in a more tasteless and rude way," Pauw declared of this codex. There was no trace of shading or perspective, or a real imitation of nature. The images of plants, animals, and people lacked proper proportions. Pauw concluded that "the Mexicans had made almost no progress in the arts." Dismissing the Codex Mendoza as "this enigma," he mocked the attempts by the likes of Samuel Purchas and others to claim that they knew what the Mexican paintings represented, given the linguistic barriers involved. "We are not sure that the Mexican manuscript [the Codex Mendoza] contains a single word of what is claimed to be within it; perhaps it concerns the eight mistresses of Montezuma." Equally scornful was the abbé Raynal's *Histoire philosophique et politique, des établissements et du commerce des Européens dans les deux Indes* (1770), which likewise condemned the indigenous people of the New World for their degeneracy. Enfeebled by the hostile climate, the native Mexicans were unable to climb the ladder of civilization. Both these works were translated into English and received a wide readership around the Atlantic.[11]

Still more influential in the English-speaking world, however, was the work published on the heels of Pauw and Raynal: the Scottish historian William Robertson's *The History of America* (1777). A number of Scottish philosophers of the eighteenth century briefly mentioned the indigenous Mexicans in their published works, but only Robertson treated the Mexicans and the codices in a systematic way. Robertson's *The History of America* was a publishing sensation, reprinted numerous times and translated into several European languages. Though published in the bleak early years of the American Revolution, it rose to immediate popularity in the United States and was read in a variety of languages and contexts.[12]

To the well-traveled Benjamin Franklin, Robertson was one of the many "Friends in Scotland" he had acquired on his visit there from London. Partly as a gesture of friendship, Franklin made sure to acquire Robertson's book immediately after its publication. John Adams read the French translation on the ship that bore him from France back to America in 1779, and his son John Quincy—then just fourteen—studied it in English in 1781. James Madison inserted Robertson's *History of America* into his report on books for Congress in 1783. In 1800—a full generation after its first publication—Jefferson was still pressing it on one of his young protégés. So influential was "the Scottish Historian," as Robertson came to be known, that for many decades after the publication of *The History of America* commentators on the indigenous Mexicans felt that they were writing with Robertson looking over their shoulders, and they continued to respond to his ideas with objections and clarifications of his main points.[13]

Although the grand title of Robertson's work hinted at something broader, *The History of America* covered only Spain's New World colonies (pending the resolution of the American Revolution, when more could be conclusively said about British America). Among his contemporaries in Scotland, Robertson was uniquely well read in Spanish-language sources, especially published Spanish sources on the American Indians. Based on his extensive reading, Robertson pronounced Spanish America "the most splendid portion of the American story," one that formed "a perfect whole by itself." Written in the wake of Buffon, Raynal, and Pauw's depressing American climatic theories, Robertson's major argument offered some hope for the New World. In spite of the unfavorable climate, argued Robertson, the civilizations of the Mexicans and Peruvians among all the indigenous Americans had advanced the farthest. These Americans had not yet attained the level of civilization of "enlightened" Europe—the gold standard by which the Scottish historian measured humankind—but they were certainly more civilized than the nomadic Indian tribes of North America. "The empires of Peru and Mexico, though their progress in civilisation, when measured by the European and Asiatic standards, was inconsiderable, acquired such an ascendancy over the rude tribes around them" that they deserved to be considered somewhat civilized.[14]

Robertson's *History of America* epitomized the new quest for empirically based historical method. Writing for an English-speaking audience with limited direct knowledge of Spain's New World colonies, Robertson proudly detailed the enormous amount of research he had done in the quest for what he called "scrupulous accuracy." Striving for the fastidious new research standards set by his contemporary Edward Gibbon, whose *History of the Decline and Fall of the Roman Empire* had begun to appear in 1776, Robertson tapped contacts at the British embassy in Madrid to gain access to what he called "several valuable manuscripts" and rare sixteenth-century Spanish books. He formulated a questionnaire that his Madrid contacts distributed to Spaniards who had spent time in the New World colonies. "Did they in their works of art discover any considerable degree of industry and ingenuity?" read one question in his list of forty-four queries about Indian customs in Spanish America. He complained of the Spanish king's unwillingness to open his royal archives to him; Spain "has uniformly thrown a veil over her transactions in America."[15]

Yet there were limits to Robertson's ability to acquire archival knowledge of the Mexicans. Most glaringly, Robertson was unaware of the location of the Codex Mendoza, which now lay forgotten at Oxford, and he had to cite the Purchas version in his *History of America.*[16]

Not just archivally rich, Robertson's *History of America* was also a bibliographic tour de force, doing more than any other text at that time to introduce English speakers to the scholarship that had been written about the indigenous peoples of Mexico since the sixteenth century. By the late eighteenth century, a number of important Spanish-language works about Spanish America had been translated into English, including those by José de Acosta, Antonio de Solis, and Antonio de Herrera y Tordesillas, and these were acquired in the United States by such readers as Jefferson, James Madison, and Alexander Hamilton. But Robertson's elegant and readable history expanded the audience for Spanish American history much more than these other texts. Robertson proudly acknowledged his bibliographic achievement by publishing a catalogue of the Spanish books that he consulted.[17]

Robertson's *History of America* also introduced English-language readers to major Mexican intellectuals, helping to break down the barrier that had loomed between the British colonies in North America and Spain's New World colonies. Especially important in this new flow of information was the rich archive of indigenous Mexican manuscripts in the possession of the eighteenth-century Italian antiquarian Lorenzo Boturini Benaduci.

Boturini had arrived in Mexico from Europe in 1735 and soon became interested in tracing the historical origins of Our Lady of Guadalupe. Spending seven years studying Nahuatl and indigenous Mexican culture, he also amassed the most important collection of native Mexican codices and manuscripts in Mexico City. Boturini's collection was built upon the indigenous manuscripts collected by two seventeenth-century predecessors in Mexico, Fernando de Alva Ixtlilxochitl and the Mexican-born Jesuit polymath Carlos de Sigüenza y Góngora. In 1746, Boturini published a list of the manuscripts in his collection, a treasure trove from the Mexican past.

Careful to distinguish Indian from Spanish authors, Boturini listed hundreds of Indian manuscripts: calendars, tribute lists, dictionaries, and what Boturini called *mapas* (probably pictorial manuscripts). An engraving of Boturini shows his right hand hovering over one of these Mexican manuscripts as he unfurls an image of the Virgin of Guadalupe. Almost as conspicuous was Boturini's record of his own labors to maintain and expand his collection: copying in his own hand manuscripts he could borrow but could not keep, traveling far and wide to unearth obscure antiquities. Readers in the new United States came first to know Boturini through Robertson's *History of*

The eighteenth-century Italian antiquarian Lorenzo Boturini Benaduci with an Aztec manuscript. Boturini lived for many years in New Spain, where he learned Nahuatl and amassed a large collection of indigenous Mexican manuscripts. From Laurentius eques Boturini Benaduci Dominus de Turre et Hono *(1746). (Courtesy of the John Carter Brown Library at Brown University)*

America and thereafter continued to cite Boturini's collection and its importance for uncovering the remote Mexican past.[18]

Yet for all Robertson's careful research, and the very real achievement of bringing a growing English-language bibliography on Mexican history to the attention of the Anglophone world, Robertson ultimately agreed with Buffon, Pauw, and Raynal: the hostile climate of the Americas stifled the life force, so that even the most civilized, enlightened Mexicans had not been able to rise to the level of European society. As part of his evidence, Robertson cited the Codex Mendoza, what he called "the Mexican paintings in Purchas" in which the Mexican girls were learning to weave. This style of weaving was just as primitive as that of the North American Indians, he opined. "A loom was an invention beyond the ingenuity of the most improved Americans," Robertson concluded of the Mexicans.[19]

The Enlightened Mexicans as Mound Builders?

With U.S. independence from Britain secured in 1783, learned people in the new republic immediately began to rebut European theories of American degeneracy and assert the possibility of enlightened civilization in the Americas. As they expanded westward beyond the Appalachians—a national policy they termed "enlightened"—they stumbled upon increasing numbers of enormous earthen mounds dotting the terrain around the Mississippi and Ohio Rivers, and debated whether the mounds were evidence of a past, glorious civilization. Their accounts highlighted the fact that the existing Indians seemed to know nothing about them. Ezra Stiles sent to Jefferson in Paris a memoir by Samuel Parsons about the large mounds in the Ohio country: "The numerous mounds of Earth erected in conical forms, to the height of 70 or 80 F., containing the bones of the Dead, are proofs of this Country's having been peopled heretofore by those who had some knowledge of the Arts; and the trees grown up in those fortresses are of a size which leaves little room to doubt that the works were abandoned long before this country was discovered by the Europeans. The present Inhabitants having no knowledge of the Arts or tradition respecting the fortifications leaves a doubt whether the present are the Immediate descendants of the former Inhabitants."[20]

What to make of these curious mounds? Reaching for answers, learned people in the United States built on the antiquarian research of Mexican scholars. They used the work of these scholars to argue that an enlightened early American people called the Toltecs had once lived in North America and built the mounds, and had then migrated south to found the civilized cities of central Mexico. Focused on the past, this argument had everything to do with emerging U.S. policy toward the modern-day Indians of North America, as it implicitly denied that the modern Indians living near the mounds were civilized. Lacking cities, writing, and all memory of the mound builders, the North American Indians must be savages, doomed to expire before the onslaught of U.S. civilization. Although their predecessors had been enlightened, the modern Indians could never become so.

Mound builder theorists in the early national United States were most influenced by Francesco Saverio Clavigero, whose *Storia antica del Messico* sympathetically and exhaustively laid out the deep history of the early peoples of Mexico. Born in Mexico in 1731, Clavigero entered the Society of Jesus as a young man; living in regions heavily populated by indigenous Mexicans, he also learned Nahuatl, one of their major languages. At the College of Saint Peter and Saint Paul in Mexico City, one of Clavigero's teachers directed his attention to the collection of documents on Mexican history and antiquities deposited there by Sigüenza y Góngora and Boturini. When the Society of Jesus was expelled from Mexico in 1767, Clavigero sailed to Bologna, where he sat down to write what became his history of ancient Mexico.[21]

Studded with engravings of ancient Mexican marvels such as the great temple in Tenochtitlán, Clavigero's history was a wholesale rebuke to the American degeneracy theories of Buffon, Pauw, Raynal, and Robertson. Clavigero mocked the armchair European philosophical historians who painted the American canvas in broad strokes while knowing nothing of the local terrain. He explained in his preface that he had lived in Mexico for thirty-six years, had learned Nahuatl, had studied ancient Mexican paintings and manuscripts, and had consulted with relevant locals. Rebutting the argument that only a few of the codices (such as the Codex Mendoza) had been spared the flames of the Spanish missionaries, Clavigero insisted that numerous codices had survived to undergird the many histories of Mexico written to date, not just by the Spanish but by Mexicans themselves, whose names he listed for the benefit of ignorant Europeans. Grounded in local evidence, these works could rebut what Clavigero called the massive blunders of the abbé Raynal and William Robertson (who lived long enough to take offense at Clavigero's accusations and to charge in turn that Clavigero had crafted "improbable narratives and fanciful conjectures"). Warming to the idea that American evidence was the best evidence, Clavigero patiently walked his readers through a detailed examination of the content and current location of the precious Mexican codices. The Codex Mendoza, he warned, had been inaccurately reproduced in some editions such as Thévenot's, so readers needed to be careful.[22]

Clavigero also sneered at Pauw's description of the codices, attacking especially Pauw's reckless reading of the Codex Mendoza. He explained that the definitions of "writing" and "history" should be expanded in light of the Mexican paintings. Learned Mexicans and Spaniards who knew the ancient Mexican language confirmed that history writing could be anything that explained something to absent persons or to posterity by symbolic means, be they figures, hieroglyphs, or characters. In fact the whole practice of history needed to be reassessed in light of the Mexican paintings, argued Clavigero. What were the historical paintings of the Mexicans but durable signs to transmit the memory of distant places and distant ages to posterity? Pauw had seen only the crude copies of the codex reproduced in Purchas, not the original paintings of the Mexicans that were essential to an accurate reading.[23] All the Europeans who had used Purchas's version of the Codex Mendoza as their baseline had rested their conclusions on a single, faulty piece of evidence. By contrast, charged Clavigero, historians who had been to America and studied the ancient paintings themselves realized that Egyptian hieroglyphs were not the only standard for judging representational writing.

Clavigero likewise rescued Mexican plants and animals from the withering criticism of the comte de Buffon. In his influential *Histoire naturelle*, Buffon had maintained that the cold and humid climate of the Americas caused animals to degenerate into smaller

Il Tempio maggior di Messico.

A relic of the preconquest era, the great temple of Tenochtitlán is depicted as
a symbol of Aztec civilization in Francesco Saverio Clavigero's Storia antica
del Messico *(1780–81). (Huntington Library)*

and less fertile versions of their European cousins. The two great
exceptions were insects and reptiles, "watery beings" that grew into
enormous and monstrously fertile varieties amid the "humid and
unwholesome exhalations" of America. Clavigero objected to this
universalizing, Eurocentric judgment about American life forms
and offered instead uniquely Mexican animals such as the jaguar-
like tlacocelotl for his readers to ponder.[24] Clavigero's lesson was

1. *Tigre Mess.ⁿᵃ* 2. *Tlacocelotl.* 3. *Itzcuintepotzotli.* 4. *Istrice Mess.ⁿᵒ* 5. *Re de' Zopi= loti.* 6. *Axolotl.* 7. *Occhione.* 8. *Tepajaxin.* 9. *Anfisbena Mess.ⁿᵃ* 10. 11. *Temolin.*

New World animals and insects from Clavigero's Storia antica del Messico,
*displayed to prove that they were not inferior versions of European fauna,
as European philosophers such as the comte de Buffon had charged.*
(Huntington Library)

clear: no European philosopher could hope to grasp anything accurate about the ancient Mexicans without on-site inspection of the Mexican archives and knowledge of a major indigenous Mexican language.

Translated into English by the Scottish scholar Charles Cullen as *The History of Mexico* (1787), Clavigero's work became the first history of Mexico in English that presented a sympathetic view of the pre-Hispanic Mexicans. The son of the celebrated Edinburgh physician William Cullen (a connection that elevated him to the highest levels of scholarly networking), Charles Cullen appears to have received the original Italian edition from the third earl of Bute, to whom Cullen dedicated his English translation.[25]

Cullen explained in his preface why an English version of Clavigero's history was necessary. However great the Scottish historian William Robertson's *History of America* had been, it suffered all the disadvantages of "distance from that continent": Robertson was "unacquainted with its languages, productions, or people" and lacked the documents "preserved in archives of the new world." The Spanish historians of the past two centuries had been utterly unhelpful, since they had been blinded by "Partiality, prejudice, ignorance, and credulity." By contrast, Clavigero had "resided near forty years in the provinces of New Spain, examined its natural produce, acquired the language of the Mexicans and other nations, gathered many of their traditions, studied their historical paintings, and other monuments of antiquity."[26] The Cullen translation reproduced the beautiful engravings of the original Italian edition, providing readers with tantalizing glimpses of the social, natural, and physical world of the ancient Mexicans, from maps of the extraordinary lagoon of Tenochtitlán to engravings of ancient Mexicans playing musical instruments, grinding corn, arrayed in noble costume, and fighting.

Clavigero's history fundamentally transformed the opinion of learned people in the early national United States about the ancient Mexicans and the peoples who may have built the earthen mounds west of the Appalachians. Both in English translation and the original Italian, it immediately attracted notice in the United States, inspiring a wide-ranging conversation about the "enlightened" peoples of early America who might have built the mounds.

Thomas Jefferson played a major role in spreading the word. In the wake of independence from Britain, Jefferson had begun to express increasing dissatisfaction with the European degeneracy theories, and Clavigero gave him ammunition. In a protracted rant to the marquis de Chastellux in 1785, Jefferson dismissed the major European theorists—Buffon, Pauw, and Robertson—saying they knew nothing because they had never been to America. He especially condemned Robertson's lack of "respectable evidence" concerning the alleged "inferiority of genius" of the "Aboriginal man of America." Robertson "never was in America, he relates nothing of his own knowledge, he is a compiler only of the relations of others, and a mere translator of the opinions of Monsr. de Buffon." Jefferson contrasted these Europe-bound theorists with explorers such as Antonio de Ulloa, who had been to America and "wrote of what he saw."[27]

Jefferson also despaired at the difficulties North Americans had in getting information about the Indians of Central and South America, whose cities might provide the most convincing evidence of civilization to urban Europeans. "Of the Indian of South America I know nothing," he wrote in the *Notes on the State of Virginia* (1787), a work he composed at the prompting of the French legation to supply knowledge about the local American scene. Stationed in Paris during the years 1784–89, Jefferson began to stockpile what soon became the largest private library of books about Spanish America in the United States at that time. "Having been very desirous of collecting the original Spanish writers on American history, I commissioned Mr. Carmichael to purchase some for me," he told James Madison in 1787.[28]

It was probably while he was in Paris that he acquired his copy of Clavigero, the Italian first edition of 1780–81. The marginal comments he made in his personal copy of the *Notes on the State of Virginia* suggest that he read Clavigero carefully. He alerted his correspondent Joseph Willard in 1789 to the ways in which Clavigero's theories overturned the American degeneracy theories of Robertson and others. "Clavigero, an Italian also, who has resided thirty six years in Mexico, has given us a history of that country, which certainly merits more respect than any other work on the same subject. He corrects many errors of Dr. Robertson and tho sound philosophy will disapprove many of his ideas, we must still consider it as an useful work, and assuredly the best we possess on the same subject."[29]

By the late 1780s and early 1790s, Clavigero's history had become an important weapon in the growing U.S. arsenal opposing European degeneracy theories. In his *Political Inquiries* (1791), Robert Coram used it to dispute Buffon, Raynal, and others. European libraries were "stuffed with such monstrous caricatures of the American," and Raynal and Buffon were "full of the most glaring prejudice and absurdity." Only Clavigero and a few others came close to telling the truth about America. "Excepting Clavigero's history of Mexico, the short account given by Mr. Jefferson, Carver's travels, the history of the five nations, and Bancroft's history of Guiana, I do not recollect an account of the Americans, which deserves the name of history."[30]

In addition to its use in dismissing European degeneracy theorists, Clavigero's text was routinely cited in the growing number of publications on the mound builders of North America. U.S. intellectuals seeking to understand the mounds focused in particular on Clavigero's account of the origin of the earliest documented Mexicans: the Toltecs. Acknowledging that much of the Toltecs' origin was wrapped in "fable," Clavigero nonetheless insisted on the need to trust the accounts of the indigenous Mexicans themselves about their own history. Based on their reports, Clavigero argued that the Toltecs had come from "the more northern parts of America, where their ancestors had been settled for many ages." The ancestral lands were difficult to pinpoint with any precision, but Clavigero offered the "north-west of Mexico" and "the North of America" as possibilities. The Toltecs then began to migrate south into central Mexico.[31]

In Clavigero's telling, the Toltecs were the ancient Greeks of the New World. Possessed of a "superior civilization," they inspired every subsequent people who migrated into central Mexico. Preferring art to war, the Toltecs built magnificent cities, founded kingdoms regulated by laws, perfected agriculture, cut fine gems, and crafted beautiful vessels of silver and gold. About six hundred years later, in the twelfth and thirteenth centuries C.E., the Toltecs and other peoples of central Mexico were joined by a new group migrating from the north, the "Aztecas," so called because their land of origin was called Aztlán, "a country situated to the north of the gulf of California." These Mexicans built the city of Tenochtitlán in the reed-choked lake that filled the volcano-rimmed valley of central Mexico, creating what became known to Europeans as the Venice of the New World. "Such was the beginning of the city of Tenochtitlan," wrote Clavigero, "which in future times was to become the court of a great empire, and the largest and most beautiful city of the new world."[32] Like the Romans to the Greeks, the people of Tenochtitlán looked admiringly on the refined artistic and intellectual culture handed to them by the Toltecs.

Clavigero's significance for intellectuals in the early United States was that he handed them a group of civilized, enlightened Indians—the Toltecs—as possible builders of the mysterious North American mounds. As U.S. political priorities shifted to the trans-Appalachian West, Clavigero provided reassurance that the Indians currently living there were not civilized. Disconnected from the mounds, they remained mired in barbarity, and might be treated accordingly. So it was that from 1787 on, U.S. theorists seized upon Clavigero to make their case that the current Indians of the trans-Appalachian West were not related to the mound builders; the mounds rather represented the reality that a great civilization had once thrived there in the past and could possibly do so again.

The first publication in the United States to make the new connection was Benjamin Smith Barton's *Observations on Some Parts of Natural History* (1787), a work often mocked today for Barton's theorizing that America had been populated by the Danes. But Barton's theory of Danish origin was in fact a small piece of a much more significant event: North Americans' acceptance of a Mexican theory of Indian origins—that is, of Clavigero's laudatory account of the great civilizations built by the indigenous Mexicans. The North American mounds, argued Barton, proved that central North America had "formerly been inhabited by a people, who had made considerable advances towards those arts which are almost inseparable from the dawn of CIVIL SOCIETY." But who? Here Barton laid out his case for "the learned Abbé Saverio Clavigero," quoting *The History of Mexico* at length. Barton defended Clavigero as an American eyewitness, with true, on-site knowledge that thoroughly debunked the "frivolity" and "fallacy" of European philosophers such as Pauw, "the most angry and the most petulant of philosophes." Clavigero showed that "there can be little doubt that" the mounds in North America and the pyramids of Mesoamerica "have been constructed by the same people, and for the same purposes." The implication was clear: "that the DANES have contributed to the peopling of AMERICA; and that the TOLTECAS, or whatever nation it may have been that constructed the eminences and fortifications in that continent, were their descendants."[33]

Over the next half century, as more English-language editions of Clavigero's *Storia antica del Messico* were published in the United States, Clavigero's name became synonymous with the Toltec theory of enlightened mound builder origins. Thaddeus Harris's *Journal of a Tour into the Territory Northwest of the Alleghany Mountains* (1805) approvingly quoted a source that had announced Clavigero's history to be "one of the most valuable works that has ever been published on the subject of America." Harris thought the mounds had "considerable resemblance to those described by Clavigero, to which antient accounts in Mexico have attributed that appropriation." Fifteen years later, Caleb Atwater endorsed Clavigero's theory that the North American and Mexican works "were erected by the same people." He observed that "we see a line of ancient works, reach from the south side of lake Ontario across this State, on to the banks of the Mississippi; along the banks of that river; through the upper part of the province of Texas, around the Mexican gulf, quite into Mexico." To the philologist John Pickering, Clavigero was "this intelligent author" to whom Americans were indebted for "a refutation of the unfounded opinions of eminent naturalists and philosophers respecting the degeneracy of the animal and other productions of the continent." In his *Ancient Monuments of North and South America* (1838), the polymath and philologist Constantine Samuel Rafinesque did not specifically cite Clavigero but wrote of the need to view the North American mounds and Mesoamerican pyramids within the same frame: "These facts may confirm the Mexican traditions, stating that the nations of Anahuac (now Mexico) once dwelt further north, in our fruitful Western plains, where wood abounded and stones were scarce, wherefore they built their cities and temples of wood, raising altars, platforms, walls and entrenchments of earth or clay." Samuel George Morton's monumental *Crania Americana* (1839) cited Clavigero and Boturini in extensive discussions of the migration of the Toltecs south to Mexico, where a "demi-civilisation" eventually flourished. By the middle of the nineteenth century, by which time the U.S. program of North American Indian removal was well under way, Clavigero's theory had become dogma. Citing Clavigero, Brantz Mayer's *Mexico as It Was and as It Is* (1844) announced that the Toltecs had left the north to found the capital of the Mexican empire as well as a dynasty "celebrated for its wisdom, knowledge, and extensive civilisation."[34]

Published at the conclusion of the Mexican-American War, which greatly expanded the western claims of the United States, Ephraim G. Squier and Edwin H. Davis's influential *Ancient Monuments of the Mississippi Valley* (1848) was a kind of summa of the accumulated knowledge from Clavigero on the mounds. Squier and Davis cited the "*American Edition*" of Clavigero in a number of specific instances. "They bear a close resemblance to the Teocallis of Mexico," the authors wrote of the North American mounds. They went on argue that "the defences of the nations of the central portion of the Continent, and especially those of the Mexicans and Peruvians, so far as we are informed concerning them, bore a close resemblance to those of the mound-builders, although exhibiting a superiority entirely consonant with the further advance which we are justified in supposing they had made in all the arts, including the art of defence." Charles Eliot Norton's review of Squier and Davis cited Clavigero's Toltec origin theory to "prove a connection between the mound builders and the ancient inhabitants of Mexico." It was necessary, said Norton, to value the legends of the "ancient inhabitants of Mexico" regarding their own origins, and to accept that the Toltecs living in the Mississippi valley "were dwellers in the country for several centuries" and "left the indelible impress of their civilization" upon that region before migrating south to a warmer and more productive climate.[35]

Clavigero's long influence on the mound builder theories served to connect the expanding United States and Mexico in a larger ethnographic story of the origins of the peoples and civili-zations of the Americas. But by severing the link between the cur-rently living Indians of the trans-Appalachian West and the ostensibly enlightened ancient mound builders, it cleared a path for the expanding "civilization" of the United States. While the present Indians of North America were barbaric, observed Ira Hill in his *Antiquities of America Explained* (1831), their "enlightened" mound-building predecessors had left the Ohio country to found in Mexico "a city which in extent and grandeur, might vie with the most magnificent cities of that period in the old world."[36]

The Calendar Stone, Symbol of the Enlightened Aztecs

Just as Clavigero's Mexican history was suggesting the possibility of enlightenment in America, another ancient Mexican artifact came to light that added fuel to the debate about the future promise of the Americas for civilization. In 1790, workers in Mexico City lifted an elaborately carved twenty-four-ton basalt stone from the mud in the main plaza of the city. Buried sometime in the century after the Spanish conquest as a symbol of Indian idolatry, the basalt sculpture reemerged in the eighteenth century to become a cause célèbre around the Atlantic, igniting new theories about the sophisticated astronomical achievements of the early Mexicans. Called the *piedra del sol* (sun stone) in Spanish, the sculpture became known in English as the Aztec Calendar Stone. In the hands of its eighteenth-century Mexican and U.S. interpreters, the Aztec Calendar Stone became an example of what a modern anthropologist has called the "defining sample": the single object that is believed to sum up a whole civilization.[37]

The reception of the Aztec Calendar Stone in the early national United States reveals how the indigenous, pre-Hispanic Mexicans (now becoming known as Aztecs) became closely tied to the political fortunes of modern Mexico, which achieved independence from Spain in 1821. As Mexico emerged as a major diplomatic priority for the United States, so too was created the first major U.S. archive housing scholarship concerning modern and ancient Mexico, at the American Philosophical Society. This archive was created by a cadre of men who were at once politically involved with modern Mexico and intellectually interested in the Aztec past: the Prussian explorer Alexander von Humboldt; the American physician and diplomat William E. Hūlings; the U.S.

minister to Mexico, Joel R. Poinsett; and Thomas Jefferson himself, who lived long enough to see his interests in Spanish American history intersect with the new political reality of an independent Mexico. All these Americans focused especially on the question of what the Aztecs symbolized about a hemisphere that was gradually being released from the fetters of European imperialism and free to chart its own path. Who would be the true heirs of Aztec glory: the modern Mexicans or the people of the new United States, both aspiring imperial powers?

The Aztec Calendar Stone achieved transatlantic renown thanks to the Mexican scholar Antonio de León y Gama, who published a picture of it in his *Descripción histórica y cronológica de las dos piedras* (Historical and Chronological Description of the Two Stones, 1792). As its title suggested, the *Descripción* discussed two objects, the Calendar Stone and another carved stone exhumed at the same time, the so-called Coatlicue ("serpent skirt"), a squat stone sculpture of a pre-Hispanic Mexican goddess. Engravings of both sculptures by the Mexican artist Francisco de Agüera appeared in León y Gama's work.[38] Of the two sculptures, the Calendar Stone attracted by far the most attention outside Mexico, since its apparent use as an astronomical device suggested the possibility of ancient Mexicans' rationality. By contrast, the confusing, monstrous, feminine Coatlicue seemed to be the very incarnation of ancient Mexicans' irrationality, earthiness, and barbarity.

Born and raised in Mexico City, León y Gama was a leading member of a group of intellectuals in eighteenth-century Mexico who published works in astronomy, linguistics, and natural history. Some of them specialized in the field of Mexican antiquities: this group included not just Clavigero but also the cleric and natural scientist José Antonio de Alzate y Ramírez, who initially published the findings of the Calendar Stone and Coatlicue in the *Gaceta de literatura de México* in December 1790 and January 1791. This journal helped expose a learned Mexican readership to international currents of thought, publishing, for example, Spanish translations of Benjamin Franklin's scientific letters. In an age of increasingly widespread print circulation, these Mexican intellectuals helped popularize a storehouse of indigenous Mexican materials that challenged Spanish imperial assertions of Mexican inferiority.[39] They

The Aztec Calendar Stone, which allegedly symbolized ancient Mexican rationality, as reproduced in Antonio de León y Gama's Descripción histórica y cronológica de las dos piedras *(1792), a text known to erudite Americans in the early United States. (Jay I. Kislac Collection, Rare Book and Special Collections Division, Library of Congress)*

became known to readers in the early national United States as allies in the effort to refute the American degeneracy theories of European figures such as Buffon, Robertson, and Pauw.

León y Gama published his work on the Calendar Stone because he was anxious to establish the ancient Mexicans as a civilized people, builders of what he called "many precious monuments of Mexican antiquity." He was inspired by the recent excavations of Herculaneum and Pompeii, which had been launched under the aegis of his king, Carlos III of Spain, who for part of his reign also claimed title as ruler of the kingdom of Naples, near where the

*The sculpture called Coatlicue was thought to represent the irrationality of the
early Mexicans, in contrast to the allegedly rational Aztec Calendar Stone. From
León y Gama,* Descripción histórica y cronológica de las dos piedras. *(Jay I.
Kislac Collection, Rare Book and Special Collections Division, Library of Congress)*

ancient Roman cities were being exhumed from volcanic rock. The
alleged mathematical rationality of the Calendar Stone as a symbol
of ancient Mexican civilization formed a contrast to Coatlicue,
which was taken to represent the sensuous irrationality of pre-
Hispanic Mexican religion. Neither sculpture, however, was
celebrated by learned Europeans as "art" in the sense of a work of
individual Mexican genius, usable by Europeans artists in their
own works. The transformation of pre-Hispanic Mexican objects
into "art"—what are today known as pre-Columbian antiquities—
did not occur until the late nineteenth century. In the decades
after their discovery, both the Calendar Stone and Coatlicue were

interpreted as representations of a people's collective mentality rather than a particular artist's originality and virtuosity.[40]

Even today, the function of the so-called Calendar Stone remains mysterious, but its earliest interpreters soon became obsessed with the idea that it must have been an astronomical calendar that helped the civilized Aztecs chart the complex movements of the stars and planets and mark their religious and royal festivals. León y Gama's description of the Calendar Stone soon came to the attention of learned people in the United States. In 1809, Benjamin Smith Barton, an expert on North American Indian languages, informed Thomas Jefferson that he possessed León y Gama's work, a text that would help to rebut the American degeneracy theories of Buffon and Pauw and that he thought should be immediately translated into English:

> You will, I think, be pleased to hear, that I have received from Mexico, a very important pamphlet on the Astronomy of the ancient Mexicans. It is not a fanciful work, such as an ingenious man might write in his closet, from the *traditions* of Indians, or the vague facts and reports of others. It is truly historical, and is principally founded upon the discovery of the "Mexican Century," a vast stone monument, which was discovered in Mexico, in the year 1790. The work is written by one Gama, a man of real learning; and will serve to overturn many an ingenious theory, the work of such historians and writers as Robe[r]tson, DePauw &c.

Jefferson immediately replied to Barton, expressing his enthusiasm for this artifact from Mexico, "one of the most interesting countries of our hemisphere."[41]

The friend to whom Barton alluded was the Philadelphia physician William Hūlings, who served as U.S. vice-consul to Spanish Louisiana in 1798–99 and, in 1803, after the United States acquired New Orleans from France, as acting vice-consul. Hūlings was proficient enough in Spanish to be able to undertake the translation of León y Gama's work, which he completed in manuscript form in 1806. Signaling a major reason for U.S. interest in the Aztecs, Hūlings added his own query at the end of his translation, identifying the early Mexicans as the mound builders of North America. "May not the Mounds discovered in the western parts of our Country, which bear the appearance of regular fortifications, have been the works of some of the *Nations* since settled in Mexico; constructed during the *frequent stops* made by them in their journeys from their *Country Aztlan*, which, in some places, were extended to a period of many years? This appears to me more than probable as *Aztlan* is said to have been *somewhere* on the North West Coast of America, & peopled perhaps *originally* from Asia, by the way of Bhering's Straits, or otherwise."[42]

Hūlings's speculation about the Aztecs as mound builders remained confined to his unpublished manuscript, but the ideas of León y Gama about the magnificence of ancient Mexican civilization as defined by the Calendar Stone were popularized in the early national United States by Alexander von Humboldt. Humboldt, one of the most famous scientific figures of the era, arrived in the United States in 1804 after his celebrated five-year expedition to Spanish America (1799–1804), where he had inspected ancient Mexican monuments and manuscripts closely. Through his massive, lavishly illustrated work, the *Vues des Cordillères, et monumens des peuples indigènes de l'Amérique* (Views of the Andes, and Monuments of the Indigenous Peoples of America, 1810), which was published in English translation in 1814, Humboldt ignited attention among leading North Americans regarding Mexican antiquities. The book appeared on the heels of his 1804 visit to Washington, D.C., where he had personally met Jefferson and Barton, who shared his interest in Mexico and its ancient people.

Humboldt's study was the first major English-language publication to use the term *Aztecs* (or, as Humboldt had it, *Aztecks*), signaling the hardening of what had previously been loosely called the "ancient Mexicans" into a distinct civilization whose name recalled the mythical northern ancestral home of Aztlán. Offering Aztec monuments, sculptures, and codices as evidence, Humboldt asserted that the Aztecs had ascended to an impressively high point on this scale of civilization, the highest the New World had achieved before the arrival of the Europeans. Inspired by the rising tide of neo-Hellenism sweeping Europe in the late eighteenth and early nineteenth centuries, which had defined the ancient Greeks as artists possessed of a unique genius, Humboldt situated the Aztecs midway on the ascending scale of civilization. A spark of individuality had inspired the ancient Greeks, "to whose creative genius belong all that the arts possess of [the] beautiful and sublime!" By contrast, the Aztecs excelled only at "servilely copying" and so had been slow—as "half civilized" people were—to adopt European stylistic techniques. As the productions of a collective psychology rather than an individual genius, Aztec monuments could not be judged according to the aesthetic category of "style," Humboldt argued. As for the writing on display in the Mexican paintings such as the Codex Mendoza, they had not yet achieved the "perfection" of ancient Egyptian hieroglyphics. At this point the precise location of the Codex Mendoza was no longer certain. But building upon what he could see of it in works by Purchas, Thévenot, and others, Humboldt declared that the Codex Mendoza showed the "sameness of will" among the Aztecs that "placed barriers to the progress of intellectual improvement and individual happiness."[43]

What rescued the Aztecs from this dismal verdict about their capacity for individual genius, happiness, and civilization was the Calendar Stone, which Humboldt claimed to have studied in person. "A people who regulated its festivals according to the motion of the stars, and who engraved its *fasti* on a public monument, had no doubt reached a degree of civilization superior to that which has been allowed by Pauw, Raynal, and even Robertson, the most judicious of the historians of America," he wrote. "These writers consider every state of society as barbarous, that did not bear the type of civilization, which they, according to their systematic ideas, had formed. We cannot admit these abrupt distinctions into barbarous and civilized nations." Substituting a more lavish European engraving for the original versions by the Mexican engraver Agüera that had appeared in León y Gama's *Descripción*, Humboldt praised the astronomical sophistication of the Aztecs. He lamented that León y Gama's work was "very scarce in Europe" and hoped that the Calendar Stone would excite the attention of learned Europeans and expand the range of Mexican artifacts of civilization known to them beyond what Robertson's *History of America* had supplied. Humboldt reiterated León y Gama's supposition that the stone was an astronomical device and sign of Aztec civilization.

"Among the number of monuments which seem to prove that the people of Mexico, at the time of their conquest by the Spaniards, had attained a certain degree of civilization, we may assign the first rank to the calendars, or different divisions of time, adopted by the Toltecks and the Aztecks."[44]

Humboldt's esteem for the Calendar Stone as a symbol of Aztec rationality and civilization found many adherents in the United States, none as politically important as the first United States minister to the newly independent state of Mexico, Joel Poinsett. Poinsett (today immortalized in the name of the red flowering plant he brought back from his stay) served as a special envoy to Mexico from 1822 to 1823 and was appointed the first U.S. minister to Mexico in 1825. In his *Notes on Mexico* (1824), Poinsett celebrated the "enlightened men" of the new nation of Mexico who were attempting to apply the political principles of "the most enlightened republics" to their country. He also revered the Mexicans' enlightened Aztec past. Secretary of State Henry Clay informed Poinsett that U.S. policy toward modern Mexico rested in part on the certainty that there had been "progress . . . towards civilization" among the Mexican "Aborgines" in the time of the Spanish invasion. "The United Mexican States, whether we regard their present posture, or recall to our recollection their ancient history, and fortunes, are entitled to high consideration." Poinsett concurred, singling out Alzate y Ramírez, Clavigero, Humboldt, and "the enlightened and celebrated traveller Boturini" for their services to the cause of preserving and furthering knowledge of the enlightened Mexican past. Poinsett made several visits to the Aztec Calendar Stone in Mexico City, vowing to translate Alzate y Ramírez's book on the subject.[45]

In the wake of Mexico's independence, Poinsett and others also acquired Mexican documents for the American Philosophical Society, which they envisioned as the major archival center of the United States. Before his visit to Mexico, Poinsett had deposited Hülings's translation of León y Gama with the American Philosophical Society, along with "a curious Collection of Spanish MSS." In 1826, an expert on American Indian languages, Peter Stephen Du Ponceau, asked Poinsett to help the APS secure Mexican antiquities, especially Aztec codices, since the Codex Mendoza reproductions in Purchas left so much to be desired: "The

Society is very anxious to possess some of the ancient Mexican hieroglyphical paintings," Du Ponceau urged. "There are none, I believe, in this Country, & they would greatly help our researches. While the *savans* of Europe are successfully endeavoring to decipher the Egyptian hieroglyphics, it seems Americans should make a similar attempt on those of our hemisphere. I have paid much attention to them from the imperfect engravings that we have in Purchas &c. I greatly wish I might have an opportunity of studying the originals."[46]

Poinsett deposited a variety of artifacts at the American Philosophical Society, including a collection of documents and pamphlets on South America, the original 1792 edition of León y Gama, a large number of Mexican stone sculptures, pottery, and jewelry, Mexican "Hieroglyphic Paintings," and wax copies of a number of statues in the National Museum of Mexico, including the Calendar Stone.[47] The effort by U.S. intellectuals to uncover an enlightened Mexican past had yielded this treasure trove: the first major Mexican archive in the United States.

This archive undergirded the works of the next generation of historians and ethnologists, who placed the U.S. conquest of Mexico at the center of a new national narrative of divinely ordained western expansion. The most influential of these intellectuals was William H. Prescott, whose *History of the Conquest of Mexico* (1843) rested on an impressive command of the material concerning Mexican thought as it had become available in the United States. Prescott had set for himself what he called a "hard job": "extracting civilization from the semi-civilized races of Anahuac [early Mexico]." He spent years preparing to write the history, immersing himself in the extensive secondary literature on the subject, much of it written by indigenous Mexican authors. He was impressed by the "rich & very curious materials" owned by Boturini, whose history he read, but cringed at the histories written by indigenous and creole Mexican historians in the seventeenth century, likening them to "the annals of barbarians." Taking extensive notes on the English translation of Clavigero's history of ancient Mexico, Prescott praised the work for its "sound principles of criticism" and judged it "probably worth all other native accounts put together." Prescott also devoured Humboldt's work on the antiquities of Mexico, saying that Humboldt did "more than any—I might say all—other

European writers" to throw light on the physical history of Mexico's "primitive races."[48]

Initially Prescott had feared that he might not have enough archival material for his history, confessing to Poinsett that he might have to content himself with "printed works." Reluctant to travel to Mexico himself, Prescott was nonetheless able to tap contacts in the United States, Mexico, and Spain to help him obtain archival material. When he began working on a new edition of his book, Prescott also benefited from the advice given to him by the Mexican translators of *The History of the Conquest of Mexico*. Despite Prescott's immersion in Mexican sources, one of these translators, José Fernando Ramírez, criticized his preference for Spanish sources over indigenous Mexican ones, as well as for his terming the indigenous Mexicans "*barbarians*" and "*savages.*" Ramírez set out "to defend the authenticity and value of the historical sources of our country, and to vindicate the memory of our Indians."[49]

Prescott did more than any other author of his time in the United States to popularize the idea of the Aztecs as a mighty but vanished people. Like the ancient Greeks to whom Prescott compared them, the Aztecs had died out, leaving only a "conquered race" in their wake. Prescott expressed his immense admiration for Aztec civilization even as he buried it in the past. "Their civilization was of the hardy character which belongs to the wilderness. The fierce virtues of the Aztec were all his own. They refused to submit to European culture,—to be engrafted on a foreign stock. His outward form, his complexion, his lineaments, are substantially the same. But the moral characteristics of the nation, all that constituted its individuality as a race, are effaced for ever."[50]

The implications of Prescott's words were clear: the best and most civilized features of the Aztec past were now dead and buried, and only the allegedly degenerated modern Mexicans remained. (This would have been a familiar narrative to early-nineteenth-century Americans, who admired the civilization of the ancient Greeks while sneering at the allegedly degenerated modern inhabitants of Greece.) The U.S. victory in the Mexican War encouraged Americans to read modern events in light of the Aztec past laid out in Prescott's *History*. After reading it, Caleb Cushing told Prescott that he saw "many points of analogy" between Cortés's first conquest and this "second Conquest" by the United States.[51] In this way, the United States by the middle of the nineteenth century had found a way to make the history of the ancient Mexicans relevant to modern America.

Prescott's *History* also reveals how quickly the writings of key Mexican intellectuals were forgotten in the United States. There was no organized scheme of suppression, but several factors worked simultaneously to erase them from national memory. First, by the 1840s, the survival of the United States as an independent republic was no longer in question, and the ideas of Clavigero and his cohort were no longer vital for proving to Europeans that a civilization could thrive in the Americas in the wake of European colonialism. Second, older works gradually fell out of favor as new ones replaced them. Prescott's version of the Aztecs' past quickly became among the most influential in the nineteenth-century United States, but the bibliography upon which it rested did not survive with it. Later studies of the ancient and modern Mexicans—such as the British anthropologist Edward Burnet Tylor's *Anahuac* (1861)—cited Prescott's massive influence but few of his Mexican sources.

Yet while they were soon forgotten in the United States, Mexican scholars such as Boturini and Clavigero helped learned people in the early national United States craft a particular form of nationalism that depended on a sweeping view of a shared, pan-American antiquity. Through intensive studies of the ancient Mexicans, a people that over time they celebrated as "enlightened Aztecs," educated North Americans found a means by which to refute the degeneracy theories of European philosophers. The Aztecs, safely embalmed in the darkness of antiquity, became the great civilization of all the Americas, a shared ancestor who seemed to prove that because their hemisphere had once achieved enlightenment, it could do so again. The losers in this new narrative were the modern Indians of North America, who were deemed to be the barbaric counterpart of the civilized, enlightened Aztecs. The ethnological categories developed in the age that called itself enlightened thus rescued some while condemning others, all in the name of an expanding, imperial civilization in the United States.

CHAPTER FOUR

The Science of Statistics and the Invention of the "Indian Population"

EUROPEANS HAD COUNTED THE Indians of North America since the moment of contact. As children, women, men, warriors, slaves, families, empires, tribes, republics, nations, villages, towns, and converts to Christianity, the Indians were counted again and again for hundreds of years. It is no exaggeration to say that the Indians are the most counted people in American history. But it was not until the second half of the eighteenth century that the North American Indians became a *population,* a potent new concept Americans mobilized as they strove to become what one writer in 1805 called "an enlightened people."[1] As distinct from the long-standing and varied programs of counting the native peoples of North America, the idea of an "Indian population" suggested that the North American Indians were a particular group of human beings who shared certain traits and could be counted within a circumscribed geographical boundary and then "improved" through the use of empirical data and statistical analysis. Built upon the foundation of older ideas, the concept of an "Indian population" was nonetheless new in the late eighteenth century, and it transformed transatlantic conversations about the essential nature and destiny of the North American Indians.

The idea of an Indian population formed part of the new eighteenth-century "science" of population, which embodied the enlightened faith that the self-conscious application of reason to society would better the human condition. Equipped with questionnaires, tables, pie charts, and forecasts, champions of the new science of population saw it as a means to increase the wealth of nations and create happy societies. The science of population promised release from an earlier age of faith and superstition, when questions of population were governed by biblical injunctions to avoid the sin of David, the king who lived to regret his presumption that the people of Israel were his to count rather than God's.[2]

In the second half of the eighteenth century, the term *population* began to decorate the titles of a clutch of influential new works about the well-being of the United States, Britain, Germany, France, and other European nations. The most famous today is Thomas Malthus's *Essay on the Principle of Population* (1798), remembered for its gloomy prediction that the ever growing numbers of humans would inevitably outstrip the food supply. Yet in his day Malthus was one of many optimistic theorists who saw the potential for the human sciences of population and statistics to increase what they called the quantum of happiness. The new United States offered a prime staging ground for this theory. In the early nineteenth century, the Scottish political economist William Playfair announced that the United States government was the best suited in the world to collect and perfect "statistical knowledge" because it was supported by a growing "population" of "enlightened people" who were unfettered by "antiquated customs."[3]

Although many features of the North American Indians—their religions, their languages, their customs—had been the subject of learned conversations around the Atlantic for over two centuries, the new question of the "Indian population" rested on an especially rich body of empirical evidence culled from America itself at a time when airy philosophical speculation about the Indians still colored much European writing.[4] Resting on the new theory that all societies progressed through stages from nomadic "savagery" to settled farming and thence to urban, commercial civilization, the notion of a North American Indian population suggested that the Indians could improve themselves as Europeans had done over the previous millennia. We have seen that the Indians of central Mexico were deemed at least semi-civilized because they lived in large cities, where they built complex societies, engaged in a form of writing, and created something resembling what Europeans recognized as art. The Indians of North America, by contrast, were thought to be savages because they appeared to lack the urbanizing impulse and the higher population densities that encouraged refinements in society and the arts. But by practicing settled agriculture in higher-density societies, the Indians might slowly ascend the scale of social evolution and perhaps ultimately become "civilized."

The key point in the new theory of social evolution was that the savage state was not just one of low numbers but also one of low population density, which doomed the Indians to constant hunger, war, misery, and crude social organization. The Scottish jurist Henry Home, Lord Kames, explained the theory neatly: "Paucity of inhabitants explains clearly why the North-American tribes remain hunters and fishers, without advancing to the shepherd-state." By contrast, civilized commercial societies were by definition not just numerous but also densely peopled. Europeans became obsessed with measuring the population densities of their greatest cities as an index of their relative merit compared to the Greco-Roman world, whose numbers were now fiercely debated by David Hume and Edward Gibbon, among others.[5]

Emerging in the 1780s, the new idea of an Indian population gripped a group of educated Americans and Europeans immersed in the new science of statistically based and empirically informed population studies that aimed to create enlightened societies. Although they did not form a unified movement, these thinkers all put their faith in the idea that the disciplined application of reason to social questions could create social happiness. In America, this motley group included the New England Congregationalist minister Ezra Stiles, the geographer Jedidiah Morse, the United States secretary of war Henry Knox, the explorers Meriwether Lewis and William Clark, and James Madison and Thomas Jefferson. Their various writings were read across the Atlantic by philosophers and social theorists eager to know how local American data might support the idea that population was an enlightened science of human improvement. The European group included Adam Smith, Richard Price, William Godwin, and Thomas Malthus. Along with the statistical measurements of other populations in Europe and elsewhere, the North American Indian population became an important empirical reference point for these thinkers, who used Indian numbers in larger conversations about how measuring human populations could create a better world.

Beginning as a mere trickle of references in the late eighteenth century, allusions to a distinct Indian population abounded after the 1820s. At that point it became common to refer even to pre-contact Indians as a population, retroactively placing them in a category that no one before the end of the eighteenth century would have understood.[6] Today historians and anthropologists routinely speak of the Indian population of the prehistoric and colonial eras. Yet at its birth in the late eighteenth century the idea of an Indian population was highly controversial because it directly confronted the question of whether the American Indians were capable of "improvement" and "civilization."

In sum, the new idea of an Indian population showed postrevolutionary Americans grappling with the basic problem of defining what kinds of peoples the Indians were and what relationship they bore to the sovereign people enshrined in the ostensibly enlightened new federal and state governments established in the wake of independence. Article 1, section 2, of the federal Constitution relegated some Indians to the opaque category of "Indians not taxed" for purposes of representation in the House of Representatives. The Indian Commerce Clause designated the federal government as the proper authority for dealing with "the Indian Tribes." These formulations had been efforts to improve on the vague wording of the Articles of Confederation, which had declared the federal government rather than the states the sole power responsible for dealing with "the Indians, not members of any of the States," a phrasing so nebulous that James Madison mocked it in essay 42 of *The Federalist* as "obscure and contradictory." He went on: "What description of Indians are to be deemed members of a State, is not yet settled; and has been a question of frequent perplexity and contention in the federal councils."[7]

Madison's words were prophetic. For the Indians to become members of the new republic, they also had to fall under the rubric of the state and federal governments. To do this, they had to become a *population* willing and able to climb the ladder of civilization so as to join other citizens in the procedures of ostensibly enlightened republican governance. Yet as the years passed, many Indians did not appear to be ascending on any scale of social measurement; most glaringly, their total numbers and population densities appeared to be declining. The problem became especially obvious during the era of Indian removal as large numbers of Indians were displaced. The Indians continued to be counted as often as in the past, though now under the banner of the new science of statistics. But no one seemed sure how the Indian population fit into the rest of the U.S. population from which it was being removed. As though summing up the puzzling legacy of the enlightened science of Indian population, a U.S. senator in the Indian removal debates of 1830 attempted to clarify the new logic of population as it applied to the Indians. "It is still to be proved that an Indian nation within a State, is a part of the population of that State. How can this be seriously pretended? The population of a State is the population which constitutes the community which constitutes the State. . . . But an Indian nation within a State is not a part of that community."[8] How did that peculiar situation come about?

Before Population: The Indian Counts of Early America

Before the emergence of the idea of an Indian population, there were Indian counts, the many numerical tallies Europeans undertook of the Indians of North America. Today, few historical topics remain more controversial than the number of Indians who lived in the Americas immediately prior to and then after European contact. Hardly anyone disputes the idea that Indian numbers declined after contact. The question is one of scale, and whether the drop in Indian numbers was so massive that it can be termed a genocide. The trail of evidence is so vast, fragmentary, and ambiguous that it can support any number of interpretations. One modern scholar has despaired that most Indian counts from this era may be "numbers from nowhere."[9]

In fact, however, the Indian counts are in many cases numbers from somewhere. That somewhere is the variety of European conventions for collecting data about human groups, conventions deeply influenced by historical and literary precedents inherited from Mediterranean antiquity and the Middle Ages. To say that the Indian counts were in many cases conventional and sometimes symbolic is not to dismiss them as inherently implausible. It is rather to place them in the historical contexts that produced them so that we can understand them on their own terms rather than ours and see them as the product of a complex array of motivations, conventions, and strategies. It was in the late eighteenth century that the old practice of counting was repackaged for the new purpose of creating enlightened polities.

The most important context for the North American Indian counts was European colonization, which extended European practices of human enumeration into new areas of the globe. During the early seventeenth century, France, Britain, and the Netherlands were establishing a foothold in North America in order to challenge Spain's supremacy to the south. The North American Indian counts assembled as part of that effort form one of the largest annals of information about the North American Indians surviving to this day. The Indian counts appear in a staggering variety of published and unpublished written records from the seventeenth century on: the colonial censuses, travelers' and soldiers' accounts, missionary reports such as the *Jesuit Relations*, and maps, to name just some. Nearly every North American Indian count was made in one or more of these contexts and was shaped by them.

The late-eighteenth-century idea of a North American Indian population grew from this older practice, in which Indians were counted for a variety of urgent European religious, military, and civil purposes. So valuable was the information on the North American Indian counts that it was frequently called "intelligence." In contrast to the vague impressions undergirding many European speculations about the North American Indians—ideas Jefferson later mocked as being "just as true as the fables of Æsop"—the Indian counts supplied information that was of immediate practical utility at the highest levels of government. In the midst of the American Revolution, King George III personally pressed his exiled royal governor Thomas Hutchinson for information on the number of Indians in Massachusetts.[10]

British Americans counted many kinds of people, especially after 1670, when the Board of Trade in England tightened its surveillance of colonial activities. At least 124 censuses of the population in British America were made between 1623 and 1775, most from the period after 1670. These colonial censuses usually provided only estimates of total population, though they often also broke down the population by race (black and white), sex, age, and military manpower. The concern was not to assess the state of the "average man," a concept that did not emerge until the nineteenth century, but rather to answer basic survival question such as who could be taxed and who was "fit to bear arms," as the Board of Trade put it in 1701.[11]

Illuminated by this information, British theorists by the late seventeenth century had concluded that populous colonies bolstered national well-being. The English political economist William Petty coined the term "political arithmetick" to describe the important relationship between quantitative data about human beings and the health of the state. Petty's many works celebrated Britain's rising power relative to France, where the Sun King was thought to rule over the most populous country in Europe. But in *Essays in Political Arithmetick* (1711) Petty pointed out that if one included Britain's American colonies, Britain was mightier than empires of greater geographical compass, an attractive possibility that he whittled into an axiom of political economy: "That a small Countrey and few People, by its Situation, Trade and Policy, may be equivalent in Wealth and Strength, to a far great People and Territory." Petty was intensely interested in American colonization. He peppered William Penn with frequent requests for information on the peopling of Pennsylvania, including a series of "Quaeries Concerning the Nature of the Natives of Pensilvania" that probed far beyond total numbers into smaller breakdowns such as sex.[12]

The archive of British American Indian counts that emerged from these concerns, large and chaotic as it is, can be sorted into a number of conventions and genres that illuminate its European origins, adaptations to pressing North American circumstances, and promise for use by thinkers drawn to the idea that human numbers could inform schemes for social improvement.

The first convention was the practice of counting warriors more often than other kinds of Indians. In contrast to the French and Spanish imperial pressures to count Indians in order to convert them to Catholicism, counting Indians in British America was often a form of military knowledge. The British did attempt to convert Indians to Protestantism, but on the whole this effort paled next to those of the Catholic European powers. Early on, warrior counts emerged as the dominant Indian counts in British America. Captain John Smith's 1612 description of Virginia's Indians repeatedly gave priority to "fighting men." The focus on warriors persisted over half a century later, when the first Virginia census listed Indians warriors by reference to wolf heads. Indians were often indirectly counted by way of the practice of giving presents or diplomatic gifts intended to forge alliances that would prevent warfare. Sir William Johnson, the British agent to the Iroquois in the middle of the eighteenth century, kept detailed daily records of the costs of "sundrys given" to Indians. Johnson's contemporary George Croghan, agent for the British to the Indians of North America, recorded in his diary the precise number of Indians who received presents of clothing. "I gave a Suit of Indian Cloaths to each Indian; being in the whole one hundred and Sixty four Men Sixteen Women and Eighteen Boys and Girls."[13]

The second convention—especially common in the warrior counts in written documents and maps—was to round Indian numbers to the nearest ten, hundred, or thousand. This practice was not new to the Americas; it appears in Greco-Roman antiquity and in the Middle Ages, and was already well established in the earliest *Jesuit Relations*. During the second half of the seventeenth century, rounded Indian military numbers appear with growing frequency in the official correspondence between the British North American colonies and the imperial center. During this time, the crown attempted to impose more control over the North American colonies, demanding ever more accurate information from colonial governors and other on-site agents.[14]

Examples of rounded Indian counts reported from the colonies to Britain appear in the imperial records beginning in the middle of the seventeenth century. They were also reported in British publications such as the *London Gazette* and the *Scots Magazine*. A ship returning to Britain from Maryland in 1676 brought intelligence that "the Indians there have been very troublesome, and the Susquehannas had built a fort at the head of the Potomac, and with about 200 of them kept it two months, notwithstanding 7 or 800 lay before it." Lord Culpeper's estimate of the population of the colony of Virginia shows that amid a series of rounded population numbers the military strength of the Indians stood out as what was to be especially counted. "An estimate of the population of Virginia, viz., about seventy or eighty thousand, of which fifteen thousand servants, three thousand blacks, and the remainder free men, women, and children; and an estimate of the strength of the Indians, as follows: None of our neighboring Indian nations can make above two hundred fighting men, except the Occanagees, about three hundred; the Tuscarores, towards Carolina, six or eight thousand, but these are peaceable; and the Senecas, a fierce and dangerous race, about four thousand." Finally, Indians themselves appear often to have been pressed for their numbers; whatever was actually said by the Indians, it was often recorded in the rounded form. At Fort Johnson in New York, a Nanticoke Indian brought what was called intelligence in the form of "400. Indians from the Westward."[15]

The third convention was the practice of calculating a rough ratio of Indian warriors to the rest of the Indians in a particular area. Again, this practice was not confined to enumerations of the American Indians, but rather used across the board for human counts in the seventeenth and eighteenth centuries. Within the North American Indian counts, this ratio was usually anywhere between two and five other people for each warrior. The convention is evident in some of the earliest North American Indian counts in the *Jesuit Relations*, suggesting that it may have existed prior to them as a practice in Europe. As one of the Jesuit accounts put it, "In this Village there are computed to be about seven hundred men; that is to say, three thousand souls, since to one man there are at least three or four other persons, namely, women and children." The practice was also reproduced in British America. In his *New Voyage to Carolina* (1709), John Lawson seems to have multiplied warriors by 2.5 to calculate total Indian numbers. "Now, there appears to be one thousand six hundred and twelve Fighting Men ... and probably, there are three Fifths of Women and Children, not including

Old Men, which amounts to four thousand and thirty Savages, besides the five Nations lately come," he wrote. The Connecticut historian Benjamin Trumbull used a similar ratio at the end of the eighteenth century, though he was not certain when the practice had begun. Writing of the Indians of early Connecticut, he wrote, "If we reckon every third person a bowman, as some have imagined, then the whole number of Indians, in the town and tract mentioned would be nine thousands; but if there were but one to four or five, as is most probable, then there were twelve or fifteen thousands."[16]

In addition to these conventions, the Indian counts can also be roughly divided into two genres. The first might be called "far-off Indians" (as Governor George Clinton of New York called them in 1749).[17] These were Indians who lived largely beyond the pale of intensive European settlement, whose numbers could only be discerned in the broadest strokes and who were by definition much less accurately counted. The far-off Indian counts could easily number into the thousands and even tens of thousands, as they did in Baron de Lahontan's counts of the Iroquois, which appeared in his *New Voyages to North-America* (1703). "Each Village or Canton contains about fourteen thousand Souls," Lahontan reported, "i.e., 1500 that bear Arms, 2000 Superannuated Men, 4000 Women, 2000 Maids, and 4000 Children; Tho' indeed some will tell you, that each Village has not above 10000 or 11000 Souls."[18] The book's image of Indians massed for war shows how the far-off numerical convention also influenced contemporary illustrations.

The second genre into which Indian counts fit can be called "nearby" Indians (to vary Clinton's wording). These were attempts to count Indians who lived within or near European settlement or who came into close contact with Europeans. Nearby Indians were counted with great specificity (that is, without perceptible rounding) by Europeans traveling or living among the Indians. They often appear as part of colonial censuses. With blacks, Indians were specifically counted as slaves in the 1708 South Carolina census, for example. But they also crop up at random in a variety of other sources. "During the evening the Onondagas came. There were six old men and four women," reported a traveler in Mohawk country in 1635.[19]

The Seven Years' War brought a new sense of urgency and organization to this chaotic stock of information about the Indians.

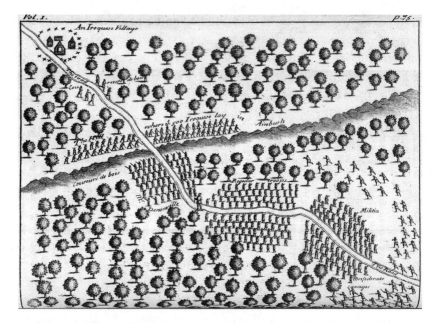

This image from Baron de Lahontan's New Voyages to North-America
*(1703) shows the visual and verbal conventions by which the numbers of
American Indian warriors were rounded, often to the nearest hundred.
The words "The Hill where ye 500 Iroquese lay in Ambush" appear next
to the double column of armed men. (Huntington Library)*

With the fate of Britain's North American empire on the line, royal
governors and other imperial officials pressed locals for "intelligence" about the number of Indians. Lieutenant Governor Francis
Fauquier of Virginia, for example, told William Byrd in 1758, "I
desire to have an exact Account of all the Indians who have been
with you, and of all who remain with you at this Day distinguish-
ing their Nations." The Peace of Paris in 1763, which gave Britain
control of most of the Atlantic seaboard of North America,
brought the need to continue to gauge the strength and numbers
of Indians west of the Proclamation Line, which ran north to south
roughly through the Appalachians. As a result of these military necessities, Indian warrior counts continued to pour into London not
just in official correspondence to Whitehall but in publications
available to the public, who followed the war with interest. "The

number of Indians that inhabit round Lake Huron is about 3000, 600 of which are warriors, or fighting men," reported the ranger Robert Rogers in his *Concise Account of North America*, published in London in 1765.[20]

Among those interested readers was a group of Scottish philosophers who after mid-century used this numerical intelligence to prepare theoretical works about the evolution of humankind from savagery to civilization. The Scots are often thought of as armchair theoreticians: never setting foot in North America, they rather grounded their grand stadial histories in perusals of such popular accounts of North American life as Joseph-François Lafitau's *Moeurs des sauvages amériquains* (1724) and Pierre-François-Xavier de Charlevoix's *Histoire et description generale de la Nouvelle France* (1744). In fact, however, their theories were also grounded in careful consultation of the numerical intelligence regarding the Indians that had accumulated as a result of the Seven Years' War. Nor were their goals purely theoretical. They were also hoping to discover Scotland's place in the new organization of Atlantic commercial powers by determining the preconditions that led to successful commercial and social development. North America had the Indians, but Scotland had the Highland clans, groups that seemed to offer instructive parallels for how societies evolved from ostensibly primitive forms of social organization to commercial complexity.[21]

Adam Smith was among the earliest to weigh in on the larger historical significance of the North American Indians. In the first major Scottish publication to make use of the American Indians for a general theory of social development, Smith defined them essentially as warriors. His *Theory of Moral Sentiments* (1759), published during the Seven Years' War, reflected the kind of intelligence that was pouring out of North America. Writing about the variety of human customs found around the world, he argued that "the savages of North America" were in "continual danger" from a combination of war, hunger, and general misery. All their social customs emerged from these hard facts. "Every savage is said to prepare himself from his earliest youth" for war and torture, Smith wrote. He embellished these views in his *Inquiry into the Nature and Causes of the Wealth of Nations* (1776), where he outlined his theories about human social development and argued that the lowest, hunter stage was unsuited for large armies. "An army of hunters can seldom exceed two or three hundred men," he observed, while a settled society of shepherds could support a much larger army.[22] He then moved to a specific case he knew well: "Nothing can be more contemptible than an Indian war in North America."[23]

Adam Smith's library shows that he kept up to date on information about the Indians of North America. He owned the New York lawyer William Smith's *History of the Province of New-York* (1757), published in London two years before the *Theory of Moral Sentiments* appeared. Dedicated to Lord Halifax, the president of the Board of Trade, William Smith's history was meant to slake the "*present Thirst in Great-Britain after American Intelligences*," and included not just general reports about the "innumerable Tribes of Savages" but more specific warrior counts sprinkled throughout. Smith offered an extensive description of the "Character" of the Iroquois, described as a people with a "warlike Disposition" who trained even women and children to scalp and torture their enemies: "No people in the World perhaps have higher Notions than these *Indians* of military Glory," he argued.[24]

As data continued to arrive from North America after the Seven Years' War, learned Scots also incorporated empirical data about the Indians into their stadial histories of society. Adam Ferguson, author of *An Essay on the History of Civil Society* (1767), relied on the eyewitness reports of Charlevoix, Lafitau, and Cadwallader Colden to affirm the warlike nature of the North American Indians. Citing Charlevoix, Ferguson argued that "the nations of North America, who have no herds to preserve, nor settlements to defend, are yet engaged in almost perpetual wars, for which they can assign no reason, but the point of honour, and a desire to continue the struggle their fathers maintained." Ferguson's interests were more than theoretical. He was deeply interested in North America, completing his *Essay on the History of Civil Society* the same year that he entertained the idea of becoming governor of the colony of West Florida, just acquired from Spain during the Seven Years' War. The Scottish historian and philosopher David Hume—who at this time was undersecretary to the secretary of state for the Northern Department—helped promote Ferguson's book among his coterie of admiring readers in the British government, such as Lords Bute, Mansfield, Chesterfield, and Lyttelton, and finally Lord Shelburne, the man then formulating American Indian policy as secretary of state for the Southern Department. Shelburne, according to Hume, declared Ferguson's book "one of the best he ever read."[25]

Similarly, John Millar's *Observations Concerning the Distinction of Ranks in Society* (1771) relied on travel accounts for descriptions of the North American Indians. Millar was blunt concerning the importance of basic empirical information about the Indians, encouraging what he called "real experiments" rather than "abstracted metaphysical theories" for the understanding of "human nature." Millar was especially keen to refute Buffon and Pauw's insistence that the low population density of the North American Indians resulted from the cold, damp American climate, which allegedly withered their reproductive organs. Instead, Millar offered a sociological argument: Indian tribes were so small that males could satisfy their lust with so little trouble that they became bored by the process. "He must have little regard for pleasures which he can purchase at so easy a rate," Millar wrote. The sexual drive was increased as societies moved up the ladder of civilization and men and women became more particular and refined in their interactions. "Thus the original society is gradually enlarged into a village or tribe," he wrote of savage peoples. "And, according as it is placed in circumstances which favour population, and render its condition prosperous and flourishing, it becomes proportionably extensive."[26]

By the middle of the eighteenth century, the complex intellectual and military situation in British America had made the Indian counts a trove of valuable information both in the colonies and in Britain. From these widely disseminated raw data, compiled largely for military and strategic purposes, Scottish theorists built some of the first general theories of human societal development. Soon British Americans also joined the conversation about the meaning of the Indian counts. Their great innovation was to suggest that the Indians could not only be counted, but that they also formed a *population*.

From Indian Counts to Indian Population

In 1783, Ezra Stiles coined the term "Indian population." As president of Yale College, the Congregationalist minister enjoyed both a local and an international reputation as a man thoroughly attuned not just to new intellectual currents generally but to the new science of population specifically. His neologism sprang from the conjunction of two long-standing interests both in population studies and in counting Indians. Stiles's achievement was to connect these two interests and to publish his ideas in a form that attracted the attention of European theorists who were equally engaged in exploring how the science of population could create social happiness.

Ezra Stiles embodied the prospects and limitations of intellectual life in eighteenth-century North America. Sensitive to his colonial status, he constantly looked to Europe for intellectual inspiration and approval. He was thrilled to receive an honorary degree from the University of Edinburgh in 1765, a coup engineered by the Edinburgh historian William Robertson and Stiles's friend Benjamin Franklin (who referred to the degree as "the Doctorate I procur'd for you").[27] Samuel King's portrait of 1771 captures the minister's omnivorous intellectual interests. Sitting quietly in his ministerial black, Stiles holds a book that was probably pulled from the shelves behind him, which are packed with works on Newtonian science, theology, and Roman and Chinese history. The pillar at left features a model of the solar system, with a comet's path clearly delineated. A glowing sphere stuffed with religious symbolism hovers nearby, literally enlightening the minister and his intellectual pursuits.

Committed to his demanding theology, Stiles was both deeply learned and intellectually omnivorous. His linguistic triumphs were legendary: he could read Latin, Greek, Arabic, Chaldee, and Syriac. Not only did he preach in Hebrew at a nearby synagogue and teach it to undergraduates at Yale, he invited rabbis to preach from his pulpit. So capacious were his sympathies that he eventually supported not just the American Revolution but the French ("Yea, I am a Jacobin").[28]

Transatlantic in his intellectual interests, Stiles himself was a homebody, seldom straying far from the small towns and tidy farms that dotted Connecticut and Rhode Island. Instead, he brought the international republic of letters to his doorstep, entertaining an endless parade of visitors who ventured from near and far to meet the learned doctor. He was forever concocting local

Samuel King's portrait of the polymath minister Ezra Stiles from 1771 shows the minister sitting contentedly among his favorite books on Newtonian science, Greek philosophy, and Chinese and Roman history. A diagram of the solar system showing the path of a comet appears on the column. Hovering to the minister's right is a glowing orb printed with a cross and the Hebrew phrase "All Happy in God." (Yale University Art Gallery)

scholarly schemes, including a learned society in the 1760s that in his own honor he christened the Societas Eruditorum Stilensiana. As librarian of Newport's Redwood Library for twenty years, he ordered crates of books from Europe and begged more from his friends living in London and Paris.[29]

In a life of many intellectual fascinations, his greatest appears to have been counting, as though God's wondrous world might best be apprehended by quantifying it. It seemed that nothing—no farm, no town, no building, no animal—escaped the eye of the tireless human yardstick that was Ezra Stiles. More than anything else, Ezra Stiles counted people. He also measured them, his own waistline being a frequent target. In a diary that sometimes reads like an arithmetic primer, he recorded numbers of churchgoers, numbers of tithable people, children in school, twins born in New England, emigration from New Haven, living alumni of American colleges, and the probable populations of Bengal, Philadelphia, Edinburgh, Rome, Rhode Island, France, and Louisiana. Heavily represented on the long list of subjects to be investigated at the Societas Eruditorum Stilensiana was what Stiles called "the whole Theory of Population": investigations into the "Facts" of smallpox spread and inoculation; birth, death, and immigration rates; census returns; the reasons for rising and "degenerating population." He loved receiving census data from correspondents in other colonies and states, who apologized obsequiously for possible inaccuracies, which they knew would irritate the vigilant counter of Connecticut.[30]

Stiles was among the first British Americans to see population as a "pleasurable" science governed by laws akin to those in the natural world. In 1761 he jotted this brief note to himself:

> I cannot but remark that Population; or the Laws of human increase and degeneracy are as properly a subject of systematical Science, as botany, the theory of agriculture, or raising and improving stock—and like all other branches of philosophy is to be founded on experiments. These experiments in all their variety are already made to our hands in the sufficiently authentic history of the last 3000 years in different parts of the world. There remains the classing and generalizing of experiments or facts, and pursuing their obvious

inductions to certain general Laws: with which we may be prepared for useful and interesting applications. These researches will not only [be] very pleasurable, but lead to several Things of great moment, hitherto little attended to by politicians, philosophers, or divines.[31]

Stiles became a clearinghouse for the transatlantic flow of information on population as a science. He joined Franklin as one of the first British Americans to publish an internationally received work on the importance of population studies. Franklin's *Observations Concerning the Increase of Mankind* (1751)—a short essay arguing that the population of America would double every twenty-five years— had found numerous enthusiastic readers in England and Scotland. Using Franklin's earlier work on population, Stiles published *A Discourse on the Christian Union* (1761), which gleefully predicted enormous increases in the numbers of Congregationalists in British America. Stationed in London on imperial business, Franklin was so delighted with Stiles's essay that he proposed to circulate it among his "ingenious Friends" in Britain. Stiles's published findings were also disseminated in England in Thomas Short's *A Comparative History of the Increase and Decrease of Mankind* (1767) and was cited approvingly (along with Franklin's work) in Richard Price's compilation of European and American vital statistics, *Observations on Reversionary Payments* (1771). Stiles in turn helped disseminate this knowledge in America: Price's *Observations on Reversionary Payments* appeared in the Yale College library during Stiles's tenure as president.[32]

Stiles's broad-gauged population study extended to the Indians of North America, whose numbers he counted with a frequency bordering on the neurotic. Stiles shared the interests of others in his era in the origins and languages of the North American Indians. Like his contemporaries he believed (from linguistic and archaeological evidence) that the Indians were descended from Old World populations, probably the Phoenicians or the Ten Lost Tribes of Israel.[33] He read about the large earthen mounds in the Ohio country. Yet his interest in the Indians fell especially in the realm of numbers; his diaries and letters are filled with tables of census data and verbatim reports about Indian numbers, quite a few pulled from reports provided by the Indians themselves.

Stiles's Indian counts fall roughly into the two genres typical of this time, the "far-off" Indians and the "nearby" Indians. To ascertain the numbers of far-off Indians, he pressed correspondents for information about their travels and military engagements. In the early 1770s he read with interest an interview of Colonel Thomas Goldthwaite from Fort Pownall in northern Maine with an Indian. Question: "Are your Indians numerous?" Answer: "They are very numerous, and they occupy great space of Country." Question: "Are there many Indian nations between Montreal and the Mataguissawack Country?" Answer: "There are a great many." In 1775 he received a visit from Bernard Romans, whose *Concise Natural History of East and West Florida* (1775) recorded Indian numbers in North and South America. "Conversed largely on the Indians, their Origin, and Customs," Stiles recorded of the visit, then jotted down a list of rounded Indian numbers he received from Romans, followed by a table of warrior counts ("fencible Men"), all rounded to a number ending in zero.[34]

Stiles was especially careful about recording numbers of the nearby Indians of New England, who frequently appeared in the colonial censuses. As a young man, Stiles had considered becoming a missionary to the settlement at Stockbridge, Massachusetts, formed in the 1730s to Christianize and educate the Indians. Here the number of Indians was precisely known, including breakdowns by sex and current standing within the church: "The Number of Indians now residing here is upwards of 90," reported the theologian Samuel Hopkins. "We have of *Indians* in regular standing in the Church 35, 13 *Males* and 22 *Females*, besides five or six under a temporary Suspension from the Communion." Stiles's visit to Stockbridge sparked his interest in the local Indians of New England. Across the bay from his home in Newport lived the Indians in Narragansett County; he wondered about their origins, once digging up graves with Indian bones. Stiles filled his notebooks and letters with counts of the New England Indians. In 1762 he received a letter from Jonathan Trumbull with a count of the Indians in Connecticut censuses of 1756 and 1762, in which the Indians were enumerated by town. Scrawling "omitted" in the margins of Trumbull's letter, the ever vigilant Stiles dutifully noted blunders in Trumbull's census information. Consulting in 1774 with a midwife, who informed him of recent births, Stiles attempted to tally the number of Indians, whites, and blacks in Newport. The total count he ended up with—9,209—included a breakdown of Indians by sex. Stiles was able to correct the erroneous Pequot Indians numbers in Thomas Hutchinson's *The History of the Colony of Massachusets-Bay* (1764).[35]

At the close of the American Revolution, Stiles fused his two interests in population and Indian counts when he coined the term "Indian population," which appeared in his bombastic sermon *The United States Elevated to Glory and Honor* (1783), a celebration of the present and projected magnificence of the new United States. As Stiles used it, the term drew directly on his deep reading in the Indian counts: the British military counts, the colonial censuses, and the more speculative numbers derived from Lahontan and Carver.

From these various counts, Stiles attempted to calculate the Indian population of North America. By "population" he meant not just total numbers but density, both of which could help to predict the Indians' contribution to the "publick weal." "By an accurate numeration made in 1766 and returned into the Plantation-office in *London*, it appeared, that there was not *forty* thousand souls, Indians, from the Missisippi to the *Atlantick*, and from *Florida* to the Pole. According to Mr. *Carver*, there are about thirty, and certainly not forty Indian tribes, west of the Senecas, and Six Nation confederacy, and from the *Missisippi* and *Ohio* northward to *Hudson's* bay, and from *Niagara* to the Lake of the Woods." He then argued that "the ratio of Indian population in the very heart of the Continent, is similar to that on this side of the missisippi." The key observation was not just the total number but the "spare thin settlement" of Indians who eked out a "very inconsiderable value" from the land. By contrast, "protestant *Europeans*" were a "numerous *population*" whose "*industry*" gave "value to land." To the Indians' small numbers, low density, and failure to improve the land, European settlers offered the possibility of "future increase" in numbers and density.[36]

In the years after Stiles published his sermon, others in America and Europe took the general idea of an Indian population and sorted out its implications. The whole enterprise was gripped by uncertainty about which Indians to count and how to count them, a problem articulated by the geographer Jedidiah Morse. "I have not been able to ascertain the exact state of the Indian population in Massachusetts and New Hampshire," he declared in his *American Geography* (1789). The problem was the same on the national scale. "The amount of Indian population, in America, can only be guessed at," he wrote in the *American Gazetteer* in 1797.[37] Still, now that there was an *American* population, it seemed that there surely had to be an *Indian* population; learned Americans rushed in to address the matter.

Among the first was Thomas Jefferson's *Notes on the State of Virginia* (1787). Responding to French queries about American numbers with a section on "population," Jefferson compiled a series of North American Indian counts into numerical tables. Like others before him, Jefferson used warrior counts—in this case the warrior counts from the Seven Years' War and the American Revolution compiled by George Croghan, Henry Bouquet, Thomas Hutchins, and John Dodge. In the table Indians were divided into categories similar to "far-off" and "nearby," which Jefferson delineated as tribes "Northward and Westward of the United States" and those "Within the Limits of the United States." Curiously, Jefferson did not mention that the numbers were warrior counts rather than total counts, simply billing them as "the nations and numbers of the Aborigines which still exist in a respectable and independent form."[38]

Just as important as total counts for Jefferson was the population density of the Indians, the key determinant of their place on the ladder of civilization according to the emerging theories of social evolution. Jefferson used the report of Captain John Smith from early-seventeenth-century Virginia to argue that the whole of the Powhatan confederacy consisted of "about 8000 inhabitants, which was one for every square mile." This was a much lower population density than that of the United States or Britain: it was "about the twentieth part of our present population in the same territory, and the hundredth of that of the British islands." Eager to refute the comte de Buffon's thesis that the allegedly cold and humid American climate depressed the Indians' fertility, Jefferson countered that their low fertility was by their own choice. They "multiply less than we do," he wrote, because they used methods such as abortion "for the purpose of restraining their numbers within certain bounds."[39]

TRIBES.	Croghan. 1759.	Bouquet. 1764.	Hutchins. 1768.	Dodge. 1779.	Where they reside.
Mohocks	—	—	160	100	Mohocks river. [of Sufquehanna.
Oneidas	—	—	300		E. fide of Oneida L. and head branches
Tufcaròras	—	—	200	400	Between the Oneidas and Onondagoes.
Onondàgoes	—	1550	260	230	Near Onondago L. [of Sufquehanna.
Cayùgas	—	—	200	220	On the Cayuga L. near the N. branch
Sènecas	—	—	1000	650	On the waters of Sufquehanna, of Ontario, and the heads of the Ohio.
Aughquàgahs	—	—	150	—	Eaft branch of Sufquehanna, and on Aughquagah.
Nànticocs	—	—	100	—	Utfanango, Chaghtnet, and Owegy, on the Eaft branch of Sufquehanna.
Mohìccons	—	—	100	—	In the fame parts.
Conòies	—	—	30	—	In the fame parts.
Sapòonies	—	—	30	—	At Diahago and other villages up the N. branch of Sufquehanna.
Mùnfies	—	—	150	*150	At Diahago and other villages up the N. branch of Sufquehanna.

This table of Indian counts from Thomas Jefferson's Notes on the State of Virginia *(1787) shows the convention of rounding that was common in enumerations of the "Indian population." (Courtesy Department of Special Collections, Stanford University Libraries)*

Although it was achieved by conscious choice, this low population density, according to Jefferson, was a retarding factor in the North American Indians' climb toward civilization. In Europe, the population had achieved greater density two thousand years earlier than it had among the present-day Indians of North America; yet little in the way of literature had emerged among these early Europeans. So how could the Indians be expected to have moved up the scale of civilization? Given time and greater population densities, however, they would surely soon produce "geniuses," as the Europeans had. "Before we condemn the Indians of this continent as wanting genius, we must consider that letters have not yet been introduced among them," Jefferson cautioned. He counseled patience, arguing through a comparison with the Roman era that higher populations were required to produce civilized art and literature:

Were we to compare them [the Indians] in their present state with the Europeans North of the Alps, when the Roman arms and arts first crossed those mountains, the comparison would be unequal, because, at that time, those parts of Europe were swarming with numbers; because numbers produce emulation, and multiply the chances of improvement, and one improvement begets another. Yet I may safely ask, How many good poets, how many able mathematicians, how many great inventors in arts or sciences, had Europe North of the Alps then produced? And it was sixteen centuries after this before a Newton could be formed.[40]

Indian population density theories also helped Americans to project probable battle success rates on the western frontier. Secretary of War Henry Knox, responsible in the late 1780s for managing relations with the Indians resident in lands claimed by the new United States, articulated the nation's early federal Indian policy in letters to George Washington. Knox believed that the Indians were sovereign rulers and possessors of the lands they occupied and that the federal government, rather than the states or individual citizens, should deal with them.

Sovereign nations or not, the Indians' low population density doomed them to recede in the face of populations of greater density, Knox argued. In letters to George Washington, Knox, a former bookseller, sounded as though he had been reading deeply in Scottish and English population theory and pondering how it might apply to the American Indians. He appealed to what he called "fixed principles" to argue that the "population" of the Indians was based on access to hunting grounds. Knox worried that the rising white population would reduce the amount of game near the borders of Indian territory, leading the Indians to become "extinct." Conceding that the "civilization of the Indians" would be a difficult process requiring time and knowledge, he argued that it could nonetheless be achieved. The "human character," even under the "stubborn habits" of the Indians, was capable of "melioration and change." One had only to look at Europe to see "the progress of society from the barbarous ages to its present degree of perfection."[41]

Thomas Malthus put the weight of population theory behind these ideas in *An Essay on the Principle of Population* (1798). Malthus mocked the optimism of social theorists such as Condorcet in France and William Godwin in England. These prophets of the "perfectibility of society" envisioned a sunny future in which humanity would forever increase both in numbers and in happiness.

Malthus by contrast soberly unveiled the ominous "law of our nature": that "the power of population is indefinitely greater than the power in the earth to produce subsistence for man." Population increased geometrically, food only arithmetically. Citing Ezra Stiles through Richard Price's work, Malthus drew attention to the doubling of the American population every twenty-five years; in the backcountry it was every fifteen years.[42] Who would grow the food to feed all these hungry mouths?

Crucial to Malthus's theory were the North American Indians. Applying the principle of population to their case revealed timeless truths about the laws of nature. "In estimating the happiness of a savage nation," argued Malthus, theorists should take into account that constant war, hunting, and drudgery ensured that "misery is the check that represses the superior power of population." Yet the danger of overpopulation still lurked even among the Indians, so powerful was the principle of population. Directly refuting John Millar's theory that the North American Indians were sexually in-ert, Malthus argued that even the Indians would eventually over-whelm their food supply as they ascended through the scale of civilization and began to farm:

> In the rudest state of mankind, in which hunting is the principal occupation, and the only mode of acquiring food; the means of subsistence being scattered over a large extent of territory, the comparative population must necessarily be thin. It is said, that the passion between the sexes is less ardent among the North American Indians, than among any other race of men. Yet notwithstanding this apathy, the effort towards population, even in this people, seems to be always greater than the means to support it. This appears, from the comparatively rapid population that takes place, whenever any of the tribes happen to settle in some fertile spot, and to draw nourishment from more fruitful sources than that of hunting.[43]

Malthus's theories gained an enthusiastic following among learned Americans during the next decades, especially after the second edition of his book—which softened some of his harshest conclusions—made its way into American libraries.[44] Americans appreciated Malthus's anti-mercantilist views and comforted themselves by insisting that the free availability of land in America rendered Malthus's theories invalid there—or at least inapplicable for many ages to come. In the meantime, Americans' research into the Indian population continued to be refined and expanded—and then published for an international audience, ensuring that the American Indian population remained a key factor in the transatlantic science of population.

The Lewis and Clark Expedition Sets the Indian Population Within an International Context

The key text that ensured the ongoing relevance of the North American Indians to debates on human population emerged from the important Indian counting project of the Lewis and Clark Expedition (1804–6). Stalled for five snowy months at Fort Mandan in present-day North Dakota during the winter of 1804–5, Meriwether Lewis and William Clark set about compiling a large, handwritten table they titled "The Estimate of the Eastern Indians." This document assembled information about the Indians living in the vast area between the western Great Lakes and east of the Rocky Mountains. The numbers of Indians who lived there had long eluded precise counts and were known to British Americans only from the often fantastical far-off Indian counts of authors such as Lahontan. President Jefferson used Lewis and Clark's "Estimate of the Eastern Indians" to prepare his published report on the expedition for Congress in 1806. Within a few years a version had been published in London, bringing the counts of the American Indians in the middle of the North American continent to international attention.[45]

Lewis and Clark's "Estimate of the Eastern Indians" was just one of many scientific projects undertaken during their journey to the Pacific Ocean. They had received instructions from Jefferson concerning what kinds of information to collect about the commercial possibilities and natural history of the new Louisiana Purchase, and the Indians were central to both. In his instructions to Lewis and Clark, Jefferson spelled out the need to determine

Indian numbers. "The commerce which may be carried on with the people inhabiting the line you will pursue, renders a knolege of those people important. You will therefore endeavor to make yourself acquainted, as far as a diligent pursuit of your journey shall admit. with the names of the nations & their numbers." They were also to collect Indian artifacts and information on Indian languages, monuments, religion, and traditions. All this they recorded in the form of maps, journals, vocabularies, and drawings. A great deal was brought back east to help in gathering "useful knowledge"—the stated purpose of the American Philosophical Society. Jefferson hoped that later expeditions would then use this information to "civilize and instruct" the Indians, thereby lifting them out of savagery.[46] The "Estimate of the Eastern Indians" thus formed merely one segment of the larger commercial, military, and scientific goals of Lewis and Clark's expedition.

Clark created the table—which measured approximately two feet by three feet—by pasting together seven sheets of letter paper. There he carefully documented nineteen categories of data about the Indians living east of the Rocky Mountains and west of the Great Lakes, including their tribal names, languages, relations with other tribes, and trading practices. Clark described this information as "being thought important at present in a governmental point of view."[47]

Four of the nineteen queries concerned Indian numbers: numbers of villages, numbers of tents and lodgings, numbers of warriors, and finally a category described as "The probable Number of Souls of this Numbr. deduct about 1/3 generally." It is not clear what Clark meant by this last category, but it usually included two notations: the first a larger number that appeared to be calculated by multiplying the warrior counts by anything from about three to six; the second number was usually that total reduced by a third. These four kinds of enumeration were recorded in the traditional format of rounded numbers. Lewis and Clark gathered their information on Indian numbers in many of the same ways their predecessors had: by talking to the Indians, sometimes directly and often through intermediaries. Their long winter stay allowed them to consult with a variety of Indians who lived nearby, including the Mandan and Indians passing through the area, such as the Assiniboine,

Cheyenne, and the westward-ranging Hidatsa, who could offer estimates of the numbers and locations of the more distant Crow, Shoshone, and Nez Perce. The second kind of Indian count was an assessment of the Indians' commercial possibilities. This count was an estimate in dollars of "the amount of Merchandise necessary for their annual consumption" and "annual returns."[48]

In short, Lewis and Clark's "Estimate of the Eastern Indians" was in many ways a conventional document: it was essentially an Indian count resembling many produced in the previous century and a half. Its major emphasis was on warrior counts and on counting Indians for commercial and diplomatic purposes. The mathematical ratios used for estimating total numbers were likewise traditional.

What made the Lewis and Clark count dramatically new was that the published version included the phrase "a Statistical Account" in the title. This new term—*statistical*—emerged from the idea of applying social knowledge to public policy, a view that had become commonplace by the late eighteenth century amid the quest to form enlightened polities. Enlightened polities in turn enjoyed a measurable amount of happiness, what the Scottish politician Sir John Sinclair called a "quantum of happiness." A friend and correspondent of Jefferson, Sinclair had popularized the new word *statistics* in the 1790s. His *Statistical Account of Scotland* (1791–99), based on widely distributed questionnaires about the population of Scotland, had defined the new terms: "Many people were at first surprised, at my using the new words, *Statistics* and *Statistical*," Sinclair noted, explaining that statistics was "an inquiry into the state of a country, *for the purpose of ascertaining the* quantum *of happiness enjoyed by its inhabitants, and the means of its future improvement.*"[49]

Sinclair encouraged Jefferson's interests in increasing the "quantum of happiness," pressing copies of his books onto his American friend. "I wish we had a statistical survey of America, similar to the one I am now carrying on in Scotland," he wrote to Jefferson in 1792. Of Sinclair's 160 queries about Scotland, a number explicitly concerned what he called "population": totals, broken down by sex, birthrate, death rate, occupation, religion, and many more categories. The great object of all the queries, Sinclair assured the sometimes reluctant Scottish clergymen who distributed the queries, was "to ascertain what means are the most likely to promote the real interests of its inhabitants." In the decades after the 1790s, numerous statistical studies of European populations were published. Through the principle of the "Statistical Scale," as noted in one of them, governments could "accurately discover not only the relative situation and greatness of each State, but unerringly measure the respective wisdom of the Governments of all." Through statistics the hope to increase the "quantum of happiness" could be realized.[50]

Statistical views of the United States became increasingly popular in the early 1800s along with new aesthetic solutions to the problem of representing the abundant numerical information resulting from efforts at enlightenment. Innovations such as the pie chart deployed simple, abstract geometric shapes whose meanings the eye could instantly grasp.[51] In 1805 a "Statistical Representation of the United States" in the form of a pie chart appeared, with each piece representing the square mileage of the United States and the "Western Territory." Created by the Scottish political economist William Playfair, the image clearly announced its goal: to show the proportions of each part of the nation in "a Striking Manner." Whatever political power the eastern states might wield, the pie chart seemed to scream, the western territories dominated the national agenda by their sheer size, practically demanding that their human population be enumerated.

The Lewis and Clark expedition marked a major turning point in the meaning of the American Indian numbers, as these were transformed from warrior counts into the objects of a "statistical view" that might somehow increase the "quantum of happiness" of humanity. After the published account of the Lewis and Clark expedition appeared in a London edition, European theorists of population seized on the new information about the trans-Missouri Indians to refine their population debates.

Among the most influential was the British political philosopher and social reformer William Godwin, who used the Lewis and Clark Indian counts to rebut Thomas Malthus's depressing forecasts about populations inevitably exceeding food supply. In his *Essay on the Principle of Population* two decades earlier, Malthus had openly attacked Godwin and others, arguing that the number of

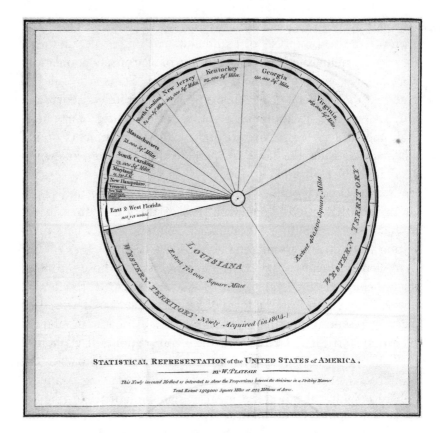

Called a "divided circle" at the time, William Playfair's statistical representation of the United States was among the first pie charts. (Huntington Library)

American Indians would begin to swell the moment that they cast aside their "savage" hunting habits and settled down to farm. With the published accounts of the Lewis and Clark expedition now in hand, Godwin was able to formulate an empirically based refutation of Malthus's arguments in his essay *Of Population* (1820). Godwin learned from the expedition reports that many farming North American Indians were experiencing a "thinness of population" nonetheless. "But the nations on the banks of the Missouri all raise corn," Godwin asserted by way of refuting Malthus's thesis that farming would increase numbers, "and yet this tract of country is at this hour more thinly peopled than we almost any where read of."[52]

For Godwin, this new empirical evidence about the North American Indians proved that Malthus had blundered in proposing that settled agriculture inevitably led to deadly overpopulation. Godwin concluded triumphantly: "The facts observed by captains Clarke and Lewis on the banks of the Missouri will hardly be disputed. Their total discordance with the theories of Mr. Malthus is sufficiently evident." So wrong was Malthus's theory that it was unworthy of this "enlightened age."[53]

James Madison immediately disputed Godwin's grasp of the facts about the American Indians. Madison himself had never traveled west beyond the Appalachians, but he kept abreast of the census data pouring in from the state and federal counts. So when Richard Rush, the American ambassador to Britain, sent Madison a copy of Godwin's *Of Population*, Madison replied to Rush with a searing refutation of Godwin's understanding of the American Indians' farming techniques. Godwin imagined enormous, complex farms in the European style, whereas the Indians (argued Madison) only coaxed measly vegetables from tiny scraps of land:

> Mr. G. could not have given a stronger proof of the estrangement of his ideas from the Indian character & modes of life than by his referring to the Missouri Tribes, which do not multiply, "altho' they cultivate corn." His fancy may have painted to him fields of Wheat, cultivated by the Plough & gathered into Barns, as a provision for the year. How wd he be startled at the sight of little patches of Maize & squashes, stirred by a piece of Wood, and that by the Squaws only; the hunters & warriors spurning such an occupation, & relying on the fruits of the Chase for the support of their Wigwams? "Corn Eaters" is a name of reproach given by some tribes to others beginning under the influence of the Whites to enlarge their cultivated spots.

Despite the evidence of corn-farming Indians, Madison hewed to the view that the American Indians were fundamentally a population of hunters and that whatever farming they did hardly deserved the name. The Indians remained therefore a low-density population. "In the savage state where wild animals are the chief food," Madison explained to Rush, "the population must be the thinnest."[54]

That singular commitment to the idea of population density—not just total population counts—in the end remained the fundamental conundrum contributed by population theorists to the place of the American Indians in what was ostensibly the "enlightened" polity of the United States. In combination with the stadial theory of human social development from savagery to civilization, the idea that the Indians were fundamentally a hunting, warrior, and low-population-density people suggested that they were unable to be a *population* in the same way that farming citizens of the United States were a population. As low-density hunting savages, the Indians could not be civilized; they could not be enlightened. The newly discovered "laws" of population suggested that higher densities would always push out lower densities. Citing the "irresistible power of numbers," the marquis de Barbé-Marbois put the matter succinctly in *The History of Louisiana* (1830), arguing that it was ridiculous to allow a single family to live on a large tract of land when it could sustain many thousands of people. "Even the Indian population is but thinly scattered over the immense space which extends from the great river [the Mississippi] to the Western Ocean; and the Americans find few obstacles in pushing on their settlements over regions which, in spite of the richness of the soil, have been long useless to man. Whatever may be our respect for the ancient rights of property, it is difficult to admit those of a single family to ten square leagues, where ten thousand persons could be supported in abundance."[55]

It is in the context of the enlightened population debates that the confusing statements made during the years of Indian Removal in 1830s begin to make more sense. Of course there could be two populations, an Indian population and an American population. Both consisted of human beings who could be counted and assessed through statistical methods that predicted their future development on the ladder of civilization and their future quantum of happiness. And there was encouraging news that the Indians were becoming "more enlightened and civilized" by being taught to read and write. Yet while the Indian tribes might be sovereign nations that showed evidence of climbing toward enlightenment, the new science of population suggested that their small and low-density populations would forever consign them to a lower rung on the scale of civilization. Thus when a senator debating Indian removal asked in 1830, "But are the Indian nations within the States included in that population?" he could immediately answer his own question: "Never."[56]

The new enlightened science of population had delivered the verdict on the North American Indians: they should rightly yield by the laws of social evolution to denser populations higher on the scale of civilization. Counted and counted as they might be, the North American Indians would never be anything but a problematic population. Whatever quantum of happiness lay in store for other Americans, the gloomy laws of the enlightened science of population would forever doom the Indians to a quantum of misery.

CHAPTER FIVE

Slavery in an Enlightened Age

ETWEEN THE ARRIVAL OF Columbus in 1492 and the late
eighteenth century, millions of Africans were loaded onto
ships and brought to labor in the plantations and cities of
the Americas. African slavery—both the trade itself and the
treatment of Africans—immediately attracted commentary, but it
was not until the second half of the eighteenth century that the institution came under sustained attack around the Atlantic. Raising
their voices in outrage, self-described enlightened people pleaded,
urged, cajoled, and shouted to the world that the worst abuses
of slavery had no place in an "enlightened age," as one British
writer in 1789 called his era.[1] The worst cruelties of slavery should
become relics of a barbarous past, since they offended reason,
progress, Christian charity, and natural rights.

People living in British America and later the United States
repeatedly claimed that their own eyewitness experience of slavery
mattered to this larger transatlantic debate about slavery and enlightenment. The great slave plantations, groaning with the sor-
rows of millions of African men, women, and children, lay in the
Americas, not in Europe. In contrast to what they believed to be
the abstractions of some of the European theorists of slavery,
Americans claimed time and again that their empirical knowledge
of slaves and slavery contributed useful insights to the increasingly

rancorous debates about whether slavery belonged in an age of enlightenment. In a variety of formats, from scientific treatises to private letters to boxes of specimens, they mustered local American
data about the particulars of black anatomy and physiology, the living conditions on the slave plantations, the realities of the slave
markets, and the logistics of mass emancipation. They shipped this
information, insistently and expectantly, to the great scientific societies and well-connected eminences across the Atlantic. In an international conversation that repeatedly sought universalizing
schemas about human nature and society, American data served as
a persistent reminder that slavery was not an abstract phenomenon
but an institution deeply rooted in time and place.

The result of this stubborn localism was that those who described themselves as *enlightened* about slavery did not think in only
one way. From Puritan Boston in the early 1700s to mid-century
Virginia and Rhode Island in the revolutionary era, local, variable
conditions shaped the way Americans imagined what an enlightened
future for slaves and slavery might entail. The outcome of this diversity of opinion was that no consensus had emerged by the early
nineteenth century on what to do about slavery. Even as a growing
number of Americans came to believe that they lived in an age of enlightenment, on the question of slavery they receded from consensus
rather than moving closer to it.

Slavery in the Republic of Letters

By the time King Charles II plucked a pineapple from the out-
stretched arms of his groveling gardener in 1675, African slavery
had taken firm hold in Britain's American colonies. These colonies
produced not just pineapples but the luxuries that transformed
daily life in Europe and the Americas: sugar, tea, coffee, chocolate,
cod, timber, and tobacco. As the royal pineapple was changing
hands, Britain's holdings in the Caribbean and the mainland had
fewer than 30,000 slaves. A century later, slavery had become the
bedrock of the Atlantic economy. In British North America in
1770, there were 450,000 slaves in a total population of 2.1 million.
In the British Caribbean, 85 percent of the 500,000 inhabitants
were enslaved.[2]

Hendrick Danckerts, Charles II Being Presented with a Pineapple, *1675.*
(Royal Collection Trust / © Her Majesty Queen Elizabeth II 2015)

Slavery transformed not just the economic structure of the Atlantic world but the republic of letters as well. Atlantic-facing cities such as Bristol, Liverpool, Nantes, Bordeaux, Newport, New York, and Philadelphia swelled in size and wealth as they became major ports of the slave trade, launching the slave ships and receiving the colonial products of slavery for redistribution. These secondary cities further increased the power and wealth of capital cities such as London and Paris by funneling reports about colonial slavery to the imperial center. The economic and intellectual facets of the Atlantic slave system thus overlapped, with plantations, ports, small cities, and major capitals together forming enormous networks of exchange.

Plantation slavery hindered the development of large cities in the British Caribbean, Virginia, and the Carolinas, but a few southern towns grew to importance as a result of the slave trade. Named for King Charles II, Charles Town (later Charleston), in the colony of Carolina, rose from the swamps to become the largest British American city south of Philadelphia in the eighteenth century. A map of Charles Town from around 1711 shows the harbor already bustling with ships. By the time the Charleston Library Society opened its doors in 1748, signaling the new importance of a learned community in that southern city, the colony's population was already majority slave—around forty thousand blacks to twenty thousand whites. Even in the British Caribbean, where slaves formed an even greater majority of the population, white planters kept abreast of the books setting fire to the learned world. The Saint-Domingue coffee planter Nicholas Lejeune worried about which ideas would "enlighten" his slaves enough to make them rise up in revolt.[3] When Benjamin Franklin brought his two slaves to London in 1757, and Jefferson his two slaves to Paris three decades later, they all traveled along the intertwined Atlantic networks of the slave trade and the republic of letters.

Scientific knowledge began to flourish in the seventeenth century alongside slavery in Britain's expanding Atlantic empire. The interlocking memberships of the first British slave-trade monopolies and London's Royal Society—both chartered by Charles II—tell a great deal. Of the sixty-six names listed in the charter of the African trading company the Royal Adventurers (founded 1660), nine either were or became fellows of the Royal Society. Similarly, the Royal African Company (founded 1672) had at least seven members who were or became fellows of the Royal Society. The slave ships themselves became floating laboratories; it has been estimated that a fifth of the mariners who collected specimens for the eminent British naturalist James Petiver were directly involved in the slave trade.[4]

Natural historians drew on the growing number of eyewitness accounts of New World slave plantations. Their numerous publications slaked the thirst of a curious public eager for scientific knowledge about the exotic plants, peoples, and places of the Americas. Natural histories of the British Caribbean such as Richard Ligon's *True & Exact History of the Island of Barbados* (1657) dipped into an array of topics that defy easy categorization into the later genres

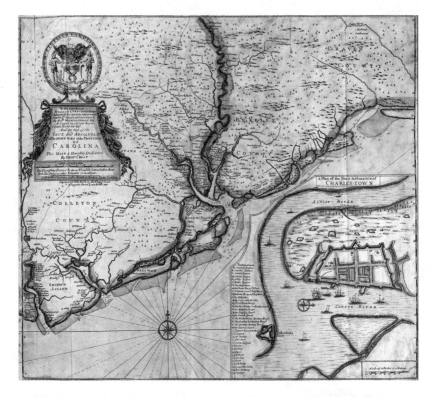

The bustling port of Charles Town, from A Compleat Description of the
Province of Carolina in 3 parts *(1711?). (Geography and Map Division,
Library of Congress)*

of anti- or proslavery polemics. Ligon found many Africans so
beautiful that he compared them to the German Renaissance artist
Albrecht Dürer's drawings of ideal humans; he described the planters' dilemma in converting their slaves to Christianity (fearing to
enslave Christians, they would not Christianize their slaves); and he
described the punishing work routines involved in cultivating
sugar-cane. Hans Sloane's *A Voyage to the Islands Madera, Barbados,
Nieves, S. Christophers and Jamaica* likewise offered a feast of knowledge about the Africans in the Caribbean plantations: their customs, food, diseases, and the healing practices of a group he called
"Negro Doctors." While in the West Indies, Sloane collected plants
and other specimens that eventually made their way into his cabinet
of curiosities in London, the seed of the future British Museum.

Over time Sloane acquired artifacts relating specifically to West Indian slaves, such as a whip and a noose; he even owned specimens of African skin. Eventually the mainland British American colonies weighed in: in the 1690s the *Philosophical Transactions* of the Royal Society published the account by the Virginia planter William Byrd of a local "Negro-Boy" who had slowly turned white. It was through such publications and artifacts that eyewitness accounts of plantations and the Africans on them became known to a broader pubic in Britain's Atlantic empire, not yet as part of the later pro- and antislavery polemics but rather as curiosities.[5]

By the early eighteenth century, the first dense, local debates about African slavery were beginning to take place in Britain's American colonies. Chief among these were the tract wars in Boston, whose high concentration of ministers, booksellers, scholars, and merchants made the port town of about seven thousand a miniature republic of letters in its own right. Writing to their educated colleagues in Britain and the Continent, Bostonians also looked to their own region and its local concerns—which by now included concern about the growing number of African slaves there. Slaves numbered approximately two hundred in Massachusetts in 1676; by 1708, four hundred black slaves lived in Boston alone, accounting for slightly over 5 percent of the town's population. Some of these slaves belonged to prominent Bostonians, such as the minister Cotton Mather, whose slave Onesimus (an "Intelligent Fellow," according to Mather) supplied Mather with information on smallpox inoculation. These slaves formed part of a larger group that also included war refugees and Native Americans whose presence raised difficult legal and moral questions about social and religious status and contributed to the increasing dehomogenization of Boston's formerly Puritan-majority population by 1700.[6]

In addition to these local concerns, ominous reports of Caribbean slavery's troubling moral and theological dimensions had begun to reach Boston by the late seventeenth century. The Anglican missionary Morgan Godwyn's *Negro's and Christian's Advocate* (1680)—the fruit of his harrowing years ministering to parishes in Virginia and Barbados—had urged planters to Christianize their slaves. The Bible was inconclusive about whether slavery was theologically sanctioned or not, but Godwyn accused planters who thought their slaves were not quite human of the heresy of pre-Adamism. This was the controversial theory proposed by the French theologian Isaac de La Peyrère, who had speculated in his *Praeadamitae* (1655) that a separate race of Gentiles had been created before Adam, the father of the Hebrews.[7]

The Boston merchant and jurist Samuel Sewall expressed his views on New England slavery in a short tract, *The Selling of Joseph* (1700), the first work published in New England that opposed slavery. Although Sewall's terms were religious—the title of the work refers to the biblical Joseph, who was sold into slavery by his jealous brothers—the work sprang from modern regional concerns about the rise of African slavery in New England and the misery it caused among blacks. "The Numerousness of Slaves at this day in the Province, and the Uneasiness of them under their Slavery, hath put many upon thinking whether the Foundation of it be firmly and well laid; so as to sustain the Vast Weight that is built upon it," Sewall wrote. He had recently helped negotiate the release of white New Englanders held as slaves in Africa, and he extended his reasoning to the African slaves in Boston. Bemoaning "the barbarous Usage of our Friends and Kinsfolk in *Africa*," Sewall asked "whether we are not culpable in forcing the *Africans* to become Slaves amongst our selves." Sewall tucked spare copies of *The Selling of Joseph* into his overseas correspondence, joining Boston to the international conversation about the morality of slavery.[8]

In 1701, the year after Sewall's pamphlet appeared, the Boston merchant and slaveholder John Saffin found a Boston press to publish a rebuttal to Sewall's arguments. Saffin conceded that the Bible prohibited Christians from enslaving Christians but asserted that "lawful Captives" of "Heathen Nations may be made Bond men." Mustering examples from the Bible, Saffin argued that in a hierarchical society it was lawful to keep servants and that white Christians need not "love and respect all men alike," though all should be treated with "Christian prudence." Saffin pointed out the logistical problems of massive manumission, arguing that unless freed slaves were "all sent out of the Country" they would be a "plague." And would masters who had set slaves free "be Re imbursed out of the Publick Treasury"? Cotton Mather joined in a few years later with *The Negro Christianized* (1706), a short tract arguing that the main obligation of masters was to Christianize their slaves—though Christianizing them would not make them free.[9]

Geographically, this early conversation went essentially no-where. Barely heard beyond Boston's borders, it did not form the clear beginning of a great international antislavery movement. The number of slaves continued to grow in Boston thereafter, and the city became ever more committed to the slave trade.

Boston's brief pamphlet war was significant nonetheless. London had by now become Britain's imperial headquarters of knowledge about and policy toward slavery and the slave trade. The pamphlet war makes clear that it was on the edges of European empires—in secondary cities and plantations far from London, Paris, Naples, Amsterdam, and Madrid—that slavery was most often experienced in its day-to-day realities and that new local communities of direct knowledge about Africans and slavery were beginning to congeal. What is also remarkable about this early outpouring of concern over slavery in Boston is how many of the arguments that would later be mustered for and against slavery were already in place: the concern about large-scale manumission, the questions about what role Christianity played in slave societies, the sense that the local experience of slavery was tied to a much larger slave system that also had claims on a person's moral per-spective. Over the course of the eighteenth century, learned people in these secondary cities and regions began to form new connec-tions to one another. Chains of correspondence among individuals far from the large imperial capitals led to new conduits of infor-mation exchange about slaves and slavery. Such was the case with Virginia and Bordeaux.

The Bordeaux-Virginia Connection

Like Boston, the provincial French city of Bordeaux was altered by New World slavery. Like Boston, its wharves welcomed the ships of the Atlantic slave trade. Like Boston, its civic and intellectual life became enmeshed in the intellectual networks of the republic of letters that flourished with the slave trade. This combination of learned culture and slavery made Bordeaux influential not just for British Americans generally but for Virginians specifically. Firmly committed to plantation slavery by the eighteenth century, Virginia also supported an educated planter elite that looked to Britain and Europe for ideas. A Bordeaux-Virginia intellectual connection formed and dissolved in the middle of the eighteenth century, offering a glimpse of how ideas that were later termed enlightened and universalizing emerged from specific local contexts of slavery.

Nestled in a bend of the deep Garonne River about fifty miles from the Atlantic, Bordeaux had by 1740 become the second most important slave port in France, trailing only Nantes as the chief entry and exit point for ships bound for Africa and the French Caribbean. By the end of the seventeenth century, France's Caribbean colonies had made the nation self-sufficient in sugar, part of French finance minister Jean-Baptise Colbert's plan to use the colonies for the good of the mother country. A sleepy wine-trading town at the close of the Middle Ages, Bordeaux entered a golden age in the early modern period with the growth of the Caribbean colonies. The city's population nearly tripled over the course of the eighteenth century as elegant buildings and squares became the public face of the new mercantile wealth extracted from the Atlantic trade. Civic life flourished with the founding of academies such as the Bordeaux Académie des sciences, belles-lettres et arts in 1712 and its internationally known publication, the *Journal des sçavans*.[10]

It was for this august French body that the Virginia physician and naturalist John Mitchell prepared an essay on the causes of differences in human skin color. If Bordeaux was now the origin point for slaving voyages to Africa, Virginia was one of the destinations for the tens of thousands of slaves who disembarked in the rich tidal lands of the Chesapeake. Virginia had shifted decisively in the early eighteenth century to an economy based on tobacco production through African slave labor. Between 1700 and 1740, slave ships brought fifty-four thousand Africans into Virginia and Maryland. Mitchell was born into this world in 1711, in a slaveholding family living among the lush tobacco farms at the mouth of the Rappahannock River, one of Virginia's doorways to Chesapeake Bay and the Atlantic beyond. Perhaps because of his family's Scottish connections, Mitchell chose in the early 1720s to attend the University of Edinburgh, where he studied botany, mathematics, Isaac Newton's theory of optics, microscopy, anatomical dissection, and astronomy.[11]

Mitchell returned ten years later to Virginia. He bought a stately property in Urbanna, a small village across the Rappahannock from his childhood home, and furnished it with an apothecary shop, a chemical laboratory, and a steady supply of books in several languages on anatomy and natural history. He purchased a number of indentured servants and slaves during an abrupt demographic shift in Virginia. During the 1730s, Chesapeake slaves were beginning to reproduce their population naturally, a development that allowed slave imports directly from Africa to slow and the first African American communities to form. Riding out to tend to the sick on nearby plantations, Mitchell would have witnessed the demographic shift in its most intimate manifestations. And as Virginia's tidewater lands were transformed by tobacco plantations, Mitchell immersed himself in the details of plant taxonomy that were preoccupying Linnaeus and others. He collected local plants and sent word of his findings to an international circle of correspondents that included Peter Collinson. He bought books by European naturalists and anatomists and dissected dead animals in his house, once storing a pair of opossums for two years. It was probably during this time that he also began to dissect human skin, both black and white.[12]

In short, Mitchell was an eyewitness to a human and natural world being fundamentally transformed by slavery and tobacco. Who better than Mitchell, then, to begin work on essay intended for Bordeaux's *Journal des sçavans* in answer to the pressing question it had posed to the learned world in 1739: "What is the physical cause of *nègres'* color, of the quality of their hair, and of the degeneration of the one and of the other?" As African slavery transformed the demography of the Americas, the question of the origin of skin color had now become the target of the international scholarly community's attention. The Bordeaux academy was offering a prize for the best essay on this topic; missing the deadline because he was so engrossed in his research, Mitchell published his essay instead in the Royal Society's *Philosophical Transactions*, a coup engineered by his friend Collinson.[13]

Brimming with his knowledge of European scientific theories in anatomy and optics, Mitchell's essay was a brief for on-site local observations of "the Cause of the Colour of the Negroes." He explained in the cover letter to Collinson that accompanied his essay that he had "several times" made experiments on living human subjects. "With great Care I have made the Experiments and Observations on purpose to find out the Truth," he went on. "I must own I was surprised at first to see them differ from the Opinions of some learned Men." His observations and experiments had led him to dismiss as mere "Opinion" the conclusion of the renowned seventeenth-century Italian physician Marcello Malpighi that black skin color resulted from black juices flowing under the skin. Mitchell instead provided American facts: he had "macerated the Skins of Negroes" and failed to extract black juices. He then cited the research of the French anatomist Alexis Littré, who had also failed to extract a black juice from human skin, even when aided "by more powerful Dissolvents." Instead of seeking black skin color in skin juices, Mitchell turned to the *Opticks* of "the great *Newton*"— and his own dissections of Virginia blacks—to insist instead that it was the relative thickness of skin that, by transmitting light differently, resulted in different skin colors. The color of the skin was in some sense an optical illusion, the result not of an underlying difference in color but simply a difference in the skin's ability to transmit color. "*The Part of the Skin which appears black in Negroes, is the* Corpus reticulare Cutis, *and external* Lamella *of the* Epidermis: *And all other Parts are of the same Colour in Them with those of white People*," Mitchell maintained.[14]

Inspired by Newtonian science, Mitchell's essay remained influential even forty years after its publication, mostly among those lobbying for the increasingly politicized antislavery movement, such as Thomas Clarkson, who cited it in his antislavery manifesto, *An Essay on the Slavery and Commerce of the Human Species* (1786).[15] But while his work was later commandeered for the abolitionist cause, Mitchell's observations were not made for that purpose. He wrote to participate in an increasingly complex transatlantic conversation about the nature of human diversity. Mitchell's contribution was to show that Virginians' observations about the causes of human skin color—informed by close contact with slaves—had relevance within the broader world of learning, from Bordeaux to London.

The reverse also was true: knowledge from Bordeaux became relevant to mid-eighteenth-century Virginians, as the example of the Virginian reception of Montesquieu's *De l'esprit des loix* (1748) reveals. Most often invoked today to track Americans' growing interest in the idea of separation of powers, Montesquieu's treatise also resonated widely around the Atlantic as one of the first sustained examinations of slavery, one that fundamentally altered future discussions of the question. Montesquieu's chapter on slavery formed just part of the work, which pulled from the confusion of history a clear schema for understanding how human governments emerged from human societies. Montesquieu categorized different governments (monarchical, republican, despotic) according to the "spirit" of the people living in them. This spirit in turn depended on factors such as climate. Those laws were best that were best adapted to the spirit of a people—hence the title, "the spirit of laws." Based on his experiences in 1729–30 living in the constitutional monarchy of England, which formed a notable contrast to the absolutism of his own king, Louis XV, Montesquieu argued that human liberty could be best secured by the separation of the judicial, legislative, and executive powers of government. *De l'esprit des loix* stood as a monument to the new idea that human governments arose from the primal conditions of nature and climate rather than the decrees of the deity. One reader at the time spoke for many when he praised Montesquieu for showing how mankind could become more just, more free, and therefore happier.[16]

In chapter 15, Montesquieu turned to slavery, showing that like human governments this practice had emerged from human history and not by divine decree. Slavery had not been ordained by God, he argued; it was the invention of rational human beings who tolerated its injustices and horrors. And because it had been created by humans, it could therefore be understood and perhaps eliminated through human efforts. Even if positive law had concocted elaborate slave codes over the past two millennia, slavery violated natural law, corrupting slave and master alike. And while types of slavery differed according to climate and government, the practice could not be justified in any kind of regime, whether democratic, despotic, or monarchical. The opening lines of chapter 15 boldly announced Montesquieu's argument: "Slavery, properly so called, is the establishment of a right which gives to one man such a power over another, as renders him absolute master of his life and fortune. The state of slavery is bad of its own nature: it is neither useful to the master nor to the slave; not to the slave, because he can do nothing thro' a motive of virtue; not to the master, because he contracts all manner of bad habits with his slaves, he accustoms himself insensibly to the want of all moral virtues, he grows fierce, hasty, severe, choleric, voluptuous, and cruel." Over the next half century, Americans and Britons cited Montesquieu on slavery as a bible of reasoned reportage on the vexing ancient question of human bondage.[17]

Philosophe he may have been, but Montesquieu's mind had turned to slavery for the same reason that the subject fired so many other imaginations in the eighteenth century: it touched him personally. He was born and raised a half-day's walk from Bordeaux in the moated fortress castle of La Brède, whose lush vineyards produced the wine that was eventually loaded into Bordeaux's waiting ships, bound for the tables of France, Britain, and the Caribbean. Montesquieu was sent to Bordeaux for his early schooling, and he returned there throughout his life for civic and business errands, including presiding over the Bordeaux academy to which John Mitchell had written. The city's transformation by the slave trade would have been obvious to him. He could hardly have missed the mascarons, the sculptured busts of African heads that now stared down from Bordeaux's stately new buildings, which had been built in part with the profits from the slave trade. Montesquieu knew where the real money was in the wine business: England provided a promising market, but it was trade with the French Caribbean islands that kept him financially solvent.[18]

Montesquieu's library at La Brède—at thirty-eight hundred volumes one of eighteenth-century Europe's largest private libraries—bore the imprint of the French slave trade. On one shelf sat Jean Melon's *Essai politique sur le commerce* (1734), whose chapter on slavery argued that the use of slaves in the French colonies was contrary neither to religion nor to morality. Some had to suffer for the benefit of the state; the only relevant question was whether slavery should be extended everywhere: "Equality amongst Men, is a Chimera, which can scarce bring forth an ideal

Commonwealth," wrote Melon. The book appeared in English translation four years later. On another shelf lay the French Dominican priest Jean-Baptiste Labat's *Nouveau voyage aux isles de l'Amérique* (6 vols., 1722), a work Montesquieu cited in his discussion of slavery in the *Esprit des loix*. Illustrated with engravings of windmills, sugarcane processing factories, and exotic fruits, Labat's *Nouveau voyage* resulted from the twelve years, from 1693 to 1705, the priest had spent in Martinique and other islands of the French Caribbean. Labat explained every aspect of life and labor on the sugar islands, including the economic links that now tied the fate of France to its Caribbean islands. From these local facts and his own theories about governments arising from the particularities of human societies, Montesquieu built his rambling denunciation of slavery into the *Esprit des loix*.[19]

Thirty years later, back in Virginia, which was now independent of British rule, the young Virginian slaveholder and legislator Thomas Jefferson found himself gripped by Montesquieu's thoughts on slavery. Jefferson had recently written the *Summary View of the Rights of British America* (1774) and the Declaration of Independence, both of which had attacked the slave trade as part of a general opposition to King George III. Jefferson shared with many in Virginia's planter gentry an intellectual commitment to ending slavery coupled with a fear of the consequences of large-scale manumission. By now there were more slaves than ever in Virginia: in many counties, 50 percent of the population consisted of black slaves, afire with the possibility that the revolutionary language of rights might also extend to them. Jefferson himself was deeply enmeshed in Virginia's slave society. A recent inheritance had just doubled his land holdings and tripled his slave count: he dutifully penned in his farm book in 1774 that he now owned exactly 187 slaves.[20]

Amid these pressing anxieties, Jefferson reached for Montesquieu's *De l'esprit des loix*, copying great swaths of the chapter on slavery into a little notebook. He bought a copy of Labat's *Nouveau voyages*, perhaps because he had seen it cited by Montesquieu in the slavery chapter. Jefferson did not copy many of Montesquieu's more abstract, philosophical meditations on slavery into his notebook. Instead, he focused on the immediate, day-to-day operation of a slave plantation where masters and slaves lived cheek by jowl, just as he did with his own slaves at Monticello. Montesquieu counseled that masters and slaves who were irritated with one another should be separated; a citizen who mistreated the slave of another citizen should be hauled before a judge.[21]

Among the longest passages Jefferson copied from Montesquieu concerned slave emancipation. Emancipation now loomed especially large in Jefferson's mind, as revolutionary ideology had stirred Quakers, Baptists, and Methodists to encourage their congregations to free their slaves, potentially vastly enlarging the number of free blacks in Virginia, where they now formed only about 1 percent of the population. If there were too many slaves in a republic, wrote Montesquieu, it was difficult to control them; but if there were too many emancipated slaves, they could not find ways to make a living. A state should not suddenly emancipate too many slaves, Montesquieu warned, citing the example of the people of Volsinii in ancient Rome; there, emancipated slaves had immediately passed a law allowing them to defile the wives of other men. How to reintegrate slaves into free society and even extend them republican citizenship? There were many ways, wrote Montesquieu, such as by teaching them useful skills like commerce or navigation. In a revealing addition of his own to his notebook, Jefferson added this thought: if too many slaves were emancipated, the state would also be in danger.[22]

Jefferson remained preoccupied by slavery and race throughout the rest of his life, uttering a series of contradictory public and private pronouncements on the topic. He wrote frequently of his desire for slave emancipation but also of his fear of losing his economic livelihood and setting thousands of uneducated people free. He penned extravagant statements about human equality, yet used data about the sources of black skin color that he may have read in John Mitchell's essay to cast doubts on whether blacks were the intellectual equals of whites.[23] He is thought to have fathered six children with his slave Sally Hemings, keeping them as slaves at Monticello alongside his free white children and grandchildren. Until his death, he read widely on the subject of slavery and corresponded with Europeans and Americans on the subject.

It is easy to overlook the significance of Jefferson's early jottings on slavery from Montesquieu, made when he was in his early

thirties and just entering public life. His most famous pronouncements about slavery and race lay in his future. But these thoughts
show him struggling to understand the institution of slavery in both
its broadest and its most personal manifestations. For this he turned
to Montesquieu, a contemporary who, like Jefferson, was preoccupied by slavery for both philosophical and pragmatic reasons. Put in
a context that includes the Virginia physician John Mitchell,
Jefferson's reading of Montesquieu illuminates the moment when
the French city of Bordeaux helped shape the thought of mid-
eighteenth-century Virginians. Over time, Bordeaux receded in importance for North Americans, and Montesquieu's discussion of
slavery became detached from the particular geographical context
that produced it, as it was consecrated as an abstract, philosophical
text. But while it lasted, for a few brief decades in the eighteenth
century, the Bordeaux-Virginia connection showed how the transformations in thinking about slavery that would soon grandly be
called *enlightened* emerged from the diverse, local Atlantic geogra-
phies of African slavery.

Searching for Human Nature in Scotland and New Jersey

For British Americans, another channel of communication about
slavery opened in the last third of the eighteenth century. This was
Scotland, the home of philosophers such as David Hume, Adam
Smith, and Lord Kames, and a destination for young American
men who aspired to a career in medicine they hoped would begin
at the famous medical school in Edinburgh.

One of those aspiring American physicians sounded an early
alarm about the slave trade: the young Philadelphian Benjamin
Rush. As he sailed into Liverpool harbor in the fall 1766 on his
way to Edinburgh, he recoiled at the sight of hulking slave ships
massed in the busy port. "Liverpool has been hitherto supported
by the African Trade," Rush wrote in his journal. "At the present
time they have near a 100 [? illegible] ships employed in [? illegi-
ble] Trade. Inhuman practise! That men should grow rich by the
calamities of their fellow creatures!"[24] First entering the slave trade
around 1700, Liverpool was now one of the largest slave ports in
Europe, and the origin of hundreds of slaving voyages.

Seven years later, Rush poured his private outrage at the "Inhuman practise" into a pamphlet condemning the evils of slave keeping and the slave trade. Published in Philadelphia, New York, and Boston in 1773, *An Address to the Inhabitants of the British Settlements in America, upon Slave-Keeping* was one of the first British American publications openly to oppose the practice. It was influential enough to inspire a wholesale rebuttal defending West Indian planters. Reflecting the influence of Montesquieu, Rush mentioned the philosophical problems posed by slavery. But then he turned to a concrete example much closer to home in British America: the former slave Phillis Wheatley of Boston, whose poems had been published in London that same year to international acclaim and astonishment (Voltaire called Wheatley "une Négresse qui fait de très-bons vers anglais"). Wheatley's "singular genius and accomplishments are such as not only do honor to her sex, but to human nature," wrote Rush. God had "created man free"; slavery was an outrage against "human nature."[25]

Rush had put his finger on the new preoccupation of his era: human nature. To discover human motivations in conduct and misconduct, the rights and duties of humans in society, the strings of attachment and sentiment that allowed people to come together to form societies over time: these questions rose to prominence in the late eighteenth century as the full diversity of humanity was made palpable after two centuries of global imperial development by Europeans. To discover general principles of human nature amid this bewildering diversity became one of the great objects of learned people around the Atlantic.

Eighteenth-century Scottish philosophers were among those who most intensively developed the study of human nature. Their inquiry formed part of the larger "science of man": an attempt to discern the progressive development of human morality and behavior in societies over time. There were particular reasons why Scottish thinkers thought deeply about these questions in the eighteenth century. Unlike France or England, Scotland had not established successful New World colonies, but the causes of the country's rapid economic development engrossed intellectuals at universities in Edinburgh, Aberdeen, and Glasgow. How, Scottish thinkers wondered, had human societies developed over time from a primitive state to the complex commercial society that a city like Edinburgh seemed to embody? From all over the world they amassed a library of evidence that helped them develop what they called a science of man based on observation of humanity itself. They believed that this science could inform planning of all kinds, from legislation to the structures and operations of government. Followed by enlightened rulers, they believed, a science of man could transform the course of human destiny.[26]

Benjamin Rush helped bring Scottish philosophy—and a Scottish philosopher—to British America. While in Scotland, Rush met Hume, William Robertson, and the celebrated physician William Cullen, a gallery of luminaries that stirred his ambition to make Philadelphia *the Edinburgh of America.* Rush gushed to a friend back home that "the whole world I believe does not afford a set of greater men than are present united in the College of Edinburgh." Chief among these "greater men" was the Presbyterian minister John Witherspoon, whom Rush successfully lured to America to head the College of New Jersey in Princeton in 1768. During Witherspoon's long presidency, the professors stamped the precepts of Scottish moral, social, and economic thought onto hundreds of students. Influenced by the Scottish moral philosophers Thomas Reid and Francis Hutcheson, Witherspoon departed from Calvinist orthodoxy by asserting that principles of duty and obligation derived from the "nature of man"; to study moral philosophy was not just to contemplate the perfections of the Deity but to study "human nature."[27]

Few Scottish inquiries into the essential nature of humanity caused a greater furor in Rush's day than Lord Kames's *Sketches of the History of Man* (1774). A prominent jurist, Kames seldom went far from Scotland, but he was fascinated by travelers' reports of human diversity in the world. In a letter to James Lind, a ship's doctor who was packing his bags to join Captain James Cook's second circumnavigation of the world, Kames whispered his creeping suspicion that the Bible story of a single human creation might be incorrect. As he peered into every corner of the earth, Kames asked, could Lind discover why "there is no known plant or animal equally fitted for every climate"? Reading and experience had showed Kames that all beings withered when transplanted from their original climate to a foreign one. Look no farther than Charles Town, South Carolina, Kames told Lind. This city was so "unkindly to the constitution of Europeans" that "not a single Descendant of the first settlers" remained.[28]

Kames's *Sketches of the History of Man* refuted Montesquieu, a "most formidable antagonist," who had insisted that human variability stemmed from "the effect of soil and climate" rather than innate difference. "There are different races of men as well as of dogs," Kames countered, each "fitted for different climates." The present diversity of human species could not have emerged from a single pair "without a miracle." All human beings emerged from different stocks, and "Providence has placed these nations each of them in its proper climate." The blacks of Africa and the Americas were a prime example of this principle. "The colour of Negroes . . . affords a strong presumption of their being a different race from the Whites," he concluded.[29]

For Kames this could only mean that the Genesis story of a single creation must be false. Instead he proposed a scenario of multiple creations, a belief later known as polygenism: "That God created many pairs of the human race, differing from each other both externally and internally; that he fitted these pairs for different climates, and placed each pair in its proper climate; that the peculiarities of the original pairs were preserved entire in their descendents." Moses was simply confused, or perhaps wrong. "Tho' we cannot doubt of the authority of Moses, yet his account of the creation of man is not a little puzzling, as it seems to contradict every one of the facts mentioned above."[30]

The highly inflammatory statements in Kames's *Sketches* roiled a generation of scholars. Kames had amassed what he called "facts" from around the world to argue that Moses's utterances were not a little puzzling, and that there might have been several creations rather than one, each fitted for its own particular climate, a theory guaranteed to infuriate an audience weaned on the Bible and Montesquieu.

No American met the challenge of Kames with more energy than the Presbyterian minister Samuel Stanhope Smith. An early exponent of the idealism of Jonathan Edwards and Bishop Berkeley, Smith was soon won over by the Scottish philosophy of commonsense realism of his own professor at the College of New Jersey, Witherspoon, whose daughter Smith married. As professor and then president of the college after Witherspoon, from 1779 to 1813, Smith schooled a generation of Americans in the various sciences—moral, political, natural—of the Scots. All of this was in the service of advancing the glorious cause of the new United States, a Christian republic that he was sure would lead the world from ignorance to civilization. Smith taught his students that the "science" of moral philosophy would increase "the order and happiness of the world."[31]

It was not a world that Smith himself had seen much of, since he never traveled abroad. But he had experienced firsthand the human diversity of the middle regions of the east coast of North America. He spent several years before coming to teach at the college among the Indian missions in New Jersey and Pennsylvania, and among blacks in Virginia and New Jersey. Their appearance might have struck him as meaningfully different from his own. Tall and blue-eyed, Smith was an unusually handsome man who shunned the drab black garb of the minister in favor of stylish clothes. One minister gushed that Smith was the most elegant person he had ever seen. The world of Samuel Stanhope Smith was a great mirror, perpetually calling to his conscious attention the subject of the human form, none more so than his own. Why did human beings look so different? The books in the Princeton library offered no sure answers. Griffith Hughes's *The Natural History of Barbados* (1750)—which appeared in the 1760 library catalogue—reported that the origins of black and Indian skin colors would remain elusive even to on-site observers like himself: "And therefore, as those Men who pretend to account for the Origin of the *Blacks*, or *Indians*, bring neither Proof nor Authority to strengthen their Opinions, these must be looked upon [as] at best but uncertain Conjectures."[32] Smith could be sure of only one thing: that religion and reason were compatible and the Bible story of humankind's origin in a single pair must be correct.

Smith's interests in religion, science, and human appearance dovetailed in 1787 when he delivered a searing rebuke to Lord Kames in an address to the American Philosophical Society, soon published as *An Essay on the Causes of the Variety of Complexion and Figure in the Human Species* (1787). The essay was reprinted in

Edinburgh and London the year after its publication, a sign of the growing importance of American ethnology to European audiences.

Smith offered up his own experience as an American in a slave-holding region to rebut the dangerously unorthodox views of a Scottish theorist who had never set foot near a slave plantation. In place of Kames's separate creations, Smith attempted to vindicate the biblical doctrine of the unity of the human race. Echoing Buffon and Montesquieu, Smith asserted that all human difference, whether moral or physical, was due to differences in climate, the state of society, or the manner of living. Darker skin color was merely a "universal freckle" growing and shrinking with rising and falling temperatures. His on-site experience of American slavery formed a key part of his critique of Lord Kames. "I have myself been witness" to "slaves in the southern states," Smith argued, and they were people whose habits prepared their children for the heat and humidity of the climate. Kames by contrast had strayed from the words of the Bible and utterly ignored the facts of America. "If his lordship had seen America," wrote Smith, he would have seen Americans of all kinds changing their locations not for the worse but for the better. "But his lordship has not seen them, and he speaks of the savage state without understanding it, and of human nature, in the beginning of time, without knowing how it would operate then, or how it has operated, in similar situations in later periods." No wonder Kames, like other "philosophers," formed "wrong conclusions."[33]

Smith's essay marked a watershed in the Atlantic debate about race-based slavery as a topic for empirical analysis. Not only had he mounted a major theological defense of monogenesis, he had used American facts to do so, effectively countering the universalizing tendencies of European philosophers with local data. Those local, American data became increasingly important as a flourishing post-revolutionary publication industry now began to support a wide-ranging debate by American authors on the subject of American slavery and race. Americans continued to absorb and respond to ideas that emerged from abroad, such as those of Johann Friedrich Blumenbach, Pieter Camper, Jean-Baptiste Lamarck, and Georges Cuvier. But it was in the wake of Smith's *Essay* of 1787 that the first large-scale American conversation about race-based slavery emerged, with authors speaking both to a European public and to one another in dense networks of exchange. It was now, in the wake of American independence, that the first people in the United States to call themselves "enlightened" about slavery emerged.

Varieties of Enlightenment in Rhode Island and Virginia

The search for self-described "enlightened" responses to slavery emerged in the decades after the American Revolution as the term gained traction to describe progress toward human happiness. Natural rights rhetoric had linked the twin issues of slave emancipation and ascent toward an "enlightened age," as students at Harvard put it in a debate in 1773. Newspapers during the Revolutionary War demanded "the enlightened equity of a free people," and pointed out the contradictions of fighting for freedom and rights when so many remained in chains. The press urged Americans to look forward to a better age, "the Time when it shall be said the United States of America are too enlightened to exercise, or suffer to be exercised an uncontrouled Authority of one Class of Men over the Persons and Property of another."[34]

Conditions for some blacks in the United States suggested grounds for optimism about the possibility of slave emancipation, as the example of the free black astronomer and almanac maker Benjamin Banneker showed. Jefferson sent one of Banneker's almanacs to Condorcet, the author of the radical antislavery manifesto, *Réflexions sur l'esclavage des Nègres* (1781), in which Condorcet called blacks his brothers and refused even to term colonial whites human beings.[35] Jefferson told Condorcet that "instances of moral eminence" among blacks such as Banneker could prove that "the want of talents observed in them is merely the effect of their degraded condition, and not proceeding from any difference in the structure of the parts on which intellect depends."[36]

Yet no consensus emerged about what it meant to be enlightened about slavery, or what an enlightened age would hold for those currently held in bondage. For planters in the British Caribbean worried about gathering antislavery forces, the progress of reason and happiness meant improving conditions for their slaves, efforts that would yield a more humane slave system and more bountiful crops. These planters began to publish an array of pamphlets urging the reform of agriculture by means of a variety of innovations including gentler treatment of slaves, what Samuel Martin of Antigua called the "rational method of treating negroes." The planter David Collins argued that the desire to "reform" the treatment of slaves in fact originated not in the metropole but in the colonies, a happy development the "resulted from the progress of the human mind." Gordon Turnbull of Grenada likewise urged the proper treatment of slaves as an aid to "their happiness."[37]

In the United States, variable local conditions continued to produce a range of responses to slavery. The political break with Britain gave some coherence to the idea of "enlightenment" in America on the slave question: the commitment to natural rights and republican government suggested that slavery was incompatible with the political ideals for which blood had been shed. Yet writers from up and down the eastern seaboard interpreted this declaration in different ways. Two responses in particular, from Rhode Island and Virginia, showed that within the republican commitment to slave emancipation as a form of human liberty lay different interpretations of enlightenment based on local pressures as experienced in the international context of the antislavery debates.

One strand of enlightenment mixed Congregationalism with a new concern for social benevolence. This was the so-called New Divinity of the New England Congregationalist minister and theologian Samuel Hopkins. Theologically complex, the New Divinity attempted to realign Calvinism—with its emphasis on humanity's depravity and utter powerlessness—with the eighteenth century's new faith in humanity's ability to improve the self and the world without God's direct intervention. Hopkins was deeply influenced by the theologian Jonathan Edwards but feared that Edwards's concept of "true virtue" was overly abstract and aestheticized, militating against action in this world. But Hopkins did not agree with religious rationalists such as the earl of Shaftesbury and Francis Hutcheson, who had proposed that human beings could regulate their social behavior through an innate "moral sense" without the need for supernatural grace. Hopkins's particular contribution was to locate true virtue less in the exalted contemplation of an ideal

Being than in hands-on social betterment. What was true holiness, he asked in a sermon in 1773: "This is love to God and our neighbour, including ourselves; and is universal benevolence, or friendly affection to all intelligent beings." Since God's glory depended on the happiness of mankind, social reform and social activism became new paths to holiness.[38]

Hopkins applied these principles to what he saw in Newport, Rhode Island, one of the leading ports of the New England slave trade. By the first decade of the nineteenth century, Rhode Islanders had launched at least a thousand slaving voyages. Nearly fifty years old when he moved to Newport from his parish in rural Massachusetts, Hopkins was shocked by the scenes he witnessed on the docks, where chained slaves were unloaded and sold amid stories about the horrors of the journey from Africa. Yet all around stood the opulent mansions purchased by Newport's Christian slave traders.[39]

Fired by the injustices staring him in the face, Hopkins began to preach to his Newport congregation about the immorality of the slave trade, publishing an important antislavery tract in 1776, *A Dialogue, Concerning the Slavery of the Africans.* He dedicated it to the Continental Congress to seek reassurance that that body's 1774 resolution prohibiting the slave trade issued not just from political expediency but from the view that slavery was unrighteous and cruel with regard to "benevolence."[40]

Hopkins's example shows that by the late eighteenth century Calvinism could turn outward into a program of social reform that deployed the language of human rights in a way that included slavery. Speaking to the Providence society for abolishing the slave trade, Hopkins again rejected slavery in 1793 as a "violation of all the rights of man." Hopkins's logic of the workings of heaven showed the influence of the Scottish scheme of human social and moral development on conceptions of sociability in this world and salvation in the next. He argued that when "heaven ... finds [men] in a state of savage ignorance and barbarity, it civilizes them, and forms them to be intelligent and good members of society." The spreading influence of heavenly benevolence united people "together into a happy society." Nothing but "the depravity of mankind" had kept this from happening since the death of Christ.

Hopkins rejected the view propagated since the late seventeenth century that slavery was a way to Christianize African heathens. Instead, he became an early promoter of African colonization by freed American slaves. They should return to Africa to save it from "barbarity" and to create there a "civilized, Christian and happy people." This was "the cause of God and human nature."[41]

Hopkins's Christian vision of enlightenment and antislavery contrasted with the political, secular vision outlined by his contemporary in Virginia, the jurist St. George Tucker. Few other Americans of this generation—the generation that had lived through a republican revolution waged in the name of liberty and equality—worked with such diligence to think through how a major slaveholding state such as Virginia could emancipate its slaves. Tucker wanted to liberate the slaves in Virginia because he thought slavery inconsistent with the principles of the American Revolution. As he wrote in the edition he published of *Blackstone's Commentaries*, Tucker believed that he lived in an "enlightened age," in which science, learning, rational religion, observation, and travel had spread civilization and good government far and wide. Yet the weight of his views on blacks and climate, the data he collected about emancipation schemes elsewhere, and his fears of the disruption emancipation would cause to white society in Virginia led him to propose a colonization scheme quite the opposite of Hopkins's: not to Africa (where former slaves might then enlighten Africans with Christianity) but west to the Louisiana territory. Tucker believed the Louisiana climate to be better suited to blacks' "natural constitutions." There, without civil rights, they would be discouraged from indulging in excessive political ambition.[42]

Tucker lived his whole life among slaves. Born in 1752 in Bermuda to a slaveholding family, he moved to Virginia in 1772 at the moment when revolutionary principles of equality and liberty were beginning to shake up the slaveholding aristocracy. He attended the College of William and Mary, where he studied with the eminent legal scholar George Wythe. In 1790, he succeeded Wythe as professor of law while also serving on the newly reorganized General Court. Yet while he taught his students that slavery contradicted the principles of the Revolution, Tucker acquired more than a hundred slaves upon his marriage to Frances Bland

Randolph, and he owned, bought, and sold slaves throughout his life. The aftermath of revolution brought disaster for Virginia's planter gentry, including Tucker: the soil on their sprawling plantations exhausted by overplanting, they also faced a disastrously depressed international market for their tobacco. This bleak economic picture spurred Tucker to sell much of his land in 1788 and move to Williamsburg with his family and house slaves.[43]

In 1796 Tucker published *A Dissertation on Slavery: With a Proposal for the Gradual Abolition of It, in the State of Virginia*. This was the most extensively researched treatise on slavery published in North America up to that time. Dedicated and delivered to the General Assembly of Virginia—which immediately tabled it without discussion or referral to a committee—the proposal represented Tucker's effort to find a workable plan for slave emancipation in Virginia after the Revolution had shown "the incompatibility of a state of slavery with the principles of our government." Like a generation of Americans before him, he quoted the "enlightened" Montesquieu's chapter on slavery from the *Esprit des loix* in an epigraph on the title page of the *Dissertation on Slavery:* "Slavery not only violates the Laws of Nature, and of civil Society, it also wounds the best Forms of Government: in a Democracy, where all Men are equal, Slavery is contrary to the Spirit of the Constitution."[44]

Tucker mustered an army of facts in his *Dissertation*. The year before its publication, he had sent a letter full of questions to Jeremy Belknap of Massachusetts, a "sister state" that had "wholly exterminated" slavery. Belknap then printed copies of the queries, which concerned such matters as the population of blacks in Massachusetts, and distributed them among "such gentlemen as it was supposed would assist in answering them." These gentlemen included Prince Hall, "a very intelligent black man," who was consulted about slave populations. Belknap replied with what he called "facts." The results of these queries appeared throughout Tucker's lavishly footnoted proposal to the Virginia legislature. Reaching deep into the past—to the age of Justinian—Tucker carried his readers forward to the present age in which the tolerance of slavery could be a sign of nothing less than "the weakness and inconsistency of human nature." All should rise to the great cause of "the restoration of human nature to its inalienable right."[45]

But significant barriers remained to widespread emancipation in Virginia, where a third of the population was enslaved. The number of slaves there was so large—Tucker reckoned nearly three hundred thousand and predicted 1.2 million in sixty years—that to free them all at once he deemed imprudent. He cited Jefferson's *Notes on the State of Virginia* to argue that slavery stifled the moral and intellectual development of blacks, and that emancipating this degraded people would cause "intestine wars, which would terminate only in their extirpation, or final expulsion." How then to choose a "middle course" between tyrannical slavery and turning "loose a numerous, starving, and enraged banditti, upon the innocent descendants of their former oppressors"?[46]

Tucker proposed a scheme of gradual emancipation in which former Virginia slaves would be colonized in the Louisiana territory. At a stroke this would remove a volatile population from Virginia, while settling blacks in a climate suited to their "natural constitutions":

> Though I am opposed to the banishment of the Negroes, I wish not to encourage their future residence among us. By denying them the most valuable privileges which civil government affords, I wished to render it their inclination and their interest to seek those privileges in some other climate. There is an immense unsettled territory on this continent [the Louisiana territory] more congenial to their natural constitutions than ours, where they may perhaps be received upon more favourable terms than we can permit them to remain with us.

In Louisiana their condition would be no worse than that of the laboring poor in other countries; the freed slaves might even find "happiness." Once the nation had discovered effective remedies to slavery such as westward colonization, a "golden age" for the United States would begin. Until then, he concluded ominously with a line from Ovid, neither slaves nor masters would be safe: "Non hospes ab hospite tutus, Non Herus a Famulis: fratrum quoque gratia rara" (Guest and host are not safe from one another, nor the master from his slaves; among brothers, even, affection is rare).[47] Two decades later, with the question of bringing slaves into the new territories of the cotton South gripping the nation, the Baltimore attorney Joseph D. Learned reaffirmed Tucker's vision of the future, acknowledging the incompatibility of slavery with "this enlightened period" while also arguing that slaves enjoyed the most protection from laws in free, enlightened governments.[48]

The Ambiguity of Enlightenment

Tucker and Learned's vision of what constituted an enlightened attitude toward slavery seems surprising today, when the idea of enlightenment is associated with the worldview of the abolitionists who sought to end slavery immediately. Our modern attitude is indebted to abolitionists such as Thomas Clarkson, the British antislavery activist whose 1808 history of the slave trade identified abolitionism as the goal of "enlightened men." For Clarkson, enlightenment in the future meant the end of slavery now. Eventually, the abolitionists of the 1830s and beyond took up the language of enlightenment as something that logically made slavery intolerable. In her ringing denunciation of slavery, *An Appeal in Favor of that Class of Americans Called Africans* (1833), Lydia Maria Child framed abolitionism as a contradiction within the enlightened polity of the United States. "In the modern world, England and America are the most conspicuous for enlightened views of freedom, and bold vindication of the equal rights of man; yet in these two countries slave laws have been framed as bad as they were in Pagan, iron-hearted Rome," she wrote. Similarly, on the eve of the Civil War, William Lloyd Garrison called abolitionism a sign of "enlightened public opinion."[49]

But Tucker's enlightenment too flowed into the future, watering the fields of the Cotton Kingdom that rolled westward with the republic. In Tucker's vision, free blacks would pour into the new lands of the Southwest, living in a kind of second-class citizenship removed from a hostile white America. This too was a kind of enlightenment, when viewed from the vantage point of Virginia's waning planter gentry. Tucker's vision of enlightenment also flourished in the movement to colonize freed slaves in Africa. Africa, wrote one proponent of colonization in 1817, "opens a wide field for the improvements in civilization, morals, and religion, which the humane and enlightened memorialists have conceived it possible in process of time, to spread over that great continent." In 1833 African colonization was being cheered as embodying the "enlightened sentiment" of Europe and America, and as the best means of spreading civilization to Africa through the transplantation there of "civilized black men."[50]

This vision of enlightenment eventually found expression in the proslavery propaganda that emerged from the 1830s on in the South. These publications put forth an alternative conception of what it meant to be enlightened about slavery. Reminding readers that slavery had thrived in Greco-Roman antiquity—widely understood to be the most enlightened age of the past—they urged Americans to imagine a slaveholding republic as the heir to that enlightened past. In 1836 William Drayton accused abolitionists of failing to see that slavery had been an institution during "the most enlightened ages" of the ancient world and so should thrive now too. Others built on the accumulating racial science of the previous century to argue that blacks could not fully participate in the social and political rites of an enlightened nation like America. It was *"impolitic"* to educate blacks for citizenship in *"an enlightened country,"* wrote Richard Colfax in 1830, because science had shown that their brains were smaller and incapable of improvement. Enlightenment should be available only to those who could reasonably achieve it. In 1860, on the eve of the Civil War, another proslavery advocate called the enslavement of Africans in America "enlightened philanthropy" because it allowed masters to protect their slaves from their own "self-destroying passions." This kind of "ENLIGHTENED LOVE," argued Marcus Bell, was what "speeds the car of civilization."[51]

In short, the idea of enlightenment led not simply to abolitionism and the moral opposition to slavery but to a variety of visions for the American future, some of which included slavery or second-class citizenship for free blacks. The idea that only freedom and racial equality accorded with the "meaning of America" as a promised land was the invention of scholars of the mid-twentieth century.[52] But for the first enlightened Americans of the late eighteenth and early nineteenth centuries, enlightenment could also imply a future of slavery and racial hierarchy.

CHAPTER SIX

Religion in the Age of Reason

ODAY WE USE "the age of reason" as a synonym for "the age of enlightenment." But in fact the term's modern usage was popularized in the 1790s by Thomas Paine, who meant it to shock—and it did. For at least a century, "age of reason" had referred to the stage of life at which children became able to tell right from wrong. It was Paine who applied this schoolroom idea to the totality of civilization, suggesting that all humanity could march forward to an era when the institutions of human society would be built on reason rather than custom, compulsion, and superstition. In *The Age of Reason* (1794), Paine targeted what he thought was one of the most arbitrary despotisms of all: religion. The notion that reason should play a role in religious belief had been born in the seventeenth century and flourished in the eighteenth. But it took Paine's title to put the phrase "age of reason" into broad circulation. Soon it had become another name for "the age of enlightenment"—both terms insisting that reason could lead to happiness in the earthly sphere.

It was in the study of myth that Americans confronted some of the most disturbing implications of what it meant to worship in the age of reason. By "myth" they generally meant stories inherited from the past that concerned an event, a practice, or a hero, and many people were familiar with the myths of the classical world.

The question now became whether Christianity itself was a concatenation of myths rather than a privileged body of truths revealed by God. As the myths of so-called primitive peoples around the world—including the Americas—began to be better known during the eighteenth century, a troubling new question emerged: What was the difference between myth and religion? If Christianity were just one of many myths shared by people past and present, then Christianity itself might not be *the* truth but rather *a* truth. Calling Christianity "the Christian mythology," Paine's *Age of Reason* erupted in the middle of the international controversy about mythology and the status of belief in the age of reason, with reverberations that rocked the new American republic.[1]

The Rise of Natural Religion

Of all the institutions organizing American public and private life during the eighteenth century, religion was by the far the most important. Protestant clergymen still enjoyed widespread public authority, the calendar was organized around fast days and other religious observances, and religious writings such as sermons, catechisms, and theological tracts formed the largest category of printed matter circulating in British America.[2] Woodcuts and engravings of the skylines of America's principal eighteenth-century cities show the many church spires poking up from cramped streets, a reminder that much of daily life at this time was still lived in the shadow of the church.

Yet by the late eighteenth century, the spectrum of religious possibilities within Protestantism in America had substantially expanded from the previous century. At the most basic level, there were more varieties of Protestantism represented in British North America and the early United States. Before 1680, Congregationalists in New England and Anglicans in the southern colonies formed the majority of mainland congregations. Over the next century, the Protestant denominations swelled in size and number. Congregationalists, Quakers, and Presbyterians were now joined by Lutherans, Amish, Mennonites, Moravians, Methodists, and Baptists. A vibrant print culture also helped new religious ideas to blossom by increasing the genres in which belief could be investigated, debated, and disseminated. New Bibles made especially for children, for example, adapted Lockean ideas about the development of human reasoning capacity specifically to the scriptures. The printer Isaiah Thomas's *A Curious Hieroglyphick Bible* (1788), which substituted pictures for words and concepts, recognized that the unfolding of reason could be harnessed to the affirmation of religious belief.[3]

Americans were also influenced by new ideas about the relationship between religion in the state. The most important of these was the notion of religious toleration, which had emerged during the sixteenth century as European governments sought to distance themselves from the relentless sectarian violence that flared up after the Protestant Reformation. So devastating were the wars of religion that states concluded that the business of governing and wealth creation could be best achieved by allowing some freedom of conscience to be tolerated within the realm. In Britain in the second half of the seventeenth century, a circle of clerics and scholars known as Latitudinarians sought to transcend sectarian strife by focusing less on doctrinal specifics and more on the general, underlying commonalities among all Protestants. John Locke's *A Letter Concerning Toleration* (1689) argued that government should not involve itself in matters of religion (which he defined as "the inward and full Perswasion of the mind") and that the civil power should not attempt to coerce souls since church membership ought to be voluntary.[4]

The idea of religious toleration soon spread to Congregationalist-dominated Massachusetts. The founders of Boston's new Brattle Street Church, established in 1699, repudiated the idea that visible church societies of any size or type were covenanted with God. They declared themselves hostile to doctrinal polemics and receptive to new ideas, including those of the natural sciences. Their founding manifesto openly affirmed that the "Law of nature" dictated the relations within their church, which they defined simply as a "Society of Christians."[5]

Ministers and lay readers throughout the colonies became especially interested in the writings of John Tillotson, archbishop of Canterbury from 1691 to 1694. Preaching virtue, morality, and reason over redemption by Christ, Tillotson's sermons may have been the most popular religious works in the colonies between 1690 and 1770. They formed part of the movement away from mystery and wonder, as opponents of religious strife sought decorum in the social, religious, and natural orders by focusing on regularity and clarity rather than the mysterious, marvelous, and strange. Tillotson reassured readers that although no text, including the Bible, could be free of misinterpretation, lucid prose (what he called "clear and certain words") could give most people grounds for agreement on many matters including the general precepts of Christianity. In an age of massively footnoted and densely argued theological texts, Tillotson's comparatively straight-forward arguments reinforced the move toward the simple, commonsensical prose style later favored by revolutionaries such as Paine, who had explicitly argued that his *Common Sense* (1776) offered "nothing more than simple facts, plain arguments, and common sense." As early as 1733, Benjamin Franklin was recommending Tillotson's work as a model of limpid prose that used "the plainest Words."[6]

Religious toleration was realized in the United States during the American Revolution with the new commitment to separate matters of conscience from matters of state. Although some states after the Revolution maintained state funding for churches, as had been characteristic of the colonial era, the First Amendment of the federal Constitution guaranteed the free exercise of religion. New republicans described religious toleration as a characteristic of enlightened nations. "There is not an enlightened nation," argued Alexander Hamilton in 1784, "which does not now acknowledge the force of this truth, that whatever speculative notions of religion may be entertained, men will not on that account, be enemies to a government, that affords them protection and security." Some Americans began to regard the Puritan founders of New England as bigots for failing to exercise the religious tolerance valued by the enlightened age. In a section of his biography of George Washington called "Religious intolerance," Chief Justice John Marshall chided the Puritans because they "possessed a degree of bigotry in religion, and a spirit of intolerance, which their enlightened posterity will review with regret." Hannah Adams's *A Summary History of New-England* (1799) described the "astonishing" blindness of the early settlers of New England from the perspective of "us, who live in an enlightened age, where the principles of religious toleration are clearly understood."[7]

The meaning of religion also expanded to include a new attention to nature and reason. The Latitudinarians had helped shift the grounds of the defense of religion from a focus on biblical writ to how religion conformed with nature and reason. The works of Isaac Newton and others suggested that God worked through impersonal, secondary causes that could be empirically studied. This new reasonable or "natural religion" (as it came to be called) clustered around a number of new convictions: that the world operated according to God-given natural laws and that the deity worked through these mechanisms rather than through miracles or supernatural events; that human reason was sufficient to determine religious truths, including the existence of a Creator; that the ways of this reasonable God were best discerned through the examination of nature and reason rather than written revelation; that the existence of an afterlife (whether in heaven or hell) was debatable; and that the happiness of humankind was the ultimate purpose of Creation. In a controversial 1748 essay debunking miracles, David Hume declared natural religion evidence that humanity was moving toward the "enlighten'd Ages of Science and Knowledge." Skepticism about miracles became dogma among the staunchest supporters of natural religion in late-eighteenth-century America, as in Ethan Allen's *Reason the Only Oracle of Man* (1784), which argued that "miracles are opposed to, and counteract the laws of nature."[8]

The Latitudinarian insistence that nature revealed God's plan emboldened scientific investigation. Naturalists sought to use natural philosophy and natural history to prove the existence of a benevolent God: science supported religious truths rather than undermining them. The subtitle of the English scientist Robert Boyle's *The Christian Virtuoso* (1690) announced Boyle's conviction that "by being addicted to *Experimental Philosophy*, a Man is rather Assisted, than Indisposed, to be a *Good Christian*." In Britain a group known as physico-theologists took up arms against the threat they saw in mechanical materialists such as Thomas Hobbes, René Descartes, and Baruch Spinoza, who had posited a more purely mechanistic nature of matter no longer infused with spirit.

The physico-theologists recoiled from this doctrine, describing the natural and physical world in scientific terms but arguing that God's benevolence was constantly revealed in nature's beauty and elegant operations. Continental contemporaries of Britain's physico-theologists included an array of naturalists whose insights also reached the American colonies, usually through English translations. Inspired by his scientific hero Robert Boyle, Cotton Mather published *The Christian Philosopher* (1721), the first comprehensive work by an American to incorporate the latest results of the scientific revolution and natural theology. One scholar has estimated that 79 percent of Mather's *Christian Philosopher* was compiled from other authors, chiefly the British physico-theologists John Ray and William Derham.[9]

By the middle of the eighteenth century, the precepts of natural religion had become part of mainstream American science. British America's leading astronomer, John Winthrop of Harvard, declared that accurate celestial observations would achieve the scientific end of demonstrating the truth of the Copernican system while also giving deeper insight in the wondrous works of God. Winthrop's description of the transit of Venus showed how precise scientific observations could yield knowledge of the wonders of the deity. "Without this, we can never ascertain the true dimensions of the solar system and the several orbs of which it is composed, nor assign the magnitudes and densities of the Sun, the planets and comets; nor, of consequence, attain a just idea of the grandeur of the works of GOD," he wrote in 1769. The Connecticut painter Ralph Earl's portrait of the Reverend Nehemiah Strong (1790) captured the religious and the natural in one canvas. Trained in theology at Yale, Strong was for a short time a Congregational minister before briefly teaching mathematics and natural philosophy at Yale and then running an academy for young men. The author of a series of astronomical almanacs, he was also known as one of the leading cosmologists of New England.[10] In Earl's portrait, the minister sits in his academic robe in front of a bookcase full of astronomy and mathematics texts, resting his right hand on an astronomical globe.

Just as human reason might detect the laws of the cosmos, so might it also discover universal laws that applied to human beings.

The Reverend Nehemiah Strong sits with his astronomical globe and astronomy books in a portrait by Ralph Earl from 1790. (Yale University Art Gallery)

Reason, that is, might discover "human nature." Though seldom defined, "human nature" presumed the existence of unique traits shared by all human beings that set them above the animals and that could be empirically observed and categorized. In contrast to the doctrine of original sin, which accepted innate depravity as part of the human condition, human nature could be morally neutral or potentially even positive, allowing some optimism about the essential capacity of human beings to shape their own destiny and even to find earthly happiness in the absence of redeeming infusions of grace.

The new quest for a science of human nature insisted on the universal character of ethical intuitions, favoring these over ecclesiastical authority as the ideal basis for morality. Hume's *Treatise of Human Nature* (1739–40) proposed what Hume called "the science of man" as the only sure foundation for all the other sciences. Not until human beings understood themselves—their human nature—could they begin to understand mathematics, natural philosophy, or religion. This optimistic understanding of human nature bore fruit during the American Revolution, which was described as an event that realized the potential of human beings for a happiness that while earthbound was also pleasing to providence. "We are fighting for the Dignity and Happiness of Human Nature," the American commissioners in Paris wrote to their colleagues back in Philadelphia in 1777.[11]

Lastly, another new area of religious possibility was the idea that religion could be a general category of inquiry rather than something that was essentially given as true. In the seventeenth and early eighteenth centuries, a few English divines had introduced the conceptual innovation that all peoples had religions, defined not as Christian truth but generically as all the customs, rules, and prohibitions by which people transacted with the divine. The age of world exploration that began in the fifteenth century had brought many new religions to the attention of educated Europeans and Americans. As Christian doctrinal differences receded in favor of a new emphasis on beliefs common to humanity, ideas and practices that earlier could be dismissed as pagan (the beliefs of the Egyptians, Greeks, and Romans) or savage devil worship (the beliefs of the American Indians) could now be approached as fully developed religions to be explored and understood, even though they might still be judged inferior to Christianity. It was also thought that the non-Christian beliefs ("myths") of societies remote in time and place could shed light on the primitive, natural religion that God had given to the first humans at the dawn of the world. In this way, the belief systems of non-Christians moved to the center of educated thought around the Atlantic. To study myth was to accept the idea that different societies legitimately embraced different truths, however false or strange those truths might appear to outsiders.[12]

One influential work along these lines was the French Jesuit priest Joseph-François Lafitau's *Moeurs des sauvages amériquains, comparées aux moeurs des premiers temps* (Customs of the American Indians, Compared with the Customs of Primitive Times, 1724), the product of Lafitau's five years living among the Iroquois in Canada between 1712 and 1717. A massive compendium of knowledge about the North American Indians by an on-site observer, Lafitau's *Moeurs* became widely known within Jesuit circles but also among Protestants throughout Europe and America. It was featured on James Madison's list of books for the U.S. Congress to purchase for its reference library.[13]

Lafitau maintained that all humanity had knowledge of God: no nation—including the Iroquois—was so barbaric as to have no religion at all. Not only did the Indians have a religion, Lafitau went on, but this religion bore a close resemblance to the myths of classical antiquity—so close that both must have the same source in the dawn of the world when the first parents of humanity, Adam and Eve, had been created by God and imprinted with knowledge of the deity. Thus Iroquois religion was based on essentially the same principles as the mythology of the Greeks and Romans. To show how religion was the root of every human endeavor both among the ancients and among the Iroquois, Lafitau wrote his book about "customs" (moeurs): all customs, from warfare to styles of clothing, ultimately derived from religious beliefs.[14] Thus the book, though its title advertised customs, was really about the religion of the American Indians, a rebuke to earlier chroniclers who had dismissed Indian worship as mere devil worship.

A term whose usage soared during the eighteenth century and later, *mythology* opened the possibility that non-Christian religions could be studied rationally with the aim of exposing the universal truths that ostensibly undergirded every religion in the world. But now that some kinds of belief were regarded as myth, what then was religion? What was to distinguish the worship of ancient Egyptians or American Indians from the worship of Christians? This was the question that the self-described enlightened or natural religion had placed on the table by the middle of the eighteenth century.

Myth Versus Religion

Americans first confronted the most disturbing implications of mythology during the revolutionary era. Throwing off kings and aristocrats, revolutionaries in America, like their counterparts in France, searched for new forms of political legitimacy. These they found in nature. Their goal was to discover the original religion of nature upon which to ground not only modern belief but also modern politics.

A clutch of publications about mythology published in England, France, and the United States in the last third of the eighteenth century historicized natural religion in ways that made the connection to political revolution abundantly clear. In the earliest ages of humanity, the authors of these works declared, an ancient mythology had existed that sprang entirely from nature. Modern societies seeking revolutionary change should look to this primordial era to rediscover a natural religion suitable for the new natural politics of republicanism. Barely a few years into building a republic authorized by what the Declaration of Independence had called "the Law of Nature and Nature's God," Americans took these mythologists very seriously indeed. Having grounded their government in principles of natural rights, natural law, and an ostensibly scientific understanding of human nature, some now also strove to ground the republic's religion in a primordial nature. For this exciting but dangerous project they looked abroad to England and France, to a group of scholars who plumbed the earliest depth of recorded human time to discover a natural religion appropriate for one of the world's newest polities.

These European scholars are not household names today, but they captured the imaginations of some of the most influential thinkers in revolutionary America. They included the English writers Jacob Bryant, Hugh Farmer, and Joseph Priestley and the French authors Antoine Court de Gébelin, the comte de Volney, and Charles-François Dupuis. Between 1774 and 1795, they published a number of books that turned to remote antiquity—the pre-Christian world of the ancient Middle East, Greece, and Egypt—to unveil a primordial world of ritual, practice, and belief. Looking closely in a historical and comparative way at the religions of the

most ancient civilizations, they suggested that pagan myths underlay some of the principal stories of the Bible, such as the great
earth-drowning flood. A few in France went so far as to suggest that
all religions had their root in an original, natural worship of the sun
to which modern peoples should return in order to create perfect
societies. By restoring their societies' most natural forms through
revolution, history would be brought to an end. The contingency of
human, event-driven history would be rendered obsolete in the
mythic present of nature itself.[15] Events in France—where some
revolutionaries hoped to rid the state of all vestiges of Christianity
and install instead a civic religion based on the worship of nature
and reason—added to the suspicion that religious skepticism led
straight to social and political chaos. Americans, flush with the success of their own revolution, looked first with hope and then with
panic as revolution gave way to the Terror and then to the megalo-
mania of Napoleon. Was this to be the new religion of nature?

The floodgates of American anxiety about ancient mythology
opened with the publication of Paine's *Age of Reason*. Published in
three parts in 1794, 1795, and (under a different title) 1807, the
work spectacularly demolished revealed religion and made Paine's
name a byword for religious infidelity. Billing his work as an investigation into true and "fabulous" theology, Paine announced that
the logical outcome of political revolution would be religious revolution. Thus the age of reason was not just the age at which children left behind fanciful notions but the historical era during which
nations banished political and religious despotism. Part of Paine's
religious emancipation involved his own declaration of independence from authority and tradition. Like his unfootnoted *Common
Sense*, *The Age of Reason* appeared to float directly from the oracle of
his mind. "My own mind is my own church," Paine asserted.[16]

The new idea of mythology lurked everywhere in *The Age of
Reason*. Calling Christians "Christian mythologists," Paine argued
that their beliefs differed little from those of the "ancient mythologists," the pagans of ancient Egypt, Rome, and Greece. All had developed pantheons and objects of worship. But the Christians were
far more nefarious a force than the ancient pagans, for the
Christian mythologists had then built a despotic system of religious
and political control atop the foundation of ancient mythology. In

the modern world, Christianity had become the most objectionable religion ever fashioned: it was insulting to God, oppressive to humanity, and repugnant to reason. It was "an engine of power," serving only "the purpose of despotism." In fact, Paine argued later in a work on the origins of freemasonry, Christianity and freemasonry both had "one and the same common origin, the ancient worship of the sun." Every "enlightened mason" should know these facts about natural religion.[17]

There is little doubt that Paine was influenced by the English deists of the earlier part of the century, such as John Toland, Matthew Tindal, and Conyers Middleton. But it is also likely that he had absorbed the more unsettling work of the French mythologists published in the second half of the eighteenth century, when these works began to be known in the United States. Among the few authors that Paine cited in *The Age of Reason* was the French engineer and conchyliomaniac Nicolas-Antoine Boulanger, best known for his *L'Antiquité dévoilée* (Antiquity Unveiled, 1766), in which Boulanger had attempted to locate the origin of all human religious practices in a great, primordial, shell-scattering flood. After his death, Boulanger's name was used as a pseudonym by the alleged French atheist Baron d'Holbach and his coterie (who liked to call themselves the *boulangerie*) to circulate controversial works of critical mythology such as *Le Christianisme dévoilé* (Christianity Unveiled, 1767).[18]

All this strenuous unveiling attracted the attention of Americans predisposed to mythological perspectives. From Germany, Joel Barlow praised the English translation of *Le Christianisme dévoilé* as an antidote to "Christian mummery." This English translation of Holbach used the term "Christian Mythology," which was similar to Paine's "Christian mythologists." The semantic clustering around the idea of Christianity as myth suggests the fertility of the "age of reason" for creating a vocabulary to discuss Christianity in the context of larger belief systems. A number of Americans also owned the English deist Jacob Bryant's *A New System, or, An Analysis of Ancient Mythology* (1774), which was essentially a plagiarism of recent works of French mythologists, including Boulanger and his flood thesis. Bryant's *New System* was among the forty most annotated books in the library of John Adams, and it was bequeathed to Thomas Jefferson by his revered law teacher, George Wythe.[19]

Immersed in the milieu of French mythologists, Paine was probably also aware of the most influential mythologist of them all: the Protestant scholar and freemason Antoine Court de Gébelin. Court de Gébelin was widely admired for his massive nine-volume quasi-encyclopedia *Monde primitif, analisé et comparé avec le monde moderne* (The Primeval World, Analyzed and Compared with the Modern World, 1773–82), which had enshrined ancient paganism as the true, original, most natural religion of humanity. Court de Gébelin claimed nature as his only guide, calling it the unchanging road to truth and the sole determiner of the course of human history. Poring over the evidence from language, customs, laws, religion, and archaeology, Court de Gébelin proposed that the ancients had practiced a form of monotheism by worshipping the sun and the moon. This primordial monotheism had then transmogrified over the centuries into the worship of God.[20] Christianity was therefore a corruption of paganism, the true, natural religion of humanity—which was more or less the same argument Paine was making in *The Age of Reason* and in his later book on the origins of freemasonry.

Although it is not possible to trace a direct line of influence from Court de Gébelin to Paine since Paine was reluctant to cite intellectual authorities, the French mythographer was well known to the American revolutionaries stationed in Paris by the time Paine alighted there in 1781, just as Court de Gébelin's fame was cresting. In his short visit to France in the spring of that year—when he accompanied congressional envoy John Laurens—Paine spent much of his time at Franklin's villa in Passy, on the outskirts of Paris. Franklin and Court de Gébelin had by now become collaborators. A supporter of the American Revolution, Court de Gébelin had worked with Franklin on the journal *Affaires de l'Angleterre et de l'Amérique* (1776–79), which kept French readers up to date on war news. Franklin in turn became a subscriber to Court de Gébelin's *Monde primitif.* As each new volume was published, Court de Gébelin pressed a copy upon Franklin, offering extras to pass on to John Adams. Court de Gébelin's admiring secretary during some of the time in which he wrote *Monde primitif* was the young linguist Pierre-Étienne Du Ponceau, who decamped to United States during the American Revolution and eventually established himself as a

leading scholar of American Indian languages under the Anglicized
name Peter Stephen Du Ponceau.[21]

Paine returned to America later in 1781, just when *Monde
primitif* was capturing the attention of American readers for its
startling proposal that the ancient seafaring Phoenicians were the
ancestors of the American Indians. Largely forgotten today,
the Phoenician origin theory enjoyed widespread popularity in the
eighteenth century, for it helped explain the presence in the New
World of civilized, city-building Indians such as the Aztecs and the
Incas and suggested appealing connections between the peoples of
the New World and the civilizations of the ancient Mediterranean.
Court de Gébelin's proposal offered a precise point of disembarka-
tion for the Phoenicians: Massachusetts. Allegedly dropping anchor eons earlier in Narragansett Bay, the Phoenicians had
purportedly carved words and figures into a large boulder that was
now partially covered by water. In 1768, the Harvard professor of
Hebrew languages, Stephen Sewall, had made a drawing of what
he believed were Phoenician inscriptions on that rock, and sent a
copy of his drawing to Court de Gébelin.[22]

This was an extraordinary find: here on the coast of
Massachusetts was hard proof that the mighty Phoenicians of antiquity had peopled the New World, an idea that helped explain
not just the paganism of the Indians but their deep connection to
an originary religion of the ancient Mediterranean. It was a testament to the growing importance of British America in European

*The Harvard Hebrew scholar Stephen Sewall made this drawing in 1768 of the
allegedly Phoenician inscriptions on Dighton Rock in Massachusetts. (© 2015
President and Fellows of Harvard College, Peabody Museum of Archaeology and
Ethnology, PM# 967-28-10/45474 [digital file# 99270006])*

*Stephen Sewall sent his drawing of the allegedly Phoenician inscriptions on a
Massachusetts rock to France, where it was published in the French mythologist
Antoine Court de Gébelin's* Monde primitif, *a work that was in turn read and
discussed in the United States. (Courtesy Department of Special Collections,
Stanford University Library)*

intellectual life that this piece of New World evidence was pub-
lished for an international readership in Court de Gébelin's famous
Monde primitif. In 1782, the Reverend James Madison of Virginia
commented on the Phoenician theory to his cousin James
Madison, praising Court de Gébelin as a man of "very great
Reputation." Court de Gébelin's theories were influential enough
in America that he was elected a foreign honorary member of the
American Academy of Arts and Sciences.[23]

There is thus good reason to believe that Thomas Paine was influenced by late-eighteenth-century French mythologists such as Court
de Gébelin in writing *The Age of Reason.* But dressed up for American
readers—complete with a publication date rendered according to the
louche revolutionary French calendar—the French mythology in
Paine's latest work inspired immediate outrage in the United States.
The press flogged him for opening the door not just to religious infidelity but to the political mayhem gripping France. Counterattacks
proliferated from Boston to New York to London, in which revelation
and miracles were ardently defended. One minister assured Paine that
the book of Revelation itself had foretold the French Revolution,
God's way of drowning popery in the flood of infidelity.[24]

Unsettling as Court de Gébelin's work was, two even more
alarming treatises on French mythology also flanked Paine's assault
on Christianity. These were Constantin-François de Chasseboeuf,
comte de Volney's *Les Ruines; ou, Méditation sur les révolutions des*

empires (1791), first published in English translation as *The Ruins; or, A Survey of the Revolutions of Empires* (1792), and Charles-François Dupuis's *Origine de tous les cultes; ou, Réligion universelle* (The Origin of All Beliefs; or, Universal Religion, 1795).

Of the two works, Volney's had far greater influence in the United States. A historian, an Orientalist, and a philosopher, Volney was also a passionate idealist eager to see a new social order emerge in his lifetime. There is no reason entirely to disbelieve the charming rumor that Volney advertised his political sympathies in a self-created surname, which was said to have combined Voltaire (his hero) with Ferney (Voltaire's Geneva estate). After moving to Paris from the French provinces as a young man and beguiling the grandes dames of the salons, Volney embarked in 1782 for Egypt and Syria. His three-year tour culminated in his magnificent *Voyage en Syrie et en Egypte* (1787), which captivated audiences in both Europe and the United States and became a major new source for knowledge of the Near East. Returning to France, Volney was soon swept up in the ferment of the French Revolution, an experience that resulted in his manifesto against despotism, *Les Ruines*.[25]

Incendiary and eloquent, Volney's *Ruines* elevated its author to international fame. English translations soon appeared from London and American presses, and around the Atlantic Volney's name became synonymous with the dangers and possibilities of the French Revolution. Volney himself eventually arrived in the United States in 1795, broken and frightened in the aftermath of the Terror, hoping to forget everything in this new world and trusting his fate to his bosom friend Thomas Jefferson, whom he had met in the Paris salon of the celebrated Madame Helvétius. In Philadelphia he rose like a brilliant sun from the large cadre of French nobles, artisans, and intellectuals who crowded into the city in the years after the French Revolution. He became the toast of the Francophile wing of Philadelphia high society, leaving a trail of Volneyesque mementos in his wake. He was disappointed in Gilbert Stuart's prim portrait of him, having hoped that Stuart would show him with his shirt open at the neck, like his hero Voltaire. After Volney pronounced Charles Willson Peale's Philadelphia museum "the Temple of God!" because it held "nothing but Truth and Reason," Peale proudly added a copy of Volney's portrait to the museum's walls. Expelled under the Alien and Sedition Acts in 1798, Volney returned to France and later sent Jefferson a tiny cork reproduction of the great pyramid of Cheops at Giza, a daily reminder to the American president of the explosive potential of pagan antiquity for modern republics. Jefferson was so captivated by the learned attack on political despotism in Volney's *Ruines* that he secretly collaborated with Joel Barlow on an English translation of the work, which was published in Paris in 1802.[26]

What was so revolutionary about Volney's *Ruines?* Looking into the pagan past that had been so palpably revealed in the crumbling ruins of Egypt and Syria, Volney built up a scathing critique of modernity. The builders of pagan empires, those worshippers of the sun and stars, had thrived for hundreds of years by conforming to the laws of nature, Volney charged, and moderns should take heed. "Solitary ruins, sacred tombs, ye mouldering and silent Walls, all hail!" Volney intoned in what became the famous opening lines of *The Ruins.* Only the laws of nature would lead humanity to understand "the principles of individual happiness and of public felicity." The only true religion was natural law and human nature, which if consulted would lead to an "enlightened" future. He added impishly: "If such is impiety, what is true belief?"[27] Guided by the light of reason and nature, Volney would expose the shams of Christianity and priestcraft, uncovering in the ruins of lost civilizations a natural guide for the modern reconstruction of society.

Volney's taunts were destructive enough, but the pièce de résistance in this feast of French mythology was Dupuis's colossal *Origine de tous les cultes,* published in 1795. A scholar equally at home in mathematics and ancient languages, Dupuis was elected to the French National Convention, where he played a role in creating the French revolutionary calendar that substituted a nature-based system for the despised Gregorian calendar—or as his contemporaries put it, substituted "for visions of ignorance the realities of reason, and for sacerdotal prestige the truth of nature."[28]

Similar hopes to make nature the ultimate guide animated Dupuis's *Origine de tous les cultes,* in which the author argued not only that all religious worship had its origins in the worship of nature but that all religions specifically originated in fertility cults. The breast, the phallus, the testicles: all played their role in

Dupuis's sexualized version of mythology. His startling suggestions ("Christ will be for us what Hercules, Osiris, Adonis, and Bacchus were") drew strength from the vivid realism of the ancient world that was now being exposed by the excavations of Pompeii and Herculaneum. Among other wonders, pornographic wall paintings and vases had emerged from the ash, setting the gods and heroes of antiquity in a sensual new context, as was extravagantly revealed in the *Collection of Etruscan, Greek, and Roman Antiquities* (1766–67) by the rakish, self-styled Baron d'Hancarville.[29] Like Volney, Dupuis turned the gaze of his classically learned readers to a vision of antiquity that was neither beautiful nor comforting but instead erotic, violent, and potentially alarming in its implications for Christianity, which had emerged from this sensual pagan world.

A quiet scholar at heart, Dupuis never enjoyed the international fame of the swashbuckling Volney. His *Origine de tous les cultes*—rambling, chockablock with unfamiliar names from antiquity—was shocking only to those who could wade through its French prose and confusing illustrations of zodiacs. But it did not escape the attention of intellectuals in the United States attuned to the dangerous implications of the French mythology. Both John Adams and the Boston scholar and bibliophile William Bentley owned the book, and one of Jefferson's French friends sent him a copy. Other thinkers were also aware of it, and this familiarity helps explain Joel Barlow's obsession with the Liberty Tree and the French liberty cap as phallic symbols with origins in the Egyptian fable of Osiris.[30]

The upshot was this: by 1795, three French works—by Volney, Dupuis, and Court de Gébelin—had formed a battering ram of destructive mythology that threatened the very core of Christian belief. Americans watched with horror as war broke out between Britain and revolutionary France in 1793, an event that underscored the links among political disorder, an assault on inherited social order, and attacks on traditional Christianity. It appeared to many that religious infidelity was sweeping west from France. In alarm, an army of American ministers soon rose up to defend orthodox Christianity against the peculiar doctrines of the French mythologists and their ilk. In 1798, Timothy Dwight, the president of Yale College, warned the susceptible youth of the graduating class to beware *"lest you become a prey to the Philosophy, which opposes the Gospel."*[31]

But the most learned rebuttal to the French mythologists—and the most impassioned defenses of revealed religion—came not from the center of orthodoxy but from the fringes of natural religion: the English Dissenting minister, chemist, and political theorist Joseph Priestley. The controversy aroused by his candid support of the French Revolution and his commitment to open and rational inquiry into theological questions caused him to decamp to the United States in 1794. In 1796, he gave a series of lectures in Philadelphia at the Universalist church and encouraged the founding of the first Unitarian church in the city. When his library went up for sale after his death, buyers found it packed with the new works on comparative religion and treatises by Holbach, Voltaire, and Condorcet.[32]

Yet despite these rather alarming credentials, Priestley ultimately hoped to vindicate the superiority of Christian revelation. During the 1790s, Priestley launched a barrage of publications that took direct aim at this new trifecta of what he called "infidelity": Paine's *Age of Reason*, Volney's *Ruines*, and Dupuis's *Origine*. Like them, he reached far back into antiquity, to the mythology of Egypt and the Hindus. But what he found there was not nature but God. Priestley took it upon himself to define religion in an age where its meaning had become cloudy: "By the *fear of God* we may very well understand *religion* in general, and there can be no doubt but that by religion Solomon meant such principles of it as he held to be the best founded, or the revelation by Moses," Priestley argued in his Philadelphia lecture. Nature was not God, but rather God was nature, Priestley urged, against the teachings of the French mythologists. Reason and enlightenment pointed not to a primordial religion of nature but rather to Christian revelation, whose "superiority in sentiment and practice to any thing that the most enlightened of mankind have ever devised is so great, that it cannot be rationally accounted for, but by supposing it to have had a truly divine origin."[33]

Is This Religion?

In the twilight of their lives, when the French Revolution had become a distant memory, John Adams and Thomas Jefferson debated what the new mythology entailed for traditional conceptions of religion. They discussed this still smoldering topic in a remarkable series of letters exchanged between 1813 and 1826, when both were old men retired from public careers with time enough on their hands to collapse into their armchairs and read enormous books about ancient Egyptian mythology and fertility cults.

Each came to this epistolary exchange with distinctive views about religion. Although raised as an Anglican in Virginia, Jefferson had believed from an early age in the supremacy of reason and the freedom of conscience. "Fix reason firmly in her seat," he advised his nephew Peter Carr in 1787, "and call to her tribunal every fact, every opinion. Question with boldness even the existence of a god; because, if there be one, he must more approve the homage of reason, than that of blindfolded fear." Jefferson had served on the committee that drafted Virginia's Statute for Religious Freedom, adopted in 1785, which declared religious liberty a "natural right" not subject to temporal powers. Jefferson hoped that this achievement would be remembered as one of his three major life accomplishments.[34] Partisan accusations abounded in the 1790s and during his presidency that he was an atheist, run amok with the anticlerical excesses of the French Revolution.

Weakly theistic as he may have been, however, Jefferson did believe in a god, though not the trinity central to orthodox Christianity. He protested that he was "a *real Christian*, that is to say, a disciple of the doctrines of Jesus." His goal was what he called a "rational Christianity," the teachings of Jesus stripped of the scriptural padding that concealed genuine ethical truths. Razor in hand, he cut up a Bible and glued together extracts from the New Testament to make booklets he called "The Philosophy of Jesus" (1804) and "The Life and Morals of Jesus" (1819–20), which excluded most mentions of supernatural acts and all miracles performed by Jesus. He remained a lifelong skeptic of organized religion. "The religion-builders have so distorted and deformed the doctrines of Jesus," he wrote in 1821 to Timothy Pickering, "so muffled them in mysticisms, fancies and falsehoods, have caricatured them into forms so monstrous and inconcievable, as to shock reasonable thinkers, to revolt them against the whole, and drive them rashly to pronounce it's founder an imposter."[35]

By contrast, Adams could trace a direct line of descent from the earliest Puritan settlers of the Massachusetts Bay Colony, and his fa-

ther had served as a Congregational deacon. Raised in the long sunset of Congregationalist supremacy in New England, he left for
Harvard at the age of sixteen with his family's expectation that he
would become a minister. Pondering his career choice after gradua-
tion, he chose law because among ministers he found "the pretended sanctity of some absolute dunces." He ultimately dropped
belief in predestination, eternal damnation, the divinity of Christ,
and much of the rest of the Calvinist belief structure. While remaining essentially committed to basic Christian principles throughout
his life, he loathed dogmatism, seeing it as a cloak for political op-
pression. He nurtured a pet theory that since antiquity, priests and
other fanatics had been burning all the books that would undermine
the doctrines of their despotic religious regimes. Knowledge was the
antidote to all oppressions, whether political or religious. "Let the
pulpit resound with the doctrines and sentiments of religious liberty," he commanded in "A Dissertation on the Canon and the
Feudal Law" (1765), a passionate denunciation of Catholicism and
feudal restraints. The work identified the Protestant Reformation
and the British peopling of North America as the two great events
that had emancipated Americans from the fetters of Catholic tyranny and feudalism and freed them to establish institutions better
aligned with what he called "human nature."[36]

Jefferson and Adams had read widely in ancient history and
ethics throughout their lives, and now in the leisure of their retirement years they turned to the many new books on the subject of
comparative mythology from France and England: the works of
Dupuis, Farmer, Bryant, Court de Gébelin. They read them, exchanged them, debated them, and wrote in them. Each remarked
numerous times that this new work in mythology had made him
reconsider his own faith and the larger truths of Christianity.
Would the world be better if there were no religion in it, Adams
wondered to Jefferson after paging through Bryant and company.
Was all this learned lumber necessary for salvation?[37]

Finally Adams scrawled the key question of his era in Bryant's
New System. At the foot of a picture of ancient Egyptians carrying a
ship bearing the goddess Isis, he wrote, "Is this Religion? Good God!"

Beyond Jefferson and Adams, the wider influence of this new
mythology and its associated skepticism began to wane in American

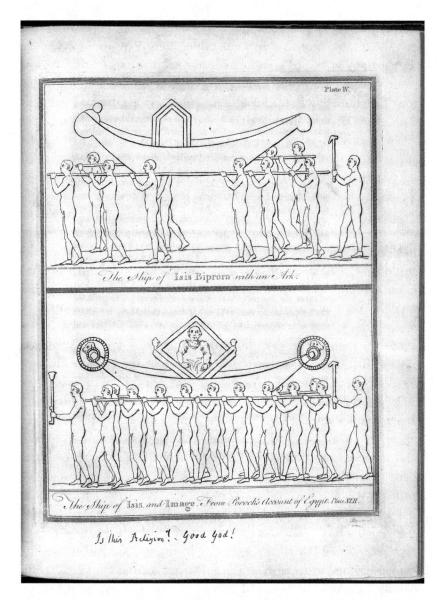

The Ship of Isis Biprora with an Ark.

The Ship of Isis. and Image. From Pocock's Account of Egypt. Plate XLII.

Is this Religion? Good God!

John Adams scrawled "Is this Religion? Good God!" at the bottom of this image of the goddess Isis in Jacob Bryant's A New System, or, An Analysis of Ancient Mythology (1775), one of the forty most annotated books in Adams's library. (Courtesy of the Trustees of the Boston Public Library/Rare Books)

culture after 1800. The various political and religious threats posed
by France receded dramatically after Napoleon's decisive defeat and
the restoration of the Bourbon monarchy. By then, republicanism
in the United States had been firmly linked to Christianity, a particularly American fusion that created what one historian has called
a "moral language of liberty." This moral language united a large
variety of Protestant denominations with a republican vocabulary
that allowed them to find common moral and political ground
for their particular visions of the national future. Evangelical
Protestant denominations such as the Baptists and the Methodists
grew rapidly in numbers between the Revolution and the Civil
War, affirming the primacy of biblical authority and its usefulness
as a moral guide for the regeneration of self and society.[38]

Reason now took a backseat to morality—principles of upright
conduct—as the foundation of American political liberties. The
French Revolution had failed, declared the Unitarian minister
William Ellery Channing in the late 1820s, because the French
lacked "moral preparation for liberty." By contrast, he went on,
America's revolutionaries had triumphed because like George
Washington they possessed what Channing called "sublime moral
qualities." In the American colleges of the period 1800–1860, the
Scottish philosophy of common sense realism, encapsulated in the
works of Thomas Reid and his disciple Dugald Stewart, comforted
Americans anxious about the nature of belief with the certainty
that their minds perceived true morality.[39] The great reform movements of the mid-nineteenth century hinged on the idea that science and religion worked together for the greater glory of God.
Abolitionism, feminism, phrenology, and temperance all yoked religion and science to assist the nation's progress toward salvation.

But the skeptical fringe of natural religion did not die out entirely after 1800, nor did its core question: In an age of reason,
what was belief? Americans began to accept the idea of myth
(rather than paganism or devil worship) as a way to understand the
religious systems of non-Christians. American Indians were no
longer servants of Satan, the Greeks and Romans no longer merely
pagans preparing for the arrival of Christ. All were now practitioners of "mythology," a word Jefferson used perhaps for the first
time in a letter in 1812 to Adams to describe Lafitau's *Moeurs des*

sauvages, a work that by then was nearly a century old but was still a testament to Lafitau's insight that the Indians had a fully formed religious system in common with ancient peoples and indeed all humanity.[40]

The idea of myth and the study of mythology became the seeds of the emerging new studies of ethnology, comparative religion, and anthropology that emerged in such works as Max Müller's *Comparative Mythology* (1856). By the second half of the nineteenth century, a new "science of myth" developed that rested on the view that religious belief could be studied empirically, and that no particular sect or creed was necessarily truer than others. Soon the new idea took root in the new departments of comparative religion that flourished in twentieth-century universities. Anthropologists honed the conceptual distinction between the sacred and the profane, one that would have been unimaginable without the first sallies of the deists in the seventeenth century, who began to imagine their way out of a world that pitted Christianity against paganism and devil worship. In the seventeenth century "belief" meant Christianity; by the nineteenth century, "belief" could mean many other things, from the naturalism of the Transcendentalists to what was now grandly called the "theology of the Iroquois," laid out by the American anthropologist Lewis Henry Morgan in *The League of the Ho-de-no-sau-nee or Iroquois* (1851). Ralph Waldo Emerson aligned Christianity with all other "mythologies" in his essay "Religion" (1867), explaining that "the religious impulse is the most revolutionary principle in human experience."[41]

In the Gifford Lectures on natural religion in 1902, the psychologist William James affirmed religious feeling as a distinct part of what he called "human nature," a term whose popularity had soared during the eighteenth century as part of the new faith in a universal, positive humanity but which now, a century or more later, seemed unremarkable, so common had it become to imagine that all human beings shared essential traits including the yearning for belief in a transcendent, sacred truth. The title of James's resulting publication encapsulated the revolution wrought by the expansion of the ideas of religion and human nature in the eighteenth century: *The Varieties of Religious Experience: A Study in Human Nature* (1902). "It is as if there were in the human consciousness *a sense of the reality, a feeling of objective presence, a per-ception* of what we may call *'something there,'* more deep and more general than any of the special and particular 'senses' by which the current psychology supposes existent realities to be originally revealed," James argued.[42]

William James thought he was rescuing "the unseen powers" of religious experience from the new regime of scientific facts. Religion, he lamented, was one of the "things which no enlight-ened man can nowadays believe in."[43] But James had his genealogy backward. For it was those who had worked for what they called enlightenment in the seventeenth and eighteenth centuries who had helped forge a richer conceptual vocabulary for understanding belief. By pushing the conversation about belief beyond the con-fines of the Bible and Christianity to a new, more expansive arena of "human nature," these self-described enlightened thinkers had made religion a subject shared among all of humanity and not just Christians. This, in the end, was the most significant legacy of the quest to discover an enlightened religion in the age of reason.

CHAPTER SEVEN

The Futuristic Farmers of
America

DURING THE EIGHTEENTH CENTURY, farmers in Europe and America suddenly began viewing agriculture in a new light. They drew charts of their fields, rotated their crops with military precision, dissected the insects that gorged on them, and unleashed a flood of treatises arguing that farmers were the very bedrock of modern human societies, not to mention God's favored children. "Those who labour in the earth are the chosen people of God, if ever he had a chosen people, whose breasts he has made his peculiar deposit for substantial and genuine virtue," intoned Thomas Jefferson, whose friends mailed pestilential worms to Washington, D.C., for the president's inspection.[1]

All nations should respond to the dictates of nature by throwing open their ports for the free circulation of crops and other products, the enlightened agriculturalists argued. Free trade would unshackle nations from the chains of mercantilism, the reigning trade policy of the past century that had helped Britain, France, the Netherlands, Spain, and Portugal to build vast new blue-water empires by jealously confining trade to individual nations and their colonies. Hoping to fill their national coffers by exporting more than they imported, mercantilist European nations had waged nearly constant warfare to protect their precious cargoes in a theater of violence that now reached around the world into Asia, Africa, and the Americas. But in the middle of the eighteenth century a chorus of voices arose in dissent, proposing instead a natural and enlightened world of free trade. Resting on the nourishing bounty of farmers and unimpeded commercial flow across national borders, this enlightened world of trade would unlock the true generative powers of humanity. Now fruitful, humanity would multiply as God had commanded, building happy societies based on the natural rights of man.

Such, at least, was the dream of the enlightened agriculturalists. Their sermonizing about manure ratios and turnip yields appears quaintly earnest today, yet at the time the agriculturalists formed the vanguard of the new, enlightened science of political economy. What were the nature and causes of the wealth of nations? How was national wealth to be defined and measured? How was it created and increased? Such questions of political economy were momentous indeed, involving nothing less than the perfectibility of societies and the governing of nations. The modern concept of "the economy" as a field separate from society and government did not emerge until the early twentieth century. Before then, the term *economy* retained its original meaning of thrift or the proper husbanding of resources. Thus political economy in the long eighteenth century concerned itself with the proper economy—or husbanding of resources—of a political entity. The agenda of political economy was expansive, urgent, and fundamental to the creation of social happiness.[2]

In the second half of the eighteenth century, a group of theorists around the Atlantic began to define political economy as a particularly enlightened science based on factual inquiry rather than superstition, received opinion, or prejudice. Among the first books with the term "political economy" in its title was the Scottish baronet James Steuart's *Inquiry into Political Economy* (1767). An exponent of government intervention in economic policy, Steuart explained his purpose as "reducing to principles, and forming into a regular science, the complicated interests of domestic policy." Political economy thus encompassed a vast array of concerns: population, agriculture, trade, coinage, taxes, tariffs—everything that contributed to the success and happiness of human societies increasingly linked by transoceanic trade. Steuart affirmed that the discovery of the New World had opened a new era and "altered the plan of government every where." Economy and government were now seen to be intertwined, a happy marriage that could be scrutinized by a science of political economy based on "*observation*" and "*reflection*" rather than "prejudice."[3]

Nine years later, Steuart's fellow Scot Adam Smith also ventured a definition of political economy as a science in *An Inquiry into the Nature and Causes of the Wealth of Nations* (1776). Although he disagreed with Steuart's interventionist approach to economic policy, Smith too saw political economy as a science of human flourishing. "Political oeconomy, considered as a branch of the science of a statesman or legislator, proposes two distinct objects," Smith explained. It would help the sovereign by filling the national coffers while also providing a means of subsistence for "the people." Smith urged his readers to establish a "reasonable system" of political economy rather than succumb to wishful—or worse, religious—thinking. "The laws concerning corn may every where be compared to the laws concerning religion," he advised. "The people feel themselves so much interested in what relates either to their subsistence in this life, or to their happiness in a life to come, that government must yield to their prejudices, and, in order to preserve public tranquillity, establish that system which they approve of."[4]

Among the local conditions shaping British Americans' perspectives on political economy, two stand out. First, as a collection of colonies, British America's primary purpose was to supply the mother country with staple agricultural products such as tobacco, wheat, and sugar. Brushing aside religious explanations for the colonization of North America, Adam Smith moved agriculture to the center of Britain's colonizing agenda. "Agriculture is the proper business of all new colonies," he argued in *Wealth of Nations*, "a business which the cheapness of land renders more advantageous than any other." Smith's comment reflected the rising importance of British American agricultural exports. By 1763, the close of the Seven Years' War, agricultural production for export markets undergirded the British American economy, accounting for 80 to 90 percent of the labor force. The American population likewise grew 83 percent between 1750 and 1770, and roughly the same percentage again between 1770 and 1790, despite the disruptions of the Revolutionary War.[5] If Britain was a nation of shopkeepers, as Smith had declared, then America was a nation of farmers, with a stake in the transatlantic debates about the place of enlightened farming in the new science of political economy.

The second particularly American emphasis in these wider debates was caused by the abrupt liberation of the United States from British mercantilist policies in 1776. Newly independent Americans now interpreted economic ideas in the context of their hopes and anxieties about republican nation formation. The distinctive feature of the American conversation after 1783 was its dependence on concerns about the fate of the young republic: Would America be a nation of farmers or of manufacturers? This dispute eventually helped split the political spectrum into two competing parties in the 1790s, the agriculturally oriented Democratic-Republicans and the Federalists, who favored the greater development of manufacturing. Yet amid their local concerns about political economy, Americans remained connected to the international conversation about enlightened agriculture. As he plied George Washington with pamphlets on silkworms and copies of his periodical *The Bee*, the Scottish agriculturalist and plow innovator James Anderson urged the American president not to "slacken our endeavours" to improve the standard of living in Britain and America through the international trade in new crops. "No man can estimate the benefits that Britain has derived from the introduction of the culture of Broad Clover—Turnips, and potatoes into this island; and the benefits that America has derived from the culture of Rice is notorious—To obtain *one* other such article would be a sufficient recompence for thousands of abortive trials." Americans discovered that in order to help their new republican government succeed and its people to prosper, they needed to participate robustly in the Atlantic commerce in crops and ideas. They hoped to forge a new science of human happiness through what Americans as late as the 1830s were still describing as "an enlightened system of cultivation."[6]

The First Economists

Surveying his soggy Connecticut farm in 1748, the farmer and minister Jared Eliot praised the "great Improvements in *Husbandry* far and wide." Eliot's *Essay upon Field-Husbandry in New-England*, the first of many similar works to issue from his pen, ranks as the first important agricultural book to be published in the British American colonies. Hundreds of miles away, on his sprawling Virginia plantation, Landon Carter had come to the same conclusion about the forward march of husbandry. Carefully perusing the French naturalist René-Antoine Ferchault de Réaumur's *Art of Hatching* (1750), which described a kiln that could efficiently warm large numbers of eggs without need of hens, who could then be freed to produce more eggs, Carter proposed a similar kiln for wheat that would roast fly-weevil eggs to a deadly crisp. He called his repurposed kiln "an Hypothesis to be proved by practice." Carter owned half as many books as he did slaves, but he was convinced that America would become the "granary" of Europe and so set about trying to fill the mahogany shelves of his library with the latest agricultural improvement treatises published abroad.[7]

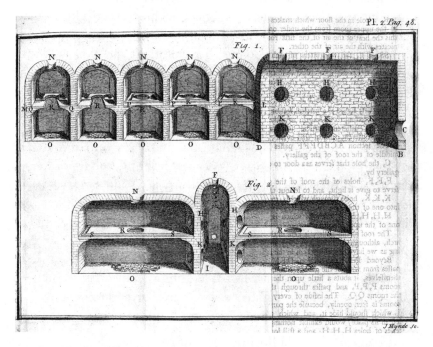

The Virginia planter Landon Carter took inspiration from this hen-free egg-warming kiln, depicted in René-Antoine Ferchault de Réaumur's The Art of Hatching *(1750). (Courtesy Department of Special Collections, Stanford University)*

Eliot and Carter stood at the fringes of a great Atlantic-wide dispute about the reigning gospel of what the nineteenth century would christen *mercantilism*, the policy of jealously guarded trade and national wealth that had developed over the previous two centuries as European powers launched their global empires. (Before the nineteenth century, this loosely organized system of policies was generally called the mercantile system.) The system's most influential single exponent had been Jean-Baptiste Colbert, the self-assured chief economic minister under Louis XIV. Through a system of preferential taxes to manufacturers and other dirigiste measures, Colbert had nurtured the development of the French economy and military at the expense of powerful rivals such as the Dutch. In England the mercantile system was explained with somewhat less fanfare by the East India merchant Thomas Mun in his *England's Treasury by Forraign Trade* (written around 1630, and published in 1664), in which he advised his king to "sell more to strangers yearly than wee consume of theirs in value." Mun hoped that growing colonial possessions and a favorable *"Ballance of the Trade"* would divert gold and silver into Britain's coffers, enriching both king and kingdom.[8]

Although critics had taken particular features of the mercantile system to task since the era of the Sun King, by the 1750s and 1760s a new generation had emerged to challenge its central doctrines. Shocked by the sheer destruction caused by unceasing wars in defense of colonial trade, these critics thrust the earth itself—its fertile soil, its bountiful crops, its stalwart farmers—to the top of national priorities. All believed, more or less, that agriculture determined the wealth of nations and that free trade in crops should be encouraged through a variety of means, including low taxes on farmers.

The most conspicuous advocates of these views were a group of French economic theorists that included François Quesnay, Victor Riquettie, marquis de Mirabeau, Anne-Robert-Jacques Turgot, Pierre-Paul Le Mercier de La Rivière, Henri-Louis Duhamel du Monceau, Jacques Claude Marie Vincent de Gournay, and Pierre Samuel du Pont de Nemours. With access to the mightiest ears of the realm, they published a small library of books and journals that ensured that their doctrines became the talk not just of France but of Europe and eventually British America.

Today they are called *physiocrats*, a term taken from the title of Du Pont de Nemours's *Physiocracie* (1767), which literally meant "government of nature." At the time, however, they were known in French as *économistes* and in English as oeconomists. None was a professional academic economist in the sense that we know that word today; Mirabeau confessed that he was no more an economist than his cat.[9] Their major platform, pursued relentlessly from the late 1750s on in a variety of publications from Diderot and d'Alembert's *Encyclopédie* to heavy tomes brimming with intricate charts, was that the wealth of nations derived solely from the value of farmed land rather than manufactures. Celebrating free-trade agriculture as a response to the decrees of nature, they believed that only a strong central power—an enlightened sovereign—could turn theory into policy.

The physician to Madame de Pompadour (a mistress of Louis XV), François Quesnay laid out the main themes of the new agricultural doctrines of the économistes in two widely circulated articles for the *Encyclopédie*: "Fermiers" (1756) and "Grains" (1758). The first sentence of Quesnay's article on farmers established their welfare as one of the highest priorities of the kingdom of France. "Farmers are those who affirm and support the good of the countryside, and who create the wealth and the most essential resources for the health of the state; thus the labor of the *farmer* is of major importance to the kingdom, and should rivet the attention of the government." He made the same point in "Grains": agriculture was the primal source of national wealth, and all "enlightened" ministers needed to recognize this. These doctrines found more systematic expression in Quesnay's *Tableau économique* (1758–59), in which he argued that agricultural surpluses rather than trade or industry were the real sources of national wealth; taxes on productive peoples such as farmers should be lower in favor of higher taxes on less productive classes, such as landowners. Insisting that he was merely unveiling the objective truths of nature, Quesnay included a picture, or "tableau," whose zigzagging lines depicted the flow of expenditures and revenues across time. By representing the simultaneous flows of rents, wages, and purchases in a chart, the tableau made plain to the eye what language—with its dependence on sequential syntax— could capture only partially.[10]

Quesnay's entry "Hommes" (Men) raised the implications of the new science of agriculture into high relief, for here Quesnay defined man purely in the terms of political economy. "It is men who constitute the power of states. It is their needs which increase wealth: the more that nations increase the products which they need, and the more of them they consume, the more wealthy they will be." The preconditions to the political rights of man were economic: these rights could emerge only when prosperous governments—sitting atop the wealth generated by sound agricultural policies—encouraged peace, liberty, and international commerce. This new definition of man required a new definition of *society*, now conceived as the largely secular container in which human flourishing would occur. Displacing older collectivities resting on divine or royal authority, the new idea of society instead exalted nature, human activity, and order as the necessary constituents of social happiness.[11]

To link the natural law that existed outside society with human activity within it, the économistes developed the idea of the "natural order" (*l'ordre naturel*). The term featured prominently in the title of Le Mercier de La Rivière's *L'Ordre naturel et essentiel des sociétés politiques* (1767), written under the close supervision of Quesnay. The natural order, argued Le Mercier de La Rivière, dictated that human beings live in society. Societies had to grow since God had commanded humans to multiply; therefore farming should rightly underlie the economic and social order. The immutable laws of nature that propelled people to live in society also dictated that humans would become enlightened enough to know how to achieve happiness within it. Indeed, humanity's happiest moments could occur only within society.[12] The order of nature thus dictated that humans create agriculturally based societies that would grow, prosper, ensure the rights of man, and allow people to achieve happiness.

The arguments of the économistes soon became known in England and Scotland as the first major chink in the armor of the mercantile system. Soon versions of the phrase "laissez faire" began to circulate in English. These derived from the commercial doctrine of the économistes, "laissez faire, laissez passer," by which they hoped to unshackle domestic and international trade from what they considered unnatural restrictions. One of the earliest

English-language versions of the phrase appeared in George Whatley's *Principles of Trade* (1774), which rendered the opposition to Colbert's mercantile system as "Laissez nous faire."[13]

The most influential and systematic response to the économistes came from Adam Smith in his *Wealth of Nations*. Smith had arrived in Paris around Christmas 1765 as part of the European tour he was making as tutor to the young duke of Buccleuch, and the two soon became fixtures at the city's leading salons. Smith had first learned about the ideas of the économistes from Quesnay's articles in the *Encyclopédie*, and the French group now eagerly embraced the awkward but knowledgeable Scotsman. The admiration was mutual; Smith described the économistes as "the most intelligent men in France." Yet although Smith had much sympathy for the French system—later describing it as "perhaps the nearest approximation to the truth that has yet been published upon the subject of political oeconomy"—he nonetheless saw it not as a universal truth but as a particularly French reaction to Colbert's attempt to convert France from a disjointed nation of subsistence farmers into a manufacturing and trading powerhouse. Smith thought that the économistes had overreacted to Colbertism, placing too much emphasis on agriculture as the sole source of the wealth of nations.[14]

Smith sought to right the ship by identifying both agriculture and manufactures as the source of national wealth. Calling Quesnay "the very ingenious and profound author" of the system of the économistes, Smith sympathetically laid out the French position in *Wealth of Nations;* he even toyed with the idea of dedicating the book to Quesnay. Having honored the system with a fair-minded summary, however, Smith gently rebuked Quesnay and his circle for calling merchants and manufacturers unproductive parasites preying upon farmers. In fact all three groups together created the wealth of nations. "The establishment of perfect justice, of perfect liberty, and of perfect equality, is the very simple secret which most effectually secures the highest degree of prosperity to all the three classes," Smith explained. Ever cautious of the systematizing mania of the French, Smith warned that Quesnay's system relied on false analogies. As royal physician, Quesnay had succumbed to the mistaken belief that bodies thrived only under a precise regimen, and so prescribed the same rigid system for economies without realizing that they, like people, could thrive under different circumstances. "He seems not to have considered," Smith argued, "that in the political body, the natural effort which every man is continually making to better his own condition, is a principle of preservation capable of preventing and correcting in many respects the bad effects of a political oeconomy in some degree both partial and oppressive."[15]

So influential was *Wealth of Nations* in the English-speaking world that it became the filter through which the doctrines of the économistes became known among people who did not read French. Benjamin Franklin's young English friend Benjamin Vaughan confessed as much after reading *Wealth of Nations*. "Smith has an express section explaining the System of the *Oeconomistes* which much instructed me."[16]

Among British Americans, Franklin developed some of the strongest personal ties with the French économistes. Like Smith he was one of the main conduits by which their doctrines became better known across the Atlantic. It is difficult to imagine Franklin sweating at the plow. A creature of the city, he was born in Boston and helped transform Philadelphia not just into a city but into a civic organism full of societies dedicated to improvement, such as libraries, post offices, printers, hospitals, and a firehouse. When he retired from his Philadelphia printing business a wealthy man in 1748, he bought a farm near Burlington, New Jersey. Although political duties often called him away, he retained an interest in the experiments of his farm, including crop rotation, the introduction of new grasses, and limited fertilization.[17]

In the late 1740s Franklin began to correspond about his New Jersey farm with the Connecticut farmer Jared Eliot concerning what Franklin called "Improvements in Agriculture." Assuring Eliot that his essays on husbandry were better than most published by English authors who knew little of America, Franklin kept Eliot abreast of the new foreign publications, shipping him books such as Robert Maxwell's *Select Transactions of the Honourable the Society of Improvers in the Knowledge of Agriculture in Scotland* (1743). As the title of Maxwell's publication indicates, societies dedicated to improving and circulating knowledge about agriculture were already springing up in the British Isles and on the Continent.[18]

Franklin also influenced the international conversation about political economy with his *Observations Concerning the Increase of Mankind, Peopling of Countries, &c.* He wrote the essay in 1751 and first circulated it in manuscript among his friends, then published it in 1755 as an addendum to a Boston pamphlet on another subject. Reissued multiple times over the next decades, Franklin's *Observations* interested not just Americans but Europeans because it probed the relations among population growth, subsistence, and statecraft. Franklin wrote the essay in response to the passage in June 1750 of the Iron Act, which restricted the iron processing industry in the colonies because of the threat it posed to England's manufactories. The act also eliminated duties on exported colonial pig and bar iron, encouraging the export of this product, which England lacked. Franklin argued that these new restrictions would hinder America's rapidly growing population. Unlike the old, tired nation of England, Franklin asserted, the population in the vast territory of young America would double every twenty-five years. This calculation quickly became gospel truth among thinkers in both Europe and America, and was often repeated in the decades that followed in such works as *Wealth of Nations* and Malthus's *Essay on the Principle of Population.*[19]

By the time he arrived in London, in 1757, Franklin was known not only as an expert on electricity but as an authority on population and political economy. During the nearly two decades he was based in the city, between 1757 and 1775, he acquired a circle of personal contacts in England, Scotland, and Paris among the authorities on political economy and enlightened agriculture. Two trips to Scotland introduced him to its illuminati: David Hume, William Robertson, and Lord Kames, to whom Franklin described his Scotland visits as "the *densest* Happiness I have met with in any Part of my Life." Thereafter he kept the Scottish group abreast of his economic preoccupations, sending Kames a copy of his *Observations* while Kames sent him his essay on the "preferable Use of Oxen in Agriculture." The self-proclaimed authority on the local terrain of British America, Franklin explained to Kames the main difference in the political economies of England's three provinces, Scotland, Ireland, and America. "Confin'd by the Sea," Franklin wrote of Scotland and Ireland, "they can scarcely increase in Numbers, Wealth and

Strength so as to overbalance England. But America, an immense Territory, favour'd by Nature with all Advantages of Climate, Soil, great navigable Rivers and Lakes, &c. must become a great Country, populous and mighty; and will in a less time than is generally conceiv'd be able to shake off any Shackles that may be impos'd on her, and perhaps place them on the Imposers."[20]

Yet while attuned to English and Scottish writing on political economy, Franklin gradually fell under the sway of the économistes, whose publications became known in Britain especially through their journal, *Éphémérides du citoyen*. Franklin betrayed some enthusiasm for the French principle of free trade in grain as early as 1766, when he published an article in the *London Chronicle* under the pseudonym "Arator" (Plowman). The article opposed the British government's refusal to allow English farmers to export their crops to Europe, where they could get a high price because of the failed wheat crops there, requiring them instead to sell their crops at home so that the English could buy wheat more cheaply. "I Am one of that class of people that feeds you all, and at present is abus'd by you all; in short I am a *Farmer*," Franklin wrote. A French translation of the "Arator" article appeared in *Éphémérides du citoyen* in February 1767.[21]

Franklin met many of the économistes when he lived briefly in Paris in 1767, and he forged a number of lifelong friendships during this time. Arriving from London, he was immediately absorbed into Quesnay's circle. "You, the wise man, the geometrician, the physician, the man whom nature allows to unveil her secrets," cooed Du Pont de Nemours to Franklin soon after Franklin had returned to London. Encouraged by Franklin, they imagined British America—and later the United States—as the laboratory in which their theories could be tested and realized.[22]

Franklin's closest friend in this group was the physician and translator Jacques Barbeu-Dubourg. For decades after Franklin's Paris visit, the two kept up an active correspondence about many matters, including the doctrines of the "Philosophes oeconomistes," as Barbeu-Dubourg called Quesnay's circle. Barbeu-Dubourg was instrumental in introducing the new phenomenon of American political economic thought to a French readership. He published a French translation of John Dickinson's *Letters from a*

Farmer in Pennsylvania (1768), one of the first pamphlets to lay out the American case against British economic policies, thereby placing this rather narrow work of argumentation into a broader international context of economic debate. Barbeu-Dubourg also made sure that Franklin, back in London, kept up to date with the doctrines of the économistes by shipping him the most recent editions of *Éphémérides du citoyen*. "Those who nurture and perfect the arts that are particularly useful to their nation are the fathers of those nations," wrote Barbeu-Dubourg to Franklin, "but those who nurture and perfect Agriculture, that art of arts, whose utility is universal, are in some sense the fathers of humanity."[23]

Thanking Du Pont de Nemours for his new book, *Physiocracie*, Franklin declared himself smitten with the doctrines of the French économistes. "There is such a Freedom from local and national Prejudices and Partialities, so much Benevolence to Mankind in general, so much Goodness mixt with the Wisdom, in the Principles of your new Philosophy, that I am perfectly charm'd with them, and wish I could have staid in France for some time, to have studied in your School, that I might, by conversing with its Founders have made myself quite a Master of that Philosophy. . . . It is from your Philosophy only that the Maxims of a contrary and more happy Conduct are to be drawn, which I therefore sincerely wish may grow and increase till it becomes the governing Philosophy of the human Species, as it must be that of superior Beings in better Worlds."[24]

After his short stay in Paris in 1767, Franklin's letters to his Scottish and American correspondents brimmed with enthusiasm for the doctrines of the économistes. "The true Source of Riches is Husbandry," he confided to the Philadelphia physician Cadwalader Evans in 1768. "Agriculture is truly *productive* of *new wealth*; Manufactures only change Forms." The next year Franklin sent Evans four French works on silkworms and their favorite food, mulberry leaves. He encouraged Americans to persist in silkworm culture despite all obstacles, citing the model of France. He also pressed the principles of the économistes on Kames. "Food is *always* necessary to *all*," explained Franklin, "and much the greatest Part of the Labour of Mankind is employ'd in raising Provisions for the Mouth. Is not this kind of Labour therefore the fittest to be the Standard by which to measure the Values of all other Labour, and consequently of all other Things whose Value depends on the Labour of making or procuring them?" He wrote in the margins of Allan Ramsay's *Thoughts on the Origin and Nature of Government* (1769) that "the Produce of the Earth is the only Source of Revenue."[25]

By the late 1760s, colonial Americans had become increasingly enmeshed in the international debate about the nature and causes of the wealth of nations. The American Revolution culminated in a broad emancipatory agenda that included demands for political self-rule and the establishment of republican government. But its origins lay in the colonists' objections to British taxation policies within the mercantile system, which Americans understood in the context of a constitutional dispute about the nature and location of sovereignty. The writings of the French, Scots, and English on international trade in agriculture and manufactures were of great relevance to revolutionary Americans. Smith's *Wealth of Nations*, published the same year as the Declaration of Independence, reminded the world that Americans' demands for liberation from British mercantile restrictions were leading them to much broader political horizons. The American people, Adam Smith wrote, were feeling "a degree of importance which perhaps, the greatest subjects of Europe scarce feel. From shopkeepers, tradesmen, and attornies, they are become statesmen and legislators," ready to found an empire they believed would be the greatest in the world.[26] It would be up to these new statesmen and legislators to decide how to farm and how to trade in the post-independence era.

A Nation of Farmers or a Nation of Manufacturers?

Would the new United States be a nation of farmers or a nation of manufacturers—or both? This debate gripped Americans in the wake of the Revolution, which abruptly released the thirteen British colonies from mercantilist trade restrictions and freed them to trade with the rest of the world. With the economic future of the new republic in the balance, the doctrines of the French, British, and Scottish political economists now became acutely relevant.

As they had in Europe for the past several decades, agricultural societies sprang up around the United States, from South Carolina to New England. At Yale College, President Ezra Stiles wondered whether to introduce "Agriculture" into the curriculum as a requirement. The American Philosophical Society proclaimed agriculture to be "the principal source of prosperity and wealth" in the new United States. To pursue any other calling would be "perverting the order of nature, nay, opposing the will of nature's God." Americans filled their libraries with the many works from France, Scotland, England, and elsewhere on the new science of enlightened agriculture, while cautioning that the United States required its own ideas and techniques. Thomas Jefferson argued against adopting the ideas of Europeans willy-nilly when local conditions in America—especially "the immensity of land"—called for different responses. "The political oeconomists of Europe have established it as a principle that every state should endeavour to manufacture for itself: and this principle, like many others, we transfer to America, without calculating the difference of circumstance which should often produce a difference of result."[27]

Europeans watched the development of the U.S. economy with interest. They learned from J. Hector St. John de Crèvecoeur, the French expatriate who had farmed for many years in America, that the American farmer was the happiest creature on earth. Crèvecoeur's *Letters from an American Farmer* (1782), written to a fictitious "enlightened" recipient in England and soon republished in France, celebrated mild government as the cradle of prosperity. "Where is that station which can confer a more substantial system of felicity than that of an American farmer, possessing freedom of action, freedom of thoughts, ruled by a mode of government which requires but little from us?" he asked. Under the pseudonym "Normano-Americanus," Crèvecoeur also published his *Traité de la culture des pommes-de-terre, et des differens usages qu'en font les habitans des États-Unis de l'Amérique* (1782), a treatise instructing Europeans to unshackle themselves from darkness, prejudice, and despotism by pioneering the enlightened cultivation of the American potato.[28]

The most influential writer on agricultural topics for postrevolutionary Americans, in fact, was not American but English: the farmer Arthur Young. His numerous works—beginning with *The Farmer's Letters to the People of England* (1767)—advocated farming

practices based on reason, fact, and experiments to an audience
that included both American and French enthusiasts. Quesnay was
such an admirer that he sent his sons to live on Young's farm.[29]
Young's ideas resembled those of the économistes, but in English
dress, and so able to reach an American audience in a way that
Quesnay and his circle could not.

One of Young's American disciples was the Maryland planter
and judge John Beale Bordley. Bordley's *Summary View of the
Courses of Crops, in the Husbandry of England & Maryland* (1784) promoted a "Revolution in Farming" that consisted of crop rotation
along lines promoted by Young.[30] Bordley had posed in 1770 for his
friend, the painter Charles Willson Peale, in an allegorical portrait
that highlighted colonial Americans' irksome agricultural relationship with Britain. Bordley points to a statue of British liberty while
the signs of Britain's violation of American liberties—the torn documents declaiming "Imperial and Civil Law"—lie at Bordley's feet.
The tree heavy with ripe peaches signifies America's agricultural
abundance; the sheep gently grazing illustrate America's ability to
prosper without importing British woolens. English works on agricultural innovation such as Young's *Farmer's Letters* remained influential to Americans even after independence, as they sought to
align their economy with the new realities of the international market. Bordley also helped encourage the founding in 1785 of the
Philadelphia Society for Promoting Agriculture.

Arthur Young was a great self-promoter and cultivated the good
graces of every influential patron he could. He courted the attentions
of his own king, George III, while simultaneously tending to the
president of the new American republic, George Washington. Both
Georges hoped to claim to the title of farmer-in-chief of their respective realms, and they kept up to date on the latest treatises on
enlightened farming. "Farmer George," as George III became
known, maintained a farm at Windsor dedicated in particular to
experimental sheep intended to improve the quality of British wool.
From the king himself Young received the gift of a Spanish Merino
ram named Don, an event Young proudly commemorated with an
illustration in his journal, the *Annals of Agriculture*.[31]

Similarly interested in new farming practices, George
Washington struck up a correspondence with Young in which they

The elaborate symbolism surrounding the Maryland planter and judge
John Beale Bordley in Charles Willson Peale's portrait of 1770 alludes to
British America's agricultural relationship with the mother country.
(Courtesy National Gallery of Art, Washington, D.C.)

exchanged what Washington called "data": agricultural advice, books and magazines on agriculture, seeds, and plants. "The system of Agriculture (if the epithet of system can be applied to it) which is in use in this part of the United States, is as unproductive to the practitioners as it is ruinous to the landholders," Washington complained to Young. Washington considered Young's *Annals of Agriculture* a farmers' bible for grounding agricultural in "experimental knowledge" rather than "old customs." While attending the federal Constitutional Convention in 1787, Washington presented six volumes of the *Annals* to the Philadelphia Society for Promoting Agriculture. Washington worried that the abundance of

American land—and the costliness of labor both slave and free—was discouraging American farmers from exploiting the real fecundity of the soil. By contrast, in England, where land was dear and labor cheap, the farmers "improve and cultivate highly." Washington and Young's letters freely compared the precise price of slave labor in America with free labor in England (though on the whole slavery remained a relatively minor strand of this conversation). Young flattered his "brother farmer" (as he addressed George Washington), asserting that agricultural reform would make Washington's name a byword for enlightened farming around the world. Invoking the agricultural reforms of Frederick the Great of Prussia, Young reminded Washington and the "enlightened legislators" of America that the president's fame worked for the good of society and the "good of agriculture." The world would "send new votaries to the Plough because Washington has attended to it." In 1847 a volume of Young's correspondence with Washington billed the departed president as a farmer freed from "the dark ages" who was not only ahead of his own time but ahead even of the present one.[32]

Washington's interest in enlightened agriculture led him to become one of the earliest promoters of landscape painting in the United States. Influenced by such British painters as Uvedale Price, Washington admired paintings in the so-called picturesque style that mixed the controlled, rational, improved garden with the natural, untamed landscape. William Winstanley's painting of the Hudson River, which hung at Mount Vernon, epitomized the style. As dawn lights the sky, a well-fed farmer drives his horse to drink from the broad waters of the Hudson, a major commercial artery linking the Atlantic port of New York City to the American interior. Framing this scene of commercial possibility, the dark, untamed forest hints at the wild nature that was still thought to reign in the American interior. Uvedale Price sent Washington the second volume of his *Essay on the Picturesque* (1798), describing the work as peculiarly adapted to "the picturesque character of american scenery." Price assured Washington that by opposing "systematic despotism," the president had done for politics what he himself was doing for gardens, freeing them from the formal tyranny of "prevailing systems" and "the tamest uniformity."[33]

An admirer of the picturesque style of painting, George Washington hung
William Winstanley's View of the North [Hudson] River (Morning) *(1793)*
at Mount Vernon. (Courtesy of Mount Vernon Ladies' Association)

The doctrines of the économistes found their most vocal American exponent in the gentleman planter George Logan. Descended from a prominent and wealthy family of Pennsylvania Quakers, Logan was practically destined to be interested in agricultural reform. His grandfather James Logan had been secretary to William Penn, and with the fortune James Logan amassed as a Philadelphia merchant he assembled one of the largest libraries in colonial America. At nearly twenty-six hundred volumes, the Bibliotheca Loganiana (as he called it) represented the range of human learning, which by now included books on agriculture. James Logan had also performed experiments with maize that had earned the praise of Linnaeus and were published in the *Philosophical Transactions* of the Royal Society. In the 1720s, James Logan built the stately, Georgian-style mansion he christened Stenton near Philadelphia, filling its vast acreage with experimental gardens and farms. Benjamin Franklin visited James Logan at Stenton and sent him books from the Library

Company of Philadelphia, while in return Logan sent Franklin copies of Jared Eliot's pamphlets on husbandry.[34]

George Logan was born amid this intellectual ferment at Stenton in 1753. In the early years of the American Revolution, he left to study at the medical school of the University of Edinburgh. There he became acquainted with the recently popularized practice of crop rotation and bought Lord Kames's pamphlet on agriculture. On a brief journey to Paris in 1779–80, he visited his grandfather's old friend Franklin at Passy, where he may also have met some of Franklin's circle of économistes. Once back in the United States in 1780, Logan took up the task of overseeing his grandfather's library (now known as the Loganian Library), and he reassured Franklin that he hoped "to follow your laudable example in being constantly employed to the good of mankind in general, & in a particular manner to the prosperity of this rising Country." Finding the Logan family fortune much reduced, he laid aside his plans of becoming a doctor and instead turned to the project of revitalizing the exhausted fields of Stenton with a system of crop rotation, gypsum fertilizer, and potato cultivation, which he described, citing Lord Kames's publication on agriculture, as "one of the greatest improvements of modern husbandry." His promotion of gypsum fertilizer caused one contemporary to dismiss him as a "plaister of Paris philanthropist," but it earned him the admiration of Jefferson, who called Logan "the best farmer in Penylva. both in theory and practice."[35]

By the late 1780s Logan had become convinced that the principles of the American Revolution—and of nature itself—were being subverted by the rise of a new class of manufacturers and wealthy merchants who were restoring the aristocracy the Revolution had worked to demolish. Alexander Hamilton's "Report on Public Credit," issued in January 1790, which advocated funding the national debt at face value, seemed to encapsulate the new dogmas of a returning aristocracy. Consulting the books in the library of Stenton—by Quesnay, Turgot, and Le Mercier de La Rivière— George Logan poured out his frustrations on paper. Often capitalizing the *F* in *Farmer*, he issued a series of pamphlets in 1791 that exalted agriculture as a science. More than any other American of his age, he echoed the axioms of the économistes Franklin had

known in Paris. The world was "alone indebted to a few enlightened men in France" for the discovery of the "essential truths of
political economy" that promoted "the happiness of men united in
society," Logan began in his first pamphlet, *Letters, Addressed to the
Yeomanry of the United States* (1791). Issued under the pseudonym "A
Farmer," the pamphlet attacked the Federalist policy of repaying
the public debt by imposing duties on imports, what Logan called
"indirect taxes." Instead, he argued, taxes should derive from the
annual produce of the land, what he called a "direct tax." Logan
went farther than any of his American contemporaries in promoting the pet project of the économistes: the single, direct tax on land,
a measure deemed impractical by Jefferson and Franklin. According
to Logan, the direct tax was the only solution for an "enlightened
people" who wanted to support their liberty-loving government for
necessary expenses rather than "supporting the parade or extrava-
gance of the servants of the people, or in bribery and corruption."[36]

Logan's essay epitomized the kind of thinking that Hamilton
hoped to crush with his *Report on the Subject of Manufactures* (1791).
Although he had courted his future wife, Elizabeth Schuyler, with
fantasies of planting turnips by her side, Hamilton was in fact a
chronic refuter of farmers. Written when he was only twenty, his
pamphlet *The Farmer Refuted* (1775) had argued that agriculturally
based polities such as the American colonies were by definition dependent on manufacturing nations such as Britain. Sixteen years
later, as the first secretary of the treasury in a young nation struggling to survive among commercial giants, Hamilton urged that
the federal government be strengthened through both political and
economic means. His *Report on Manufactures* advocated subsidies to
industry, the regulation of trade with moderate tariffs to support
American manufactures, and the raising of revenue to pay the expenses of government. Although there is no evidence that
Hamilton read the work of the French économistes in their original form, his repudiation of their doctrines in the *Report on
Manufactures* is a paraphrase of Adam Smith's criticisms of the
French group's classification of manufactures as unproductive labor. The *Report* also shows his knowledge of the economic argu-
ments of James Steuart, the British economic writer Malachy
Postlethwayt, Montesquieu, David Hume, and Jacques Necker, the

finance minister of Louis XVI.[37] The *Report*, in short, while addressing an American question, did so in the context of a Europe-wide debate about political economy.

Hamilton opened the *Report on Manufactures* by quoting at length the arguments of the proponents of agriculture, immediately granting their major thesis. "It ought readily to be conceded," he wrote, "that the cultivation of the earth—as the primary and most certain source of national supply—as the immediate and chief source of subsistence to man—as the principal source of those materials which constitute the nutriment of other kinds of labor—as including a state most favourable to the freedom and independence of the human mind—one, perhaps, most conducive to the multiplication of the human species—has *intrinsically a strong claim to pre-eminence over every other kind of industry.*" Echoing Smith's objections to the économistes, however, Hamilton pointed out that agriculture did not have exclusive claim to productivity, and that it was encouraged rather than suppressed by manufactures. To anoint agriculture as the primary engine of national wealth required "more evidence," as well as "facts and calculations." A decade later, Hamilton continued to publicly frown upon the French supporters of an agriculturally centered political economy, mocking President Jefferson as "a disciple of *Turgot*."[38]

To George Logan, Hamilton's pro-manufacturing stance represented nothing less than a step back into the dark ages. Like all unenlightened doctrines, Hamilton's proposals were "inveloped in darkness and mystery," as Logan put it in his *Letters Addressed to the Yeomanry of the United States* (1793). Hamilton's banks, public credit, indirect taxes, and other "oracles" presaged the return to the Middle Ages when scheming ministers threw a veil of obscurity over the workings of government. "Kings, priests, and crafty financiers have been too successful in rendering government an impenetrable mystery to the people," wrote Logan. Logan argued instead that the laws of nature clearly lit the path of human happiness. His *Address on the Natural and Social Order of the World* (1798) was among the most systematic American treatments of the idea of the "natural order" that had gripped Mirabeau three decades earlier. Aiming for "the general happiness of Mankind," Logan argued that agriculture formed the basis of reasonable human government.

"The law of Nature, as supported by reason, prescribes us this course, as the only just foundation of our own individual happiness or safety," Logan intoned, while reminding his readers that eighteen of twenty Americans were farmers, while only one in twenty were mechanics and manufacturers.[39]

The Happy Science of Political Economy

After George Logan, others continued to look forward to a day when agriculture, properly pursued as part of the larger science of society, could produce a happier world. Thomas Paine, in *Agrarian Justice* (1797), which was printed in England, France, and the United States, argued that dispossession represented a denial of an individual's natural right to land, what he called man's "natural inheritance" from God himself. From Virginia, Logan's contemporary, the planter and politician John Taylor of Caroline, promoted enlightened agriculture as a way to save the nation and the South, a thesis that led him to become one of the first theorists of states' rights. His books *Arator* (1813) and *An Inquiry into the Principles and Policy of the Government of the United States* (1814) railed against the rise of the manufacturing class and an "aristocracy of paper and patronage" that was reminiscent of "the dark ages." Like Crèvecoeur before him, he held farmers up as the prophets of an "enlightened age." Agricultural societies continued to spread, publishing an array of periodicals, such as the *Agricultural Museum* (1810), the *New England Farmer* (1822), and the *Farmer's Register* (1832). Edward Hicks's painting *The Cornell Farm* (1848) commemorated the tidy rationalism of James Cornell's farm, whose livestock had been honored with a premium from the Bucks County Agricultural Society.[40]

The political economists of the nineteenth century carried forward the nugget idea of the first self-described enlightened farmers of the previous century. They too hoped that human reason could perceive the ostensibly natural workings of agriculture and commerce and harness them to create social happiness. In the wake of the pessimistic theories of the British economists Thomas Malthus and David Ricardo, which gained traction in the early decades of the nineteenth century and emphasized scarcity and the dire specter of poverty, a number of Americans upheld the more optimistic

Edward Hicks, The Cornell Farm *(1848), depicts the rational, orderly farm of James Cornell. (Courtesy National Gallery of Art, Washington, D.C.)*

contribution of the eighteenth-century économistes.[41] Continuing to cite the publications of the aging économistes, they also looked to the younger generation, who were adapting those theories to a new post–French Revolutionary context.

One of these was Jean-Baptiste Say, part of a group of French theorists swayed by Adam Smith who flourished in the wake of the French Revolution and became known as the *idéologues* because they aimed to reduce the science of society to a series of positive truths that were as empirical and certain as those in the physical sciences. Say's *Traité d'économie politique* (1803), which promoted free trade, went through numerous English-language American editions beginning with Clement Biddle's edition of 1821 and was adopted by Harvard and Yale as a textbook in the middle of the 1820s. In the sixth American edition of Say's political economy, the editor, Clement Biddle, assured readers that no other authors were "exerting a more powerful and enduring influence on the well-being" of the French and Americans as Adam Smith and Jean-Baptiste Say. Say's book announced the benefits of political economy as a "science" with "general laws" first discovered by Smith. It was saturated with modifiers for the noun *happiness:* he wrote of social happiness, national happiness, public happiness, and domestic happiness—all to be attained through the new science of political economy.[42]

Jefferson counted Jean-Baptiste Say among the group of French thinkers—both the aging économistes and their younger colleagues, the idéologues—with whom he continued to maintain a lively correspondence about political economy in the first decades of the nineteenth century. They provided a counterweight not just to Malthus and Ricardo, but also to Montesquieu's earlier exaltation of the superior constitutional monarchy of Britain in *De l'esprit des loix* (1748), a work whose "political heresies" increasingly left Jefferson cold in the years after the American Revolution. Expressing interest in buying a plantation near Charlottesville, Say sent a new edition of his work on political economy to Jefferson in 1814 with assurances that it established political economy as part of the "realm of positive knowledge" that could aid in "the improvement of the social arts and the happiness of mankind." Another friend was Du Pont de Nemours, who had fled France with his family during the French Revolution and made a home in the United States (and whose son Éleuthère Irénée du Pont in 1802 founded the company today known as DuPont). Du Pont de Nemours continued to promote the superiority and priority of the French économistes against the British school of economy represented by Malthus and Ricardo. He informed Jefferson that Thomas Malthus—whose *Essay on the Principle of Population* (1798) had forecast a growing population that would outstrip the food supply—was merely restating the truths first established by "les Economistes français": that "the measure of subsistence is the measure of population, because it is impossible to employ more workers than one can feed."[43]

Jefferson also popularized the work of the French idéologues by publishing an English translation of the work of the French philosopher Antoine Louis Claude Destutt de Tracy, a slightly older contemporary of Say. Retitling Destutt de Tracy's work *A Treatise on Political Economy* (1817), Jefferson wrote introductory notes that read like a celebratory genealogy of French progress in social thought from the économistes on. "Political economy, in modern times, assumed the form of a regular science, first in the hands of the political sect in France, called the Economists. They made it a branch only of a comprehensive system, on the natural order of Societies. Quesnia [*sic*], first, Gournay, Le Trosne, Turgot, & Dupont de Nemours, the enlightened, philanthropic, and venerable citizen now of the United States, led the way in these developments, and gave to our enquiries the direction they have since observed." Adam Smith too had published a "rational" book on political economy, charged Jefferson, but his need to insert detail about principles now generally accepted made *Wealth of Nations* "prolix and tedious." The new works from France were superior to those of Smith and the économistes. Unlike the économistes, who had imagined their system to have already reached a state of perfection because it was perfectly aligned with the unchanging dictates of nature and reason, Jefferson allowed that Say and Destutt de Tracy had advanced the subject of political economy to conform to the fluctuating realities of the world, and so displayed "greater maturity of subject." It was in part through Destutt de Tracy's work that the new terms *social science* and *ideology* were imported into the United States from their French context, which had been an exploration of the social means of achieving human happiness. *Social science* appeared in Jefferson's translation of Destutt de Tracy's *Treatise on Political Economy*, while *ideology* appeared a few years earlier in a letter Jefferson wrote describing Destutt de Tracy's work. Jefferson defended such neologisms from the French language as essential to the "progress of ideas." The court of public opinion would accept or reject the new words based on whether they were useful.[44]

The optimism of the first French economists continued to percolate through discussions of American political economy during the nineteenth century. The Scottish earl James Lauderdale's anti-mercantilist *An Inquiry into the Nature and Origins of Public Wealth* (1804) taught American readers about what he called "the works of all the Oeconomists." Lauderdale's writings deeply influenced Daniel Raymond, whose *Thoughts on Political Economy* (1820) berated his fellow Americans for failing to produce a native treatise on political economy, which he described as "the most interesting and important science" because it was the most concerned with "human happiness." Thomas Cooper's *Lectures on the Elements of*

Political Economy (1826)—the first American textbook on political economy—distinguished between the older subject of moral philosophy and the new subject of political economy, a "science" that prepared students to participate in improving national life. Cooper plunged into the work of "the French 'Economists;' at the head of whom was Dr. Francois Quesnay." Although Cooper (like Adam Smith before him) found the French system defective because it exaggerated agriculture's contributions to national wealth and underrated the value added by merchants and manufacturers, he nonetheless praised Quesnay and his circle for doing much "to introduce the genuine principles of free trade, and the liberal notions that characterize the modern science of Political Economy." Henry Carey's *Principles of Political Economy* (1837) likewise defined political economy as a science that treated "man as a reasonable animal" with the aim of increasing human "improvement" and "enjoyment." Carey distantly echoed the French économistes in his book *The Past, the Present and the Future* (1848) by declaring the law of nature to be the key to human happiness. "The volume now offered to the public is designed to demonstrate the existence of a simple and beautiful law of nature, governing man in all his efforts for the maintenance and improvement of his condition, a law so powerful and universal that escape from it is impossible, but which, nevertheless, has heretofore remained unnoticed."[45]

This then was the long American sunset of the French économistes of the eighteenth century, who with their coterie of international friends had first dared hope that human reason directed to the bounty of the warm earth might free humanity from worry and want. Their intellectual heirs continued to advance political economy as the supreme science of society, conceiving of society in its most generous terms as the vessel for the realization of human aspirations for earthly happiness. In 1849, Thomas Carlyle skewered political economy as "the dismal science." Yet American political economy was not dismal at all as it emerged from the eighteenth century but an exuberant and eclectic program for human happiness. Well into the nineteenth century, enlightened farming remained as Jefferson had defined it in 1817: "the employment of our first parents in Eden, the happiest we can follow, and the most important to our country."[46]

CHAPTER EIGHT

Republics Versus Monarchies

T HE ENLIGHTENED AMERICAN REVOLUTION was made, not given. Between 1760 and 1800, Americans invented a new political vocabulary that described their kingless republic and its people as being or becoming enlightened. In a burst of intellectual and lexical creativity, they began to modify a series of political terms with the adjective *enlightened*. In roughly their order of appearance after about 1760, *nation, people, public opinion, legislatures, statesmen, citizens,* and *policies* all began to be described by American revolutionaries as enlightened or the product of enlightenment. In pamphlets, newspapers, speeches, books, congressional debates, and private letters, the vocabulary of political enlightenment swelled in importance and explanatory power to celebrate American republicanism and its crowning document, the federal Constitution, a "luminous body" whose "light was ... so clear that nothing more was wanted."[1]

Like Adam naming the animals in the Garden of Eden, Americans after 1760 christened each new republican event, structure, hero, and document as enlightened. By 1800 they had invested the whole of the American Revolution with the language of enlightenment, not as an objective fact but as a conviction in their minds that with it they had started down the road toward an era of human happiness.

The major innovation in the new political meaning of enlightenment was that it was secular, human-centered, and historical. An intellectual scaffold rather than a program for action, political enlightenment appealed to reason and progress as the essential, external, and unimpeachable authorities against which new republican institutions were to be measured. In contrast to the earlier idea of enlightenment as a religious awakening cosmic in scale and potentially eternal in duration, political enlightenment located human beings in a human-centered history that stretched from antiquity to the present and looked to a golden future forged by human effort. This progressive view of human history acknowledged that some past eras had been enlightened but also insisted that the present—the urgent *now* that propelled so much revolutionary writing—was the most enlightened era, freed from the superstition and received authority that had literally darkened earlier ages. The idea of political enlightenment committed revolutionary Americans to a language of relentless futurity and progress, one that painted the prerevolutionary past as an age of primitive darkness and the nonrepublican present—the present of European monarchies—as the fossilized relic of a barbaric past from which the republican Revolution had delivered Americans. The *Massachusetts Gazette* of 1784 warned newly independent Americans that if they did not read the public papers to keep up with affairs, "ignorance may gradually overspread this new enlightened country, and tyranny advance as knowledge decays, until darkness and slavery wrap this glorious land in all the horrors of despotick sway."[2]

David Edwin's *Apotheosis of Washington* (1800) captured the promise of happy futurity at the core of republican enlightenment and the ease with which Americans continued to mix religious and political enlightenment. As a winged cherub lowers a wreath onto his bewigged head, the barefoot president ascends from Mount Vernon into a republican heaven, where he is greeted by the revolutionary war heroes Richard Montgomery and Joseph Warren. Wrapped in Christlike robes and gesturing toward the earth below, Washington monitors the rising glory of the young republic from his perch in the clouds.

The earliest biographies of Washington also hailed the recently deceased president as the embodiment of the enlightened republic.

David Edwin, Apotheosis of Washington, *1800. (Yale University Art Gallery)*

Mason Locke Weems's popular life of Washington praised the president's "enlightened mind" and his leadership of an enlightened people, while John Marshall's multivolume *Life of Washington* (1804–7) dwelled on the enlightened nature of the American Revolution and Washington's role in steering the enlightened republic the Revolution had secured.[3]

It would be easy to dismiss the new political use of *enlightened* as mere wordplay and insist that the real American Revolution lay elsewhere, in the ideas of natural rights and liberties that carried the colonists to independence in the first place, or on the battlefields in which they achieved military victory against Britain. Yet the new political meaning of the word became the secular, historical framework that grounded the ideas of natural rights and liberties in human time, allowing them to take seed and flourish as a result of human effort. Natural rights and liberties presumed the grand historical canvas of enlightenment for their actualization. Without enlightenment, the human condition would remain static or cyclical, forever caught in a loop of typological repetition. Enlightenment presumed progress, the development and growth of political liberties through the ages.

Seen in this way, the idea that a kingless republic was an enlightened one was not incidental to the American Revolution but fundamental to it. It set the Revolution within a framework of temporal meaning, inspiring Americans by affirming that they marched ever forward, ever upward. Americans not only had to conjure that new historical framework into existence, they had to embellish and repeatedly defend it over the next decades as they launched the modern world's first successful kingless republican government.

So thoroughly did the term *enlightened* penetrate the public papers that it became like the air Americans breathed: energized by it, revolutionaries seldom paused to explain it. Today, we often take the Prussian philosopher Immanuel Kant's essay "An Answer to the Question, What is Enlightenment?" as a universal definition of the eighteenth-century view. Published in German in 1784, Kant's essay urged the people of Prussia to use reason in both religious and governmental matters to grow out of their political immaturity: "Sapere aude!" (dare to know), he commanded. Written for an audience that included King Frederick II—who promoted legal, educational, and ecclesiastical reform in Prussia within the confines of absolutist monarchy—Kant's essay is best seen as a single, local effort to define *enlightenment* rather than a universal truth about the term. In fact, people all over Europe and the Americas were struggling to explain what it meant to be enlightened in the political realm. "What is enlightenment?" asked one of Kant's exasperated Prussian contemporaries. "This question, which is almost as important as what is truth, should indeed be answered before one begins enlightening! And still I have never found it answered!"[4]

Kant's essay was essentially unknown in revolutionary America, but its royal context is a reminder that newly republicanized

Americans asserted their enlightenment at a time when monarchs were cloaking themselves in similar language: Frederick II of Prussia, Catherine the Great of Russia, Louis XV of France, Joseph II of Austria, and Carlos III of Spain all launched reforms in the name of enlightenment. It was widely accepted in European circles that enlightened despotism was one of the few available means to secure a variety of social, religious, and educational reforms. Revolutionary Americans were not cut off from these currents of thought. Leading revolutionaries and major American libraries had copies of Frederick II's *Anti-Machiavel* (1740; English translation 1741), written in league with his protégé Voltaire, an "Antidote" to Machiavelli's *The Prince* that argued that kings could be a source of justice and good for their people. From Britain a slight variation of the theme appeared. The British fancied themselves weaned of absolutism thanks to the Glorious Revolution of 1688–89, which had placed parliamentary constraints on the power of the monarch. Yet they not only retained their royals in the age of revolutions but happily settled down to enjoy their monarchs' comforting familiarity and harmless antics. At the very moment of American independence in 1776, the British took the opportunity to announce that they inhabited an "enlightened age" that admired the "rights of human nature" and disdained war as a relic of a "barbarous" past.[5]

Americans' distinctive contribution to the Atlantic-wide debate about political enlightenment was to insist to an international audience of monarchies that a kingless, republican state could join the forward-looking nations that would leave barbarity behind in the march toward human happiness. Never universal, *enlightenment* had distinct local meanings. For Americans, it answered these urgent questions: Could the republican United States enter the enlightened age, and by what means? Could kingless republicanism and government exclusively by the people be established and perpetuated amid powerful monarchies? How should knowledge be diffused among the American people so that an enlightened public could continue to uphold republican government? Were republican institutions of enlightenment more effective at nurturing learning than the monarchical and aristocratic institutions of enlightenment that had successfully carpeted Europe with universities, museums, and learned societies since the Renaissance?

Seen in this way, revolutionary Americans' insistence that monarchs were peddlers of ignorance and that only republican institutions could secure enlightenment represented a massive propaganda campaign to make real what was in fact untried modern republican theory. It flew in the face of the lived realities of the royally sponsored institutions that had not only enlightened Europe but had also helped educate the American revolutionaries themselves, in institutions both in colonial America and in Europe. The onerous task undertaken by revolutionary Americans was to prove that republicanism rather than monarchy was the golden path to an enlightened future. In this, they were only partially successful.

Enlightened Republicans and Enlightened Monarchs

Americans had not always abhorred monarchy. In fact, anti-monarchism had come late and suddenly in the imperial crisis that until 1776 had focused primarily on taxation and the perceived violation of the colonists' rights of political self-determination. Although colonial Americans had for over a century preached a steady stream of diatribes against tyrannical kings, monarchy itself had not come under attack. As the Boston minister Charles Turner put it in 1773, Americans were trained "from their cradles, in a most affectionate dutiful respect to, and confidence in the House of Hanover."[6] Even in 1774 and 1775, many Americans assumed that George III would continue to rule them. In the ancient style of the royal petition, they directed their complaints about Parliament to their king as their protector of last resort.[7]

But abruptly in January 1776, Thomas Paine's *Common Sense* declared monarchy to be offensive to an enlightened age. In the chapter "Of Monarchy and Hereditary Succession," Paine argued that the origins of monarchy lay deep in a "delusion" in the human past when artificial distinctions began to sift a privileged few from the original equality of humanity at the Creation. Removing the "dark covering of antiquity" showed that the original king was nothing more than "the principal ruffian of some restless gang," a man of "savage manners" whose origins were forgotten in eras of "few or no records." From the moment of the first kings among the ancient Greeks and Romans, the whole institution had contradicted "the authority of scripture." Promoting war and violating the "equal right of nature," monarchy was "the popery of Government." Six months later the Declaration of Independence followed up on Paine's theories by placing the American rebellion within secular, human time ("the course of human events") and declaring the king to be a "Tyrant," a relic of an earlier, barbaric age. One of the specific charges against George III was that he used foreign mercenaries against his American subjects, an act of tyranny "scarcely paralleled in the most barbarous ages; and totally unworthy the Head of a civilized nation."[8]

The rise of American political anti-monarchism was rapid and seemingly total. "Is not the Change We have seen astonishing?" asked John Adams in August 1776. "Idolatry to Monarchs, and servility to Aristocratical Pride, was never so totally eradicated from so many Minds in so short a Time." In 1789, Thomas Jefferson assured James Madison that although "we were educated in royalism . . . [t]he rising race are all republicans." New republicans repeatedly flogged European monarchy as a barbaric, premodern, and superstitious relic overtaken by current republican events in which the rights of man were better recognized. George Washington thanked God in 1783 that "the foundation of our Empire was not laid in the gloomy age of Ignorance and Superstition, but at an Epocha when the rights of mankind were better understood and more clearly defined than at any former period." Papering over the fact that the American presidency lodged more power in the nonhereditary, elective chief executive than was enjoyed by Britain's king, Alexander Hamilton concluded his review of the office of the presidency in essay 77 of *The Federalist* with a rhetorical question: "What more can an enlightened and reasonable people desire?" Decades after revolution had secured republican government in the United States, Thomas Jefferson still took pleasure in bundling together six royal memoirs and trial records to form a "Book of Kings" that confirmed every monarch of Europe to be a "fool," an "ideot," or a "hog."[9]

But republican Americans' conviction that monarchy was a fossil relic of a dark age flew in the face of reality in Europe, where monarchies remained not just militarily powerful but culturally dynamic. It was widely accepted there that the best monarchs epitomized the enlightened age by reconciling their interests with those of their subjects. Even today, historians are wont to assume that monarchy must be a retrograde form of government. "Especially in the United States," the editors of a recent volume assert, "there is almost no recognition that anyone ever saw any redeeming value in monarchy or monarchism. . . . Many take it for granted that a real monarchy must be socially backward, politically repressive, intellectually unjustifiable, the last gasp of feudalism, and fit only for the dustbin of history." Yet the terms "enlightened monarch," "enlightened despot," and "enlightened sovereign" were coined in the late eighteenth century to explain the ongoing relevance of monarchs in the age that called itself enlightened. A number of monarchs favored some legal reforms and measures of religious toleration, condemning fanaticism and excessive censorship.[10]

Monarchies, then, were not relics of the past: they were realities of the present. For decades after the American Revolution, the United States and Haiti remained the lone kingless states in a sea of powerful Atlantic monarchies. "American Ministers are acting in Monarchies, and not in Republicks," John Adams noted correctly from Paris in 1783.[11] Americans now had to grapple with the real and demonstrable ways in which monarchy and aristocracy had facilitated the process of enlightenment and continued to do so in Europe. In the wake of independence, they struggled to differentiate what made America's republican schools, universities, presses, and libraries different from and superior to Europe's aristocratic and monarchical institutions of learning.

The monarchies of Europe acted as agents of enlightenment in a number of ways. The active, aggressive bureaucracies of eighteenth-century European monarchs helped push back the power of the church, and admiring references to the idea of a philosopher-king as the guarantor of the people's happiness appeared in some widely disseminated texts. No other bureaucratic structure in seventeenth- and eighteenth-century Europe had equivalent resources to support a thriving cultural and intellectual life, and between roughly 1500 and 1800, many European monarchs had tried to make their courts the monumental expressions of monarchical political policy and cultural patronage. In an age before universities had become the main centers of intellectual life, princely courts nurtured a staggering array of intellectual projects, from science to art and music. The patronage of Europe's monarchies—self-aggrandizing as it might have been—had produced a rich array of scientific and literary societies. Monarchs had given their princely imprimaturs to the Royal Society in Britain; to the Académie des inscriptions et belles-lettres and the Académie royale des sciences in France; to the Saint Petersburg Academy of Sciences in Russia; to the Royal Society of Sciences (founded by King George II of Britain in his capacity as Elector of Hanover) in Germany; and to the Royal Academy of Letters, History, and Antiquities in Sweden. These flourished alongside societies patronized by the higher nobility, such as the Accademia dei Lincei in Rome. "Monarchies and aristocracies are in possession of the voice and influence of every university and academy in Europe," John Adams observed.[12]

Revolutionary Americans needed only to gaze into the recent past to see that British monarchs had been engines of learning and patronage. Although the colonists were forever scorning the extravagant tyrannies of the long-dead Stuarts, the more recent monarchs of England had done much to give institutional shape to colonial intellectual life. The reign of George II (1727–60)—at thirty-three years the longest in the American colonial era—and his queen consort, Caroline, was one of enormous cultural effervescence in both Britain and the American colonies. The Hanoverian monarchs participated in the transformation of London into a modern megalopolis, both the political center of the growing empire and the cultural capital of Britain. The role of the monarch in this transformation was as patron of the arts, sciences, and letters in an increasingly diffused and porous urban culture. Cultural outlets now migrated away from the primary location of the royal court—which still dominated such Continental cities as Berlin, Lisbon, Vienna, Copenhagen, Saint Petersburg, and Stockholm—and began to be integrated into the life of the city itself. Hanoverian London saw the rise of learned societies, coffeehouses, pleasure gardens, salons, theaters, assembly rooms, debating clubs, and art galleries. Attendance at court and familiarity with court etiquette were still essential for London's beau monde, but the royal court was only one of a number of spheres for the cultivation of fashionable identity. The monarchs played a role in nurturing British culture—attending the theater and the opera, and patronizing libraries, scientists, and artists—but so too did other actors and forces: the landed elite and the rising middle orders, the expanding world of print, a vigorous mercantile and industrial base, and a robust culture of satire that thought nothing of mocking George II, his ministers, and "Magna Farta."[13]

The culturally rich and open Hanoverian court in London also became the incubator in which philosophes hatched their plans for reform. George II and Caroline supported Voltaire and Montesquieu, critics of absolutist Continental monarchies. In his *Letters Concerning the English Nation* (1733), Voltaire rhapsodized about Queen Caroline: "She appears as an amiable Philosopher on the Throne, having never let slip one Opportunity of improving the great Talents she receiv'd from Nature, nor of exerting her Beneficence."[14]

British Americans also forged strong personal, intellectual, and patronage ties with the cultural brokers in London, a city one scholar has aptly termed the capital of America. By the early 1770s, British North America ranked as the leading export market for London publishers, importing more English books than all Europe. Remembered today as an American revolutionary, Benjamin Franklin was before 1775 the incarnation of the American colonist who exploited London's possibilities for royal and aristocratic patronage, and he became the major American node connecting other ambitious Americans seeking patronage and connections there. Franklin greeted the coronation of the young King George III with high hopes for the future happiness and virtue of the British people led by the "rising Sun," their young monarch. Taking the opportunity to also heap praise on the king of Prussia's abilities, Franklin assured the London printer William Strahan that the British under George III would be "as happy as they deserve to be." The nation's virtue would rise "Ad Exemplum Regis" (according to the example of the king).[15]

The coronation of George II in 1727 had given American ministers the opportunity to glorify the new monarch and remind him of the royal thanks owed to the American colonies for extending the king's dominions and preaching the gospel in the wilderness. Although New England Puritan ministers had immediately rejected as idolatrous the Stuarts' divine right theory of kingship, they nevertheless produced a number of biblical justifications for kingship more generally. "Thanks be to God that there is the *Protestant House of Hannover* on the Throne over us, who are unto us as the *House of David*," declared the Boston minister Benjamin Colman, who could boast an impressive array of correspondents in London who would agree with his affirmations. None were more joyful at the coronation "than His People in these Colonies," wrote Cotton Mather, another colonist eager for approval in royal circles. The colonists had "improved an horrid *Wilderness* into a *Fruitful Field*, and enlarged the *British Empire* in *America* to the extent of more than Two or Three Hundred Miles." Mather reminded his king of the existence of Harvard, ever ready to receive "His Royal Rays."[16]

The royal rays of George II did reach the colonies, encouraging both directly and indirectly a period of rapid growth of learned institutions. This process was driven by the colonists but made possible by the open, exuberant culture of learning that the Hanoverians had helped nurture in London. The Library Company of Philadelphia relied upon colonists' patronage networks in London to secure a steady supply of lavish books. The American Philosophical Society was modeled on the Royal Society. Four new colleges were founded during George II's reign. Three were in the American colonies: the College of New Jersey (later Princeton, 1746), and King's College (later Columbia, 1754), both chartered by George II, and the College of Pennsylvania (1755). William Smith, in promoting the cause of King's College, noted how surprising it was that the colony of New York had existed for nearly a century in "the Hands of a civilized and enlightned People" without a public seminary of learning, and rejoiced in the "long Succession of Princes, whose Family have ever reckon'd it their greatest Glory to be the Patrons of Freedom." A society for the relief of German Protestants in Pennsylvania received a thousand pounds from George II and a hundred pounds from the princess dowager "with truly royal and princely generosity." The fourth university chartered by George II was the eponymous Georg-August-Universität in Göttingen (1734) in his home state of Hanover, the king's attempt to outdo his archrival the king of Prussia as a patron of learning. Before it became a destination university for American students in the nineteenth century, Göttingen was already helping colonial Americans forge crucial intellectual connections on the European Continent. Benjamin Franklin visited Göttingen in 1766 because he was interested in founding a similar university in Pennsylvania. There he formed what he called the "Göttingen circle" of new scholarly acquaintances: the philologist Johann David Michaelis, the scientist Rudolph Raspe, and the physician Johann Hartmann.[17] The same year Franklin was elected to the Royal Society at Göttingen.

The College of New Jersey also benefited from George II's royal patronage. It was founded by local Presbyterians to train ministers in New Light principles. But hovering above this local sectarian project was George II, whose seal—with its enormous words, "George II by the grace of God"—adorned the official charter of the college that was sent to the colony in 1748. In his funeral sermon for the departed king, the college's president, Samuel Davies, celebrated the faraway George II as the patron of New World learning. "And tho', like the Sun, He shone in a distant Sphere, we felt, most sensibly felt, His benign Influences, cherishing SCIENCE and her Votaries, in this her new-built Temple." The main university building, Nassau Hall (named for William III, prince of Orange and Nassau), housed a full-length portrait of George II.[18]

The consort of George II, Queen Caroline, also quickly established herself as Britain's chief royal patroness of New World science. More intellectually curious than her husband, whose interests tended more toward peerages and hunting, Caroline had established herself as an important advocate for culture even before George ascended the throne. During her thirteen years as the Princess of Wales, she had attempted to form an exciting and visible counterweight to the dreary, queenless court of George I, holding balls and swanning up and down the Thames in the royal barge. From afar the American colonists tracked her ascent into the pinnacle of patronage: the third edition of Joseph Addison's wildly popular play *Cato* contained a dedicatory poem to Caroline, and colonists were aware of her efforts to promote smallpox inoculation. Hans Sloane, author of *A Voyage to the Islands Madera, Barbados, Nieves, S. Christophers and Jamaica* (1707), was also royal physician; Caroline collected Sloane's maps, along with books about the Americas and the South Seas. A regular correspondent of Leibniz, Newton, and the English philosopher Samuel Clarke, Caroline eventually amassed a meticulously organized library of over 2,000 volumes that was the de facto royal library, stocking it with works by Newton, Locke, and Pierre Bayle. After her death, the king donated her collection of 10,500 books to the British Library. Childrearing manuals such as Stephen Philpot's *An Essay on the Advantage of a Polite Education* (1747) held up Queen Caroline as an exemplary modern parent, "for the most part present when Her Children were instructed."[19]

Caroline's coronation in 1727 unleashed a torrent of laudatory poems and sermons in the American colonies. "Fair Princess, Thou!" exclaimed Mather Byles, tireless American monarchist and self-appointed representative of provincial New England to the London capital of the republic of letters. Mark Catesby dedicated the first volume of his lavish *Natural History of Carolina, Florida and the Bahama Islands* (1732) to Queen Caroline. In 1730 she and the king entertained a visiting group of Cherokees at Windsor Castle, as well as Tomochichi, chief of the Lower Creeks, from the colony of Georgia. Conscious of the need to establish a Hanoverian dynastic connection to previous English royal houses, she took a personal interest in horticulture, arraying the royal gardens with statues of Tudor and Stuart monarchs. As her own dynastic contribution multiplied—she and the king produced seven living children—she became known through the empire as its mother, simultaneously bearing heirs to perpetuate the Hanoverian dynasty and gently tending her colonial children. One American minister called her "a Nursing Mother to GOD's Church and People."[20] The queen's patronage of science in the empire was memorialized in a medal that showed her watering a grove of tiny Carolina palms, encircled by the words "Growing Arts Adorn Empire/ Caroline Protecting."

Royal governors in the American colonies also established intellectual connections to the royal center. Jonathan Belcher (1681/2–1757), royal governor at various times of the colonies of Massachusetts, New Hampshire, and New Jersey, epitomized the ways in which political office could translate into the development of intellectual institutions. In a group more often noted for its

Queen Caroline's interests in promoting science across her empire are commemorated in this medal showing her watering a grove of tiny Carolina palms. (John Sigismund Tanner [1728–1775]. Jernegan's Lottery Medal: GROWING ARTS ADORN EMPIRE. 1736. British. Silver, struck. Gift of Edward Holbrook, 1906 [06.136]. The Metropolitan Museum of Art, New York, NY, U.S.A. Image copyright © The Metropolitan Museum of Art. Image Source: Art Resource, NY.)

military achievements and political machinations, Belcher stands out for his intellectual curiosity, expressed in a special fondness for gilded books about monarchy. It would be too ambitious to call Belcher a theorist or philosopher: Belcher read books but he did not ponder them; ideas to him were potential energy, ready for launching into a monarchical world. He is best apprehended as a creature of monarchism, perfectly adapted to its demanding ecological niche. Prone to haughtiness and self-pity, he varnished to a high gloss the art of groveling in the service of personal advancement and scholarly institution building. The seal he ordered to be cut for himself in London proclaimed his eternal loyalty to the crown, and his delight in serving it: "Labor ipse Voluptas," the seal declared. Labor itself is a pleasure.[21]

As a young man Belcher had spent several years in the royal courts of Europe, where he personally met three future British monarchs, including the future George II and Caroline. These personal encounters with monarchs and lavish courtly culture clarified for Belcher the ways monarchs could promote learning in America, and after he became royal governor he took pleasure in using his regal connections to promote Harvard's welfare.[22] In the portrait he commissioned to celebrate his appointment, he sported a wig and lace kerchief nearly identical to the one in the coronation portrait of his revered king, George II.

Sensing his queen's interest in New World science, Belcher leaped at the chance to curry royal favor: it had worked for Hans Sloane, he observed, so why not for him? Belcher launched a flotilla of royal presents from the New World. Off went a brace of wild geese for the queen's duck ponds at Richmond and Kensington. Two birch canoes for Robert Walpole's canals at Houghton Hall. Five squirrels to be presented by his son to the princess royal. American birds and plants for the daughter of Viscount Townshend, his "noble patron"—anything "that might be acceptable at Raynham," Townshend's stately home. A tea table made of American black ash for basically anyone of importance. Belcher's most valuable gift from the wilderness of America was his feckless son, studying law at the Inns of Court in London. Belcher nagged him to buy a wig, cast off his boorish Americanisms, and contrive a personal audience with Queen Caroline. "The Election Sermons I sent you were well composed, and I thôt wou'd be pleasing at Court; if you get one into the hands of the Queen let me know it. I have no doubt . . . you might find an opportunity of being privately introduced at the Queen's back stairs into her apartment by one of the Ladies of the Bedchamber, and present one on your knees yourself. Try this."[23]

To promote the goal of what he called "enlightening the minds" of the colony, Belcher donated his own library of 474 volumes to the College of New Jersey. He threw in his own full-length portrait and ten framed portraits of British monarchs as part of the bequest (though they would all burn to ashes during the American Revolution). Stocked primarily with historical and religious texts, the library contained both republican-friendly works such as John Locke's treatises, *Cato's Letters*, and Sidney's *Discourse on Government*, along with the florid trappings of monarchy: poems upon the marriage of the Prince of Orange to the English Princess Mary and the mirror for princes genre, represented by the Bourbon Prince of

John Faber, His Excellency, Jonathan Belcher, Esqr., 1734. (Dutch Prints Collection, Department of Rare Books and Special Collections, Princeton University Library)

Conti's *Works* (1711). The first published catalogue of the library praised the *"public-spirited Gentlemen on both Sides of the* Atlantic" who had donated the majority of the books. Belcher turned down the college trustees' offer to thank him by naming the first college building Belcher Hall. Instead he proposed naming it Nassau Hall for his hero, "the glorious King William the Third ... of the illustrious House of Nassau." He constantly sought books for Harvard's library, and urged his son in England to solicit books for Yale's: "When you have the opportunity be thoughtfull to serve Yale College by begging of some gentm a present of books."[24]

This rich tradition of royal patronage of learning in the

Studio of Charles Jervas, King George II, *c. 1727. (© National Portrait Gallery, London)*

American colonies provided the basis for the specific rebuttals by British pamphleteers in 1776 to the new claim by American republicans that monarchy was inherently backward. A point-by-point rebuttal to the Declaration of Independence published in London established monarchy as decidedly not the relic of a barbarous age but enlightened. "Ill would it become the policy of an enlightened Sovereign to appeal to other states on matters relating to his own internal government," the London barrister John Lind wrote in *An Answer to the Declaration of the American Congress* (1776). The dispute, Lind argued, was never between the colonists and the king, who could not have separate interests from his subjects; it was rather between his British subjects and his American subjects. "As a proof of tyranny or usurpation," Lind continued, the Declaration had accused George III of acts committed by his ancestors. In fact, the colonists themselves were tyrannical, aiming to bring everyone "under subjection to the worst of all tyrants—artful, selfish Demagogues." To the charge that the king had committed acts of tyranny "scarcely paralleled in the most barbarous ages," Lind cited the American practices of tarring and feathering and other new tortures "unknown even to the savage executioners of an inquisition." Another rebuttal, by an American loyalist signing as Candidus, asserted that the happiest era of humankind had existed in the American colonies from the restoration of Charles II in 1660 to 1776: happiness lay not in the republican future but in the royal past. Others also chimed in with assertions of the suitability of monarchy to modernity. In "modern times," and based on "the woeful experience of ages," asserted "Rationalis," a Paine opponent, it was clear that "hereditary is preferable to elective monarchy, on account of the terrible disorders, outrages, and confusion which usually attend the election of a king."[25]

Against the rising clamor of America's republican enlightenment, British writers continued to paint their own monarch and other monarchs as engines of royal enlightenment and public happiness. Captain James Cook openly praised George III as an "enlightened monarch" for patronizing his voyages to the Pacific Ocean. Italians at the Royal Academy of Florence likewise praised George III as an *"enlightened Monarch"* and his encouragement of *"Genius, Truth, and the public Benefit"* in 1785. "In these enlightened times," explained the former colonial American official William Knox to Parliament in 1789, "our Hereditary Monarchs can have no interest" that was "injurious to the permanent prosperity and happiness of their people." In his *History of the Reign of George III* (1803), the Scottish writer Robert Bisset praised Frederick of Prussia because he "rendered ignorant and uncivilized inhabitants an enlightened and civilized people."[26]

There was much truth to these defenses. Contrary to Paine's contention in *Common Sense* that George III was "the Royal Brute," the king ranked among the most educated monarchs ever to sit on the British throne. The king's education exceeded in depth and breadth that of many British university graduates at the time, and it far surpassed that possessed by the military man that the Americans would elect as their first president and then anoint as the epitome of enlightenment. George Washington never attended college and knew no foreign languages; by contrast, the education of the future George III had become an urgent national priority the moment his father, the Prince of Wales, died and he abruptly moved to the front of the order of succession. "Let me be ever so learned in what is necessary for a King to know," the young prince had written to his tutor, the third earl of Bute. He learned German, Latin, Greek, mathematics, history, science, art, architecture, public finance, naval science, music, and especially geography, the science of kings that gave them knowledge of their dominions.[27]

Americans affirmed these truths with on-site observations. Visiting the royal residence at Buckingham in 1783, John Adams marveled at the king's stock of books. "The king's library struck me with admiration," he observed. Not only were the books in "perfect taste and judgment," but the library also contained maps of the king's dominions, all chosen with "judgment" and "simplicity, without the smallest affectation." Bored loyalists waiting out the American Revolution in London spent much of their time contriving glimpses of the monarchs and visiting the cultural riches that the Hanoverians had helped promote, including paintings by the American expatriates Benjamin West and John Singleton Copley, who had decamped to London for the bigger stage it offered, including royal patronage. West became historical painter to the court and then surveyor of the king's pictures, and his studio and Copley's became virtual factories of royal portraiture, producing between them at least ten portraits of the royal family that flattered the king and his family as both regal and forward-looking.[28] In Benjamin West's portrait of George III of 1783, the loss of the American colonies seems to have been forgotten and Britannia rules once more. Smartly turned out in armor and ermine, gazing blankly into the future, the king clutches a spyglass as the clouds part over the bustling fleet behind him.

Queen Charlotte, meanwhile, kept abreast of the most enlightened educational trends. Born in 1744 and raised in a small duchy of the Holy Roman Empire, the queen maintained Continental connections throughout her life, bringing for example

Benjamin West (American, 1783–1820), George III, 1783. Oil on canvas, 126.5 × 101 cm. (The Cleveland Museum of Art, Gift of Mr. and Mrs. Lawrence S. Robbins 1952.17)

the Genevan geologist Jean-André Deluc to her court as French Reader and adviser on matters geological and botanical.[29] She raised her enormous brood of princelings and princesses according to the latest pedagogical theories, which advocated instilling reason in young children through appropriate education. In Allan Ramsay's portrait, the queen cradles one of her sons while another nestles in the great pink cocoon of her skirt. Resting prominently atop the piano is John Locke's popular educational manual, *Some Thoughts Concerning Education*, first published in 1693 and hugely influential throughout the eighteenth century. Rejecting theories of innate sinfulness, Locke's work was an anthem to the formative power of education in helping children unfold their reason.

In her commitment to reason-producing pedagogies, Queen Charlotte resembled her precise contemporary, the austerely republican Abigail Adams, who dismissed royals as "mere Men and Women." Born in the same year as Charlotte, Abigail consulted the same books to school her own four children in republicanism.[30] She read the Roman and Greek classics to her eldest son, John Quincy, while Queen Charlotte appeared in a royal portrait by Johan Zoffany with the toddler Prince of Wales dressed as Telemachus, son of Penelope and Odysseus. Both mothers sent those carefully educated sons to the highest office in the land: John Quincy Adams was elected the sixth president of the United States and the Prince of Wales became King George IV.

In short, the catechisms of republicanism were not so easily distinguished from the primers for monarchy. A few American revolutionaries, exposed to European courts during their diplomatic duties, paused to reconsider their misgivings about monarchs. John Adams saw the human face of monarchy clearly when he met three reigning monarchs during his ten years abroad in the American diplomatic service. "I was deeply impressed with a Character of Mildness, Goodness and Innocence in his face," Adams confessed to his diary after his audience with the young Louis XVI. "It seemed to me impossible that an ill design could be harboured in that breast." He assured the marquis de Lafayette that Louis was one of "Three Monarcks in Europe for whom I have as much Veneration as it is lawfull for one Man to have for another. The King of France, the Emperor of Germany and the King of Prussia, are constant objects

A testament to the popularity of John Locke's Some Thoughts Concerning Education *(1693), Allan Ramsay's portrait of Queen Charlotte and her two eldest sons positions Locke's text prominently atop the piano. Allan Ramsay,* Queen Charlotte with Her Two Eldest Sons, *1769. (Royal Collection Trust / © Her Majesty Queen Elizabeth II 2015)*

of my Admiration, for Reasons of Humanity Wisdom and Beneficence which need not be enlarged on." Once at the court of George III, Adams pitied the endless public duties of the monarch, "a Slavery to which no human Being ought to be subjected." His own embattled years as president heightened his sensitivity to the burdens of executive duty, whether hereditary or elective. "I never believed George to be a tyrant in disposition and in nature," he explained in 1822 to Timothy Pickering after the king's death. "I always believed him to be deceived by his courtiers on both sides of the Atlantic, and in his official capacity only, cruel."[31]

Adams's realization from his European service that monarchs were patrons of learning had lasting effects in the United States. Adams helped found the American Academy of Arts and Sciences in 1780 upon his return from France. The academy was one of the first learned institutions to be established under the new republican regime, its charter announcing its goal of promoting "every art and science" in America. Prominently featured was the republican insistence that the arts and sciences flourish best in free States ("SUB LIBERTATE FLORENT," as the academy's seal had it). But also prominent was the society's desire and need to imitate and communicate with the royal and aristocratic societies of Europe. Informing Benjamin Franklin of his election, Joseph Willard mentioned the many "similar Institutions in Europe" on which the academy was modeled—all of them royal or aristocratic.[32]

The American Academy of Arts and Sciences embodied the new republican dilemma: how to condemn monarchy and aristocracy while identifying what made America's republican schools, universities, and libraries more enlightened than Europe's aristocratic and monarchical institutions of learning. In a diary entry in the late 1780s, John Quincy Adams summed up the distinctive advantages that a monarchy presented to the cultivation of the arts and sciences over a republic:

> Let us run a parallel between the progress of a man of genius in a republic and in a Monarchy. In both Cases, he will be employ'd while young in the pursuit of literature. In the republic, he will soon be called upon to serve the public, and from that time forth, he will be obliged to relinquish

the Study of the Arts and Sciences, because the affairs of the Nation will employ all his Time. But in a Monarchy, his Talents will acquire him respect, reputation, and perhaps fortune, but they will not introduce him to a Situation which shall induce him to neglect the Sciences. On the contrary he will be continually improving his literary faculties, and his productions will do honour to himself and to his Country. This is my idea of the promotion of literature, and this is what a republic can seldom boast of.

The progress of literature, Adams concluded, "must be the greatest, where there are Men, who can employ all their days, in cultivating the Arts and Sciences"—that is, in a monarchy.[33]

The Ambiguity of Enlightenment

The outcome of the American Revolution bore out some of John Quincy Adams's concerns about the capacity of republicanism to promote learning and enlightenment. With so many paths to enlightenment in both monarchies and the new American republic, who was to say that one political system was preferable to the other for achieving the goal of creating an enlightened, happy people?

The question preoccupied politicians in the young United States who needed to legitimate the credentials of republican government to an audience of more powerful rival nations. To the considerable amusement of European observers of the American republican experiment, the U.S. House of Representatives spent many hours in December 1796 debating whether it was prudent or proper to declare the United States the most enlightened nation in the world. The context of the discussion was the House's response to George Washington's farewell address of that fall, in which the president declared his intention to retire from his second term as president. A committee of five, hoping to cover the president in glory, included this statement as part of its answer to him: "The spectacle of a whole nation, the freest and most enlightened in the world, offering by its Representatives the tribute of unfeigned approbation to its first citizen, however novel and interesting it may be, derives all its lustre . . . from the transcendent merit of which it is the voluntary testimony."[34]

Their colleagues in the House immediately seized on the problematic phrase "freest and most enlightened in the world." The Federalist Josiah Parker of Virginia moved to strike it. "Although . . . I wish to believe that we are the freest people, and the most enlightened people in the world," said Parker, "it is enough that we think ourselves so; it is not becoming in us to make the declaration to the world; and if we are not so, it is still worse for us to suppose ourselves what we are not." William Giles of Virginia (who openly confessed his low opinion of the president, and who had resisted the Jay Treaty that had secured closer economic ties with Britain) also objected to the puffed wording, reminding his colleagues that it was imprudent to say such things "in the face of the world." Giles proposed that it was not just "unnatural and unbecoming in us to exult in our superior happiness, light, or wisdom," it was in fact insulting to other "nations in their troubles." He utterly disapproved of the whole paragraph. "If I am free, if I am happy, if I am enlightened more than others, I wish not to proclaim it on the house top; if we are free, it is not prudent to declare it; if enlightened, it is not our duty in this House to trumpet it to the world: it is no Legislative concern." John Swanwick of Pennsylvania concurred with Giles, saying, "It would be much more prudent in us to let other nations discover it, and not make a boast of it ourselves." Both Britain and France, he added, "may think themselves as happy as we are: they may feel offended to hear of our comparisons," especially since both other nations seem to have profited from the trade wars of the 1790s. France had not only enriched its coffers with gold and silver through the colonial wars it fought with Great Britain; it had added "the most valuable stores of the productions of the arts; as statues, paintings, and manuscripts of inestimable worth." American boasting, in short, would only "invite new depredations upon our commerce."[35]

Others disagreed. The debates over the recent Jay Treaty between Britain and the United States had been filled with affirmations of America's prosperity and strength: Why such modesty now? The hawkish Federalist William Smith of South Carolina demanded to know which "nation was so free or enlightened as ours." In his observation of other nations, "I know of none that enjoy so much civil and religious freedom as America, or is so enlightened, especially in the affairs of Government." Fisher Ames of Massachusetts also leaped in to defend the phrasing, stating that Americans were not just declaring their superior enlightenment to other nations; more important, they were acknowledging "the beneficent hand of God," who had carried America to prosperity. It was both "natural and becoming" for Americans to acknowledge this gratefully. Americans should hang together and hold fast to their hard-won independence. "We are neither Frenchmen, nor Englishmen, but we are Americans," declared Ames. Swanwick immediately countered Ames's logic: Was it not impertinent to brazenly thank God for making Americans "wiser or more enlightened than others"? Moving from theological to military matters, Swanwick reaffirmed that given America's military weakness, Congress should not insult the superior powers of Europe by trumpeting American enlightenment. "If we read their own publications of themselves, they will tell you they are the most free and enlightened people upon earth."[36]

The next day House members resumed the debate, with William Smith paging through French publications that showed that they too used "bombastical expressions," such as proclaiming the French nation "the most enlightened in the civilized world." No, said Parker: the previous four years of the United States had shown that France was not the most enlightened nation in the world: if it had been, the government "would not have suffered such shameful spoliations on our commerce and shameful acts of cruelty to our seamen." Take "the two little monarchies of Denmark and Sweden," he said, which somehow managed to preserve their neutrality though surrounded by enemy states. Parker entirely missed the point, replied Ames. Enlightenment was not about declarations of national might but a statement of the relative learning of the people. France and England were indeed "remarkable for enlightened men." But these formed an elite group of "literati": few others in Europe among the common people could be "calculated to be in any respect enlightened." The United States had far more people proportionately who could read and write: in America, "They are enlightened enough to be free."[37]

In the end, despite many hours of debate, the wording about America's enlightenment was never included in an official American government document. But it reverberated for years around the

Atlantic as Europeans tried to make sense of what this earnest debate implied about Americans' national and intellectual pretensions. Many Europeans remained deeply skeptical of America's capacity for national enlightenment. Since their independence, Americans had "given no indications of genius," complained the Anglican cleric Sydney Smith in the *Edinburgh Review* in 1820. "In the four corners of the globe, who reads an American book? or goes to an American play? or looks at an American picture or statue?"[38]

Smith's sharp questions cut to the core of what efforts toward enlightenment had brought—and not brought—to the young republic. On the one hand, the republican Revolution that had delegitimized monarchy and aristocracy had brought some identifiable changes. A few were cosmetic. King's College was immediately renamed Columbia College and Queen's College eventually rechristened Rutgers, in part to erase their royal pedigrees. Prayers for the king and the British royal family were excised from the Book of Common Prayer. Even as they imported huge numbers of books from Britain, Americans masked their monarchical tendencies. "Fear God. Honour the King," the phrase taken from *The Instructor; or, Young Man's Best Companion,* a British manual for clerks and mechanics, became "Fear God. Honour Your Rulers," in an American edition.[39]

But other changes were structural, allowing for the free spread of knowledge in ways still not fully achieved in Europe. The new government of the United States renounced the use of state power to police public opinion. No stamp tax restricted newspapers and other written documents to an economic elite. No public authorities inspected the mail to hunt out simmering rebellion, nor did customs officers prevent threatening books from entering the United States. New colleges and universities, female academies, literary clubs, workingmen's associations, and a flourishing publishing industry of books, newspapers, and magazines encouraged the spread of knowledge. Societies with names like the Friendly Club downplayed vertical lines of patronage while highlighting the ostensibly more republican horizontal lines of friendship, sympathy, consent, unregulated conversation, like-mindedness, and affinity. In the new republican regime, Americans argued, there would be no difference between the people as politically relevant citizens and the people as part of a voluntary society coming together for education, reading, conversation, and sociability. One female academy reminded students that in England "the nobility would feel it a degradation to have their daughters educated in common with the untitled," whereas in the United States "the spirit of our republican government" rendered such distinctions "ridiculous."[40]

Yet the new American republic also remained intellectually dependent on Europe and especially London. Republican enlightenment in the United States continued to draw strength from the older centers of learning in Europe that had been built—and in many cases continued to thrive—thanks to centralized royal and aristocratic patronage. But in the United States, the new federal government did not become a patron of learning and the arts, except in cases where these directly served practical state interests, such as the Lewis and Clark expedition of 1804–6. Congress declined to establish a national university in Washington, D.C. Americans continued to import many books from Europe, and the new republican colleges, seminaries, learned societies, and social libraries remained a major market for British books into the middle of the nineteenth century.[41]

American colleges also continued to benefit from aristocratic patronage. The American-born scientist turned loyalist Benjamin Thompson—a student of the natural philosopher John Winthrop at Harvard—had made so many inroads into European courtly circles that he was elected count of the Holy Roman Empire. He went on as Count Rumford to found Britain's Royal Institution for science in 1799, which he hoped would be "a lasting monument of the liberality and enterprising spirit of an enlightened nation" (by which he meant Britain, not his birth country). Count Rumford endowed not just the Rumford medals of the Royal Society and the American Academy of Arts and Sciences but a professorship at Harvard.[42]

Printers and engravers in the early national United States continued to lag behind in the technical expertise of their counterparts across the Atlantic. Authors who yearned for a truly grand edition of works celebrating America—such as John James Audubon for his life-size hand-colored prints in the *Birds of America* (1827–38)—turned to London for printing expertise and to the royal courts of Europe for patronage. Audubon's subscribers included the monarchs of England and France and assorted European nobles, in addition to Henry Clay and Noah Webster. For decades after the American Revolution, the royal painter Benjamin West remained the major source of patronage in London for American artists who were born during or after the Revolution, such as Rembrandt Peale, Washington Allston, and Thomas Sully. At the request of the Society of the Sons of St. George in Philadelphia, a group dedicated to helping indigent English immigrants, Sully traveled to London to paint a full-length portrait of the young Queen Victoria.[43]

The enlightenment of the American Revolution was thus both a reality and a fable that the people of the new United States told about themselves. They asserted that a republic needed an enlightened people to survive, by which they seemed to mean the broad circulation of knowledge that would create an informed citizenry able to distinguish tyranny from liberty. What they did not yet know was whether a republic nurtured true intellectual distinction. Was it enough for knowledge to circulate freely, for books and magazines to expand their reach, for literacy rates to rise? Or did true enlightenment require something more, the kind of wealth, power, and magnificence—the chance at true distinction rather than endless equality—that only princely patronage could supply?

This would be the ambivalence felt by intellectuals in the United States during the first eighty years of nationhood about the republican path to enlightenment. Long after the Revolution, Americans languished in their own minds—and those of European nations—as a second-tier intellectual backwater. Their republican ideology committed them to popular education as a bulwark of popular government. But America lacked—in their words—true genius. Ironically, it would be the new American aristocracy of wealth created by the Industrial Revolution that would pump enough money into U.S. universities and libraries to bring them to greatness in the twentieth century.

Epilogue: The Tusks of the Mastodon

AMONG THE MOST INTRIGUING discoveries of the eighteenth century was the skeleton of a mastodon, an elephant-like creature whose enormous bones, teeth, and tusks, exhumed from deep in the North American mud, captured imaginations around the Atlantic. Did this monster still roam the land, somewhere in an unexplored part of the vast American continent? Were the bones vestiges of the ancient wonders of America, of giant creatures who dwarfed the glories of the ancient Greeks and Romans, of ferocious quadrupeds that would finally put to rest the American degeneracy theories of Buffon and his friends? No one could be sure. The best that could be done for the time being was to assemble the hulking skeleton and display it for a gawking public, as Charles Willson Peale did in his Philadelphia museum in the early nineteenth century.

But there was one major problem—or rather, two: the tusks. Lacking a live version of this great beast, no one was sure whether the long, curving tusks should face up or down. The decision boiled down to one's belief about the mastodon's essential nature. For those who believed that the mastodon had been a gentle plant eater, a harmless specimen of American weakness, the tusks should surely face up, like those of modern elephants known to nibble on leaves. But others were certain that the mastodon had been a

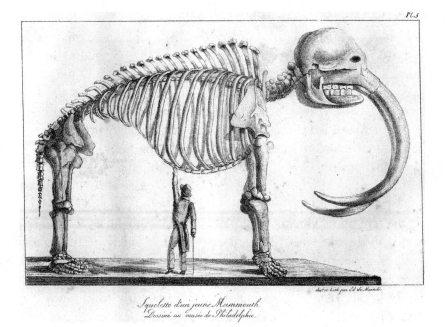

"Squelette d'un jeune Mammouth" (Skeleton of a young mammoth), *from Édouard de Montulé,* Receuil des cartes et des vues du voyage en Amérique *(1821). (Reproduction by permission of the Buffalo & Erie County Public Library, Buffalo, N.Y.)*

vicious carnivore, the relic of past American glory, when giants had stalked the land. Formidable weapons by which the mastodon gored its hapless prey, the tusks, they argued, should face down. This was the decision taken by Charles Willson Peale, who displayed his mastodon tusks facing downward. "He could have torn an animal to pieces held beneath his foot," Peale announced confidently of his fearsome American animal. An astonished French visitor to Peale's museum in 1816 sketched a picture of the tusks of Peale's mastodon.[1]

Did the tusks of the vanished creature face up or down? The same question could be asked of our modern view of the legacy of the first people who long ago called themselves enlightened: Has it been mostly positive or negative? This question has bedeviled scholars throughout the twentieth century. Some have condemned the self-described enlightened thinkers of the eighteenth century for concocting rationalist regimes of classification and control that led straight to some of the greatest collective tragedies of the twentieth century. They would point the tusks down. Others have seen the enlightened people of the eighteenth century as the first architects of universal human rights and a cosmopolitan frame of mind that have led to some of the greatest achievements for human justice in the history of the world. To them, the tusks face up.

What happened to enlightened ideas after the long eighteenth century? As more scholars are placing ideals of enlightenment in their global contexts, we are learning that the conventional understandings of the fate of enlightenment no longer hold. Enlightenment did not end with the movement called Romanticism, its ideals of reason and cosmopolitanism wilting before the onslaught of lush emotionalism, evangelical Protestantism, and rising nationalism. In the United States by the 1830s, the term *enlightened* had expanded so much that it had lost much of its novelty and critical edge, becoming essentially synonymous with progress, improvement, and reform rather than the specific goals of emancipation from superstition, revealed religion, and traditional political authority. Increasingly detached from the specific critical conversations with which it had first been associated, the ideal of enlightenment now spread broadly in American culture. Americans no longer wondered whether they were the most enlightened nation in the world, as they had in 1796. They now assumed that they were, and set about holding up the torch of enlightened American "progress" for a variety of goals. By the middle and later nineteenth century, this new semantic looseness had made enlightenment coterminous with the broad objectives of American civilization and Manifest Destiny, losing not only the critical edge of the first inventors of the term but also the sense of ambivalence and doubt that had characterized the age. By the late nineteenth century, the way was paved for the invention of "The Enlightenment" as a concrete era in the eighteenth century.[2] From an eighteenth-century question emerged a twentieth-century declaration, and from an eighteenth-century process emerged by the mid-twentieth century an era: the American Enlightenment.

Today, from every part of the political spectrum, in newspapers and magazines, in speeches and blogs, Americans express their hope that they are enlightened on a huge variety of topics: human rights, animal rights, economic austerity, capital punishment, recycling, gay rights, the pope, racism, evangelical Christianity, sodium intake, genital mutilation, universal health care, Marxism, environmentalism, the state of Israel, affluence, pornography, fathers doing housework and childcare, secularism, the Constitution, administrative techniques, democracy, human trafficking, and the purpose of universities, among other topics.[3] The twentieth-century vogue for Eastern mysticism has also introduced the notion of personal enlightenment as an emancipation from materialism and worldly concerns, but this too has meshed with the general idea of a constant search for betterment in the present world.

Americans today also routinely invoke the American Enlightenment as a glorious moment in the national past that prioritized reason, empiricism, the separation of church and state, the dignity of the individual, the defense of human rights, progress, a faith in science, and representative government. The highly nationalistic, hyper-real American Enlightenment remains foundational to modern American identity. When he was president, Barack Obama was a constant exponent of a distinct historical epoch called the Enlightenment in the United States. Hewing to a diffusionary vision of enlightenment, Obama publicly invoked the European (and especially French) roots of ideas modern Americans value, such as freedom of conscience, representative government, and the rule of law.[4]

Our modern views of the idea of enlightenment are not wrong. But they are not precisely what eighteenth-century thinkers meant by enlightenment. Tracing the views of enlightenment as they were expressed in the eighteenth century reminds us that those thinkers would probably have been surprised at our confident assessments of their legacies; they were never sure whether the tusks of the mastodon faced up or down. Enlightenment, as people in the eighteenth century recognized, was not a single event or achievement but an ongoing process fueled by a disposition of mind to believe that reason and empirical evidence might make the world a better place. But never did anyone agree on a single path to enlightenment, nor did enlightened thinkers ever agree that enlightenment had been achieved. Enlightenment was a journey that involved more questioning than answering. Doubt and wonder rather than confidence characterized the bewildering number of efforts at enlightenment.

Assessing the achievements of his era in the year of his death, Thomas Jefferson encapsulated the simultaneous hope and anxiety that dogged those who strove for enlightenment. "All eyes are opened, or opening, to the rights of man," he wrote in 1826. "The general spread of the light of science has already laid open to every view the palpable truth, that the mass of mankind has not been born with saddles on their backs, nor a favored few booted and spurred, ready to ride them legitimately, by the grace of God. These are grounds of hope for others."[5] Jefferson recognized that there were grounds for hope. But eyes were still opening; enlightenment had not yet been achieved.

As we unearth the bones of the past, we too debate how best to reassemble them. We are driven to connect the first people who called themselves enlightened to our aspirations for enlightenment today. This is an understandable goal; at times it is also an admirable one. But we should never forget that like the extinct mastodons, the people of the eighteenth century who called themselves enlightened walked a different earth from ours. We can try to re-create their world by listening to their words and scrutinizing their hearts and their minds. But in the end we are always visitors to their era. Our best hope for enlightenment today is to listen carefully to our eighteenth-century predecessors and then chart our own path, trusting that future generations will understand that we too pursued happiness for ourselves and others, hoping to realize our own particular species of enlightenment.

Abbreviations

APDE	*The Adams Papers Digital Edition*, ed. C. James Taylor. Charlottesville: University of Virginia Press, 2008– .
CLTJ	E. Millicent Sowerby, *Catalogue of the Library of Thomas Jefferson*. 5 vols. Washington, D.C.: Library of Congress, 1952–59.
PAH	Harold Syrett, ed., *The Papers of Alexander Hamilton*. 27 vols. New York: Columbia University Press, 1961–87.
PBF	Leonard W. Labaree et al., eds., *The Papers of Benjamin Franklin*. 41 vols. to date. New Haven: Yale University Press, 1959– .
PBFDE	*The Papers of Benjamin Franklin: Digital Edition.* http://franklinpapers.org/franklin//.
PGW Col	W. W. Abbot et al., eds., *The Papers of George Washington: Colonial Series*. 10 vols. Charlottesville: University Press of Virginia, 1983–95.
PGW Conf	W. W. Abbot et al., eds., *The Papers of George Washington: Confederation Series*. 6 vols. Charlottesville: University Press of Virginia, 1992–97.
PGW Pres	Dorothy Twohig et al., eds., *The Papers of George Washington: Presidential Series*. 18 vols. to date. Charlottesville: University Press of Virginia, 1987– .
PGW Ret	Dorothy Twohig et al., eds., *The Papers of George Washington: Retirement Series*. 4 vols. Charlottesville: University Press of Virginia, 1998–99.

PJMCS   William T. Hutchinson et al., eds., *The Papers of James Madison: Congressional Series.* 17 vols. Chicago: University of Chicago Press, 1962–91.

PTJ   Julian P. Boyd et al., eds., *The Papers of Thomas Jefferson.* 41 vols. to date. Princeton: Princeton University Press, 1950– .

PTJ Ret   J. Jefferson Looney et al., eds., *The Papers of Thomas Jefferson: Retirement Series.* 10 vols. to date. Princeton: Princeton University Press, 2004– .

Notes

Unless otherwise indicated, all translations are mine.

Introduction

1. Crèvecoeur, *Traité de la culture*, 18.
2. John Adams, "Thoughts on Government," April 1776, *APDE*.
3. For recent historiographical surveys of the idea of the American Enlightenment, see Winterer, "What Was the American Enlightenment?," Dixon, "Henry F. May and the Revival of the American Enlightenment," and Caron and Wulf, "American Enlightenments."
4. Koch, *Power, Morals, and the Founding Fathers*, 10; Koch, "Introduction," in Adrienne Koch, ed., *The American Enlightenment*, 19; "Adrienne Koch, Historian, Dies; Wrote on America of 1765–1815," *New York Times*, August 23, 1971, 32; Adrienne Koch, "Topics: Reflections on Independence Day," *New York Times*, July 4, 1970.
5. Becker, *The Heavenly City*, 163–68, and Cassirer, *The Philosophy of the Enlightenment*, xi; for the context of Cassirer's work, see Emily Levine, *Dreamland of Humanists*, 226. On the rise of *the Enlightenment* as an era rather than a process, see Schmidt, "Inventing the Enlightenment."
6. Bellah, "Civil Religion in America," 7; David Brion Davis, *The Problem of Slavery in Western Culture*, 3, 16. Davis followed in the wake of two works that presented American slavery as a moral "problem" antithetical to the "meaning of America" as a promised land. First was Myrdal's *An American Dilemma*, in which the author argued that "*The American Negro problem is a problem in the heart of the American*" (1: xliii). The second was Elkins, *Slavery*, which also invoked a "problem of slavery" and "our slave problem" (85, 140, 141, 174). This "problem" was distinctively American because it was conceptualized as a question of "pure morality" rather

than "institutional arrangement" (28). On the "project" of enlightenment, see Habermas, "Modernity," and MacIntyre, *After Virtue*. On the afterglow of enlightenment, see Gray, *Enlightenment's Wake*, 215.

7. Pierre Samuel du Pont de Nemours to Thomas Jefferson, August 18, 1816, in Chinard, ed., *The Correspondence of Jefferson and Du Pont de Nemours*, 1.

8. At least seven books with some version of the term *radical enlightenment* in the title have been published since 1981. For a lucid critique of presentism in enlightenment studies, see La Vopa, "A New Intellectual History?"

9. The term achieved prominence in the 1970s after the publication in 1973 of Isaiah Berlin's essay "The Counter-Enlightenment." For a critique of the term's growing popularity among modern historians, see Robert Norton, "The Myth of the Counter-Enlightenment."

10. Reid, *An Inquiry*, 169, 168, 493; on eighteenth-century American libraries that contained Reid's works, see Lundberg and May, "The Enlightened Reader in America," 288; for the importance of hearing in this era, see Leigh Eric Schmidt, *Hearing Things*.

11. Gay, *The Enlightenment*, 2: 559, 558; Horkheimer and Adorno, *Philosophische Fragmente*; Commager, *The Empire of Reason*, xi. Ernest Cassara's *The Enlightenment in America* (1975) was seldom reviewed with the other studies from this period. Since the bicentennial, numerous works on the fate of enlightenment in British America and the United States have been published. Book-length works include Burns, *Fire and Light*, Delbourgo, *A Most Amazing Scene of Wonders*, Fea, *The Way of Improvement Leads Home*, Ferguson, *The American Enlightenment*, Knott and Taylor, eds., *Women, Gender, and Enlightenment*, Marsden, *The Twilight of the American Enlightenment*, Pagden, *The Enlightenment* (which deals in part with the British America and the United States), Reid-Maroney, *Philadelphia's Enlightenment*, Richard, *The Founders and the Classics*, Justin Roberts, *Slavery and the Enlightenment in the British Atlantic*, Schmidt, *Hearing Things*, Sher, *The Enlightenment and the Book*, Spencer, ed., *The Bloomsbury Encyclopedia of the American Enlightenment*, Staloff, *Hamilton, Adams, Jefferson*, Torre, *The Political Economy of Sentiment*, Wills, *Cincinnatus*, Zakai, *Jonathan Edwards's Philosophy of History*, and Zakai, *Jonathan Edwards's Philosophy of Nature*. On the postmodern turn, see Hollinger, "The Enlightenment and the Genealogy of Cultural Conflict in the United States."

12. On enlightenment and empire in the eighteenth century, see Muthu, *Enlightenment Against Empire*, Pitts, *A Turn to Empire*, Rothschild, *The Inner Life of Empires*, and Conrad, "Enlightenment in Global History."

13. Locke, *Two Treatises of Government*, 301.

14. Geertz, "Religion as a Cultural System," 90; May, *The Enlightenment in America*, xiii.

15. James P. Byrd, *Sacred Scripture, Sacred War*, 11.
16. John Adams, diary entry for October 18, 1775, *APDE*.
17. On the meaning of natural law in the Roman world, see Lehoux, *What Did the Romans Know?*, 47–76; on the modern period, see Daston and Vidal, eds., *The Moral Authority of Nature*, and Daston and Stolleis, eds., *Natural Law*.
18. Some major works on Americans and nature (in a vast literature) include Marx, *The Machine in the Garden*, Nash, *Wilderness and the American Mind*, Cherry, *Nature and Religious Imagination*, Pole, "Enlightenment and the Politics of American Nature," Pagden, *The Fall of Natural Man*, John C. Greene, *American Science in the Age of Jefferson*, and Charles A. Miller, *Jefferson and Nature*.
19. Publius [James Madison], *The Federalist*, 2: 6, 7. On the importance of unknowns in revolutionary American political thought, see Winterer, "Model Empire, Lost City."
20. Pierre Samuel du Pont de Nemours to Thomas Jefferson, July 23, 1808, in Chinard, ed., *The Correspondence of Jefferson and Du Pont de Nemours*, 134.

Chapter One. The American Setting

1. Chase, ed. and trans., *Our Revolutionary Forefathers*, 86.
2. Greene and Harrington et al., *American Population*, 6–7.
3. Joel Barlow to Thomas Jefferson, June 15, 1787, *PTJ*, 11: 473. For this theme in Spanish America, see Gerbi, *The Dispute of the New World*, Brading, *The First America*, Cañizares-Esguerra, *How to Write the History*, Weber, *Bárbaros*, Safier, *Measuring the New World*, and Bleichmar, *Visible Empire*. For North America, see Chaplin, *Subject Matter*, and Parrish, *American Curiosity*.
4. See Crosby, *Ecological Imperialism*, Henry Lowood, "The New World and the European Catalog of Nature," in Kupperman, ed., *America in European Consciousness*, 295–323, Blackbourn, *The Conquest of Nature*, Cooper, *Inventing the Indigenous*, McNeill, *Mosquito Empires*, Jonsson, *Enlightenment's Frontier*, and Withers, *Placing the Enlightenment*.
5. For populations of North American cities, see Bridenbaugh, *Cities in the Wilderness*, 303; for city populations in Spanish America, see J. H. Elliott, *Empires of the Atlantic World*, 262; on Caribbean planters, see O'Shaughnessy, *An Empire Divided*, 19–27.
6. See Clark, *European Cities and Towns*, 121, Raven, *The Business of Books*, 9, Sher, *The Enlightenment and the Book*, 503–40, Hugh Amory, "A Note on Statistics," in Amory and Hall, eds., *The Colonial Book*, 514, Graph 7a, and Burnard, *Mastery, Tyranny, and Desire*, 107.
7. See Flavell, "Decadents Abroad," 35, 55n9, 47, 50, and Richard Beale Davis, *Intellectual Life in the Colonial South*, 1: 371. Feld, "In the Latest London Manner," 308.

8. Hugh Amory, "Reinventing the Colonial Book," in Amory and Hall, eds., *The Colonial Book*, 43; Parrish, *American Curiosity*, 128–35; John, *Spreading the News*, 8; Fea, *The Way of Improvement Leads Home*, 107.

9. See Mark Peterson, "*Theopolis Americana*," Nicholas Phillipson, "Culture and Society in the Eighteenth-Century Province: The Case of Edinburgh and the Scottish Enlightenment," in Lawrence Stone, ed., *The University in Society*, 2: 407–48, John Robertson, *The Case for the Enlightenment*, 25–26, Ferguson, *Law and Letters in American Culture*, 5, Clive and Bailyn, "England's Cultural Provinces," 206, Daniel Walker Howe, *Making the American Self*, 48–77, and Davis, *Intellectual Life in the Colonial South*, 1: 363.

10. See Goldgar, *Impolite Learning*, Bots and Waquet, *La République des lettres*, Peter N. Miller, *Pereisc's Europe*, Brockliss, *Calvet's Web*, Furey, *Erasmus*, and Shelford, *Transforming the Republic of Letters*.

11. On British American participation in the eighteenth-century republic of letters, see Winterer, "Where Is America in the Republic of Letters?," Fiering, "The Transatlantic Republic of Letters," Warner, *The Letters of the Republic*, Landsman, *From Colonials to Provincials*, 31–56, Ferguson, *The American Enlightenment*, Shields, *Civil Tongues and Polite Letters*, and David D. Hall, "Learned Culture in the Eighteenth Century," in Amory and Hall, eds., *The Colonial Book*, 411–33. On Catholics, see Stanwood, "Catholics," 220, Feingold, "Jesuits: Savants," Steven J. Harris, "Confession-Building," and Harris, "Mapping Jesuit Science."

12. The Philadelphia Quaker merchant James Logan, for example, owned the first English edition of Acosta, from 1604: see Edwin Wolf, *James Logan*, 22. On Catholics, see Walch, ed., *Early American Catholicism*, unpaginated introduction, 1–5, Luca Codignola, "The Holy See and the Conversion of the Indians in French and British North America, 1486–1760," in Kupperman, ed., *America in European Consciousness*, 213, and Stanwood, "The Protestant Moment."

13. See Butler, *Becoming America*, 186–92, Susan O'Brien, "A Transatlantic Community of Saints," and Whitefield, *A Select Collection of Letters*.

14. Kennedy, "Thomas Brattle," 589; James Logan, *Experimenta et Meletemata* (1739); Logan, *Experimenta et Meletemata* (1747); Wolf, *James Logan*, 39–40.

15. See Ditz, *Epistolary Selves*, Bannet, *Empire of Letters*, Goodman, *Becoming a Woman in the Age of Letters*, Dierks, *In My Power*, Gaul and Harris, *Letters*, Daybell, *The Material Letter*, and O'Neill, *The Opened Letter*.

16. Pearsall, *Atlantic Families*, 9. See also Eustace, *Passion Is the Gale*; and Knott, *Sensibility*.

17. On the estimate of five thousand, I am grateful for the e-mail communication from Walter Woodward, August 18, 2010, who also notes that a number of letters may not have survived. Woodward, *Prospero's America*, 3, 54, 65, 262, 263, 254.

18. Claire Rydell Arcenas and Caroline Winterer, "The Correspondence Network of Benjamin Franklin: The London Decades, 1757–1775." Ms. in possession of author.

19. On the Atlantic traffic in scientific objects, see Rice, "Jefferson's Gift of Fossils," Beall, Jr., "Cotton Mather's Early 'Curiosa Americana,' " Stearns, *Science*, Ryan, "Assimilating New Worlds," Levin, "Giants in the Earth," Prince, ed., *Stuffing Birds*, Schiebinger, *Plants and Empire*, Delbourgo and Dew, eds., *Science and Empire*, and Parsons and Murphy, "Ecosystems Under Sail."

20. On women's literacy and learning in British America and the early national United States, see Thornton, *Handwriting in America*, Kerrison, *Claiming the Pen*, Kelley, *Learning to Stand and Speak*, Monaghan, *Learning to Read and Write*, and Winterer, "Is There an Intellectual History of Early American Women?" On manuscript culture, see Shields, "The Manuscript in the British American World of Print." On the mid-Atlantic coterie of women, see Mulford, ed., *Only for the Eye of a Friend*, Blecki and Wulf, eds., *Milcah Martha Moore's Book*, and Ousterhout, *The Most Learned Woman in America*. On female worlds, see Winterer, *The Mirror of Antiquity*, 12–39, Stabile, *Memory's Daughters*, and Ring, *Girlhood Embroidery*.

21. See Zagarri, *Revolutionary Backlash*, 12–19, and Silvia Sebastiani, "Race, Women and Progress in the Scottish Enlightenment," and Sylvana Tomaselli, "Civilization, Patriotism, and Enlightened Histories of Woman," both in Knott and Taylor, eds., *Women, Gender and Enlightenment*, 75–96 and 117–35. Miller, *A Brief Retrospect*, 2: 280.

22. Barratt and Miles, *Gilbert Stuart*, 226.

23. Wollstonecraft, *A Vindication of the Rights of Woman*, 83; Murray, *The Gleaner*, 2: 280, 3: 189.

24. On European libraries, see Walker, "The State of Libraries in Eighteenth-Century Europe," 286–87; for Belcher's experiences in European libraries, see Belcher, "A Journal of My Intended Voyage & Journey to Holland, Hannover etc. Beginning at London Saturday July 8th: O.S. 1704," Massachusetts Historical Society, 74; on the contents and lending practices of private libraries in colonial America, see Hayes, *The Library of William Byrd*, 1–103, Wolf, *The Library of James Logan*, McLachlan, "The Choice of Hercules: American Student Societies in the Early Nineteenth Century," in Lawrence Stone, ed., *The University in Society*, 2: 449–94, and Lundberg and May, "The Enlightened Reader in America."

25. See Ross W. Beales and James N. Green, "Libraries and Their Users," in Amory and Hall, eds., *The Colonial Book*, 399–404.

26. Louise May Bryant and Mary Patterson, "The List of Books Sent by Jeremiah Dummer," and Anne Stokely Pratt, "The Books Sent from England by Jeremiah Dummer to Yale College," in *Papers in Honor of Andrew Keogh*, 7–44 and 423–92; Mooney, ed., *Eighteenth-Century*

Catalogues of the Yale College Library, vii–xix; Peter J. Thuesen, "Editor's Introduction," in Thuesen, ed., *Catalogues of Books*, 1–113; Anderson, ed., *Scientific and Philosophical Writings*, 164. On Edwards and natural philosophy, see Zakai, *Jonathan Edwards's Philosophy of Nature*.

27. Anderson, ed., *Scientific and Philosophical Writings*, 31–32.

28. Cohen, *Some Early Tools of American Science*, 109; Rice, *The Rittenhouse Orrery*; Mather, *The Christian Philosopher*, 164, 166.

29. Winthrop, *Two Lectures*, 29.

30. See Impey and MacGregor, eds., *The Origins of Museums*, 1–4, MacGregor, ed., *Sir Hans Sloane*, Findlen, *Possessing Nature*, Smith and Findlen, eds., *Merchants and Marvels*, and Phillips and Idiens, " 'A Casket of Savage Curiosities.' "

31. Sloan, *A New World*, 170–71; McBurney, *Mark Catesby's "Natural History" of America*, 25, 115–20; Meyers and Pritchard, eds., *Empire's Nature*.

32. John Adams to Abigail Adams, July 25, 1782, *APDE*; John Adams to Abigail Adams, April–May 1780, *APDE*; John Adams to Abigail Adams, April–May 1780, *APDE*; John Adams, diary entry for October 27, 1783, *APDE*.

33. Semonin, *American Monster*, 299.

34. Brigham, *Public Culture in the Early Republic*; Sellers, *Mr. Peale's Museum*; Rigal, "Peale's Mammoth"; Amy R. Waters, "Imposing Order on the Wilderness: Natural History Illustration and Landscape Portrayal," in Nygren, *Views and Visions*, 123–24; Hindle, "Charles Willson Peale's Science and Technology," 114.

Chapter Two. Seashells in the Appalachians

1. Samuel Miller, *A Brief Retrospect*, 184–85; Browne, *An Address*, 3.

2. The topic of shells and natural history has attracted much attention from early modern British and European historians and art historians, and comparatively little from historians of British America and the early United States. The exception is the shells of the wampum trade, which is not my main concern here. For scientific interest in shells in early America, see Stearns, *Science, passim*. On the British and European interest, see Rudwick, *Bursting the Limits of Time*, Rappaport, *When Geologists Were Historians*, 105–35, John Thackray, "Mineral and Fossil Collections," in MacGregor, ed., *Sir Hans Sloane*, 123–35, Segal, *A Prosperous Past*, 77–92, Gillespie, *Genesis and Geology*, Porter, *The Making of Geology*, Rudwick, *The Meaning of Fossils*, and Dance, *Shell Collecting*. Historians of British America and the United States have given most of their attention to megafauna fossils. Recent book-length studies include Dugatkin, *Mr. Jefferson and the Giant Moose*, Thomson, *The Legacy of the Mastodon*, Hedeen, *Big Bone Lick*, Rigal, *The American Manufactory*, and Semonin, *American Monster*. Influential article-length studies include Levin, "Giants

in the Earth," Stanford, "The Giant Bones of Claverack," and Simpson, "The Beginnings of Vertebrate Paleontology in North America." On lusus naturae, see Findlen, "Jokes of Nature." John Bartram to Peter Collinson, undated but probably November 14, 1751, in Berkeley and Berkeley, eds., *The Correspondence of John Bartram*, 334.

3. Agassiz, "America the Old World," 1. On nationalist posturing in American geology, see Bedell, *The Anatomy of Nature*, 6.

4. William Byrd II to Sir Hans Sloane, April 20, 1706, in "Letters of William Byrd II," 186.

5. Amid the larger conversation about whether the biblical flood had extended to America was an ongoing debate about whether American Indians had knowledge of the flood and if so, whether that knowledge was reliable. John Ray (who had never traveled to America) thought they did and it was: *Miscellaneous Discourses*, 100; Peter Kalm, who traveled extensively in America, frequently reported on the Indians' views of the biblical flood: *Travels into North America*, 58, 74. Mayor, *Fossil Legends of the First Americans*, is an in-depth study of the topic.

6. Adair, *The History of the American Indians*, 228, relates that some North American Indians believed that the Appalachians continued south through Peru.

7. Walter W. Woodward, *Prospero's America*, 78; Alvord and Bidgood, *The First Explorations of the Trans-Allegheny Region*, 141; Herrman, *Virginia and Maryland*; for his map see http://www.msa.md.gov/msa/educ/exhibits/images/fig18.jpg.

8. Alvord and Bidgood, *The First Explorations of the Trans-Allegheny Region*, 138; Stearns, *Science*, 206, 190.

9. Leibniz, *Protogaea*, xiv, 13.

10. These three works appear in the inventories of American private libraries and colleges. Burnet's *Telluris Theoria Sacra* and Woodward's *Essay* appear in the 1714 Dummer gift to Yale's library: see Anne Stokely Pratt, "The Books Sent from England by Jeremiah Dummer," in *Papers in Honor of Andrew Keogh*, 15–16.

11. Burnet, *The Sacred Theory*, 62–63, 65, 27, 115, 118.

12. Burnet, *The Sacred Theory*, 110, 111–13.

13. Ray, *Miscellaneous Discourses*, 99; Burnet, *The Sacred Theory*, 111.

14. Edwin Wolf, "The Dispersal of the Library of William Byrd of Westover," 59, 105; "A Catalogue of the Books in the Library at Westover belonging to William Byrd Esqr.," in Bassett, ed., *The Writings*, 415; William Byrd I to Perry and Lane, July 23, 1689, in Tinling, ed., *The Correspondence of the Three William Byrds*, 1: 111.

15. William Byrd, *History of the Dividing Line*, 1: 138.

16. William Byrd, *The Westover Manuscripts*.

17. I have come to this conclusion based on my reading of Mather's letters and texts. Thanks also to David D. Hall for his thoughts on whether

Mather had ever been to the mountains (conversation May 19, 2012, Cambridge, Mass.).

18. See Smolinski and Stievermann, eds., *Cotton Mather*, 1: 3, 337 ff., Silverman, comp., *Selected Letters of Cotton Mather*, ix, and Semonin, *American Monster*, 29–38.

19. Joseph Levine, *Dr. Woodward's Shield*, 23–24; John Harris, *Lexicon Technicum*, s.v. "Fossils."

20. Thackray, "Mineral and Fossil Collections," in MacGregor, ed., *Sir Hans Sloane;* on Lister in his American context, see Stearns, *Science*, 167–68, Segal, *A Prosperous Past*, 77–92, and Levine, *Dr. Woodward's Shield*, 49.

21. Woodward, *An Essay*, unpaginated page 4 of preface, 225.

22. Woodward, *An Essay*, 217; Cotton Mather to John Woodward, November 17, 1712, quoted in Levin, "Giants in the Earth," 757; Levine, *Dr. Woodward's Shield*, 51.

23. Levine, *Dr. Woodward's Shield*, 51, 101.

24. Mather to John Winthrop, August 15, 1716, in "Letters of Cotton Mather," 419; John Winthrop to Cotton Mather, November 5, 1716, in "Winthrop Papers," 332–33; John Woodward to John Winthrop, April 8, 1721, in "November Meeting, 1873," 110.

25. David Price, "John Woodward," 82.

26. Levine, *Dr. Woodward's Shield*, 100; Mather, *The Christian Philosopher*, 97.

27. Bartram to Collinson, April 27, 1755, Bartram to Collinson, undated but probably fall 1753, Jan Frederik Gronovius to Bartram, January 10, 1754, in Berkeley and Berkeley, eds., *The Correspondence of John Bartram*, 383, 359, 367.

28. On availability of Burnet's *Theory of the Earth* in British America, see "To be Sold by the Printer hereof, the following Books," *Pennsylvania Gazette*, March 28, 1734, Franklin to Jared Eliot, July 16, 1747, *PBF*, 3: 149, and Franklin, "A Proposal for Promoting Useful Knowledge Among the British Plantations in America," May 15, 1743, *PBF*, 2: 381; on Franklin's geological interests, see Dean, "Benjamin Franklin and Geology."

29. Bartram to Cadwallader Colden, January 25, 1745/6, Bartram to Gronovius, December 6, 1745, Bartram to Collinson, July 22, 1741, in Berkeley and Berkeley, eds., *The Correspondence of John Bartram*, 271, 267, 162.

30. Bartram, *Observations*, 70.

31. Bartram to Hans Sloane, November 14, 1742, Collinson to Bartram, June 7, 1736, Bartram to Sloane, July 22, 1741, John Fothergill to Bartram, December 23, 1743/4, Bartram to Gronovius, March 14, 1752, Fothergill to Bartram, December 22, 1743/4, in Berkeley and Berkeley, eds., *The Correspondence of John Bartram*, 207, 31, 160, 230, 339, 230.

32. The text appears on *A Map of Pensilvania, New-Jersey, New-York, and the Three Delaware Counties: by Lewis Evans* (1749), in Gipson, ed., *Lewis Evans*, second map in "Part Four: *Maps*."

33. Kalm, entry for October 16, 1748, in Benson, ed., *The America of 1750: Peter Kalm's Travels*, 1: 106–7; Kalm, entry for October 31, 1748, in Kalm, *Travels into North America*, 126. The wampum trade extended far inland from the coast where the shells were found: see Ceci, "Native Wampum."

34. Collinson to Bartram, n.d., but probably 1751 or after, Bartram to Collinson, n.d., but probably November 14, 1751, in Berkeley and Berkeley, eds., *The Correspondence of John Bartram*, 328, 333, 334.

35. Mendes da Costa, *A Natural History of Fossils*, iv. For the North American circulation of this work, see Franklin to Joseph Morris, February 20, 1761, *PBF*, 9: 275, Madison to Jefferson, November 30, 1794, *PJMCS*, 15: 396, and *CLTJ*, 1: 497.

36. I concur with Martin Rudwick's argument about European geology, which is that the influence of the Scottish geologist James Hutton has been overstated relative to other, equally influential earth theorists. Some of the blame for this can be laid at the feet of the British geologist Charles Lyell's influential *Principles of Geology*, which contains an extensive history of the rise of the earth sciences. Lyell's British-centric account, the basis on which future Anglo-American historians built their own histories of the topic, mostly ignored the early American presence in earth theorizing and also understated French influence, even though Lyell himself did extensive fieldwork in the Auvergne region of France. See Lyell, *Principles of Geology*, vol. 1, and Rudwick, *Bursting the Limits of Time*, 158.

37. Volney, *View*, 13.

38. Faujas de Saint Fond, *Histoire Naturelle*, 14; Madison, "Preliminary Draft of an Essay on Natural Order, [ca. November 10,] 1791," *PJMCS*, 14: 100, 102; Rudwick, *Bursting the Limits of Time*, 181–95. Jefferson owned Faujas de Saint Fond's *Histoire Naturelle*: *CLTJ*, 1: 300.

39. Jefferson, *Notes* (1787), 69; Dexter, ed., *The Literary Diary of Ezra Stiles*, 2: 315 (entry for December 28, 1778).

40. Buffon, *Des époques*, 3, 84; Buffon, *Oeuvres complètes*, 1: 443; Rossi, *The Dark Abyss of Time*, 108.

41. John Quincy Adams, diary entries for November 4 and 9, 1787, *APDE*; Buffon, *Oeuvres complètes*, 1: 388–51. For a digitized version of John Adams's copy with marginalia, see John Adams Library at the Boston Public Library: https://archive.org/details/oeuvrescompltesdo1buff.

42. "Editorial Note," in Madison, "Notes on Buffon's *Histoire naturelle*," completed ca. May 1786, *PJMCS*, 9: 29; Madison to Jefferson, May 12, 1786, *PJMCS*, 9: 53; Reverend James Madison to Jefferson, December 28, 1786, *PTJ*, 10: 642–43.

43. Voltaire, "Des coquilles," 115, 120, 126. For a stern rebuke to Voltaire's shell theory, see Sauvagère, *Recueil*, xviii–xxviii, a work Jefferson owned: *CLTJ*, 1: 305–6.

44. Deluc, *Lettres*, viii; Rudwick, *Bursting the Limits of Time*, 157. The English-language term *geology* appears to have been coined earlier in the eighteenth century: see Rudwick, "Geohistory."

45. Soulavie, *Histoire naturelle*; Wolf and Hayes, *The Library of Benjamin Franklin*, 744; Rudwick, *Bursting the Limits of Time*, 122.

46. Jefferson, *Notes* (1801), 34.

47. For the 1735 French expedition to Ecuador to measure the circumference of the earth, a source of major new contributions to observations of the Andes, Jefferson cited Bouguer, *La Figure de la Terre*, and Ulloa, *Noticias americanas*; for the mountains of Mexico, he cited Clavigero, *Storia antica*; for France, Voltaire, "Des coquilles"; and for Russia, Krasheninnikov, *Histoire de Kamtschatka*.

48. Jefferson, *Notes* (1787), 45.

49. Jefferson, *Notes* (1787), 49, 46, 47.

50. Jefferson, *Notes* (1787), 47, 48.

51. Jefferson, *Notes* (1787), 48–49.

52. Franklin to Soulavie, September 22, 1782, *PBFDE*.

53. Rev. James Madison to Jefferson, March 27, 1786, *PTJ*, 9: 355–57; Rev. James Madison to Jefferson, December 28, 1786, *PTJ*, 10: 642–44; Jefferson owned the 1774 edition of Hamilton, *Observations on Mount Vesuvius: CLTJ*, 1: 300; Jefferson to Marc Auguste Pictet, October 14, 1795, *PTJ*, 28: 505.

54. Jefferson, *Memorandums Taken on a Journey from Paris into the Southern Parts of France and Northern Italy in the Year 1787*, in *CLTJ*, 1: 306; Sauvagère, *Recueil*, xxviii; Jefferson to the Reverend James Madison, August 13, 1787, *PTJ*, 12: 30. Jefferson also sent a copy of Sauvagère's book to David Rittenhouse, with an enthusiastic note: Jefferson to David Rittenhouse, September 18, 1787, *PTJ*, 12: 144.

55. Jefferson quoted in Charles A. Miller, *Jefferson and Nature*, 49–50.

56. Doskey, ed., *The European Journals of William Maclure*, 343; Maclure, *Essay*, 9.

57. James Madison, "Preliminary Draft of an Essay on Natural Order," ca. November 10, 1791, *PJMCS*, 14: 103.

58. Hayden, *Geological Essays*, vi, 113, 347.

59. Temple Henry Croker to Franklin, June 11, 1787, *PBFDE*; Green, *A Monograph of the Trilobites*, 12, 14.

Chapter Three. The Civilization of the Aztecs

1. Burford, *Description*, 4. See also Sanders, *A History of the Indian Wars*, in which Mexico and Peru at the time of the conquest are described as "The most enlightened places" (113).

2. Hill, *Antiquities of America*, 130; Mill, *The History of Mexico*, 2. For developments in Spanish America, see Brading, *The First America*,

Cañizares-Esguerra, *How to Write the History*, Pagden, *Spanish Imperialism*, 91–116, Pocock, *Barbarism and Religion*, 4: 157–79, and Coronado, *A World Not to Come*. On North America, see Bauer, "The Hispanic Enlightenment."

3. On surviving codices, see Gruzinski, *Painting the Conquest*, 229. Historians and art historians debate the moral and aesthetic meanings of the post-conquest codices. Serge Gruzinski emphasizes the century after conquest as a moment not only of massive disaster but also of cultural fertility, what he calls a "Mexican Renaissance" (197). Donald Robertson likewise argues that the Codex Mendoza shows that "native traditions were enriched by Spanish contact" (*Mexican Manuscript Painting*, 45). On codices in European collections, see Detlef Heikamp, "American Objects in Italian Collections of the Renaissance and Baroque: A Survey," and Donald Robertson, "Mexican Indian Art and the Atlantic Filter: Sixteenth to Eighteenth Centuries," both in Chiappelli, Allen, and Benson, eds., *First Images of America*, 1: 455–82 and 483–94. James Lockhart urges caution when judging how representative the pictorial codices were, arguing that the postconquest Nahua (Aztecs) produced both pictographic writing and, under the influence of the Spanish, alphabetic writing. With each passing decade after 1521, the Nahua shifted ever more toward alphabetic writing and away from pictographic depictions; in fact, the bulk of postconquest pictographic documents is infinitesimal compared with the large mass of postconquest Nahua-produced alphabetic documents in Mexican archives. However, because Europeans preferred the pictographic writing for its beauty and their sense that it provided a window onto preconquest Nahua society, those pictographs were shipped to Europe preferentially over the Nahua alphabetic manuscripts. Thus the European archives became heav-ily weighted toward increasingly nonrepresentative and archaic picto-graphic documents. See Lockhart, *The Nahuas After the Conquest*, 331.

4. Mendoza's name was not specifically attached to this document until the late eighteenth century: see H. B. Nicholson, "The History of the Codex Mendoza," and Berdan and Anawalt, "Introduction," in Berdan and Anawalt, [eds.], *The Codex Mendoza*, 1: 10 and xii.

5. Purchas, *Purchas His Pilgrimage*, 803; Purchas, *Purchas His Pilgrimes*; Nicholson, "The History of the Codex Mendoza," in Berdan and Anawalt, [eds.], *The Codex Mendoza*, 1: 1–11.

6. Purchas, *Purchas His Pilgrimage*, 803, 811; Purchas, *Purchas His Pilgrimes*, 3: 1102.

7. Purchas, *Purchas His Pilgrimes*, 3: 1102.

8. Purchas, *Purchas His Pilgrimage*, 803; John Adams Library at the Boston Public Library; *CLTJ*, 4: 166–67; Warburton, *The Divine Legation*, 2: 67–70.

9. Keen, *The Aztec Image*, 217–59; Voltaire, *An Essay*, 3: 201.

10. Kagan, *Urban Images*, 9, 89–95; MacCormack, "Limits of Understanding: Perceptions of Greco-Roman and Amerindian Paganism in Early Modern

Europe," in Kupperman, ed., *America in European Consciousness*, 79–129; Diderot and d'Alembert, *Encyclopédie*, 10: 480 (s.v. "Mexico, ville de").

11. Pauw, *Recherches philosophiques sur les Américains*, 2: 197, 198; Raynal, *Histoire philosophique et politique*. On the broad outlines of this debate, see Gerbi, *The Dispute of the New World*, 45–169.

12. The indigenous Mexicans are briefly mentioned in Adam Smith, *The Theory of Moral Sentiments*, Adam Ferguson, *An Essay on the History of Civil Society*, Kames, "Sketch XII. Origin and Progress of American Nations," in his *Sketches*, 3: 80–112, and Adam Smith, *An Inquiry* (London).

13. Franklin to William Robertson, March 4, 1765, *PBF*, 12: 80; Franklin acquired the first edition from a friend sometime after June 1777: see Wolf and Hayes, *The Library of Benjamin Franklin*, 680. Diary of John Adams, entry for July 16, 1779, *APDE*; William Jackson to John Adams, October 26, 1781, *APDE*; James Madison, "Report on Books for Congress," [January 23] 1783," *PJMCS*, 6: 101; Jefferson, "A Course of Reading for Joseph C. Cabell," September 1800, *PTJ*, 32: 178. Jefferson's manuscript catalogue indicates that he owned a copy of Robertson: *CLTJ*, 1: 216. Diary of John Adams, entry for July 12, 1796, *APDE*.

14. Lenman, " 'From Savage to Scot' "; Robertson, *The History of America*, 1: vi, 27, 368–69.

15. Robertson, *The History of America*, 1: xv, viii, ix; Humphreys, *William Robertson*, 17; Duckworth, "An Eighteenth-Century Questionnaire," 41, 47.

16. Keen, *The Aztec Image*, 281.

17. Robertson, *The History of America*, 1: xvi, 2: 519–35.

18. Boturini Benaduci, *Catalogo del Museo*, 1–6, 48; Glass, "The Boturini Collection," 48; for more on Boturini, see Cañizares-Esguerra, *How to Write the History*, 135–55.

19. Robertson, *The History of America*, 1: 484.

20. Schoolcraft, *Travels*, 228; Samuel Holden Parsons to Ezra Stiles, April 27, 1786, enclosure in Ezra Stiles to Thomas Jefferson, May 8, 1786, in *PTJ*, 9: 478. On the mound builders, see Silverberg, *Mound Builders*, and Sayre, "The Mound Builders." Some early accounts of the mounds include David Jones, *A Journal*, Jones, "A Plan," and Filson, *The Discovery*.

21. The expulsion of Jesuits from Mexico produced other works on Mexican antiquities. Another Jesuit exile, Pedro José Márquez, wrote the first work on Mexican archaeology to be published in Europe: *Due antichi monumenti di architettura messicana*. See also Keen, *The Aztec Image*, 300.

22. Clavigero, *Storia antica del Messico*, 1: 1, 5, 19, 4: 222–23; Lenman, " 'From Savage to Scot,' " 205.

23. Clavigero, *Storia antica del Messico*, 4: 215–16.

24. Buffon, *The Natural History*, 2: 367; Clavigero, *Storia antica del Messico*, 4: 105–59.

25. See Almeida, *Reimagining the Transatlantic*, 40–48.

26. Clavigero, *The History of Mexico*, 1: iv, iii.

27. Jefferson to the marquis de Chastellux, June 7, 1785, *PTJ*, 8: 185.

28. Jefferson, *Notes* (1787), 96; Jefferson to Miguel de Lardizábel y Uribe, with Enclosure, July 6, 1787, *PTJ*, 11: 553–54; Jefferson to James Madison, August 2, 1787, *PTJ*, 11: 667.

29. *CLTJ*, 4: 269; Jefferson to Joseph Willard, March 24, 1789, *PTJ*, 14: 698. In his personal copy of the *Notes on the State of Virginia* (1787), Jefferson made numerous memos to himself, in which he quoted Clavigero in Italian or made general reference to Clavigero. See Jefferson, *Notes*, ed. Shuffelton, 295n28, 300n50, 302n57, 310n121, 310n125, 316n151.

30. Coram, *Political Inquiries*, 12.

31. Clavigero, *The History of Mexico*, 1: 83, 84, 90.

32. Clavigero, *The History of Mexico*, 1: 86, 90 112, 122.

33. Barton, *Observations*, 39, 50, 53, 60, 65. Barton expanded on his use of Clavigero and the southward migrations of the Toltecs in his *New Views of the Origin of the Tribes and Nations of America*.

34. Harris, *The Journal of a Tour*, 163, 158; Atwater, *Writings*, 148–49 [reprint of 1820 article from *Archaeologia Americana*]; Pickering, "Introductory Observations," 6; Rafinesque, *The Ancient Monuments*, 6; Morton, *Crania Americana*, 63, 141–44; Mayer, *Mexico as It Was and as It Is*, 261.

35. Squier and Davis, *Ancient Monuments*, 3, 45; Charles Eliot Norton, "Ancient Monuments," 492–94.

36. Hill, *Antiquities of America Explained*, 33, 46.

37. Khristaan D. Villela, Matthew H. Robb, and Mary Ellen Miller, "Introduction," in Villela and Miller, eds., *The Aztec Calendar Stone*, 1–6; Boone, "The Defining Sample."

38. See Villela, "Editor's Commentary," in Villela and Miller, eds., *The Aztec Calendar Stone*, 52.

39. Villela, "Editor's Commentary," in Villela and Miller, eds., *The Aztec Calendar Stone*, 50; Cody, "An Index to the Periodicals," 445, 455. On seventeenth-century Spanish American scholars and the pre-Hispanic past, see More, *Baroque Sovereignty*.

40. León y Gama, *Descripción*, 1, 4; on the rise of the idea of pre-Columbian "art," see Braun, *Pre-Columbian Art and the Post-Columbian World*, 21–49.

41. Barton to Jefferson, September 14, 1809, *PTJ Ret*, 1: 521; Jefferson to Barton, September 21, 1809, *PTJ Ret*, 1: 556.

42. William E. Hūlings, "An Historical and Chronological Description of Two Stones Found Under Ground, in the Great Square of the City of Mexico, in the Years 1790" (American Philosophical Society. Mss.913.72. L55). No complete English translation of León y Gama's *Descripción* has ever been published. Biographical information for León y Gama and Hūlings and a partial translation of León y Gama's *Descripción* appear in Villela and Miller, eds., *The Aztec Calendar Stone*, 52–76.

43. Humboldt, *Researches*, 1: 39, 166, 399, 127–29, 138, 161, 185.
44. Humboldt, *Researches*, 1: 408, 289, 276.
45. Poinsett, *Notes on Mexico*, 325, 299, unpaginated first page of "Advertisement," 326, 55; Henry Clay to Joel R. Poinsett, March 26, 1825, in William R. Manning, ed., *Diplomatic Correspondence*, 1: 229.
46. "Donations Received" (1825), 491, 495; Peter S. Du Ponceau to Joel R. Poinsett, November 9, 1826, quoted in Freeman, "Manuscript Sources," 531–32.
47. "Donations Received" (1830), 503; "Mexican Antiquities."
48. William Prescott to Francis Lieber, November 26, 1839, in Gardiner, ed., *The Papers of William Hickling Prescott*, 147; Gardiner, ed., *The Literary Memoranda*, 2: 9, 17, 3, 4–7, 22; Jaksić, *The Hispanic World*, 145.
49. William Prescott to Joel R. Poinsett, January 26, 1839, in Gardiner, ed., *The Papers of William Hickling Prescott*, 136 (see also Jaksić, *The Hispanic World*, 131); Jaksić, *The Hispanic World*, 151, 149.
50. Prescott, *History of the Conquest of Mexico*, 1: 58, 59.
51. On American philhellenism, see Winterer, *The Culture of Classicism*, 44–98; Cushing quoted in Jaksić, *The Hispanic World*, 154.

Chapter Four. The Science of Statistics and the Invention of the "Indian Population"

1. William Playfair, "To His Excellency Thomas Jefferson, President of the United States of America, &c. &c. &c.," in Donnant, *Statistical Account*, xi.
2. As punishment for King David's action, God sent a plague that killed thousands. The "sin of David" appears in 1 Chronicles 21 and 2 Samuel 24. The fear of the sin of David continued to haunt American census takers; after the returns of the first federal census, George Washington complained to Gouverneur Morris about the "religeous scruples" that caused some Americans to refuse to return the census lists: Washington to Morris, July 28, 1791, *PGW Pres*, 8: 383.
3. Playfair, "To His Excellency Thomas Jefferson," in Donnant, *Statistical Account*, x, xi.
4. In a large literature on the American Indians in seventeenth- and eighteenth-century thought, see especially Pagden, *The Fall of Natural Man*, Edward Gray, *New World Babel*, Honour, *The New Golden Land*, Ellingson, *The Myth of the Noble Savage*, Berkhofer, *The White Man's Indian*, Pearce, *The Savages of America*, and Slotkin, *Regeneration Through Violence*. On North American data in conjectural history, see Bickham, *Savages Within the Empire*, chap. 5. For conjectural history, see Höpfl, "From Savage to Scotsman," and Emerson, "American Indians." For general works on stadial theories, see Meek, *Social Science*, Berry, *The Social Theory*, and Bryson, *Man and Society*.

5. Kames, *Sketches*, 3: 90; Hume, "Of the Populousness of Ancient Nations," in *Essays*, 377–464; Gibbon, *The History of the Decline and Fall*, 1: 43; Souligné, *A Comparison;* Robert Wallace, *A Dissertation.*

6. Among the first books to use the term *Indian population* in its title was Coates, *Annual Discourse* (1834).

7. Anderson et al., *American Indian Law*, 108; Publius [James Madison], *The Federalist*, 2: 54.

8. "Speech of the Hon. Asher Robbins, Senator from Rhode Island, Delivered in the Senate of the United States, April 21, 1830," in *Speeches on the Passage*, 73.

9. Russell Thornton, *American Indian Holocaust;* Henige, *Numbers from Nowhere.*

10. Jefferson, *Notes* (1787), 96; the king's question was "What number of Indians had you in your Government?"; see Peter Orlando Hutchinson, ed., *The Diary and Letters*, 1: 173.

11. Wells, *The Population of the British Colonies*, 5–21 (quotation from 19).

12. Blum, *Strength in Numbers*, 6; Petty, *Essays*, 161; Landsdowne, ed., *The Petty Papers*, 2: 115–16.

13. Wells, *The Population of the British Colonies*, 7–12, 34; Luca Codignola, "The Holy See and the Conversion of the Indians in French and British North America, 1486–1760," in Kupperman, ed., *America in European Consciousness*, 196; John Smith, *A Map of Virginia*, 5; "An Act for Destroying Wolves," in Hening, *The Statutes at Large*, 2: 274–76; "Johnson's Account of Indian Expenses, Mar., 1755 to Oct., 1756," in Sullivan, ed., *The Papers of Sir William Johnson*, 2: 567; Wainwright, ed., "George Croghan's Journal," 317. For more on diplomatic gifts, see Jacobs, *Wilderness Politics.*

14. For a British American map showing this convention of rounding, see Edward Moseley, "A New and Correct Map of the Province of North Carolina" (1733) in Cumming, *The Southeast in Early Maps*, plate 54, and 200–202; for Roman rounding, see Julius Caesar, *The Conquest of Gaul*, trans. S. A. Handford, rev. ed. (New York: Penguin, 1982), 40 and passim; on medieval rounding, see Biller, *The Measure of Multitude*, 224; on rounding in colonial American censuses, see Wells, *The Population of the British Colonies*, 33; there are many examples of rounding in Thwaites, ed., *The Jesuit Relations*. On British imperial policy, see Cassedy, *Demography*, 59–90.

15. Anthony Thorold to [?] Williamson, July 3, 1676, in "Charles II: July 1676," *Calendar of State Papers Domestic: Charles II, 1676–7* (1909): 199–257, British History Online, http://www.british-history.ac.uk/report.aspx?compid=57350; J. W. F. Fortescue, ed., "America and West Indies: December 1681, 3–15," entry for December 12, 1681, *Calendar of State Papers Colonial, America and West Indies*, vol. 11: 1681–1685, no. 320. British History Online, http://www.british-history.ac.uk/report.aspx?compid=69854; Wraxall, "Indian Intelligence from Sir William Johnson," in Sullivan, ed., *The Papers of Sir William Johnson*, 2: 710.

16. Thwaites, ed., *The Jesuit Relations*, 44: 245; Lawson, *A New Voyage to Carolina*, 235; Trumbull, *A Complete History*, 1: 29.

17. George Clinton to Board of Trade, November 26, 1749, in *Journal of the Commissioners for Trade and Plantations, from January 1749/50 to December 1753* (London: His Majesty's Stationery Office, 1932), 46.

18. Lahontan, *New Voyages*, 1: 23.

19. Wells, *The Population of the British Colonies*, 167–68; "Narrative of a Journey into the Mohawk and Oneida Country, 1634–1635," in J. Franklin Jameson, ed., *Narratives of New Netherland*, 153.

20. Adam Stephen's account of 1754, cited in "Minutes of a Council of War," June 28, 1754, *PGW Col*, 1: 156n2; Francis Fauquier to William Byrd, August 17, 1758, in Reese, ed., *The Official Papers of Francis Fauquier*, 1: 61; Rogers, *A Concise Account*, 162. On British policy toward the American Indians in the 1750s and 1760s, see Shaw, *British Administration of the Southern Indians*, and Bickham, *Savages Within the Empire*, 113–67.

21. Lafitau, *Moeurs des sauvages amériquains*; Charlevoix, *Histoire et description generale de la Nouvelle France*; Jonsson, *Enlightenment's Frontier*, 12–16.

22. Adam Smith, *The Theory of Moral Sentiments*, 313, 320, 315; Adam Smith, *An Inquiry* (Dublin), 3: 45.

23. Smith, *An Inquiry* (Dublin), 3: 46.

24. William Smith, *The History of the Province of New-York*, xi, 34–35. This book is entry no. 1568 in Adam Smith, *The Glasgow Edition of the Works and Correspondence of Adam Smith: Adam Smith's Library*.

25. Colden, *The History of the Five Indian Nations*; Adam Ferguson, *An Essay on the History of Civil Society*, 33; Bickham, *Savages Within the Empire*, 181 (on Ferguson's American interests, see also Kettler, "The Social and Political Thought of Adam Ferguson," 60), and David Hume to Adam Ferguson, March 10, 1767, in Merolle, *The Correspondence of Adam Ferguson*, 1: 73.

26. Millar, *Observations*, iv, 3, 115–16; Bickham, *Savages Within the Empire*, 189–91.

27. Benjamin Franklin to William Robertson, June 2, 1765, *PBF*, 12: 165; Franklin to Ezra Stiles, July 5, 1765, *PBF*, 12: 195.

28. Ezra Stiles, entry for April 13, 1786, in Dexter, ed., *The Literary Diary of Ezra Stiles*, 3: 213; Edmund S. Morgan, *The Gentle Puritan*, 142–43, 159, 456; Mooney, ed., *Eighteenth-Century Catalogues of the Yale College Library*, xv.

29. Morgan, *The Gentle Puritan*, 159; Lutz, "Ezra Stiles and the Library," 14, 17.

30. See Morgan, *The Gentle Puritan*, 161, and Jonathan Trumbull to Ezra Stiles, July 14, 1762, in Calder, ed., *Letters and Papers of Ezra Stiles*, 9–10.

31. Morgan, *The Gentle Puritan*, 139–40.

32. Franklin to Stiles, May 29, 1763, in Calder, ed., *Letters and Papers of Ezra Stiles*, 13; Short, *A Comparative History*, iii, Richard Price, *Observations*,

203, and footnote on "Dr. Styles"; Mooney, ed., *Eighteenth-Century Catalogues of the Yale College Library*, C9, C45. For more on Franklin and population, see Hodgson, "Benjamin Franklin on Population," Houston, *Benjamin Franklin*, 106–46, Aldridge, "Franklin as Demographer," and Whelan, "Population and Ideology in the Enlightenment."

33. See Morgan, *The Gentle Puritan*, 136–39.

34. Morgan, *The Gentle Puritan*, 136; "Talk of Coll. Goldthwait of Fort Pownall with Josepsis a Mataguissawack Indian who is Now Settled among the Penobscots. August: 1771," in Calder, ed., *Letters and Papers of Ezra Stiles*, 27; Ezra Stiles, entry for March 10, 1775, in Dexter, ed., *The Literary Diary of Ezra Stiles*, 1: 524; Romans, *A Concise Natural History*.

35. Wells, *The Population of the British Colonies*, 90; Hopkins, *Historical Memoirs*, 54, 128; Morgan, *The Gentle Puritan*, 80–88, 136, 137; Jonathan Trumbull to Ezra Stiles with note in Stiles's hand, July 14, 1762, in Calder, ed., *Letters and Papers of Ezra Stiles*, 9–11; Stiles, entry for November 24, 1777, in Dexter, ed., *The Literary Diary of Ezra Stiles*, 1: 489.

36. Stiles, *The United States Elevated*, 11, 18–19, 13.

37. Morse, *The American Geography*, 159; Morse, *The American Gazetteer*, 249, s.v. "Indians."

38. Jefferson, *Notes* (1787), 153, 165.

39. Jefferson, *Notes* (1787), 152, 101.

40. Jefferson, *Notes* (1787), 106–7.

41. Henry Knox to George Washington, Enclosure Number 1, June 15, 1789, *PGW Pres*, 2: 491; Knox to Washington, July 7, 1789, *PGW Pres*, 3: 138–39.

42. Malthus, *An Essay on the Principle of Population*, 16, 13, 21, 105, 185.

43. Malthus, *An Essay on the Principle of Population*, 42, 44, 39–40.

44. See McCoy, "Jefferson and Madison on Malthus," and Spengler, "Malthusianism."

45. See Moulton, ed., *Journals*, 3: 387, 334, 386–450, *Message from the President*, and Lewis, Clark, and Mackenzie, *The Travels of Capts. Lewis & Clarke*.

46. Jefferson, "Instructions to Captain Lewis, June 20, 1803," in Merrill Peterson, ed., *Thomas Jefferson: Writings*, 1128; Ronda, "Lewis and Clark and Enlightenment Ethnography," 8.

47. Moulton, ed., *Journals*, 3: 386, 390.

48. Moulton, ed., *Journals*, 3: 388; Ronda, "Lewis and Clark and Enlightenment Ethnography," 11–13; *Message from the President of the United States*, 9–65.

49. Sinclair, *The Statistical Account of Scotland*, 20: xiii.

50. John Sinclair to Jefferson, May 18, 1792, *PTJ*, 23: 524; Sinclair, *The Statistical Account of Scotland*, 20: xxxix; Clarke, *A Statistical View of Europe*, iv–v.

51. See Tufte, *The Visual Display of Quantitative Information*.

52. Godwin does not mention which edition of the Lewis and Clark reports he read. Based on his arguments, however, we can speculate that he read the 1814 London edition: Lewis, *Travels to the Source of the Missouri River,* 251; Godwin, *Of Population,* 363.

53. Godwin, *Of Population,* 365, 2.

54. Madison to Richard Rush, April 21, 1821, in Gaillard Hunt, ed., *Writings of James Madison,* 9: 54, 48.

55. Barbé-Marbois, *The History of Louisiana,* 74.

56. Ramsay, *The History of South-Carolina,* 2: 366; "Speech of the Hon. Asher Robbins," in *Speeches on the Passage,* 74.

Chapter Five. Slavery in an Enlightened Age

1. Dickson, *Letters on Slavery,* 4.

2. See Dunn, *Sugar and Slaves,* 226; Blackburn, *The Overthrow of Colonial Slavery,* 5.

3. Wood, *Black Majority,* 152; Nicholas Lejeune quoted in Burnard, *Mastery, Tyranny, and Desire,* 137.

4. Govier, "The Royal Society," 203–4, 206, 208; Murphy, "Collecting Slave Traders," 647n20.

5. Delbourgo, "Slavery," 1–2, 15; Kriz, "Curiosities"; Iannini, *Fatal Revolutions;* Ligon, *A True & Exact History,* 51, 50, 85 ff.; Sloane, *A Voyage,* 2: 161, 342; Delbourgo, "The Newtonian Slave Body," 191; Byrd, "An Account," 781–82.

6. See Sewall, *The Selling of Joseph,* 29, Cotton Mather to John Woodward, July 12, 1716, in Kittredge, "Some Lost Works," 422, Minardi, "The Boston Inoculation Controversy," Mark Peterson, "The Selling of Joseph," 5, and Towner, "The Sewall-Saffin Dialogue."

7. Morgan Godwyn, *The Negro's & Indians Advocate,* 18; Godwyn, *A Supplement to the Negro's & Indian's Advocate,* 7; La Peyrère, *Praeadamitae.*

8. Sewall, *The Selling of Joseph,* 7, 12; Towner, "The Sewall-Saffin Dialogue," 43; see also Peterson, "The Selling of Joseph," 13. See also John Saffin, *A True and Particular Narrative by Way of Vindication of the Author's Dealing with and Prosecution of his Negro Man Servant* (1701), which has never been reprinted in full; for the first part, see "A Brief and Candid Answer to a Late Printed Sheet, *Entituled,* The Selling of Joseph," in Moore, *Notes on the History of Slavery,* 251–56; the second section is reprinted in Goodell, "John Saffin and His Slave Adam," 103–12.

9. "A Brief and Candid Answer," in Moore, *Notes on the History of Slavery,* 254, 255, 256, 253, 252; Mather, *The Negro Christianized.*

10. Mettas, *Répertoire des expéditions;* Saugera, *Bordeaux;* Pétrissans-Cavaillès, *Sur les traces;* Stein, *The French Sugar Business,* 4–8; Barrière, *Un Grand Provincial,* 42.

11. See Kulikoff, *Tobacco and Slaves,* 45–77, 320, and Berkeley and Berkeley, *Dr. John Mitchell,* 5–15.

12. See Gordon Jones, *The Library of an Early Virginia Scientist*, unpaginated 20, Berkeley and Berkeley, *Dr. John Mitchell*, 7–26, 43, and Kulikoff, *Tobacco and Slaves*, 70–72.

13. See Curran, *The Anatomy of Blackness*, 2, and Berkeley and Berkeley, *Dr. John Mitchell*, 44.

14. Mitchell, "An Essay," 102, 114, 117, 103, 109; John Mitchell to Peter Collinson cover letter, cited in Hornberger, "The Scientific Ideas of John Mitchell," 286.

15. Clarkson, *An Essay*, 205.

16. Le Chevalier D'Aydie to Montesquieu, January 6, 1749, in Gebelin, *Correspondance de Montesquieu*, 2: 90.

17. Montesquieu, *The Spirit of Laws*, 1: 336. For the reception of Montesquieu on slavery in Britain, see Fletcher, "Montesquieu's Influence on Anti-Slavery Opinion in England."

18. See Barrière, *Un Grand Provincial*, 21–24, 34–44, 78–80, 108; on mascarons, see Saugera, *Bordeaux*, 15, 68. Montesquieu to Solar, March 7, 1749, in Gebelin, *Correspondance de Montesquieu*, 2: 146.

19. Desgraves and Volphilhac-Auger, *Catalogue de la bibliothèque de Montesquieu*, 298, 338; Melon, *A Political Essay upon Commerce*, 77, 80; Labat, *Nouveau voyage*; Russell Parsons Jameson, *Montesquieu et l'esclavage*, 288–347. On France and slavery in the eighteenth century, see also Seeber, *Anti-Slavery Opinion in France*, Lafontant, *Montesquieu et le problème de l'esclavage*, Sala-Molins, *Les Misères des lumières*, Estève, *Montesquieu, Rousseau, Diderot*, DuBois, "An Enslaved Enlightenment," and Ehrard, *Lumières et esclavage*, 141–61.

20. See Kulikoff, *Tobacco and Slaves*, 340, and Stanton, *Free Some Day*, 17.

21. The passages on Montesquieu in Jefferson's "Legal Commonplace Book" (775–802) can be read online by searching the Library of Congress website (https://www.loc.gov/). It is difficult to date this document precisely, but Douglas Wilson argues that the entries on Montesquieu were probably composed in late 1776: see Wilson, "Thomas Jefferson's Early Notebooks," 447–48. It is likely that Jefferson read Montesquieu in a French-language edition of 1767; Jefferson's library shows he owned the 1767 London edition: *CLTJ*, 3: 2. Jefferson also owned the 1724 edition of Labat's *Nouveau voyage: CLTJ*, 4: 284–85. The passage on separating masters and slaves appears in Montesquieu, *Oeuvres*, 1: 343; Jefferson copied it into his Legal Commonplace Book.

22. Eva Sheppard Wolf, *Race and Liberty in the New Nation*, 3; Montesquieu, *Oeuvres*, 1: 344, 345; Jefferson, "Legal Commonplace Book."

23. Delbourgo "The Newtonian Slave Body," 199–200. Jefferson's comments on the inferiority of blacks appear in Jefferson, *Notes* (1787), 228–40.

24. Benjamin Rush, Journal, August 31, 1766–June 23, 1768 (entry for October 28, 1766), in Jonathan Williams Mss., Lilly Library Manuscript Collections, Indiana University.

25. On Philadelphia in the international context of antislavery, see McDaniel, "Philadelphia Abolitionists," and David Brion Davis, *The Problem of Slavery in the Age of Revolution*, 533–36. Voltaire quoted in Mason, Jr., ed., *The Poems of Phillis Wheatley*, 30; Rush, *An Address*, 2, 7, 28, 3. The rebuttal to Rush's pamphlet was Nisbet, *Slavery Not Forbidden by Scripture*; Rush then published a response to Nisbet's rebuttal.

26. On social thought in eighteenth-century Scotland, see John Robertson, *The Case for the Enlightenment*, Berry, *The Social Theory of the Scottish Enlightenment*, Sebastiani, *The Scottish Enlightenment*, Broadie, ed., *The Cambridge Companion to the Scottish Enlightenment*, Ahnert and Manning, eds., *Character, Self, and Sociability in the Scottish Enlightenment*, Manning and Cogliano, eds., *The Atlantic Enlightenment*, and Bryson, *Man and Society*.

27. Corner, ed., *The Autobiography of Benjamin Rush*, 49–50; Benjamin Rush to John Morgan, November 16, 1766, and Rush to Jonathan Bayard Smith, April 30, 1767, in Butterfield, *Letters of Benjamin Rush*, 1: 29, 41. For more on enlightened Scottish thought in American colleges, see Douglas Sloan, *The Scottish Enlightenment*, Morrison, *John Witherspoon*, and Noll, *Princeton and the Republic*.

28. Kames to James Lind, March 7, 1772, in Ross, *Lord Kames and the Scotland of His Day*, 334.

29. Kames, *Sketches*, 1: 31, 26, 10, 37, 32.

30. Kames, *Sketches*, 1: 38, 39.

31. Samuel Stanhope Smith, *The Lectures*, 1: 25.

32. Noll, *Princeton and the Republic*, 115, 64–65; Hudnut, "Samuel Stanhope Smith"; Wertenbaker, *Princeton*, 118; Hughes, *The Natural History of Barbados*, 14n18 (this book appears in *Catalogue of Books in the Library of the College of New-Jersey*, 17).

33. Smith, *An Essay*, 10, 35; "Strictures on the Lord Kaims's Discourse on the Original Diversity of Mankind," in Smith, *An Essay*, appendix pages 27, 28. For helpful discussions of the context of the essay, see Noll, *Princeton and the Republic*, 115–24, John C. Greene, "The American Debate," and Greene, *American Science*, 320–42.

34. *Forensic Dispute*, 4; Antibiastes, "Observations on the Slaves," 1; A Friend to Every Honourable Branch of Commerce, "For the United States Chronicle," *United States Chronicle*, January 29, 1784, 1.

35. Jefferson to Benjamin Banneker, August 30, 1791, *PTJ*, 22: 98; Condorcet [attrib.], *Réflexions sur l'esclavage des Nègres*, iii, iv.

36. Jefferson to Condorcet, August 30, 1791, *PTJ*, 22: 99.

37. Martin, *An Essay upon Plantership*, 10; Collins, *Practical Rules*, 21; Turnbull, *Letters to a Young Planter*, 36. On the broader worldview of these planters, see Justin Roberts, *Slavery and the Enlightenment*.

38. Conforti, "Samuel Hopkins," 579, 576, 577, 580; Hopkins, *An Inquiry*, 11.

39. Coughtry, *The Notorious Triangle*; Rappleye, *Sons of Providence*; Conforti, *Samuel Hopkins*, 126–27.

40. Conforti, "Samuel Hopkins," 585; Hopkins, *A Dialogue*, iii.

41. Hopkins, *A Discourse*, 3, 5, 6, 7, 11, 19, 20. On Hopkins and the African colonization movement, see Conforti, *Samuel Hopkins*, 142–58.

42. Tucker, *Blackstone's Commentaries*, 1: xii; Tucker, *A Dissertation on Slavery*, 95.

43. Finkelman, "The Dragon St. George Could Not Slay," 1218, 1220; Phillip Hamilton, "Revolutionary Principles," 532, 533; Hamilton, *The Making*, 73, 79.

44. Tucker, *Blackstone's Commentaries*, 1, appendix page 366; Tucker, *A Dissertation on Slavery*, 11 and title page. On the tabling of Tucker's *Dissertation*, see Wolf, *Race and Liberty in the New Nation*, 104. On black and Indian colonization schemes in this era, see Guyatt, " 'The Outskirts of Our Happiness.' "

45. Tucker, "Queries," 192, 199, 196; Tucker, *A Dissertation on Slavery*, 30.

46. Tucker, *A Dissertation on Slavery*, 98, 77–80, 84, 90.

47. Tucker, *A Dissertation on Slavery*, 94–95, 106.

48. Learned, *A View of the Policy*, 3, 4; Christopher Phillips, *Freedom's Port*, 186.

49. Clarkson, *The History*, 1: 139; Child, *An Appeal*, 35–36; Garrison, *The New "Reign of Terror,"* 31.

50. *View of Exertions*, 17; Harrison, *Review of the Slave Question*, 44, 45.

51. Drayton, *The South Vindicated*, 82; Colfax, *Evidence*, 26; Bell, *Message of Love*, 22, 27.

52. David Brion Davis, *The Problem of Slavery in Western Culture*, 3, 16.

Chapter Six. Religion in the Age of Reason

1. Paine, *The Age of Reason* (1794), 11, 18.

2. See Bonomi, *Under the Cope of Heaven*, 3–4.

3. Butler, *Becoming America*, 186, 189–91; *Curious Hieroglyphick Bible*. On changing ideas of reason and consent among children in revolutionary America, see Holly Brewer, *By Birth or Consent*, 8, 286–87, 348–52, and Fliegelman, *Prodigals and Pilgrims*.

4. Quentin Skinner, *The Foundations*, 2: 244–45; Locke, *A Letter*, 7.

5. Colman [attrib.], *A Manifesto or Declaration*, 3.

6. Fiering, "The First American Enlightenment," 309; Hornberger, "Benjamin Colman and the Enlightenment"; Daston and Park, *Wonders and the Order of Nature*, 329; Tillotson, *Sermons Preach'd*, unpaginated preface, 20; Paine, *Common Sense*, 17; Benjamin Franklin, "On Literary Style," *Pennsylvania Gazette*, August 2, 1733, in *PBF*, 1: 329.

7. Alexander Hamilton, *Colonel Hamilton's Second Letter*, 45; Marshall, *The Life of George Washington*, 1: 157; Hannah Adams, *A Summary History of New-England*, 102.

8. David Hume, "Of Miracles," in Hume, *Philosophical Essays*, 187; Allen, *Reason the Only Oracle of Man*, 233. On the rise of reasonable religion

in eighteenth-century British America, see James Turner, *Without God*, 28–34.

9. Boyle, *The Christian Virtuoso;* Solberg, "Introduction," in Solberg, ed., *The Christian Philosopher,* xxi, xlvii, xlix.

10. Winthrop, *Two Lectures*, 14; Kornhauser, *Ralph Earl*, 169–71.

11. Hume, *A Treatise of Human Nature*, 1: 6; American Commissioners [Benjamin Franklin and Silas Deane] to the Committee of Secret Correspondence, March 12[–April 9], 1777, *PBFDE*.

12. See Turner, *Religion Enters the Academy*, 4, Sheehan, "Sacred and Profane," 59; Lovejoy, "Satanizing the American Indian," and Manuel, *The Eighteenth Century Confronts the Gods.*

13. "Report on Books for Congress," [23 January] 1783, *PJMCS*, 6: 99.

14. Lafitau, *Moeurs des sauvages amériquains*, 1: 7, 9, 113, 17.

15. See Lynn Hunt, *Politics, Culture, and Class*, 27.

16. Paine, *The Age of Reason* (1794), 11; on Paine's lack of citations, see Davidson and Scheick, *Paine, Scripture, and Authority*, 24, 58.

17. Paine, *The Age of Reason*, (1794), 27, 17–18; Paine, *The Age of Reason* (1795), 89; Paine, *On the Origin of Free-Masonry*, 17.

18. See Boulanger, *L'Antiquité dévoilée* (1766), Manuel, *The Eighteenth Century Confronts the Gods*, 210–13, and Davidson and Scheick, *Paine, Scripture, and Authority*, 63–64.

19. Barlow's letter is quoted in Howard, *The Connecticut Wits*, 299. Holbach [attrib.], *Christianity Unveiled*, 53. On Bryant as plagiarist of Boulanger and other French mythologists, see Manuel, *The Eighteenth Century Confronts the Gods*, 274–75. On Adams's and Jefferson's ownership of Bryant, see the John Adams Library, Boston Public Library, and *CLTJ*, 1: 21.

20. Court de Gébelin, *Monde primitif*, 1: 6, 68–69; for biographical details on Court de Gébelin, see Mercier-Faivre, *Un Supplément à "l'Encylopédie";* for Court de Gébelin and the turn to ancient Egypt in revolutionary France, see Edelstein, "The Egyptian French Revolution."

21. Ziesche, "Thomas Paine," 123; Antoine Court de Gébelin to Benjamin Franklin, March 19, 1778, *PBF*, 26: 131; Antoine Court de Gébelin to Franklin, November 2, 1779, *PBF*, 31: 24; Peter Stephen Du Ponceau, entry for February 14, 1844, in Whitehead, ed., "Notes and Documents," 260–61.

22. On Sewall's 1768 drawing, see Delabarre, "Middle Period of Dighton Rock History," 57–59. See also MacLean, "Pre-Columbian Discovery of America." On Phoenician origin theories for the American Indians, see Winterer, "Model Empire, Lost City."

23. Reverend James Madison to James Madison, June 15, 1782, *PJMCS*, 4: 338.

24. Winchester, *Ten Letters*, 67, 69. For a list of contemporary responses to Paine's *Age of Reason*, see Davidson and Scheick, *Paine, Scripture, and Authority*, Appendix 2, 108–16.

25. Gaulmier, *Un Grand Témoin de la Révolution*.

26. See Anthony F. Wallace, *Jefferson and the Indians*, 113–20; *CLTJ*, 2: 20, Barratt and Miles, *Gilbert Stuart*, 198, Fanelli, *History of the Portrait Collection*, 311, "Pyramid Model in Place in Entrance Hall," *Monticello Newsletter* 14, 1 (Spring 2003): unpaginated 1–3, and Chinard, *Volney et l'Amérique*.

27. Volney, *The Ruins*, unpaginated 1, 101, 27.

28. Richardson, "Introduction," v, 23; Andrews, "Making the Revolutionary Calendar," 530.

29. Dupuis quoted in Manuel, *The Eighteenth Century Confronts the Gods*, 269; Hancarville, *Collection of Etruscan, Greek, and Roman Antiquities*.

30. See Chipley, "The Enlightenment Library of William Bentley," 11. Thomas Jefferson to Destutt de Tracy, February 14, 1806, in Chinard, *Jefferson et les idéologues*, 41. On Joel Barlow and the fertility myths of antiquity, see Beran, *Jefferson's Demons*, 76, and Alfred F. Young, *Liberty Tree*, 372–73.

31. Dwight, *The Nature and Danger of Infidel Philosophy*, 10.

32. See Priestley, *A Comparison of the Institutions of Moses*, 302, Priestley, *Discourses*, Priestley, *Letters to Mr. Volney*, and *Catalogue of the Library of the late Dr. Joseph Priestley*, 7, 11, 63, 85, 94.

33. Priestley, *Discourses*, 1; Priestley, *Letters to Mr. Volney*, 13; Priestley, *A Comparison of the Institutions of Moses*, vii.

34. Jefferson to Peter Carr, August 10, 1787, *PTJ*, 12: 15; Merrill Peterson and Robert C. Vaughan, eds., *The Virginia Statute for Religious Freedom*; Ragosta, *Religious Freedom*.

35. Jefferson to Charles Thomson, January 9, 1816, in *PTJ Ret*, 9: 341; Jefferson to Timothy Pickering, February 27, 1821, in Dickinson W. Adams, ed., *Jefferson's Extracts from the Gospels*, 402, 403.

36. John Adams to Charles Cushing, October 19, 1756, *APDE*; John Adams, "A Dissertation on the Canon and the Feudal Law," 139, 112.

37. Adams to Jefferson, April 19, 1817, and Adams to Jefferson, May 18, 1817, in Cappon, ed., *The Adams-Jefferson Letters*, 509, 515.

38. Noll, *America's God*, 88, 91, 106, 165–66, 173–74.

39. Channing, "Remarks," 130, 131; Daniel Walker Howe, *The Unitarian Conscience*; Meyer, *The Instructed Conscience*; Noll, *America's God*; Porterfield, *Conceived in Doubt*.

40. Jefferson to Adams, June 11, 1812, in Cappon, ed., *The Adams-Jefferson Letters*, 305.

41. Jackson, *The Oriental Religions*, 104; Sheehan, "Sacred and the Profane"; Lewis Henry Morgan, *League of the Ho-de-no-sau-nee*, 157; Emerson, "Religion," 3; James Turner, *Religion Enters the Academy*, 35–38.

42. William James, *The Varieties of Religious Experience*, 58.

43. James, *The Varieties of Religious Experience*, 466.

Chapter Seven. The Futuristic Farmers of America

1. Jefferson, *Notes on the State of Virginia* (1787), 274; letter to Thomas Jefferson from John Peter Van Ness, July 5, 1806, available at Founders Online, National Archives, http://founders.archives.gov/documents/Jefferson/99-01-02-3965.

2. On political economy as a widely shared discourse of enlightenment, see John Robertson, *The Case for the Enlightenment;* on historical conceptions of "the economy," see Timothy Mitchell, "Fixing the Economy," 84–85, and Mitchell, *Rule of Experts*, 4–6.

3. Steuart, *An Inquiry*, 1: v, 10, 3; on Steuart's economic thought, see Andrew Skinner, "James Steuart."

4. Smith, *An Inquiry* (London), 2: 1, 126.

5. Smith, *An Inquiry* (London), 2: 214–15; James F. Shepherd, "British America and the Atlantic Economy," and Jacob M. Price, "Reflections on the Economy of Revolutionary America," both in Hoffman, McCusker, Menard, and Albert, eds., *The Economy of Early America*, 5, 304.

6. James Anderson (1739–1808) to George Washington, August 15, 1793, *PGW Pres*, 13: 456; Hitchcock, *Report on the Geology*, 13.

7. Eliot, *An Essay upon Field-Husbandry*, 2; Grasso, "The Experimental Philosophy of Farming"; Réaumur, *The Art of Hatching;* Jack P. Greene, ed., *The Diary of Colonel Landon Carter*, 1: 186 (entry for October 25, 1757); Carter, "Observations concerning the FLY-WEEVIL," 205; Isaac, *Landon Carter's Uneasy Kingdom*, 87; xvii. For a study of eighteenth-century agricultural ideas farther to the south, see Chaplin, *An Anxious Pursuit*.

8. Mun, *England's Treasure*, 11, 30. In a large literature on mercantilism, see Istvan Hont, "Jealousy of Trade: An Introduction," in Hont, *Jealousy of Trade*, 1–156.

9. Meek, *The Economics of Physiocracy*, 15.

10. Quesnay, "Fermiers," "Grains," and "Tableau économique," in Quesnay, *Oeuvres économiques*, 1: 128, 162, 413; Vardi, *The Physiocrats*, 13–14.

11. Quesnay, "Hommes," in *Oeuvres économiques*, 1: 259; Baker, "Enlightenment and the Institution of Society."

12. Le Mercier de La Rivière, *L'Ordre naturel*, 1: xiv, 4.

13. Whatley, *Principles of Trade*, 34.

14. Phillipson, *Adam Smith*, 193, 194; see also Istvan Hont, "Adam Smith and the Political Economy of the 'Unnatural and Retrograde' Order," in Hont, *Jealousy of Trade*, 354–88.

15. Smith, *An Inquiry* (London), 2: 270, 265–66, 271; Hochstrasser, "Physiocracy and the Politics of *Laissez-Faire*," 420.

16. Benjamin Vaughan to Benjamin Franklin, December 7, 1779, *PBFDE*.

17. Earle D. Ross, "Benjamin Franklin," 55.

18. Franklin to Jared Eliot, September 12, 1751, *PBF*, 4: 193; Franklin to Eliot, December 10, 1751, *PBF*, 4: 215. See also Wolf and Hayes, *The*

Library of Benjamin Franklin, 741; on European improving societies see Stapelbroek and Marjanen, eds., *The Rise of Economic Societies.*

19. Franklin's calculation was cited in Arthur Young, *Political Arithmetic*, 68; Malthus, *An Essay on the Principle of Population*, 20; and Smith, *An Inquiry* (London), 1: 86. Franklin also sent his essay to people he admired, such as Lord Kames: Franklin to Kames, January 3, 1760, *PBF*, 9: 5. The essay is reprinted, with extended editorial notes, in *PBF*, 4: 225–34.

20. Franklin to Kames, January 3, 1760, *PBF*, 9: 9; Franklin to Kames, February 21, 1769, *PBF*, 16: 46; Franklin to Kames, February 25, 1767, *PBF*, 14: 69–70.

21. Benjamin Franklin ["Arator"], "On the Price of Corn, and Management of the Poor," November 29, 1766, in *PBF*, 13: 510–16, quotation from 512; McCoy, *The Elusive Republic*, 55.

22. Du Pont de Nemours to Franklin, May 10, 1768, *PBF*, 15: 118; Hochstrasser, "Physiocracy and the Politics of *Laissez-Faire*," 440.

23. Barbeu-Dubourg to Franklin, December 19, 1772, *PBF*, 19: 434.

24. Franklin to Du Pont de Nemours, July 28, 1768, *PBF*, 15: 181–82.

25. Franklin to Cadwalader Evans, February 20, 1768, *PBF*, 15: 52; Franklin to Evans, November 27, 1769, *PBF*, 16: 240; Franklin to Evans, July 4, 1771, *PBF*, 18: 159–61; Franklin to Kames, February 21, 1769, *PBF*, 16: 47; Franklin marginalia, *PBF*, 16: 315.

26. Smith, *An Inquiry* (London), 2: 232.

27. W. H. Brewer, "Agricultural Societies"; Ezra Stiles, entry for June 2, 1789, in Dexter, ed., *The Literary Diary of Ezra Stiles*, 3: 355; Collin, "Introduction to Vol. the Third," vii, viii; Jefferson, *Notes* (1787), 273–74.

28. Crèvecoeur, *Letters from an American Farmer*, 21, 23; Crèvecoeur, *Lettres d'un cultivateur américain*; Crèvecoeur, *Traité de la culture*, i, 13–14, 18.

29. Arthur Young, *The Farmer's Letters*, 6.

30. Bordley, *A Summary View*, 19.

31. Jane Roberts, *Royal Landscape*, 72.

32. Washington to Arthur Young, June 18[–21], 1792, *PGW Pres*, 10: 461; Washington to Young, August 6, 1786, *PGW Conf*, 4: 196; Young to Washington, February 1, 1787, *PGW Conf*, 5: 5; Washington to Samuel Powel, June 30, 1787, *PGW Conf*, 5: 237; Washington to Young, December 5, 1791, *PGW Pres*, 9: 256; Young to Washington, January 7, 1786, *PGW Conf*, 3: 499; Young to Washington, June 9, 1792, *PGW Pres*, 10: 446; Young to Washington, January 18, 1792, *PGW Pres*, 9: 479; Franklin Knight, "Introduction," in Knight, ed., *Letters on Agriculture*, 10.

33. Uvedale Price to Washington, March 31, 1798, *PGW Ret*, 2: 165–66; Uvedale Price, *An Essay on the Picturesque*. For the earliest landscape painters in the United States, see Nygren, *Views and Visions*, and Bryan Wolf, "Revolution in the Landscape: John Trumbull and Picturesque Painting," in Helen Cooper, ed., *John Trumbull*, 206–15.

34. Edwin Wolf, *The Library of James Logan;* Wolf, *James Logan,* unpaginated 2, 8; James Logan to Franklin, April 16, 1748, *PBF,* 3: 285.

35. Albertone, *National Identity and the Agrarian Republic,* 140–41; Tolles, "Unofficial Ambassador," 4–6; Tolles, *George Logan of Philadelphia,* 3–47; George Logan to Franklin, September 20, 1780, *PBF,* 33: 315; George Logan, *Fourteen Agricultural Experiments,* 25, 8, 30; William Vans Murray to John Quincy Adams, August 28, 1798, in Ford, ed., "Tenth Report," 460; Jefferson to Thomas Mann Randolph, July 28, 1793, *PTJ,* 26: 576.

36. Tolles, *George Logan of Philadelphia,* 109, 112; Logan, *Fourteen Agricultural Experiments,* 36; Logan ["A Farmer"], *Letters, Addressed to the Yeomanry of the United States,* 8, 19, 25, 20.

37. Alexander Hamilton to Elizabeth Schuyler [August 1780], *PAH,* 2: 398; Hamilton to Schuyler, September 6, 1780, *PAH,* 2: 423; Hamilton, *The Farmer Refuted;* "Report on the Subject of Manufactures: Introductory Note," in *PAH,* 10: 1, 7–8.

38. "Alexander Hamilton's Final Version of the Report on the Subject of Manufactures," December 5, 1791, *PAH,* 10: 236; Hamilton ["Lucius Crassus"], "The Examination Number IX" [January 18, 1802], *PAH,* 25: 501.

39. Logan ["An American Farmer"], *Letters Addressed to the Yeomanry of the United States,* 5, 23; Logan, *An Address on the Natural and Social Order of the World,* 3, 8.

40. Paine, *Agrarian Justice,* 7; John Taylor, *An Inquiry,* 188; on the agricultural societies, see Albertone, *National Identity and the Agrarian Republic,* 168; on the Bucks County Agricultural Society see William Watts Hart Davis, *History of Bucks County, Pennsylvania, from the Discovery of the Delaware to the Present Time* (1876; repr. New York: Lewis Publishing, 1905).

41. On antebellum political economy, see McCoy, *The Elusive Republic,* Conkin, *Prophets of Prosperity,* Sklansky, *The Soul's Economy,* and Michael O'Brien, *Conjectures of Order,* 2: 877–937. For England, see Winch, *Riches and Poverty.*

42. Chinard, *Jefferson et les idéologues,* 33–34; Albertone, *National Identity and the Agrarian Republic,* 187, 263–68; Biddle, ed., *A Treatise on Political Economy,* iv, vi, xxv, 409, 418, 426, xlvi.

43. Jefferson to Thomas Mann Randolph, Jr., May 30, 1790, *PTJ,* 16: 449; on Jefferson's evolving attitude toward Montesquieu's *De l'esprit des loix,* see Chinard, *Jefferson et les idéologues,* 3–6, Jean-Baptiste Say to Jefferson, June 15, 1814, *PTJ Ret,* 7: 417, and Pierre Samuel du Pont de Nemours to Jefferson, January 25, 1812, in Chinard, ed., *The Correspondence of Jefferson and Du Pont de Nemours,* 184.

44. Jefferson, "Prospectus," in Destutt de Tracy, *A Treatise on Political Economy,* iii, iv, vii; Destutt de Tracy, *A Treatise on Political Economy,* 14, 27; Jefferson to Thomas Cooper, July 10, 1812, *PTJ Ret,* 5: 223. The term

social science was used in English before this time, but Jefferson's usage in this case seems to have been a direct translation of the French *science sociale*.

45. Lauderdale, *An Inquiry*, 7; Raymond, *Thoughts on Political Economy*, 9; Albertone, *National Identity and the Agrarian Republic*, 192; Thomas Cooper, *Lectures on the Elements of Political Economy*, 1, 7, 8; Carey, *Principles of Political Economy*, 1: xii; Carey, *The Past*, 5.

46. Carlyle, "Occasional Discourse on the Negro Question"; Jefferson to William Johnson, May 10, 1817, *PTJ Ret*, 11: 344–45.

Chapter Eight. Republics Versus Monarchies

1. March 23, 1796 (HR), *Annals of Congress*, 4th Congress, 1st Session, 5: 688; March 22, 1796 (HR), *Annals of Congress*, 4th Congress, 1st Session, 5: 657. For this political discourse, see also Wood, "The American Enlightenment."

2. Consideration, "An Address to the citizens of America, shewing the necessity of encouraging a general circulation of NEWS-PAPERS, among all classes and denominations of people," *Massachusetts Gazette, or General Advertiser*, January 13, 1784, 2. On the temporal qualities of revolutionary American writing, see Ferguson, *The American Enlightenment*, 36.

3. Weems, *A History*, 29; Marshall, *The Life of George Washington*, 4: 191, 563, 5: 62, 89, 402.

4. Kant, "Beantwortung der Frage"; Kant, "An Answer to the Question"; James Schmidt, "The Question of Enlightenment," 272.

5. Frederick II, *Anti-Machiavel*, vi; Alexander Carlyle, *The Justice*, 16; James Murray, *An Impartial History*, 2: 55. On enlightened monarchs, see Scott, ed., *Enlightened Absolutism*, and Beales, *Enlightenment and Reform*. On monarchy in Britain in the late eighteenth century, see Colley, *Britons*, 195–236. In eighteenth-century America, the *Anti-Machiavel* of Frederick II may have been best known because it appeared in the English-language edition of Machiavelli's works by Farneworth, trans., *The Works of Nicholas Machiavel* (1762), a widely cited work that appears in a number of eighteenth-century British American libraries.

6. Charles Turner, *A Sermon*, 21.

7. Thomas Jefferson, "A Summary View of the Rights of British America" (1774), in Merrill Peterson, ed., *Thomas Jefferson*, 105–22. We still lack a full accounting of American monarchism and anti-monarchism (or royalism and anti-royalism), but see Downes, *Democracy, Revolution, and Monarchism*, McConville, *The King's Three Faces*, and Nelson, *The Royalist Revolution*.

8. Paine, *Common Sense*, 8, 12, 13, 11.

9. John Adams to Richard Cranch, August 2, 1776, *APDE*; Thomas Jefferson to James Madison, March 15, 1789, *PTJ*, 14: 661; George Washington, "Circular to the States," June 8, 1783, in Fitzpatrick,

ed., *The Writings of George Washington*, 26: 485; Publius [Alexander Hamilton], *The Federalist*, 2: 290; Jefferson to John Langdon, March 5, 1810, *PTJ Ret*, 2: 276; *CLTJ*, 1: 181–82.

10. Blom, Laursen, and Simonutti, eds., *Monarchisms in the Age of Enlightenment*, 3; Beales, *Enlightenment and Reform*, 264–66.

11. John Adams to Abigail Adams, February 27, 1783, *APDE*.

12. John Adamson, "Introduction: The Making of the Ancien-Régime Court, 1500–1700," in Adamson, ed., *The Princely Courts of Europe*, 7–41; John Howe, *The Changing Political Thought of John Adams*, 187.

13. Black, *George II*, 24. A substantial body of historiography has emerged to challenge the assessment of Isaac Kramnick and others that the combined reigns of George I and II (1714–60) are best viewed as "the age of Walpole," a reference to Robert Walpole, who dominated politics during the reigns of both kings. For this view, see Kramnick, *Bolingbroke and His Circle*, Robbins, *The Eighteenth-Century Commonwealthman*, Bailyn, *The Ideological Origins*, and Lewis Namier, who argued that George II's ministers knew "the King's (constitutional) mind better than he knew it himself": Namier, *England in the Age of the American Revolution*, 45. In contrast to this minister-centered analysis, scholars recently have begun to assert the continued relevance of royal political and cultural power in eighteenth-century Britain, one still significant if diminished from its Tudor and Stuart heyday. In this analysis, Queen Caroline, the consort of George II, is recognized for her role in cultivating the political power of Walpole. An early critic of the minister-centered analysis was John B. Owen, "George II Reconsidered," in Whiteman, Bromley, and Dickson, eds., *Statesmen, Scholars and Merchants*, 113–34; more recent assessments, in addition to Jeremy Black's noted above, include Orr, "New Perspectives on Hanoverian Britain," and Thompson, *George II*, 3–6. For more on British monarchical culture in the eighteenth century, see John Brewer, *The Pleasures of the Imagination*, Porter, *The Creation of the Modern World*, Black, *A Subject for Taste*, 25–40, Hannah Greig, "Leading the Fashion: The Material Culture of London's *Beau Monde*," in Styles and Vickery, eds., *Gender, Taste and Material Culture*, 293–313, Jane Roberts, ed., *George III and Queen Charlotte*, and Simms and Riotte, eds., *The Hanoverian Dimension in British History*.

14. Voltaire, *Letters Concerning the English Nation*, 79.

15. Flavell, *When London was Capital of America*; Robert A. Gross, "Introduction: An Extensive Republic," in Gross and Kelley, eds., *An Extensive Republic*, 13; Benjamin Franklin to William Strahan, December 19, 1763, *PBF*, 10: 407–8.

16. Breen, *The Character of the Good Ruler*, 20; Colman, *Fidelity to Christ*, 8; Mather, *Christian Loyalty*, 8, 16, 24, 25.

17. McClellan, *Science Reorganized*, 106; William Smith, *Some Thoughts on Education*, 2, vii; William Smith to Benjamin Franklin and Richard

Peters, February 1754, *PBF*, 5: 212; Samuel Chandler to James Hamilton, Benjamin Franklin, et al., March 15, 1754, *PBF*, 5: 238; McClelland, *State, Society, and University in Germany*, 37, vii; Bigelow, *The Life of Benjamin Franklin*, 1: 510a; Johann David Michaelis[?] to Benjamin Franklin, *c.* 1772, *PBF*, 19: 447.

18. Davies, *A Sermon Delivered at Nassau-Hall*, 2; Blair, *An Account of the College of New-Jersey*, 12–13.

19. See Joanne Marschner, "Queen Caroline of Anspach and the European Princely Museum Tradition" and Christine Gerrard, "Queens-in-Waiting: Caroline of Anspach and Augusta of Saxe-Gotha as Princesses of Wales," both in Orr, ed., *Queenship in Britain*, 130–42 and 143–61, Jay, "Queen Caroline's Library," Black, *George II*, 127, Clarissa Campbell Orr, "Lost Royal Libraries and Hanoverian Court Culture," in Raven, ed., *Lost Libraries*, 163–80, and Philpot, *An Essay*, 27.

20. Byles, *A Poem*, iv; *George III: Collector and Patron*, 40; Marschner, "Queen Caroline of Anspach," in Orr, ed., *Queenship in Britain*, 130–42; Black, *George II*, 32; Checkley, *The Duty of a People*, 23.

21. "The Belcher Papers," *Massachusetts Historical Society Collections*, 6th ser., 7 (1894): 22.

22. See Batinski, *Jonathan Belcher*, 63; for a group profile of the royal governors, see Labaree, *Royal Government in America*.

23. "The Belcher Papers," *Massachusetts Historical Society Collections*, 6th ser., 6 (1893): 299; 7 (1894): 108, 16–17, 58, 143.

24. Leitch, *A Princeton Companion*, 49, 50; "Governor Belcher's Library," Jonathan Belcher Collection, Mudd Library, Princeton, Box 1, folder 2; *Catalogue of Books in the Library of the College of New-Jersey*, iv; Jonathan Belcher to Jonathan Belcher, Jr., April 28, 1732, "The Belcher Papers," *Massachusetts Historical Society Collections*, 6th ser., 6 (1893): 128.

25. Lind, *An Answer*, 5, 7, 75, 79, 96, 100; Candidus [James Chalmers?], *Plain Truth*, 8; Rationalis, bound in with Candidus [James Chalmers?], *Plain Truth*, 40.

26. Cook, *A Voyage Round the World*, 3: iii; Michelangelo Gianetti, *Elogy of Captain James Cook Composed and Publickly Recited Before the Royal Academy of Florence by Michelangelo Gianetti, Translated into English by a Member of the Royal Academy of Florence* (Florence: Gaetano Cambiagi, 1785), 25; Knox, *Considerations*, 20; Bisset, *The History of the Reign of George III*, 4: 118.

27. Paine, *Common Sense*, 32; Prince of Wales to Earl of Bute, n.d., but probably September 1758, in Sedgwick, ed., *Letters from George III to Lord Bute*, 15; Brooke, *King George III*, 24; Brooke, "The Library of King George," 33; Peter Barber, "George III and His Geographical Collection," in Jonathan Marsden, ed., *The Wisdom of George III*, 263–89; Bullion, " 'George, Be a King!' "; Bullion, " 'To Know This Is the True Essential Business of a King.' "

28. John Adams, diary entry for October 27, 1783, *APDE;* Oliver, ed., *The Journal of Samuel Curwen,* 1: 42–55; Charles Knight, ed., *Biography or Third Division of "The English Cyclopaedia,"* 649.

29. Clarissa Campbell Orr, "Queen Charlotte and Her Circle," in Marsden, ed., *The Wisdom of George the Third,* 169–70.

30. Abigail Adams to John Quincy Adams, June 26, 1785, *APDE;* on Abigail Adams's reading of Locke's *Some Thoughts Concerning Education,* see Withey, *Dearest Friend,* 351.

31. Autobiography of John Adams, entry for May 8, 1778, *APDE;* John Adams to the marquis de Lafayette, May 21, 1782, *APDE;* Richard Alan Ryerson, "John Adams, Republican Monarchist: An Inquiry into the Origins of His Constitutional Thought," in Gould and Onuf, eds., *Empire and Nation,* 77.

32. American Academy of Arts and Sciences, at http://www.amacad.org/about/charter.aspx#chartermbrs; Walter Muir Whitehill, "Early Learned Societies in Boston and Vicinity," in Oleson and Brown, eds., *The Pursuit of Knowledge,* 154; Joseph Willard to Benjamin Franklin, February 9, 1781, *PBF,* 34: 361.

33. Diary of John Quincy Adams, entry for October 2, 1786, *APDE.*

34. December 14, 1796, *Annals of Congress* (HR), 4th Congress, 2d Session, 6: 1612.

35. December 14, 1796, *Annals of Congress* (HR), 4th Congress, 2d Session, 6: 1614, 1618, 1615, 1616, 1620, 1621.

36. December 14, 1796, *Annals of Congress* (HR), 4th Congress, 2d Session, 6: 1623, 1627, 1628, 1630.

37. December 15, 1796, *Annals of Congress* (HR), 4th Congress, 2d Session, 6: 1638, 1642.

38. Aldridge, *Early American Literature,* 187–88; Sydney Smith, "[Review of] *Statistical Annals of the United States of America,"* 79.

39. Gross, "Introduction," in Gross and Kelley, eds., *An Extensive Republic,* 29.

40. Gross, "Introduction," in Gross and Kelley, eds., *An Extensive Republic,* 19; Phelps, *Lectures to Young Ladies,* 96–97. For more on the rise of an American reading public in the early national period see Brown, *Knowledge Is Power,* Warner, *The Letters of the Republic,* Pasley, *"The Tyranny of Printers,"* Waterman, *Republic of Intellect,* Loughran, *The Republic in Print,* and Kaplan, *Men of Letters in the Early Republic.*

41. See Robson, *Educating Republicans,* 228–36, and Gross, "Introduction," in Gross and Kelley, eds., *An Extensive Republic,* 27.

42. Rumford, *The Complete Works of Count Rumford,* 4: 250. On the royal patronage of the Royal Institution, see Frank A. J. L. James, *Guides to the Royal Institution of Great Britain,* 3: *The Royal Institution and the Royal Family,* http://www.rigb.org/docs/royal_family_1.pdf and Caroe, *The Royal Institution.* On Rumford's patronage of American science, see Mary

Ann James, "Engineering an Environment for Change: Bigelow, Peirce, and Early Nineteenth-Century Practical Education at Harvard," in Clark A. Elliott and Margaret W. Rossiter, eds., *Science at Harvard University*, 59.

43. Wendy Moonan, "Rarae Aves: Audubon at Auction." *New York Times*, March 3, 2000; Steiner, *Audubon Art Prints*, 259; Barratt, *Queen Victoria and Thomas Sully.*

Epilogue

1. Semonin, *American Monster*, 335. Modern scientists believe that the tusks were upturned, as in modern elephants.
2. For a lucid overview of these developments outside the United States, see Conrad, "Enlightenment in Global History," 1016–19.
3. Thanks to Scott Spillman, doctoral candidate in the Department of History at Stanford University, for an extensive sampling of publications in the period 2010–15 for uses of the idea of enlightenment. Research notes in possession of author.
4. See, for example, Barack Obama, "Remarks to European Youth in Brussels, Belgium," March 26, 2014, at http://www.presidency.ucsb.edu/ws/index.php?pid=105073, Obama, "Remarks with President François Hollande of France at Monticello in Charlottesville, Virginia," February 10, 2014, at http://www.presidency.ucsb.edu/ws/index.php?pid=104731, Obama, "Remarks at the Brandenburg Gate in Berlin, Germany," June 19, 2013, at http://www.presidency.ucsb.edu/ws/index.php?pid=103842, Obama, "Proclamation 8774—Religious Freedom Day, 2012," January 13, 2012, at http://www.presidency.ucsb.edu/ws/index.php?pid=98876, Obama, "Remarks at Cannes City Hall in Cannes, France," November 4, 2011, at http://www.presidency.ucsb.edu/ws/index.php?pid=96998, and Obama, "Remarks to the Parliament in London," May 25, 2011, at http://www.presidency.ucsb.edu/ws/index.php?pid=90446.
5. Thomas Jefferson to Roger Weightman, June 24, 1826, in Merrill Peterson, ed., *Thomas Jefferson: Writings*, 1517.

Bibliography

Archival Sources

American Philosophical Society
    Hŭlings ms.
    Individually Catalogued Manuscript Maps
Bodleian Libraries, University of Oxford
    MS. Arch. Seldon
Boston Public Library
    John Adams Library, Rare Books Department
Library of Congress
    Geography and Map Division
    Jay I. Kislac Collection
Lilly Library Manuscript Collection, Indiana University
    Jonathan Williams Manuscript Collection
Massachusetts Historical Society
    Jonathan Belcher, "A Journal of My Intended Voyage"
    Byles Family Papers
Mudd Library, Princeton University
    Jonathan Belcher Collection
Stanford University Libraries
    Department of Special Collections

Printed Sources

Adair, James. *The History of the American Indians.* London: Edward and Charles Dilly, 1775.

Adams, Dickinson W., ed. *Jefferson's Extracts from the Gospels: "The Philosophy of Jesus" and "The Life and Morals of Jesus."* Princeton: Princeton University Press, 1983.

Adams, Hannah. *A Summary History of New-England, from the First Settlement at Plymouth, to the Acceptance of the Federal Constitution.* Dedham, Mass.: H. Mann and J. H. Adams, 1799.

Adams, John. "A Dissertation on the Canon and the Feudal Law." In Thomas Hollis, comp., *The True Sentiments of America: Contained in a Collection of Letters Sent from the House of Representatives of the Province of Massachusetts Bay to Several Persons of High Rank in This Kingdom Together with Certain Papers Relating to a Supposed Libel on the Governor of That Province, and a Dissertation on the Canon and the Feudal Law.* London: J. Almon, 1768. 111–43.

Adamson, John., ed. *The Princely Courts of Europe, 1500–1750: Ritual, Politics and Culture Under the Ancien Régime.* London: Weidenfeld and Nicolson, 1999.

Agassiz, Louis. "America the Old World." In Louis Agassiz, *Geological Sketches.* Boston: Ticknor and Fields, 1866. 1–28.

Ahnert, Thomas, and Susan Manning, eds. *Character, Self, and Sociability in the Scottish Enlightenment.* New York: Palgrave Macmillan, 2011.

Albertone, Manuela. *National Identity and the Agrarian Republic: The Transatlantic Commerce of Ideas Between America and France (1750–1830).* Farnham, Surrey, UK: Ashgate, 2014.

Aldridge, Alfred Owen. *Early American Literature: A Comparatist Approach.* Princeton: Princeton University Press, 1982.

Aldridge, Alfred Owen. "Franklin as Demographer." *Journal of Economic History* 9, no. 1 (May 1949): 25–44.

Allen, Ethan. *Reason the Only Oracle of Man; or, A Compenduous System of Natural Religion.* Bennington, Vt.: Haswell and Russell, 1784.

Almeida, Joselyn M. *Reimagining the Transatlantic, 1780–1890.* Surrey, UK: Ashgate, 2011.

Alvord, Clarence Walworth, and Lee Bidgood. *The First Explorations of the Trans-Allegheny Region by the Virginians, 1650–1674.* Cleveland: Arthur H. Clark, 1912.

Amory, Hugh, and David D. Hall, eds. *The Colonial Book in the Atlantic World.* Vol. 1 of *A History of the Book in America.* Cambridge: Published in Association with the American Antiquarian Society by Cambridge University Press, 2000.

Anderson, Robert T., et al. *American Indian Law: Cases and Commentary.* Saint Paul, Minn.: Thomson West, 2008.

Anderson, Wallace, E., ed. *Scientific and Philosophical Writings.* Vol. 6 of *The Works of Jonathan Edwards.* New Haven: Yale University Press, 1980.

Andrews, George Gordon. "Making the Revolutionary Calendar." *American Historical Review* 36, no. 3 (April 1931): 515–32.

Annals of Congress. From Library of Congress, *A Century of Lawmaking for a New Nation: U.S. Congressional Documents and Debates, 1774–1875.* Available at http://memory.loc.gov/ammem/amlaw/lwac.html.

Antibiastes. "Observations on the Slaves and the Indentured Servants, Enlisted in the Army, and in the Navy of the United States." *Maryland Journal*, October 7, 1777, 1–2.

"Article, Inquiries Relative to Rural Economy." *Transactions of the American Philosophical Society* 3 (1793): vii–xiii.

Atwater, Caleb. *Writings of Caleb Atwater*. Columbus, Ohio: The author, printed by Scott and Wright, 1833.

Bailyn, Bernard. *The Ideological Origins of the American Revolution*. Cambridge, Mass.: Belknap, 1967.

Baker, Keith. "Enlightenment and the Institution of Society: Notes for a Conceptual History." In *Main Trends in Cultural History: Ten Essays*, ed. Willem Melching and Wyger Velema. Amsterdam: Rodopi, 1994. 95–120.

Bannet, Eve Tavor. *Empire of Letters: Letter Manuals and Transatlantic Correspondence, 1688–1820*. Cambridge: Cambridge University Press, 2005.

Barbé-Marbois, François, marquis de. *The History of Louisiana, Particularly of the Cession of That Colony to the United States of America; with an Introductory Essay on the Constitution and Government of the United States*. Philadelphia: Carey and Lea, 1830.

Barratt, Carrie Rebora. *Queen Victoria and Thomas Sully*. Princeton: Princeton University Press, 2000.

Barratt, Carrie Rebora, and Ellen G. Miles. *Gilbert Stuart*. New York: Metropolitan Museum of Art, and New Haven: Yale University Press, 2004.

Barrière, Pierre. *Un Grand Provincial: Charles-Louis de Secondat, baron de La Brède et de Montesquieu*. Bordeaux: Éditions Delmas, 1946.

Barton, Benjamin Smith. *New Views of the Origin of the Tribes and Nations of America*. Philadelphia: John Bioren, 1797.

Barton, Benjamin Smith. *Observations on Some Parts of Natural History: To Which Is Prefixed an Account of Several Remarkable Vestiges of an Ancient Date, Which Have Been Discovered in Different Part of North America*. London: C. Dilly, 1787.

Bartram, John. *Observations on the Inhabitants, Climate, Soil, Rivers, Productions, Animals, and Other Matters Worthy of Notice. Made by Mr. John Bartram, in His Travels from Pensilvania to Onondago, Oswego and the Lake Ontario, in Canada. To Which Is Annex'd, a Curious Account of the Cataracts at Niagara. By Mr. Peter Kalm, a Swedish Gentleman Who Travelled There*. London: J. Whiston and B. White, 1751.

Bassett, John Spencer, ed. *The Writings of "Colonel William Byrd, of Westover in Virginia Esqr."* New York: Doubleday, Page, 1901.

Batinski, Michael C. *Jonathan Belcher, Colonial Governor*. Lexington: University Press of Kentucky, 1996.

Bauer, Ralph. "The Hispanic Enlightenment, Thomas Jefferson, and the Birth of Hemispheric American Studies." *Dieciocho: Hispanic Enlightenment* 4 (Spring 2009): 49–82.

Beales, Derek. *Enlightenment and Reform in Eighteenth-Century Europe.* London: Tauris, 2005.

Beall, Otho T., Jr. "Cotton Mather's Early 'Curiosa Americana' and the Boston Philosophical Society of 1683." *William and Mary Quarterly* 3d ser., 18 (1961): 360–72.

Becker, Carl L. *The Heavenly City of the Eighteenth-Century Philosophers.* 2d ed. New Haven: Yale University Press, 2003.

Bedell, Rebecca. *The Anatomy of Nature: Geology and American Landscape Painting, 1825–1875.* Princeton: Princeton University Press, 2001.

Bell, Marcus. *Message of Love. South-Side View of Cotton Is King; and the Philosophy of African Slavery.* Atlanta: Daily Locomotive Job Office, 1860.

Bellah, Robert. "Civil Religion in America." *Daedalus* 96, no. 1 (Winter 1967): 1–21.

Benson, Adolph B., ed. *The America of 1750: Peter Kalm's Travels in North America: The English Version of 1770.* 2 vols. New York: Dover, 1937.

Beran, Michael Knox. *Jefferson's Demons: Portrait of a Restless Mind.* New York: Free Press, 2003.

Berdan, Frances F., and Patricia Rieff Anawalt, [eds.]. *The Codex Mendoza.* 4 vols. Berkeley: University of California Press, 1992.

Berkeley, Edmund, and Dorothy Smith Berkeley. *Dr. John Mitchell: The Man Who Made the Map of North America.* Chapel Hill: University of North Carolina Press, 1974.

Berkeley, Edmund, and Dorothy Smith Berkeley, eds. *The Correspondence of John Bartram, 1734–1777.* Gainesville: University Press of Florida, 1992.

Berkhofer, Robert, Jr. *The White Man's Indian: Images of the American Indian from Columbus to the Present.* New York: Vintage, 1978.

Berlin, Isaiah. "The Counter-Enlightenment" (1973). In *Against the Current: Essays in the History of Ideas,* ed. Henry Hardy. London: Hogarth, 1979. 1–24.

Berry, Christopher. *The Social Theory of the Scottish Enlightenment.* Edinburgh: Edinburgh University Press, 1997.

Bickham, Troy. *Savages Within the Empire: Representations of American Indians in Eighteenth-Century Britain.* Oxford: Clarendon, 2005.

Biddle, Clement C., ed. *A Treatise on Political Economy; or, The Production, Distribution, and Consumption of Wealth. By Jean-Baptiste Say.* Philadelphia: Grigg and Elliot, 1836.

Bigelow, John. *The Life of Benjamin Franklin.* 3 vols. 1893; repr. Philadelphia: Lipincott, 1905.

Biller, Peter. *The Measure of Multitude: Population in Medieval Thought.* Oxford: Oxford University Press, 2000.

Bisset, Robert. *The History of the Reign of George III. To the Termination of the Late War. To Which Is Prefixed, a View of the Progressive Improvement of England, in Prosperity and Strength, to the Accession of His Majesty.* 6 vols. London: T. N. Longman and O. Rees, 1803.

Black, Jeremy. *George II: Puppet of the Politicians?* Exeter, UK: University of Exeter Press, 2007.

Black, Jeremy. *A Subject for Taste: Culture in Eighteenth-Century England.* London: Hambledon and London, 2005.

Blackbourn, David. *The Conquest of Nature: Water, Landscape, and the Making of Modern Germany.* New York: Norton, 2006.

Blackburn, Robin. *The Overthrow of Colonial Slavery, 1776–1848.* London: Verso, 1988.

Blair, Samuel. *An Account of the College of New-Jersey.* Woodbridge, N.J.: James Parker, 1764.

Blecki, Catherine La Courreye, and Karin A. Wulf, eds. *Milcah Martha Moore's Book: A Commonplace Book from Revolutionary America.* University Park: Pennsylvania State University Press, 1997.

Bleichmar, Daniela. *Visible Empire: Botanical Expeditions and Visual Culture in the Hispanic Enlightenment.* Chicago: University of Chicago Press, 2012.

Blom, Hans, John Christian Laursen, and Luisa Simonutti, eds. *Monarchisms in the Age of Enlightenment: Liberty, Patriotism, and the Common Good.* Toronto: University of Toronto Press, 2007.

Blum, Carol. *Strength in Numbers: Population, Reproduction, and Power in Eighteenth-Century France.* Baltimore: Johns Hopkins University Press, 2002.

Bonomi, Patricia. *Under the Cope of Heaven: Religion, Society, and Politics in Colonial America.* New York: Oxford University Press, 1986.

Boone, Elizabeth Hill. "The Defining Sample: How We Pursue the Pre-Columbian Past." In *A Pre-Columbian World*, ed. Jeffrey Quilter and Mary Miller. Washington, D.C.: Dumbarton Oaks Research Library and Collection, 2006. 21–53.

Bordley, John Beale. *A Summary View of the Courses of Crops, in the Husbandry of England & Maryland; with a Comparison of Their Products; and a System of Improved Courses, Proposed for Farms in America.* Philadelphia: Charles Cist, 1784.

Bots, Hans, and Françoise Waquet. *La République des lettres.* Paris: Belin: DeBoeck, 1997.

Boturini Benaduci, Lorenzo. *Catálogo del Museo histórico indiano del Cavallero Lorenzo Boturini Benaduci, señor de la Torre y de Hono, quien llegó a la Nueva España por febrero del año 1736.* Madrid: Juan de Zuñiga, 1746.

Bouguer, Pierre. *La Figure de la Terre, déterminée par les observations de Messieurs Bouguer, & de La Condamine, de l'Académie royale des sçiences, envoyés par ordre du Roy au Pérou, pour observer aux environs de l'Equateur.* Paris: Charles-Antoine Jombert, 1749.

Boulanger, Nicolas-Antoine ["feu"]. *L'Antiquité dévoilée par ses usages; ou, Examen critique des principales opinions, cérémonies & institutions religieuses & politiques des différens peuples de la Terre.* 3 vols. Amsterdam: Marc Michel Rey, 1766.

Boyle, Robert. *The Christian Virtuoso: Shewing, That by Being Addicted to Experimental Philosophy, a Man Is Rather Assisted, Than Indisposed, to Be a Good Christian.* London: Edward Jones, for John Taylor, 1690.

Brading, David. *The First America: The Spanish Monarchy, Creole Patriots, and the Liberal State, 1492–1867.* Cambridge: Cambridge University Press, 1991.

Braun, Barbara. *Pre-Columbian Art and the Post-Columbian World: Ancient American Sources of Modern Art.* New York: Abrams, 1993.

Breen, T. H. *The Character of the Good Ruler: A Study of Puritan Political Ideas in New England, 1630–1730.* New Haven: Yale University Press, 1970.

Brewer, Holly. *By Birth or Consent: Children, Law, and the Anglo-American Revolution in Authority.* Chapel Hill: Published for the Omohundro Institute of Early American History and Culture, Williamsburg, Virginia, by the University of North Carolina Press, 2005.

Brewer, John. *The Pleasures of the Imagination: English Culture in the Eighteenth Century.* 1997; repr. New York: Routledge, 2013.

Brewer, W. H. "Agricultural Societies, What They Are and What They Have Done." In *Annual Report of the Secretary of the Connecticut Board of Agriculture,* vol. 14 (Hartford, 1881), 98–116.

Bridenbaugh, Carl. *Cities in the Wilderness: The First Century of Urban Life in America, 1625–1742.* New York: Ronald Press Company, 1938.

Brigham, David R. *Public Culture in the Early Republic: Peale's Museum and Its Audience.* Washington, D.C.: Smithsonian Institution Press, 1995.

Broadie, Alexander, ed. *The Cambridge Companion to the Scottish Enlightenment.* Cambridge: Cambridge University Press, 2003.

Brockliss, L. W. B. *Calvet's Web: Enlightenment and the Republic of Letters in Eighteenth-Century France.* New York: Oxford University Press, 2002.

Brooke, John. *King George III.* New York: McGraw-Hill, 1972.

Brooke, John. "The Library of King George." *Yale University Library Gazette* 52, no. 1 (July 1977): 33–45.

Brown, Richard. *Knowledge Is Power: The Diffusion of Information in Early America, 1700–1865.* New York: Oxford University Press, 1989.

Browne, Peter Arrell. *An Address, Intended to Promote a Geological and Mineralogical Survey of Pennsylvania, the Publication of a Series of Geological Maps, and the Formation of State and County Geological and Mineralogical Collections.* Philadelphia: P. M. Lafourcade, 1826.

Bryant, Jacob. *A New System, or, An Analysis of Ancient Mythology.* 2 vols. London: T. Payne, 1774.

Bryson, Gladys. *Man and Society: The Scottish Inquiry of the Eighteenth Century.* Princeton: Princeton University Press, 1945.

Buffon, George Louis Leclerc, comte de. *Des époques de la Nature.* 1778; repr. Paris: Diderot, 1998.

Buffon, George Louis Leclerc, comte de. *The Natural History of Animals, Vegetables, and Minerals; with the Theory of the Earth in General. Translated from the French of Count de Buffon.* 6 vols. London: T. Bell, 1775–76.

Buffon, George Louis Leclerc, comte de. *Oeuvres complètes de M. le C[om]te de Buffon.* 25 vols. Paris: De l'Imprimerie Royale, 1774–79.

Bullion, John L. " 'George, Be a King!': The Relationship Between Princess August and George III." In *Hanoverian Britain and Empire: Essays in Memory of Philip Lawson,* ed. Stephen Taylor, Richard Connors, and Clyve Jones. Woodbridge, Suffolk, UK: Boydell, 1998. 177–97.

Bullion, John L. " 'To Know This Is the True Essential Business of a King': The Prince of Wales and the Study of Public Finance, 1755–1760." *Albion* 18, no. 3 (Autumn 1986): 429–54.

Burford, Robert. *Description of the Panorama of the Superb City of Mexico, and the Surrounding Scenery, Painted on 2700 Square Feet of Canvas, by Robert Burford, Esq. from Drawings Made on the Spot at the Request of the Mexican Government.* New York: E. Conrad, 1828.

Burnard, Trevor. *Mastery, Tyranny, and Desire: Thomas Thistlewood and His Slaves in the Anglo-Jamaican World.* Chapel Hill: University of North Carolina Press, 2004.

Burnet, Thomas. *The Sacred Theory of the Earth.* 1691. Introduction by Basil Willey. London: Centaur, 1965.

Burnet, Thomas. *Telluris Theoria Sacra: Orbis Nostri Originem & Mutationes Generales, quas Aut jam subiit, aut olim subiturus est, complectens.* London: Typis R. N., impensis Gualt. Kettilby, 1681.

Burns, James MacGregor. *Fire and Light: How the Enlightenment Transformed Our World.* New York: Thomas Dunne, 2013.

Butler, Jon. *Becoming America: The Revolution Before 1776.* Cambridge: Harvard University Press, 2000.

Butterfield, L. H., ed. *Letters of Benjamin Rush.* 2 vols. Princeton: Published for the American Philosophical Society by Princeton University Press, 1951.

Byles, Mather. *A Poem on the Death of His Late Majesty King George, of Glorious Memory. And the Accession of Our Present Sovereign King George II. To the British Throne.* Boston: s.n., 1727.

Byrd, James P. *Sacred Scripture, Sacred War: The Bible and the American Revolution.* Oxford: Oxford University Press, 2013.

Byrd, William. "An Account of a Negro-Boy That Is Dappel'd in Several Places of His Body with White Spots. By Will. Byrd, Esq, F. R. S." *Philosophical Transactions* 19 (1695–97): 781–82.

Byrd, William. *History of the Dividing Line and Other Tracts. From the Papers of William Byrd, of Westover, in Virginia, Esquire.* 2 vols. Richmond, Va.: s.n., 1866.

Byrd, William. *The Westover Manuscripts: Containing the History of the Dividing Line Betwixt Virginia and North Carolina; A Journey to the Land of Eden, A.D. 1733; and A Progress to the Mines. Written from 1728 to 1736, and Now First Published.* Petersburg, Va.: Edmund and Julian C. Ruffin, 1841.

Calder, Isabel M., ed. *Letters and Papers of Ezra Stiles, President of Yale College, 1778–1795.* New Haven: Yale University Library, 1933.

Candidus [James Chalmers?]. *Plain Truth: Addressed to the Inhabitants of America. Containing Remarks on a Late Pamphlet, Intitled Common Sense.* Philadelphia; repr. Dublin: M. Mills, 1776.

Cañizares-Esguerra, Jorge. *How to Write the History of the New World: Histories, Epistemologies, and Identities in the Eighteenth-Century Atlantic World.* Stanford: Stanford University Press, 2001.

Cappon, Lester J., ed. *The Adams-Jefferson Letters: The Complete Correspondence Between Thomas Jefferson and Abigail and John Adams.* 1959; repr. Chapel Hill: Published for the Institute of Early American History and Culture, Williamsburg, Virginia, by the University of North Carolina Press, 1988.

Carey, H. C. *The Past, the Present and the Future.* Philadelphia: Carey and Hart, 1848.

Carey, H. C. *Principles of Political Economy.* 3 vols. Philadelphia: Carey, Lea, and Blanchard, 1837.

Carlyle, Alexander. *The Justice and Necessity of the War with Our American Colonies Examined.* London: J. Murray, 1777.

Carlyle, Thomas. "Occasional Discourse on the Negro Question." *Fraser's Magazine* 40 (December 1849): 670–79.

Caroe, Gwendy M. *The Royal Institution: An Informal History.* London: John Murray, 1985.

Caron, Nathalie, and Naomi Wulf. "American Enlightenments: Continuity and Renewal." *Journal of American History* 99 (March 2013): 1072–91.

Carter, Landon. "Observations Concerning the FLY-WEEVIL, That Destroys the Wheat, with Some Useful Discoveries and Conclusions, Concerning the Propagation and Progress of That Pernicious Insect, and the Methods to Be Used to Prevent the Destruction of the Grain by It. By Colonel LANDON CARTER, of Sabine-Hall, Virginia; Transmitted by Colonel LEE. Read, and Ordered to Be Published, November 15th, 1768." *Transactions of the American Philosophical Society* 1 (1769–71): 205–17.

Cassara, Ernest. *The Enlightenment in America.* New York: Twayne, 1975.

Cassedy, James H. *Demography in Early America: Beginnings of the Statistical Mind, 1600–1800.* Cambridge: Harvard University Press, 1969.

Cassirer, Ernst. *The Philosophy of the Enlightenment.* 1932. Trans. Fritz C. A. Koelln and James P. Pettegrove. Boston: Beacon, 1955.

Catalogue of Books in the Library of the College of New-Jersey, January 29, 1760, A. Woodbridge, N.J.: James Parker, 1760.

Catalogue of the Books, Belonging to the Library Company of Philadelphia, A; to Which Is Prefixed, a Short Account of the Institution, with the Charter, Laws and Regulations. Philadelphia: Zacharia Poulson, 1789.

Catalogue of the Library of the late Dr. Joseph Priestley, Containing Many Very Scarce and Valuable Books, for Sale by Thomas Dobson. Philadelphia: s.n., 1816.

Catesby, Mark. *The Natural History of Carolina, Florida, and the Bahama Islands.* 2 vols. London: Benjamin White, 1731, 1743.

Ceci, Lynn. "Native Wampum as a Peripheral Resource in the Seventeenth-Century World-System." In *The Pequots in Southern New England: The Fall and Rise of an American Indian Nation*, ed. Laurence M. Hauptman and James D. Wherry. Norman: University of Oklahoma Press, 1990. 48–63.

Channing, William Ellery. "Remarks on the Life and Character of Napoleon Bonaparte (1827–1828)." In *The Works of William Ellery Channing*. Boston: James Munroe, 1846. 69–166.

Chaplin, Joyce. *An Anxious Pursuit: Agricultural Innovation and Modernity in the Lower South, 1730–1815*. Chapel Hill: Published for the Institute of Early American History and Culture, Williamsburg, Virginia, by the University of North Carolina Press, 1993.

Chaplin, Joyce. *Subject Matter: Technology, the Body, and Science on the Anglo-American Frontier, 1500–1676*. Cambridge: Harvard University Press, 2001.

Charlevoix, Pierre-François-Xavier de. *Histoire et description generale de la Nouvelle France, avec le journal historique d'un voyage fait par ordre du Roi dans l'Amérique septentrionnale*. 6 vols. Paris: Chez Didot, 1744.

Chase, Eugene Parker, ed. and trans. *Our Revolutionary Forefathers: The Letters of François, Marquis de Barbé-Marbois During his Residence in the United States as Secretary of the French Legation, 1779–1785*. New York: Duffield, 1929.

Checkley, Samuel. *The Duty of a People, to Lay to Heart and Lament the Death of a Good King*. Boston: Benjamin Gray, 1727.

Cherry, Conrad. *Nature and Religious Imagination: From Edwards to Bushnell*. Philadelphia: Fortress, 1980.

Chiappelli, Fredi, Michael J. B. Allen, and Robert Benson, eds. *First Images of America: The Impact of the New World on the Old*. 2 vols. Berkeley: University of California Press, 1976.

Child, Lydia Maria Francis. *An Appeal in Favor of That Class of Americans Called Africans*. Boston: Allen and Ticknor, 1833.

Chinard, Gilbert. *Jefferson et les idéologues*. 1925. Repr. New York: Arno, 1979.

Chinard, Gilbert. *Volney et l'Amérique d'après des documents inédits et sa correspondance avec Jefferson*. Baltimore: Johns Hopkins University Press, 1923.

Chinard, Gilbert, ed. *The Correspondence of Jefferson and Du Pont de Nemours, with an Introduction on Jefferson and the Physiocrats*. Baltimore: Johns Hopkins University Press, 1931.

Chipley, Louise. "The Enlightenment Library of William Bentley." *Essex Institute Historical Collections* 122 (January 1986): 2–29.

Clark, Peter. *European Cities and Towns: 400–2000*. New York: Oxford University Press, 2009.

Clarke, Thomas. *A Statistical View of Europe, in Respect to the Forms of Government, Administration of Justice, Religion and Manners, of Each Nation*. London: C. Dilly, 1791.

Clarkson, Thomas. *An Essay on the Slavery and Commerce of the Human Species, Particularly the African, Translated from a Latin Dissertation, Which Was Honoured with the First Prize in the University of Cambridge, for the Year 1784.* London: J. Phillips and T. Cadell, 1786.

Clarkson, Thomas. *The History of the Rise, Progress, & Accomplishment of the Abolition of the African Slave-Trade, by the British Parliament.* 2 vols. Philadelphia: James P. Parke, 1808.

Clavigero, Francesco Saverio. *The History of Mexico. Collected from Spanish and Mexican Historians, from Manuscripts, and Ancient Paintings of the Indians. Illustrated by Charts, and Other Copper Plates. To Which Are Added, Critical Dissertations on the Land, the Animals, and Inhabitants of Mexico. By Abbé D. Francesco Saverio Clavigero. Translated from the Original Italian, by Charles Cullen, Esq.* 2 vols. London: G. G. J. and J. Robinson, 1787.

Clavigero, Francesco Saverio. *Storia antica del Messico, cavata da' migliori storici spagnuoli, e da' manoscritti, e dalle pitture antiche degl' Indiani: divisa in dieci libri, e corredata di carte geografiche, e di varie figure: e dissertazioni sulla terra, sugli animali, e sugli abitatori del Messico.* 4 vols. bound as 2. Cesena: G. Biasini, 1780–81.

Clive, John, and Bernard Bailyn. "England's Cultural Provinces: Scotland and America." *William and Mary Quarterly* 11, no. 2 (April 1954): 200–213.

Coates, Benjamin Hornor. *Annual Discourse, Delivered Before the Historical Society of Pennsylvania, on the 28th Day of April, 1834, on the Origin of the Indian Population of America.* Philadelphia: M'Carty and Davis, 1834.

Cody, W. F. "An Index to the Periodicals Published by José Antonio Alzate y Ramírez." *Hispanic American Historical Review* 33, no. 3 (August 1953): 442–75.

Cohen, I. Bernard. *Some Early Tools of American Science: An Account of the Early Scientific Instruments and Mineralogical and Biological Collections in Harvard University.* Cambridge: Harvard University Press, 1950.

Colden, Cadwallader. *The History of the Five Indian Nations Depending on the Province of New-York in America.* New York: William Bradford, 1727.

Colfax, Richard H. *Evidence Against the Views of the Abolitionists, Consisting of Physical and Moral Proofs, of the Natural Inferiority of the Negroes.* New York: James T. M. Bleakley, 1833.

Colley, Linda. *Britons: Forging the Nation, 1707–1837.* New Haven: Yale University Press, 1992.

Collin, Nicholas. "Introduction to Vol. the Third: An Essay on Those Inquiries in Natural Philosophy, Which at Present Are Most Beneficial to the United States of North America." *Transactions of the American Philosophical Society* 3 (1793): iii–xxvii.

Collins, David. *Practical Rules for the Management and Medical Treatment of Negro Slaves, in the Sugar Colonies. By a Professional Planter.* 1803; repr. London: J. Barfield, 1811.

Colman, Benjamin. *Fidelity to Christ and to the Protestant Succession in the Illustrious House of Hannover. A Sermon Preached at Boston in New-England, the Lord's-day After the Proclaiming of King George the Second; August 9. 1727*. Boston: T. Fleet for T. Hancock, 1727.

Colman, Benjamin [attrib.]. *A Manifesto or Declaration, Set Forth by the Undertakers of the New Church Now Erected in Boston in New-England, November 17th. 1699*. Boston: B. Green and J. Allen? 1699?.

Commager, Henry Steele. *The Empire of Reason: How Europe Imagined and America Realized the Enlightenment*. Garden City, N.Y. Anchor, 1977.

Condorcet, Jean-Antoine-Nicolas de Caritat, marquis de [attrib.]. *Réflexions sur l'esclavage des Nègres*. Neufchâtel: Société Typographique, 1781.

Conforti, Joseph. "Samuel Hopkins and the New Divinity: Theology, Ethics, and Social Reform in Eighteenth-Century New England." *William and Mary Quarterly* 34, no. 4 (1977): 572–89.

Conforti, Joseph. *Samuel Hopkins and the New Divinity Movement: Calvinism, the Congregational Ministry, and Reform in New England Between the Great Awakenings*. Grand Rapids, Mich.: Eerdmans, 1981.

Conkin, Paul. *Prophets of Prosperity: America's First Political Economists*. Bloomington: Indiana University Press, 1980.

Conrad, Sebastian. "Enlightenment in Global History: A Historiographical Critique." *American Historical Review* 17, no. 4 (October 2012): 999–1027.

Cook, James. *A Voyage Round the World, Performed in His Britannic Majesty's Ships the Resolution and Adventure, in the Years 1772, 1773, 1774, and 1775*. 4 vols. Dublin: W. Whitestone et al., 1777.

Cooper, Alix. *Inventing the Indigenous: Local Knowledge and Natural History in Early Modern Europe*. Cambridge: Cambridge University Press, 2007.

Cooper, Helen, ed. *John Trumbull: The Hand and Spirit of a Painter*. New Haven: Yale University Press, 1982.

Cooper, Thomas. *Lectures on the Elements of Political Economy*. Columbia: D. E. Sweeny, 1826.

Coram, Robert. *Political Inquiries: To Which Is Added, a Plan for the General Establishment of Schools Throughout the United States*. Wilmington, Del.: Andrews and Brynberg, 1791.

Corner, George W., ed. *The Autobiography of Benjamin Rush: His "Travels Through Life" Together with His "Commonplace Book" for 1789–1813*. Princeton: Published for the American Philosophical Society by Princeton University Press, 1948.

Coronado, Raúl. *A World Not to Come: A History of Latino Writing and Print Culture*. Cambridge: Harvard University Press, 2013.

Coughtry, Jay. *The Notorious Triangle: Rhode Island and the African Slave Trade, 1700–1807*. Philadelphia: Temple University Press, 1981.

Court de Gébelin, Antoine. *Monde primitif, analisé et comparé avec le monde moderne; ou, Recherches sur les antiquités du monde*. Paris: Chez l'Auteur, 1773–82.

Crèvecoeur, J. Hector St. John de. *Letters from an American Farmer; Describing Certain Provincial Situations, Manners, and Customs, Not Generally Known; and Conveying Some Idea of the Late and Present Interior Circumstances of the British Colonies in North America*. London: Thomas Davies and Lockyer Davis, 1782.

Crèvecoeur, J. Hector St. John de ["Normano-Americanus"]. *Traité de la culture des pommes-de-terre, et des differens usages qu'en font les habitans des États-Unis de l'Amérique*. Caen: s.n., 1782.

Crèvecoeur, Michel Guillaume St. Jean de. *Lettres d'un cultivateur américain, écrites à W. S. Écuyer, depuis l'année 1770, jusqu'à 1781*. 2 vols. Paris: Cuchet, 1784.

Crosby, Alfred. *Ecological Imperialism: The Biological Expansion of Europe, 900–1900*. Cambridge: Cambridge University Press, 1986.

Cumming, William P. *The Southeast in Early Maps: With an Annotated Check List of Printed and Manuscript Regional and Local Maps of Southeastern North America During the Colonial Period*. Princeton: Princeton University Press, 1958.

Curious Hieroglyphick Bible, A; or, Select Passages in the Old and New Testaments, Represented with Emblematical Figures, for the Amusement of Youth. Worcester, Mass.: Isaiah Thomas, 1788.

Curran, Andrew S. *The Anatomy of Blackness: Science and Slavery in an Age of Enlightenment*. Baltimore: Johns Hopkins University Press, 2011.

Dance, S. Peter. *Shell Collecting: An Illustrated History*. Berkeley: University of California Press, 1966.

Daston, Lorraine, and Katherine Park. *Wonders and the Order of Nature, 1150–1750*. New York: Zone Books, 1998.

Daston, Lorraine, and M. Stolleis, eds. *Natural Law and Laws of Nature in Early Modern Europe: Jurisprudence, Theology, Moral and Natural Philosophy*. Farnham, Surrey, UK: Aldershot, 2008.

Daston, Lorraine, and Fernando Vidal, eds. *The Moral Authority of Nature*. Chicago: University of Chicago Press, 2004.

Davidson, Edward H., and William J. Scheick. *Paine, Scripture, and Authority: The Age of Reason as Religious and Political Idea*. Bethlehem: Lehigh University Press, 1994.

Davies, Samuel. *A Sermon Delivered at Nassau-Hall, January 14, 1761. On the Death of His Late Majesty King George II. By Samuel Davies, A.M., Late President of the College of New-Jersey. To Which is Prefixed, a Brief Account of the Life, Character, and Death, of the Author. By David Bostwick, A.M. Minister of the Presbyterian Congregation in New-York*. Philadelphia: William Bradford, 1761.

Davis, David Brion. *The Problem of Slavery in the Age of Revolution, 1770–1823*. Ithaca: Cornell University Press, 1975.

Davis, David Brion. *The Problem of Slavery in Western Culture*. Ithaca: Cornell University Press, 1966.

Davis, Richard Beale. *Intellectual Life in the Colonial South, 1585–1763*. 3 vols. Knoxville: University of Tennessee Press, 1978.

Daybell, James. *The Material Letter in Early Modern England: Manuscript Letters and the Culture and Practices of Letter-Writing, 1512–1635*. Houndmills, Basingstoke, Hampshire, UK: Palgrave Macmillan, 2012.

Dean, Dennis R. "Benjamin Franklin and Geology." In *The Revolution in Geology from the Renaissance to the Enlightenment*, ed. Gary D. Rosenberg. Boulder: Geological Society of America, 2009. 209–23.

Delabarre, Edmund Burke. "Middle Period of Dighton Rock History." *Publications of the Colonial Society of Massachusetts: Transactions* 19 (1916–17): 46–149.

Delbourgo, James. *A Most Amazing Scene of Wonders: Electricity and Enlightenment in Early America*. Cambridge: Harvard University Press, 2006.

Delbourgo, James. "The Newtonian Slave Body: Racial Enlightenment in the Atlantic World." *Atlantic Studies* 9, no. 2 (June 2012): 185–207.

Delbourgo, James. "Slavery in the Cabinet of Curiosities: Hans Sloane's Atlantic World." Available at http://www.britishmuseum.org/pdf/ delbourgo%20essay.pdf.

Delbourgo, James, and Nicholas Dew, eds. *Science and Empire in the Atlantic World*. New York: Routledge, 2008.

Deluc, Jean-André. *Lettres physiques et morales sur les montagnes et sur l'histoire de la terre et de l'homme: adressées à la Reine de la Grande Bretagne*. The Hague: Detune, 1778.

Desgraves, Louis, and Catherine Volphilhac-Auger. *Catalogue de la bibliothèque de Montesquieu à La Brède*. Paris: Universitas, 1999.

Destutt de Tracy, Antoine Louis Claude. *A Treatise on Political Economy; to Which Is Prefixed a Supplement to a Preceding Work on the Understanding; or Elements of Ideology; with an Analytical Table, and an Introduction on the Faculty of the Will … Translated from the Unpublished French Original*. Georgetown [Washington, D.C.]: Joseph Milligan, 1817.

Dexter, Franklin Bowditch, ed. *The Literary Diary of Ezra Stiles, D.D., LL.D.* 3 vols. New York: Scribner's, 1901.

Dickson, William. *Letters on Slavery, by William Dickson, Formerly Private Secretary to the Late Hon. Edward Hay, Governor of Barbadoes. To Which Are Added, Addresses to the Whites, and to the Free Negroes of Barbadoes; and Accounts of Some Negroes Eminent for Their Virtues and Abilities*. London: J. Phillips, 1789.

Diderot, Denis, and Jean Le Rond d'Alembert. *Encyclopédie; ou, Dictionnaire raisonné des sciences, des arts et des métiers*. Neufchâtel: Samuel Faulche, 1765.

Dierks, Konstantin. *In My Power: Letter Writing and Communications in Early America*. Philadelphia: University of Pennsylvania Press, 2009.

Ditz, Toby. *Epistolary Selves: Letters and Letter-Writers, 1600–1945*. Aldershot, UK: Ashgate, 1999.

Dixon, John M. "Henry F. May and the Revival of the American Enlightenment: Problems and Possibilities for Intellectual and Social History." *William and Mary Quarterly* 3rd ser., 71, no. 2 (April 2014): 255–80.

"Donations Received by the American Philosophical Society, Since the Publication of Vol. I—New Series." *Transactions of the American Philosophical Society* 2 (1825): 481–502.

"Donations Received by the American Philosophical Society, Since the Publication of Vol. II.—New Series." *Transactions of the American Philosophical Society* 3 (1830): 487–509.

Donnant, Denis François. *Statistical Account of the United States of America. By D. F. Donnant. Member of the Atheneum of Arts, &c. &c. at Paris. Translated from the French, by William Playfair: With an Addition on the Trade to America. For the Use of Commercial Men, by the Same. Illustrated by a Divided Circle, Representing the Proportional Extent of the Different States, the Eastern Country, and the Newly Acquired Territory of Louisiana.* London: Greenland and Norris, 1805.

Doskey, John S., ed. *The European Journals of William Maclure.* Philadelphia: American Philosophical Society, 1988.

Downes, Paul. *Democracy, Revolution, and Monarchism in Early American Literature.* New York: Cambridge University Press, 2002.

Drayton, William. *The South Vindicated from the Treason and Fanaticism of the Northern Abolitionists.* Philadelphia: H. Manly, 1836.

DuBois, Laurent. "An Enslaved Enlightenment: Rethinking the Intellectual History of the French Atlantic." *Social History* 31 (2006): 1–14.

Duckworth, Mark. "An Eighteenth-Century Questionnaire: William Robertson on the Indians." *Eighteenth-Century Life* 11 (February 1987): 36–49.

Dugatkin, Lee. *Mr. Jefferson and the Giant Moose: Natural History in Early America.* Chicago: University of Chicago Press, 2009.

Dunn, Richard S. *Sugar and Slaves: The Rise of the Planter Class in the English West Indies, 1624–1713.* Chapel Hill: Published for the Institute of Early American History and Culture, Williamsburg, Virginia, by the University of North Carolina Press, 1972.

Dupuis, Charles-François. *Origine de tous les cultes; ou, Religion universelle.* Paris: H. Agasse, An 3 de la République [1795].

Dwight, Timothy. *The Nature and Danger of Infidel Philosophy, Exhibited in Two Discourses, Addressed to the Candidates for the Baccalaureate, in Yale College, September 9th, 1797.* 1798; repr. New Haven: George Bunce, 1799.

Edelstein, Dan. "The Egyptian French Revolution: Antiquarianism, Freemasonry and the Mythology of Nature." In *The Super-Enlightenment: Daring to Know Too Much*, ed. Dan Edelstein. Oxford: Voltaire Foundation, 2010. 215–41.

Edelstein, Dan. *The Enlightenment: A Genealogy.* Chicago: University of Chicago Press, 2010.

Ehrard, Jean. *Lumières et esclavage: l'esclavage colonial et l'opinion publique en France au XVIIIe siècle.* Bruxelles: André Versaille éditeur, 2008.

Eliot, Jared. *An Essay upon Field-Husbandry in New-England as It Is or May Be Ordered*. New London, Conn.: T. Green, 1748.

Elkins, Stanley. *Slavery: A Problem in American Institutional and Intellectual Life*. Chicago: University of Chicago Press, 1959.

Ellingson, Ter. *The Myth of the Noble Savage*. Berkeley: University of California Press, 2001.

Elliott, Clark A., and Margaret W. Rossiter, eds. *Science at Harvard University: Historical Perspectives*. Bethlehem, Pa.: Lehigh University Press, 1992.

Elliott, J. H. *Empires of the Atlantic World: Britain and Spain in America, 1492–1830*. New Haven: Yale University Press, 2006.

Emerson, Ralph Waldo. "Religion." In *Sketches and Reminiscences of the Radical Club of Chestnut Street, Boston*, ed. Mrs. John T. [Mary Elizabeth Fiske] Sargent. Boston: James R. Osgood, 1880. 3–20.

Emerson, Roger L. "American Indians, Frenchmen, and Scots Philosophers." *Studies in Eighteenth-Century Culture* 9 (1979): 211–36.

Estève, Laurent. *Montesquieu, Rousseau, Diderot: du genre humain au bois d'ébène; les silences du droit naturel*. Paris: Éditions Unesco, 2002.

Eustace, Nicole. *Passion Is the Gale: Emotion, Power, and the Coming of the American Revolution*. Chapel Hill: Published for the Omohundro Institute of Early American History and Culture, Williamsburg, Virginia, by the University of North Carolina Press, 2008.

Fanelli, Doris Devine. *History of the Portrait Collection, Independence National Historical Park*. Philadelphia: American Philosophical Society, 2001.

Farneworth, Ellis, trans. *The Works of Nicholas Machiavel, Secretary of State to the Republic of Florence*. 2 vols. London: Thomas Davies, 1762.

Faujas de Saint Fond, Barthélemy. *Histoire naturelle de la Montagne de Saint-Pierre de Maestricht*. Paris: H. J. Jansen, 1798–99.

Fea, John. *The Way of Improvement Leads Home: Philip Vickers Fithian and the Rural Enlightenment in Early America*. Philadelphia: University of Pennsylvania Press, 2008.

Feingold, Mordechai. "Jesuits: Savants." In *Jesuit Science and the Republic of Letters*, ed. Mordechai Feingold. Cambridge: MIT Press, 2003. 1–45.

Feld, Stuart. "In the Latest London Manner." *Metropolitan Museum of Art Bulletin* 21 (May 1963): 296–308.

Ferguson, Adam. *An Essay on the History of Civil Society*. Dublin: Boulter Grierson, 1767.

Ferguson, Robert A. *The American Enlightenment, 1750–1820*. Cambridge: Harvard University Press, 1997.

Ferguson, Robert A. *Law and Letters in American Culture*. Cambridge: Harvard University Press, 1984.

Fiering, Norman S. "The First American Enlightenment: Tillotson, Leverett, and Philosophical Anglicanism." *New England Quarterly* 54, no. 3 (September 1981): 307–44.

Fiering, Norman S. "The Transatlantic Republic of Letters: A Note on the Circulation of Learned Periodicals to Early Eighteenth-Century America." *William and Mary Quarterly* 3d ser., 33 (October 1976): 642–60.

Filson, John. *The Discovery, Settlement and Present State of Kentucke.* Wilmington, Del.: James Adams, 1784.

Findlen, Paula. "Jokes of Nature and Jokes of Knowledge: The Playfulness of Scientific Discourse in Early Modern Europe." *Renaissance Quarterly* 43, no. 2 (Summer 1990): 292–331.

Findlen, Paula. *Possessing Nature: Museums, Collecting, and Scientific Culture in Early Modern Italy.* Berkeley: University of California Press, 1994.

Finkelman, Paul. "The Dragon St. George Could Not Slay: Tucker's Plan to End Slavery." *William and Mary Law Review* 47, no. 4 (2006): 1213–43.

Fitzpatrick, John, ed. *The Writings of George Washington from the Original Manuscript Sources, 1745–1799.* 39 vols. Washington, D.C.: United States Government Printing Office, 1931–1944.

Flavell, Julie. "Decadents Abroad: Reconstructing the Typical Colonial American in London in the Late Colonial Period." In *Old World, New World: America and Europe in the Age of Jefferson,* ed. Leonard J. Sadosky, Peter Nicolaisen, Peter S. Onuf, and Andrew J. O'Shaughnessy. Charlottesville: University of Virginia Press, 2010. 32–60.

Flavell, Julie. *When London Was Capital of America.* New Haven: Yale University Press, 2010.

Fletcher, F. T. H. "Montesquieu's Influence on Anti-Slavery Opinion in England." *Journal of Negro History* 18, no. 4 (October 1933): 414–25.

Fliegelman, Jay. *Prodigals and Pilgrims: The American Revolution Against Patriarchal Authority, 1750–1800.* Cambridge: Cambridge University Press, 1982.

Ford, W. C., ed. "Tenth Report of the Historical Manuscript Commission: Letters of William Vans Murray to John Quincy Adams, 1797–1803." *Annual Report of the American Historical Association for 1912.* Washington, D.C.: U.S. Government Printing Office, 1914. 341–708.

Forensic Dispute on the Legality of Enslaving the Africans, A, Held at the Public Commencement in Cambridge, New-England, July 21st, 1773. By Two Candidates for the Bachelor's Degree. Boston: John Boyle, for Thomas Leverett, 1773.

Franklin, Benjamin. *Experiments and Observations on Electricity, Made at Philadelphia in America, by Mr. Benjamin Franklin, and Communicated in Several Letters to Mr. P. Collinson, of London, F.R.S.* London: E. Cave, 1751.

Frederick II, King of Prussia. *Anti-Machiavel; or, An Examination of Machiavel's Prince.* London : T. Woodward, 1741.

Freeman, John Finley. "Manuscript Sources on Latin American Indians in the Library of the American Philosophical Society." *Proceedings of the American Philosophical Society* 106, no. 6 (December 12, 1962): 530–40.

Furey, Constance. *Erasmus, Contarini, and the Religious Republic of Letters*. New York: Cambridge University Press, 2006.

Gardiner, Harvey C., ed. *The Literary Memoranda of William Hickling Prescott*. 2 vols. Norman: University of Oklahoma Press, 1961.

Gardiner, Harvey C., ed. *The Papers of William Hickling Prescott*. Urbana: University of Illinois Press, 1964.

Garrison, William Lloyd. *The New "Reign of Terror" in the Slaveholding States, for 1859–60*. New York: American Anti-Slavery Society, 1860.

Gaul, Theresa Strouth, and Sharon M. Harris. *Letters and Cultural Transformations in the United States, 1760–1860*. Farnham, Surrey, UK: Ashgate, 2009.

Gaulmier, Jean. *Un Grand Témoin de la Révolution et de l'Empire: Volney*. Paris, Hachette, 1959.

Gay, Peter. *The Enlightenment: An Interpretation*. 2 vols. New York: Knopf, 1966–69.

Gebelin, François, avec la Collaboration de M. André Morize. *Correspondance de Montesquieu*. 2 vols. Paris: Édouard Champion, 1914.

Geertz, Clifford. "Religion as a Cultural System." In Geertz, *The Interpretation of Cultures: Selected Essays*. New York: Basic, 1973. 87–125.

George III: Collector and Patron. London: Queen's Gallery, Buckingham Palace, 1974.

Gerbi, Antonello. *The Dispute of the New World: The History of a Polemic, 1750–1900*. Trans. Jeremy Moyle. 1955; Pittsburgh: University of Pittsburgh Press, 1973.

Gibbon, Edward. *The History of the Decline and Fall of the Roman Empire*. 6 vols. London: W. Strahan and T. Cadell, 1776–88.

Gillespie, Charles. *Genesis and Geology: A Study in the Relations of Scientific Thought, Natural Theology, and Social Opinion in Great Britain, 1790–1850*. Cambridge: Harvard University Press, 1951.

Gipson, Lawrence Henry, ed. *Lewis Evans, to Which Is Added Evans' "A Brief Account of Pennsylvania."* Philadelphia: Historical Society of Pennsylvania, 1939.

Glass, John B. "The Boturini Collection and the Council of the Indies, 1780–1800." *Contributions to the Ethnohistory of Mexico*, no. 4. Lincoln Center, Mass.: Conemex Associates, 1976.

Godwin, William. *Of Population: An Enquiry Concerning the Power of Increase in the Numbers of Mankind, Being an Answer to Mr. Malthus's Essay on That Subject*. London: Longman, Hurst, Rees, Orme, and Brown, 1820.

Godwyn, Morgan. *The Negro's & Indians Advocate, Suing for Their Admission into the Church; or, A Persuasive to the Instructing and Baptizing of the Negro's and Indians in Our Plantations*. London: J.D., 1680.

Godwyn, Morgan. *A Supplement to the Negro's & Indian's Advocate; or, Some Further Considerations and Proposals for the Effectual and Speedy Carrying on of the Negro's Christianity in Our Plantations (Notwithstanding the Late*

Pretended Impossibilities) Without any Prejudice to Their Owners. London: J.D., 1681.

Goldgar, Anne. *Impolite Learning: Conduct and Community in the Republic of Letters, 1680–1750*. New Haven: Yale University Press, 1995.

Goodell, Abner C. "John Saffin and His Slave Adam." *Publications of the Colonial Society of Massachusetts* 1 (March 1895): 85–112.

Goodman, Dena. *Becoming a Woman in the Age of Letters*. Ithaca: Cornell University Press, 2009.

Gould, Eliga H., and Peter S. Onuf, eds. *Empire and Nation: The American Revolution in the Atlantic World*. Baltimore: Johns Hopkins University Press, 2005.

Govier, Mark. "The Royal Society, Slavery, and the Island of Jamaica: 1660–1700." *Notes and Records of the Royal Society of London* 53, no. 2 (May 1999): 203–17.

Grasso, Christopher. "The Experimental Philosophy of Farming: Jared Eliot and the Cultivation of Connecticut." *William and Mary Quarterly* 3d ser., 50, no. 3 (July 1993): 502–28.

Gray, Edward. *New World Babel: Languages and Nations in Early America*. Princeton: Princeton University Press, 1999.

Gray, John. *Enlightenment's Wake: Politics and Culture at the Close of the Modern Age*. London: Routledge, 1995.

Green, Jacob. *A Monograph of the Trilobites of North America: With Coloured Models of the Species*. Philadelphia: J. Brano, 1832.

Greene, Evarts B., and Virginia D. Harrington. *American Population Before the Federal Census of 1790*. New York: Columbia University Press, 1932.

Greene, Jack P., ed. *The Diary of Colonel Landon Carter of Sabine Hall, 1752–1778*. Charlottesville: Published for the Virginia Historical Society by the University Press of Virginia, 1965.

Greene, John C. "The American Debate on the Negro's Place in Nature, 1780–1815." *Journal of the History of Ideas* 15, no. 3 (June 1954): 384–96.

Greene, John C. *American Science in the Age of Jefferson*. Ames: Iowa State University Press, 1984.

Gross, Robert A., and Mary Kelley, eds. *An Extensive Republic: Print, Culture, and Society in the New Nation, 1790–1840*. Vol. 2 of *A History of the Book in America*. Chapel Hill: Published in association with the American Antiquarian Society by the University of North Carolina Press, 2010.

Gruzinski, Serge. *Painting the Conquest: The Mexican Indians and the European Renaissance*. Paris: Unesco: Flammarion, 1992.

Guyatt, Nicholas. " 'The Outskirts of Our Happiness': Race and the Lure of Colonization in the Early Republic." *Journal of American History* 95, no. 4 (March 2009): 986–1011.

Habermas, Jürgen. "Modernity: An Unfinished Project." Trans. Nicholas Walker. In *Habermas and the Unfinished Project of Modernity: Critical Essays* on *"The Philosophical Discourse of Modernity,"* ed. Maurizio Passerin d'Entrèves and Seyla Benhabib. Cambridge: MIT Press, 1997. 38–55.

Hamilton, Alexander. *Colonel Hamilton's Second Letter, from Phocion to the Considerate Citizens of New-York, on the Politics of the Times, in Consequence of the Peace: Containing Remarks on Mentor's Reply.* Philadelphia: Robert Bell, 1784.

Hamilton, Alexander. *The Farmer Refuted; or, A More Impartial and Comprehensive View of the Dispute Between Great-Britain and the Colonies, Intended as a Further Vindication of the Congress: In Answer to a Letter from A. W. Farmer, Intitled a View of the Controversy Between Great-Britain and Her Colonies: Including a Mode of Determining the Present Disputes Finally and Effectually, &c.* New York: James Rivington, 1775.

Hamilton, Phillip. *The Making and Unmaking of a Revolutionary Family: The Tuckers of Virginia, 1752–1830.* Charlottesville: University of Virginia Press, 2003.

Hamilton, Phillip. "Revolutionary Principles and Family Loyalties: Slavery's Transformation in the St. George Tucker Household of Early National Virginia." *William and Mary Quarterly* 3d ser., 55, no. 4 (October 1998): 531–56.

Hamilton, William. *Observations on Mount Vesuvius, Mount Etna, and Other Volcanos.* London: T. Cadell, 1772.

Hancarville, Pierre François Hugues, baron d'. *Collection of Etruscan, Greek, and Roman Antiquities from the Cabinet of the Hon. Wm. Hamilton.* 4 vols. Naples: François Morelli, 1766–67.

Harris, John. *Lexicon Technicum.* London: D. Brown et al., 1704.

Harris, Steven J. "Confession-Building, Long-Distance Networks, and the Organization of Jesuit Science." *Early Science and Medicine* 1, no. 3 (October 1996): 287–318.

Harris, Steven J. "Mapping Jesuit Science: The Role of Travel in the Geography of Knowledge." In *The Jesuits: Cultures, Sciences, and the Arts, 1540–1773,* ed. John W. O'Malley, Gauvin Alexander Bailey, Steven J. Harris, and T. Frank Kennedy. Toronto: University of Toronto Press, 1999. 212–40.

Harris, Thaddeus. *The Journal of a Tour into the Territory Northwest of the Alleghany Mountains; Made in the Spring of the Year 1803. With a Geographical and Historical Account of the State of Ohio.* Boston: Manning and Loring, 1805.

Harrison, Jesse Burton. *Review of the Slave Question, Extracted from the American Quarterly Review, Dec. 1832.* Richmond: T. W. White, 1833.

Hayden, Horace H. *Geological Essays; or, An Inquiry into Some of the Geological Phenomena to Be Found in Various Parts of America, and Elsewhere.* Baltimore: J. Robinson, 1820.

Hayes, Kevin J. *The Library of William Byrd of Westover.* Madison, Wisc.: Madison House, 1997.

Hedeen, Stanley. *Big Bone Lick: The Cradle of American Paleontology.* Lexington: University Press of Kentucky, 2008.

Henige, David. *Numbers from Nowhere: The American Indian Contact Population Debate.* Norman: University of Oklahoma Press, 1998.

Hening, William W. *The Statutes at Large: Being a Collection of All the Laws of Virginia, from the First Session of the Legislature in the Year 1619.* 13 vols. Richmond: Samuel Pleasants, 1809–23.

Herrman, Augustin. *Virginia and Maryland as It Is Planted and Inhabited This Present Year 1670 Surveyed and Exactly Drawne by the Only Labour & Endeavour of Augustin Herrman Bohemiensis.* London: Augustin Herrman and Thomas Withinbrook, 1673.

Hill, Ira. *Antiquities of America Explained.* Hagerstown, Md.: William D. Bell, 1831.

Hindle, Brooke. "Charles Willson Peale's Science and Technology." In *Charles Willson Peale and His World,* ed. Edgar P. Richardson, Brooke Hindle, and Lillian B. Miller. New York: Abrams, 1983. 107–69.

Hitchcock, Edward. *Report on the Geology, Mineralogy, Botany, and Zoology of Massachusetts.* Amherst: J. S. and C. Adams, 1833.

Hochstrasser, T. J. "Physiocracy and the Politics of *Laissez-Faire.*" In *The Cambridge History of Eighteenth-Century Political Thought,* ed. Mark Goldie and Robert Wokler. Cambridge: Cambridge University Press, 2006. 419–42.

Hodgson, Dennis. "Benjamin Franklin on Population: From Policy to Theory." *Population and Development Review* 17, no. 4 (December 1991): 639–61.

Hoffman, Ronald, John J. McCusker, Russell R. Menard, and Peter J. Albert, eds. *The Economy of Early America: The Revolutionary Period, 1763–1790.* Charlottesville: University Press of Virginia for the U.S. Capitol Historical Society, 1988.

Holbach, Paul-Henri Thiry, baron d'. *L'Antiquité dévoilée par ses usages; ou, Examen critique des principales opinions, cérémonies & institutions religieuses & politiques des différens peuples de la Terre. Par feu M. Boulanger.* Amsterdam: Marc Michel Rey, 1766.

Holbach, Paul-Henri Thiry, baron d' [attrib.]. *Christianity Unveiled; Being, an Examination of the Principles and Effects of the Christian Religion. From the French of Boulanger, Author of Researches into the Origins of Oriental Despotism. By W. M. Johnson.* New York: Columbian Press, 1795.

Hollinger, David A. "The Enlightenment and the Genealogy of Cultural Conflict in the United States." In *What's Left of Enlightenment? A Postmodern Question,* ed. Keith Baker and Peter Hanns Reill. Stanford: Stanford University Press, 2001. 7–18.

Honour, Hugh. *The New Golden Land: European Images of America from the Discoveries to the Present Time.* New York: Pantheon, 1975.

Hont, István. *Jealousy of Trade: International Competition and the Nation-State in Historical Perspective.* Cambridge, Mass.: Belknap, 2005.

Höpfl, H. M. "From Savage to Scotsman: Conjectural History in the Scottish Enlightenment." *Journal of British Studies* 17, no. 2 (Spring 1978): 19–40.

Hopkins, Samuel. *A Dialogue, Concerning the Slavery of the Africans; Shewing It to Be the Duty and Interest of the American Colonies to Emancipate All Their African Slaves: with an Address to the Owners of Such Slaves.* Norwich, Conn.: Judah P. Spooner, 1776.

Hopkins, Samuel. *A Discourse upon the Slave-Trade, and the Slavery of the Africans.* Providence: J. Carter, 1793.

Hopkins, Samuel. *Historical Memoirs, Relating to the Housatunnuk Indians.* Boston: S. Kneeland, 1753.

Hopkins, Samuel. *An Inquiry into the Nature of True Holiness.* Newport, R.I.: Solomon Southwick, 1773.

Hornberger, Theodore. "Benjamin Colman and the Enlightenment." *New England Quarterly* 12, no. 2 (June 1939): 227–40.

Hornberger, Theodore. "The Scientific Ideas of John Mitchell." *Huntington Library Quarterly* 10, no. 3 (May 1947): 277–96.

Horkheimer, Max, and Theodor Adorno. *Philosophische Fragmente.* 1944; Amsterdam: Querido, 1947.

Houston, Alan. *Benjamin Franklin and the Politics of Improvement.* New Haven: Yale University Press, 2008.

Howard, Leon. *The Connecticut Wits.* Chicago: University of Chicago Press, 1943.

Howe, Daniel Walker. *Making the American Self: Jonathan Edwards to Abraham Lincoln.* Cambridge: Harvard University Press, 1997.

Howe, Daniel Walker. *The Unitarian Conscience: Harvard Moral Philosophy, 1805–1861.* Cambridge: Harvard University Press, 1970.

Howe, John. *The Changing Political Thought of John Adams.* Princeton: Princeton University Press, 1966.

Hudnut, William H. "Samuel Stanhope Smith: Enlightened Conservative." *Journal of the History of Ideas* 17, no. 4 (1956): 540–52.

Hughes, Griffith. *The Natural History of Barbados.* London: Printed for the Author, 1750.

Humboldt, Alexander von. *Researches Concerning the Institutions & Monuments of the Ancient Inhabitants of America, with Descriptions & Views of Some of the Most Striking Scenes in the Cordilleras! Written in French by Alexander de Humboldt, & Translated into English by Helen Maria Williams.* 2 vols. London: Longman, Hurst, Rees, Orme and Brown, J. Murray and H. Colburn, 1814.

Humboldt, Alexander von. *Vues des Cordillères, et monumens des peuples indigènes de l'Amérique.* 2 vols. Paris: F. Schoell, 1810.

Hume, David. *Essays: Moral, Political, and Literary,* ed. Eugene F. Miller. Indianapolis: Liberty Classics, 1985.

Hume, David. *Philosophical Essays Concerning Human Understanding.* London: A. Millar, 1748.

Hume, David. *A Treatise of Human Nature: Being an Attempt to Introduce the Experimental Method of Reasoning into Moral Subjects*. 2 vols. London: John Noon, 1739–40.

Humphreys, Robert Arthur. *William Robertson and His "History of America."* London: Hispanic and Luso-Brazilian Councils, 1954.

Hunt, Gaillard, ed. *The Writings of James Madison, Comprising His Public Papers and His Private Correspondence, Including Numerous Letters and Documents Now for the First Time Printed*. 9 vols. New York: Putnam's, 1900–1910.

Hunt, Lynn. *Politics, Culture, and Class in the French Revolution*. Berkeley: University of California Press, 1984.

Hutchinson, Peter Orlando, ed. *The Diary and Letters of His Excellency Thomas Hutchinson, Esq*. 2 vols. London: S. Low, Marston, Searle and Rivington, 1883–86.

Hutchinson, Thomas. *The History of the Colony of Massachusets-Bay, from the First Settlement Thereof in 1628. Until Its Incorporation with the Colony of Plimouth, Province of Main, &c., by the Charter of King William and Queen Mary, in 1691*. Boston: Thomas and John Fleet, 1764.

Iannini, Christopher. *Fatal Revolutions: Natural History, West Indian Slavery, and the Routes of American Literature*. Chapel Hill: Published for the Omohundro Institute of Early American History and Culture, Williamsburg, Virginia, by the University of North Carolina Press, 2012.

Impey, Oliver R., and Arthur MacGregor, eds. *The Origins of Museums: The Cabinet of Curiosities in Sixteenth- and Seventeenth-Century Europe*. Oxford: Clarendon, 1985.

Isaac, Rhys. *Landon Carter's Uneasy Kingdom: Revolution and Rebellion on a Virginia Plantation*. New York: Oxford University Press, 2004.

Jackson, Carl T. *The Oriental Religions and American Thought: Nineteenth-Century Explorations*. Westport, Conn.: Greenwood, 1981.

Jacobs, Wilbur R. *Wilderness Politics and Indian Gifts: The Northern Colonial Frontier, 1748–1763*. Lincoln: University of Nebraska Press, 1950.

Jaksić, Iván. *The Hispanic World and American Intellectual Life, 1820–1880*. New York: Palgrave Macmillan, 2007.

James, William. *The Varieties of Religious Experience: A Study in Human Nature. Being the Gifford Lectures on Natural Religion Delivered at Edinburgh in 1901–1902*. 1902; repr. New York: Longmans, Green, 1905.

Jameson, J. Franklin, ed. *Narratives of New Netherland, 1609–1664*. New York: Scribner's, 1909.

Jameson, Russell Parsons. *Montesquieu et l'esclavage: étude sur les origines de l'opinion antiesclavagiste en France au XVIIIe siècle*. 1911; repr. New York: B. Franklin, 1971.

Jay, Emma. "Queen Caroline's Library and Its European Contexts." *Book History* 9 (2006): 31–55.

Jefferson, Thomas. *Notes on the State of Virginia*. London: John Stockdale, 1787.

Jefferson, Thomas. *Notes on the State of Virginia. With an Appendix.* 8th ed. Boston: David Carlisle, 1801.

Jefferson, Thomas. *Notes on the State of Virginia.* Ed. Frank Shuffelton. New York: Penguin, 1999.

John, Richard. *Spreading the News: The American Postal System from Franklin to Morse.* Cambridge: Harvard University Press, 1995.

Jones, David. *A Journal of Two Visits Made to Some Nations of Indians on the West Side of the River Ohio, in the Years 1772 and 1773.* Burlington, N.J.: Isaac Collins, 1774.

Jones, David. "A Plan of an Old Fort and Intrechment in the Shawanese Country, Taken on Horse Back, by Computation Only. October 17, 1772." *Royal American Magazine* 2, no. 1 (January 1775): 29–30.

Jones, Gordon. *The Library of an Early Virginia Scientist: Dr. John Mitchell, F.R.S. (1711–1768).* Fredericksburg: E. Lee Trinkle Library, Mary Washington College of the University of Virginia, 1971.

Jonsson, Fredrik Albritton. *Enlightenment's Frontier: The Scottish Highlands and the Origins of Environmentalism.* New Haven: Yale University Press, 2013.

Journal of the Commissioners for Trade and Plantations, from January 1749/50 to December 1753. London: His Majesty's Stationery Office, 1932.

Kagan, Richard. *Urban Images of the Hispanic World, 1493–1793.* New Haven: Yale University Press, 2000.

Kalm, Peter. *Travels into North America.* Trans. John Reinhold Forster. 1770; repr. Barre, Mass.: Imprint Society, 1972.

Kames, Henry Home, Lord. *Sketches of the History of Man.* 4 vols. Dublin: James Williams, 1774–75.

Kant, Immanuel. "An Answer to the Question: What Is Enlightenment?" (1784). In *Practical Philosophy,* ed. and trans. Mary Gregor. Cambridge: Cambridge University Press, 1996. 11–22.

Kant, Immanuel. "Beantwortung der Frage: Was ist Aufklärung?" *Berlinische Monatsschrift* (December 1784): 481–94.

Kaplan, Catherine O'Donnell. *Men of Letters in the Early Republic: Cultivating Forums of Citizenship.* Chapel Hill: Published for the Omohundro Institute of Early American History and Culture, Williamsburg, Virginia, by the University of North Carolina Press, 2008.

Keen, Benjamin. *The Aztec Image in Western Thought.* New Brunswick, N.J.: Rutgers University Press, 1971.

Kelley, Mary. *Learning to Stand and Speak: Women, Education, and Public Life in America's Republic.* Chapel Hill: Published for the Omohundro Institute of Early American History and Culture, Williamsburg, Virginia, by the University of North Carolina Press, 2006.

Kennedy, Rick. "Thomas Brattle and the Scientific Provincialism of New England, 1680–1713." *New England Quarterly* 63, no. 4 (December 1990): 584–600.

Kerrison, Catherine. *Claiming the Pen: Women and Intellectual Life in the Early American South*. Ithaca: Cornell University Press, 2006.

Kettler, David. "The Social and Political Thought of Adam Ferguson: An Intellectual and the Emergence of Modern Society." Ph.D. diss., Columbia University, 1960.

Kittredge, George L. "Some Lost Works of Cotton Mather." *Proceedings of the Massachusetts Historical Society* 45 (1911–12): 419–20.

Knight, Charles, ed. *Biography or Third Division of "The English Cyclopaedia."* Vol. 6. London: Bradbury Evans, 1868.

Knight, Franklin, ed. *Letters on Agriculture from His Excellency George Washington President of the United States to Arthur Young, Esq. F.R.S. and Sir John Sinclair, Bart., M.P. with Statistical Tables and Remarks, by Thomas Jefferson, Richard Peters, and Other Gentlemen, on the Economy and Management of Farms in the United States*. Washington, D.C.: Franklin Knight, 1847.

Knott, Sarah. *Sensibility and the American Revolution*. Chapel Hill: Published for the Omohundro Institute of Early American History and Culture, Williamsburg, Virginia, by the University of North Carolina Press, 2009.

Knott, Sarah, and Barbara Taylor, eds. *Women, Gender and Enlightenment*. Houndmills, Basingstoke, UK: Palgrave Macmillan, 2005.

Knox, William. *Considerations on the Present State of the Nation*. London: J. Debrett, 1789.

Koch, Adrienne. *Power, Morals, and the Founding Fathers: Essays in the Interpretation of the American Enlightenment*. Ithaca, N.Y.: Great Seal Books, 1961.

Koch, Adrienne, ed. *The American Enlightenment: The Shaping of the American Experiment and a Free Society*. New York: Braziller, 1965.

Kornhauser, Elizabeth Mankin. *Ralph Earl: The Face of the Young Republic*. New Haven: Yale University Press, and Hartford: Wadsworth Athenaeum, 1991.

Kramnick, Isaac. *Bolingbroke and His Circle: The Politics of Nostalgia in the Age of Walpole*. Cambridge: Harvard University Press, 1968.

Krasheninnikov, Stepan Petrovitch. *Histoire de Kamtschatka des Isles Kurilski, et des contrées voisines, publiée à Petersbourg, en langue russienne, par ordre de Sa Majesté Impériale*. Lyons: B. Duplain, 1767.

Kriz, Kay Dian. "Curiosities, Commodities, and Transplanted Bodies in Hans Sloane's 'Natural History of Jamaica.'" *William and Mary Quarterly* 3d ser., 57, no. 1 (January 2000): 35–78.

Kulikoff, Alan. *Tobacco and Slaves: The Development of Southern Cultures in the Chesapeake, 1680–1800*. Chapel Hill: Published for the Institute of Early American History and Culture, Williamsburg, Virginia, by the University of North Carolina Press, 1986.

Kupperman, Karen Ordahl, ed. *America in European Consciousness, 1493–1750*. Chapel Hill: Published for the Institute of Early American History and

Culture, Williamsburg, Virginia, by the University of North Carolina Press, 1995.

Labaree, Leonard W. *Royal Government in America: A Study of the British Colonial System Before 1783.* New Haven: Yale University Press, 1930.

Labat, Jean-Baptiste. *Nouveau voyage aux isles de l'Amérique.* 6 vols. Paris: Chez Guillaume Cavelier fils, 1722.

Lafitau, Joseph-François. *Moeurs des sauvages amériquains, comparées aux moeurs des premiers temps.* 2 vols. Paris: Chez Saugrain l'aîné, 1724.

Lafontant, Julien J. *Montesquieu et le problème de l'esclavage dans l'Esprit des lois.* Sherbrooke, Quebec: Naaman, 1979.

Lahontan, Louis Armand de Lom d'Arce, baron de. *New Voyages to North-America.* 2 vols. London: H. Bonwicke, 1703.

Landsdowne, Henry William Edmund Petty FitzMaurice, marquis of, ed. *The Petty Papers: Some Unpublished Writings of Sir William Petty.* 2 vols. London: Constable, 1927.

Landsman, Ned. *From Colonials to Provincials: American Thought and Culture, 1680–1760.* New York: Twayne, 1997.

La Peyrère, Isaac de. *Praeadamitae. Sive Exercitatio super Versibus Duodecimo, Decimotertio, & Decimoquarto, Capitis Quinti Epistolae D. Pauli ad Romanos. Quibus Inducuntur Primi Homines ante Adamum Conditi.* Amsterdam: s.n., 1655.

Lauderdale, James Maitland, earl of. *Inquiry into the Nature and Origin of Public Wealth, and into the Means and Causes of Its Increase.* Edinburgh: A. Constable, 1804.

La Vopa, Anthony J. "A New Intellectual History? Jonathan Israel's Enlightenment." *Historical Journal* 52, no. 3 (2009): 717–38.

Lawson, John. *A New Voyage to Carolina; Containing the Exact Description and Natural History of That Country: Together with the Present State Thereof.* London: s.n., 1709.

Learned, Joseph D. *A View of the Policy of Permitting Slaves in the States West of the Mississippi: Being a Letter to a Member of Congress.* Baltimore: J. Robinson, 1820.

Lehoux, Daryn. *What Did the Romans Know? An Inquiry into Science and Worldmaking.* Chicago: University of Chicago Press, 2012.

Leibniz, Gottfried Wilhelm. *Protogaea* (1696). Ed. and trans. Claudine Cohen and Andre Wakfield. Chicago: University of Chicago Press, 2008.

Leitch, Alexander. *A Princeton Companion.* Princeton: Princeton University Press, 1978.

Le Mercier de La Rivière, Pierre-Paul. *L'Ordre naturel et essentiel des sociétés politiques.* 2 vols. London: Nourse, and Paris: Desaint, 1767.

Lenman, Bruce P. " 'From Savage to Scot' via the French and the Spaniards: Robertson's Principal Spanish Sources." In *William Robertson and the Expansion of Empire,* ed. Stewart J. Brown. Cambridge: Cambridge University Press, 1997. 196–209.

León y Gama, Antonio de. *Descripción histórica y cronológica de las dos piedras que con ocasión del nuevo empedrado que se está formando en la plaza principal de México, se hallaron en ella el año de 1790.* Mexico City: Felipe de Zúñiga y Ontiveros, 1792.

"Letters of Cotton Mather." *Massachusetts Historical Society Collections*, 4th ser., 8 (1868): 383–462.

"Letters of William Byrd II, and Sir Hans Sloane Relative to Plants and Minerals of Virginia." *William and Mary Quarterly* 2d ser., 1, no. 3 (July 1921): 186–200.

Levin, David. "Giants in the Earth: Science and the Occult in Cotton Mather's Letters to the Royal Society." *William and Mary Quarterly* 3d ser., 45, no. 4 (October 1988): 751–70.

Levine, Emily. *Dreamland of Humanists: Warburg, Cassirer, Panofsky, and the Hamburg School.* Chicago: University of Chicago Press, 2013.

Levine, Joseph. *Dr. Woodward's Shield: History, Science, and Satire in Augustan England.* Berkeley: University of California Press, 1977.

Lewis, Meriwether. *Travels to the Source of the Missouri River and Across the American Continent to the Pacific Ocean.* London: Longman, Hurst, Rees, Orme and Brown, 1814.

Lewis, Meriwether, William Clark, and Sir Alexander Mackenzie. *The Travels of Capts. Lewis & Clarke, from St. Louis, by Way of the Missouri and Columbia Rivers, to the Pacific Ocean; Performed in the Years 1804, 1805, & 1806, by Order of the Government of the United States.* London: Longman, Hurst, Rees, and Orme, 1809.

Ligon, Richard. *A True & Exact History of the Island of Barbados.* London: Humphrey Moseley, 1657.

Lind, John. *An Answer to the Declaration of the American Congress.* London: T. Cadell, 1776.

Locke, John. *A Letter Concerning Toleration: Humbly Submitted, &c.* London: Awnsham Churchill, 1689.

Locke, John. *Two Treatises of Government.* Ed. Peter Laslett. 1960; repr. Cambridge: Cambridge University Press, 2010.

Lockhart, James. *The Nahuas After the Conquest: A Social and Cultural History of the Indians of Central Mexico, Sixteenth Through Eighteenth Centuries.* Stanford: Stanford University Press, 1992.

Logan, George. *An Address on the Natural and Social Order of the World, as Intended to Produce Universal Good; Delivered Before the Tammany Society, at Their Anniversary, on the 12th of May, 1798.* Philadelphia: Benjamin Franklin Bache, 1798.

Logan, George. *Fourteen Agricultural Experiments, to Ascertain the Best Rotation of Crops: Addressed to the "Philadelphia Agricultural Society."* Philadelphia: Francis and Robert Bailey, 1797.

Logan, George ["An American Farmer"]. *Letters Addressed to the Yeomanry of the United States, Containing Some Observations on Funding and Bank*

Systems: By an American Farmer. Philadelphia: Francis Childs and John Swain, 1793.

Logan, George ["A Farmer"]. *Letters, Addressed to the Yeomanry of the United States: Shewing the Necessity of Confining the Public Revenue to a Fixed Proportion of the Net Produce of the Land: and the Bad Policy and Injustice of Every Species of Indirect Taxation and Commercial Regulations.* Philadelphia: Eleazer Oswald, 1791.

Logan, James. *Experimenta et Meletemata de Plantarum Generatione.* Leiden: Cornelium Haak, 1739.

Logan, James. *Experimenta et Meletemata de Plantarum Generatione . . . Translated from the Original Latin.* London: C. Davis, 1747.

Loughran, Trish. *The Republic in Print: Print Culture in the Age of U.S. Nation Building, 1770–1870.* New York: Columbia University Press, 2007.

Lovejoy, David S. "Satanizing the American Indian." *New England Quarterly* 67, no. 4 (December 1994): 603–21.

Lundberg, David, and Henry F. May. "The Enlightened Reader in America." *American Quarterly* 28 (1976): 262–93.

Lutz, Cora. "Ezra Stiles and the Library." *Yale University Library Gazette* 56 (October 1981): 13–21.

Lyell, Charles. *Principles of Geology, Being an Attempt to Explain the Former Changes of the Earth's Surface, by Reference to Causes Now in Operation.* 3 vols. London: J. Murray, 1830–33.

MacGregor, Arthur, ed. *Sir Hans Sloane: Collector, Scientist, Antiquary, Founding Father of the British Museum.* London: British Museum Press in Association with Alistair McAlpine, 1994.

MacIntyre, Alasdair. *After Virtue: A Study in Moral Theory.* 3rd ed. 1981; Notre Dame, Ind.: University of Notre Dame Press, 2008.

MacLean, J. P. "Pre-Columbian Discovery of America." *American Antiquarian and Oriental Journal* 14, no. 4 (July 1892): 189–96.

Maclure, William. *Essay on the Formation of Rocks, or an Inquiry into the Probable Origin of their Present Form and Structure.* New-Harmony, Ind.: Printed for the Author, 1832.

Malthus, Thomas R. *An Essay on the Principle of Population, as It Affects the Future Improvement of Society. With Remarks on the Speculations of Mr. Godwin, M. Condorcet, and Other Writers.* London: J. Johnson, 1798.

Manning, Susan, and Francis D. Cogliano, eds. *The Atlantic Enlightenment.* Aldershot, UK: Ashgate, 2008.

Manning, William R., ed. *Diplomatic Correspondence of the United States Concerning the Independence of Latin-American Nations.* 3 vols. New York: Oxford University Press, 1925–26.

Manuel, Frank. *The Eighteenth Century Confronts the Gods.* Cambridge: Harvard University Press, 1959.

Márquez, Pedro José. *Due antichi monumenti di architettura messicana.* Rome: Presso Il Salomoni, 1804.

Marsden, George. *The Twilight of the American Enlightenment: The 1950s and the Crisis of Liberal Belief.* New York: Basic, 2014.

Marsden, Jonathan, ed. *The Wisdom of George the Third: Papers from a Symposium at the Queen's Gallery, Buckingham Palace, June 2004.* London: Royal Collection Publications, 2004.

Marshall, John. *The Life of George Washington.* 5 vols. Philadelphia: C. P. Wayne, 1804–7.

Martin, Samuel. *An Essay upon Plantership, Humbly Inscrib'd to All the Planters of the British Sugar-Colonies in America.* 1749; 2d ed., Antigua: T. Smith, 1750.

Marx, Leo. *The Machine in the Garden: Technology and the Pastoral Ideal in America.* New York: Oxford University Press, 1964.

Mason, Julian D., Jr., ed. *The Poems of Phillis Wheatley.* Rev. and enl. ed. Chapel Hill: University of North Carolina Press, 1989.

Mather, Cotton. *Christian Loyalty.* Boston: T. Fleet, 1727.

Mather, Cotton. *The Christian Philosopher: A Collection of the Best Discoveries in Nature, with Religious Improvements.* London: Emanuel Matthews, 1721.

Mather, Cotton. *The Negro Christianized: An Essay to Excite and Assist the Good Work, the Instruction of Negro-Servants in Christianity.* Boston: B. Green, 1706.

Mather, Cotton. *Winter Meditations.* Boston: Benjamin Harris, 1693.

Mather, Cotton. *The Wonderful Works of God Commemorated.* Boston: S. Green, 1690.

Maxwell, Robert, ed. *Select Transactions of the Honourable the Society of Improvers in the Knowledge of Agriculture in Scotland.* Edinburgh: Sands, Bryner, Murray, and Cochran, 1743.

May, Henry F. *The Enlightenment in America.* New York: Oxford University Press, 1976.

Mayer, Brantz. *Mexico as It Was and as It Is.* New York: J. Winchester, 1844.

Mayor, Adrienne. *Fossil Legends of the First Americans.* Princeton: Princeton University Press, 2005.

McBurney, Henrietta. *Mark Catesby's "Natural History" of America: The Watercolors from the Royal Library, Windsor Castle.* Houston: Museum of Fine Arts, Houston, in Association with Merrell Holbertson, 1997.

McClellan, James E., III. *Science Reorganized: Scientific Societies in the Eighteenth Century.* New York: Columbia University Press, 1985.

McClelland, Charles E. *State, Society, and University in Germany, 1700–1914.* Cambridge: Cambridge University Press, 1980.

McConville, Brendan. *The King's Three Faces: The Rise and Fall of Royal America, 1688–1776.* Chapel Hill: Published for the Omohundro Institute of Early American History and Culture, Williamsburg, Virginia, for the University of North Carolina Press, 2006.

McCoy, Drew. *The Elusive Republic: Political Economy in Jeffersonian America.* 1980; repr. New York: Norton, 1982.

McCoy, Drew. "Jefferson and Madison on Malthus: Population Growth in Jeffersonian Political Economy." *Virginia Magazine of History and Biography* 88 (July 1980): 259–76.

McDaniel, W. Caleb. "Philadelphia Abolitionists and Antislavery Cosmopolitanism." In *Antislavery and Abolition in Philadelphia: Emancipation and the Long Struggle for Racial Justice in the City of Brotherly Love*, ed. Richard Newman and James Mueller. Baton Rouge: Louisiana State University Press, 2011. 149–73.

McNeill, John Robert. *Mosquito Empires: Ecology and War in the Greater Caribbean, 1620–1914*. Cambridge: Cambridge University Press, 2010.

Meek, Ronald. *The Economics of Physiocracy: Essays and Translations*. 1962; repr. London: Routledge, 2003.

Meek, Ronald. *Social Science and the Ignoble Savage*. Cambridge: Cambridge University Press, 1976.

Melon, Jean. *A Political Essay upon Commerce: Written in French by Monsieur M*** Translated, with Some Annotations, and Remarks. By David Bindon, Esq.* Dublin: Philip Crampton, 1738.

Mendes da Costa, Emanuel. *A Natural History of Fossils*. London: L. Davis and C. Reymers, 1757.

Mercier-Faivre, Anne-Marie. *Un Supplément à "l'Encylopédie": Le "Monde primitif" d'Antoine Court de Gébelin*. Paris: Honoré Champion, 1999.

Merolle, Vincenzo, ed. *The Correspondence of Adam Ferguson*. 2 vols. London: Pickering and Chatto, 1995.

Message from the President of the United States, Communicating Discoveries Made in Exploring the Missouri, Red River and Washita, by Captains Lewis and Clark, Doctor Sibley, and Mr. Dunbar; with a Statistical Account of the Countries Adjacent. Washington, D.C.: A. & G. Way, 1806.

Mettas, Jean. *Répertoire des expéditions négrières françaises au XVIIIe siècle*. Ed. Serge and Michele Daget. Vol. 2: *Ports autres que Nantes*. Paris: Société française d'histoire d'Outre-Mer, 1984.

"Mexican Antiquities." *Transactions of the American Philosophical Society* n.s., 3 (1830): 510–11.

Meyer, Donald H. *The Democratic Enlightenment*. New York: Putnam, 1976.

Meyer, Donald H. *The Instructed Conscience: The Shaping of the American National Ethic*. Philadelphia: University of Pennsylvania Press, 1972.

Meyers, Amy R. W., and Margaret Beck Pritchard, eds. *Empire's Nature: Mark Catesby's New World Vision*. Chapel Hill: Published for the Omohundro Institute of Early American History and Culture and the Colonial Williamsburg Foundation, Williamsburg, Virginia, by the University of North Carolina Press, 1998.

Mill, Nicholas. *The History of Mexico, from the Spanish Conquest to the Present Aera*. London: Sherwood, Jones, 1824.

Millar, John. *Observations Concerning the Distinction of Ranks in Society*. Dublin: T. Ewing, 1771.

Miller, Charles A. *Jefferson and Nature: An Interpretation.* Baltimore: Johns Hopkins University Press, 1988.

Miller, Peter N. *Pereisc's Europe: Learning and Virtue in the Seventeenth Century.* New Haven: Yale University Press, 2000.

Miller, Samuel. *A Brief Retrospect of the Eighteenth Century.* 2 vols. New York: T. and J. Swords, 1803.

Minardi, Margot. "The Boston Inoculation Controversy of 1721–1722: An Incident in the History of Race." *William and Mary Quarterly* 3rd ser., 61, no. 1 (January 2004): 47–76.

Mitchell, John. "An Essay upon the Causes of the Different Colours of People in Different Climates; by John Mitchell, M.D. Communicated to the Royal Society by Mr. Peter Collinson, F.R.S. Read at Several Meetings, from May 3 to June 14, 1744." *Philosophical Transactions of the Royal Society of London* 43 (1744–45): 102–50.

Mitchell, Timothy. "Fixing the Economy." *Cultural Studies* 12, no. 1 (2010): 82–101.

Mitchell, Timothy. *Rule of Experts: Egypt, Techno-Politics, Modernity.* Berkeley: University of California Press, 2002.

Monaghan, E. Jennifer. *Learning to Read and Write in Colonial America.* Amherst: University of Massachusetts Press, in Association with the American Antiquarian Society, 2005.

Montesquieu, Charles de Secondat, baron de. *Oeuvres de Monsieur de Montesquieu, nouvelle édition, revue, corrigée & considérablement augmentée par l'auteur.* 3 vols. London: Chez Nourse, 1767.

Montesquieu, Charles de Secondat, baron de. *The Spirit of Laws. Translated from the French of M. de Secondat, Baron de Montesquieu.* 2 vols. London: J. Nourse, and P. Vaillant, 1750.

Mooney, James E., ed. *Eighteenth-Century Catalogues of the Yale College Library.* New Haven: Yale University Beinecke Library, 2001.

Moore, George H. *Notes on the History of Slavery in Massachusetts.* New York: Appleton, 1866.

More, Anna. *Baroque Sovereignty: Carlos de Sigüenza y Góngora and the Creole Archive of Colonial Mexico.* Philadelphia: University of Pennsylvania Press, 2012.

Morgan, Edmund S. *American Slavery, American Freedom: The Ordeal of Colonial Virginia.* New York: Norton, 1975.

Morgan, Edmund S. *The Gentle Puritan: A Life of Ezra Stiles, 1727–1795.* 1974; repr. New York: Norton, 1983.

Morgan, Lewis Henry. *League of the Ho-de-no-sau-nee, or Iroquois.* Rochester: Sage and Brother, 1851.

Morrison, Jeffry. *John Witherspoon and the Founding of the American Republic.* Notre Dame, Ind.: University of Notre Dame Press, 2005.

Morse, Jedidiah. *The American Gazetteer.* Boston: S. Hall, 1797.

Morse, Jedidiah. *The American Geography.* Elizabethtown: Printed for the author, 1789.

Morton, Samuel George. *Crania Americana; or, A Comparative View of the Skulls of Various Aboriginal Nations of North and South America: To Which Is Prefixed an Essay on the Varieties of the Human Species.* Philadelphia: J. Penington, 1839.

Moulton, Gary E., ed. *The Journals of the Lewis and Clark Expedition.* 13 vols. Lincoln: University of Nebraska Press, 1983–2001.

Mulford, Carla, ed. *Only for the Eye of a Friend: The Poems of Annis Boudinot Stockton.* Charlottesville: University Press of Virginia, 1995.

Mun, Thomas. *England's Treasure by Forraign Trade.* London: J. G. for Thomas Clark, 1664.

Murphy, Kathleen S. "Collecting Slave Traders: James Petiver, Natural History, and the British Slave Trade." *William and Mary Quarterly* 3rd ser., 70, no. 4 (October 2013): 637–70.

Murray, James. *An Impartial History of the Present War with America.* 2 vols. Newcastle upon Tyne: T. Robson, 1779.

Murray, Judith Sargent [Constantia]. *The Gleaner.* 3 vols. Boston: I. Thomas and E. T. Andrews, 1798.

Muthu, Sankar. *Enlightenment Against Empire.* Princeton: Princeton University Press, 2003.

Myrdal, Gunnar. *An American Dilemma: The Negro Problem and Modern Democracy.* 2 vols. New York: Harper and Brothers, 1944.

Namier, Lewis. *England in the Age of the American Revolution.* 1930; 2d ed. London: Macmillan, 1963.

Nash, Roderick. *Wilderness and the American Mind.* New Haven: Yale University Press, 1967.

Nelson, Eric. *The Royalist Revolution: Monarchy and the American Founding.* Cambridge, Mass.: Belknap, 2014.

Nisbet, Richard ["A West-Indian"]. *Slavery Not Forbidden by Scripture.* Philadelphia: John Sparhawk[?], 1773.

Noll, Mark. *America's God: From Jonathan Edwards to Abraham Lincoln.* New York: Oxford University Press, 2002.

Noll, Mark. *Princeton and the Republic, 1768–1822: The Search for a Christian Enlightenment in the Era of Samuel Stanhope Smith.* Princeton: Princeton University Press, 1989.

Norton, Charles Eliot. "Ancient Monuments in America." *North American Review* 68 (1849): 466–96.

Norton, Robert. "The Myth of the Counter-Enlightenment." *Journal of the History of Ideas* 68, no. 4 (October 2007): 635–58.

"November Meeting, 1873." *Massachusetts Historical Society Proceedings* 13 (1873–75): 104–22.

Nygren, Edward J., with Bruce Robertson. *Views and Visions: American Landscape Before 1830.* Washington, D.C.: The Corcoran Gallery of Art, 1986.

O'Brien, Michael. *Conjectures of Order: Intellectual Life and the American South, 1810–1860.* 2 vols. Chapel Hill: University of North Carolina Press, 2004.

O'Brien, Susan. "A Transatlantic Community of Saints: The Great Awakening and the First Evangelical Network, 1735–1755." *American Historical Review* 91, no. 4 (October 1986): 811–32.

Oleson, Alexandra, and Sanborn C. Brown, eds. *The Pursuit of Knowledge in the Early American Republic: American Scientific and Learned Societies from Colonial Times to the Civil War.* Baltimore: Johns Hopkins University Press, 1976.

Oliver, Andrew, ed. *The Journal of Samuel Curwen, Loyalist.* 2 vols. Cambridge: Harvard University Press for the Essex Institute, 1972.

O'Neill, Lindsay. *The Opened Letter: Networking in the Early Modern British World.* Philadelphia: University of Pennsylvania Press, 2015.

Orr, Clarissa Campbell. "New Perspectives on Hanoverian Britain." *Historical Journal* 52, no. 2 (June 2009): 513–29.

Orr, Clarissa Campbell, ed. *Queenship in Britain, 1660–1837: Royal Patronage, Court Culture and Dynastic Politics.* Manchester, UK: Manchester University Press, 2002.

O'Shaughnessy, Andrew Jackson. *An Empire Divided: The American Revolution and the British Caribbean.* Philadelphia: University of Pennsylvania Press, 2000.

Ousterhout, Ann M. *The Most Learned Woman in America: A Life of Elizabeth Graeme Fergusson.* University Park: Pennsylvania State University Press, 2004.

Pagden, Anthony. *The Enlightenment: And Why It Still Matters.* New York: Random House, 2013.

Pagden, Anthony. *The Fall of Natural Man: The American Indian and the Origins of Comparative Ethnology.* Cambridge: Cambridge University Press, 1982.

Pagden, Anthony. *Spanish Imperialism and the Political Imagination: Studies in European and Spanish-American Social and Political Theory, 1513–1830.* New Haven: Yale University Press, 1990.

Paine, Thomas. *The Age of Reason. Being an Investigation of True and of Fabulous Theology.* New York: T. and J. Swords, 1794.

Paine, Thomas. *The Age of Reason. Part the Second. Being an Investigation of True and of Fabulous Theology.* London: H. D. Symonds, 1795.

Paine, Thomas. *Agrarian Justice, Opposed to Agrarian Law, and to Agrarian Monopoly.* Philadelphia: R. Folwell, for Benjamin Franklin Bache, 1797.

Paine, Thomas. *Common Sense.* Philadelphia: R. Bell, 1776.

Paine, Thomas. *Examination of the Passages in the New Testament, Quoted from the Old, and Called Prophecies Concerning Jesus Christ: To Which Is Prefixed an Essay on Dream, Shewing by What Operation of the Mind a Dream Is Produced in Sleep, and Applying the Same to the Account of Dreams in the New Testament; with an Appendix Containing My Private Thoughts of a Future State, and Remarks on the Contradictory Doctrine in the Books of Matthew and Mark.* New York: Printed for the author, [1807]. [Republished in 1811 and 1819 as part 3 of *The Age of Reason.*]

Paine, Thomas. *On the Origin of Free-Masonry.* New York: Elliot and Crissy, 1810.

Papers in Honor of Andrew Keogh, Librarian of Yale University. New Haven: Yale University Library, 1938.

Parrish, Susan Scott. *American Curiosity: Cultures of Natural History in the Colonial British Atlantic World.* Chapel Hill: Published for the Omohundro Institute of Early American History and Culture, Williamsburg, Virginia, by the University of North Carolina Press, 2006.

Parsons, Christopher M., and Kathleen S. Murphy. "Ecosystems Under Sail: Specimen Transport in the Eighteenth-Century French and British Atlantics." *Early American Studies: An Interdisciplinary Journal* 10, no. 3 (Fall 2012): 503–39.

Pasley, Jeffrey. *"The Tyranny of Printers": Newspaper Politics in the Early American Republic.* Charlottesville: University Press of Virginia, 2001.

Pauw, Cornelius. *Recherches philosophiques sur les Américains.* 2 vols. Berlin: George Jacques Decker, 1768.

Pearce, Roy Harvey. *The Savages of America: A Study of the Indian and the Idea of Civilization.* Baltimore: Johns Hopkins Press, 1953.

Pearsall, Sarah. *Atlantic Families: Lives and Letters in the Eighteenth Century.* Oxford: Oxford University Press, 2008.

Pearson, E. S., ed. *The History of Statistics in the Seventeenth and Eighteenth Centuries Against the Background of Intellectual, Scientific and Religious Thought.* New York: Macmillan, 1978.

Peterson, Mark. "The Selling of Joseph: Bostonians, Antislavery, and the Protestant International, 1689–1733." *Massachusetts Historical Review* 4 (2002): 1–22.

Peterson, Mark. *"Theopolis Americana:* The City-State of Boston, the Republic of Letters, and the Protestant International, 1689–1739." In *Soundings in Atlantic History: Latent Structures and Intellectual Currents, 1500–1830,* ed. Bernard Bailyn and Patricia L. Denault. Cambridge: Harvard University Press, 2009. 329–70.

Peterson, Merrill, ed. *Thomas Jefferson: Writings.* New York: Library of America, 1984.

Peterson, Merrill, and Robert C. Vaughan, eds. *The Virginia Statute for Religious Freedom: Its Evolution and Consequences in American History.* Cambridge: Cambridge University Press, 1988.

Pétrissans-Cavaillès, Danielle. *Sur les traces de la traite des noirs à Bordeaux.* Bordeaux: DiversCités; Paris: L'Harmattan, 2004.

Petty, William. *Essays in Political Arithmetick.* London: Henry and George Mortlock, 1711.

Phelps, Almira H. Lincoln. *Lectures to Young Ladies, Comprising Outlines and Applications of the Different Branches of Female Education, for the Use of Female Schools, and Private Libraries Delivered to Pupils of the Troy Female Seminary.* Boston: Carter, Hendee, 1833.

Phillips, Christopher. *Freedom's Port: The African American Community of Baltimore, 1790–1860.* Urbana: University of Illinois Press, 1997.

Phillips, Ruth B., and Dale Idiens. " 'A Casket of Savage Curiosities': Eighteenth-Century Objects from North-Eastern North America in the Farquharson Collection." *Journal of the History of Collections* 6, no. 1 (1994): 21–33.

Phillipson, Nicholas. *Adam Smith: An Enlightened Life.* New Haven: Yale University Press, 2010.

Philpot, Stephen. *An Essay on the Advantage of a Polite Education Joined with a Learned One.* London: Printed for the author, 1747.

Pickering, John. "Introductory Observations." In *A Grammar of the Massachusetts Indian Language. By John Eliot. A New Edition: With Notes and Observations, by Peter S. DuPonceau, Ll. D., and An Introduction and Supplementary Observations, by John Pickering. As Published in the Massachusetts Historical Collections.* Boston: Phelps and Farnham, 1822.

Pitts, Jennifer. *A Turn to Empire: The Rise of Imperial Liberalism in Britain and France.* Princeton: Princeton University Press, 2005.

Pocock, J. G. A. *Barbarism and Religion.* 5 vols. Cambridge: Cambridge University Press, 1999–2015.

Poinsett, Joel R. *Notes on Mexico, Made in the Autumn of 1822.* Philadelphia: H. C. Carey and I. Lea, 1824.

Pole, J. R. "Enlightenment and the Politics of American Nature." In *The Enlightenment in National Context,* ed. Roy Porter and Mikuláš Teich. Cambridge: Cambridge University Press, 1981. 192–214.

Porter, Roy. *The Creation of the Modern World: The Untold Story of the British Enlightenment.* New York: Norton, 2000.

Porter, Roy. *The Making of Geology: Earth Science in Britain, 1660–1815.* New York: Cambridge University Press, 1977.

Porterfield, Amanda. *Conceived in Doubt: Religion and Politics in the New American Nation.* Chicago: University of Chicago Press, 2012.

Prescott, William H. *History of the Conquest of Mexico, with a Preliminary View of the Ancient Mexican Civilization, and the Life of the Conqueror, Hernando Cortés.* 3 vols. New York: Harper and Brothers, 1843.

Price, David. "John Woodward and a Surviving British Geological Collection from the Early Eighteenth Century." *Journal of the History of Collections* 1, no. 1 (1989): 79–95.

Price, Richard. *Observations on Reversionary Payments.* London: T. Cadell, 1771.

Price, Uvedale. *An Essay on the Picturesque, as Compared with the Sublime and Beautiful; and, on the Use of Studying Pictures, for the Purpose of Improving Real Landscape.* London: J. Robson, 1796.

Priestley, Joseph. *A Comparison of the Institutions of Moses with Those of the Hindoos and Other Ancient Nations; with Remarks on Mr. Dupuis's Origin of all Religions, the Laws and Institutions of Moses Methodized, and an Address to the Jews on the Present State of the World and the Prophecies Relating to It.* Northumberland, Pa.: A. Kennedy, 1799.

Priestley, Joseph. *Discourses Relating to the Evidences of Revealed Religion, Delivered in the Church of the Universalists, at Philadelphia, 1796.* Philadelphia: T. Dobson, 1796.

Priestley, Joseph. *Letters to Mr. Volney, Occasioned by a Work of His Entitled Ruins, and by His Letter to the Author.* Philadelphia: Thomas Dobson, 1797.

Prince, Sue Ann, ed. *Stuffing Birds, Pressing Plants, Shaping Knowledge: Natural History in North America, 1730–1860.* Philadelphia: American Philosophical Society, 2003.

Publius [Alexander Hamilton, John Jay, and James Madison]. *The Federalist.* 2 vols. New York: J. and A. M'Lean, 1788.

Purchas, Samuel. *Purchas His Pilgrimage.* London: William Stansby for Henrie Fetherstone, 1614.

Purchas, Samuel. *Purchas His Pilgrimes.* 4 vols. London: William Stansby for Henrie Fetherstone, 1625.

Quesnay, François. *Oeuvres économiques complètes et autres textes,* ed. Christine Théré, Loïc Charles, and Jean-Claude Perrot. 2 vols. Paris: L'Institut National d'Études Démographiques, 2005.

Rafinesque, Constantine Samuel. *The Ancient Monuments of North and South America.* 2d ed. Philadelphia: Printed for the author, 1838.

Ragosta, John. *Religious Freedom: Jefferson's Legacy, America's Creed.* Charlottesville: University of Virginia Press, 2013.

Ramsay, David. *The History of South-Carolina, from Its First Settlement in 1670, to the Year 1808.* 2 vols. Charleston: David Longworth, 1809.

Rappaport, Rhoda. *When Geologists Were Historians, 1665–1750.* Ithaca: Cornell University Press, 1997.

Rappleye, Charles. *Sons of Providence: The Brown Brothers, the Slave Trade, and the American Revolution.* New York: Simon and Schuster, 2006.

Raven, James. *The Business of Books: Booksellers and the English Book Trade, 1450–1850.* New Haven: Yale University Press, 2007.

Raven, James, ed. *Lost Libraries: The Destruction of Great Book Collections Since Antiquity.* New York: Palgrave Macmillan, 2004.

Ray, John. *Miscellaneous Discourses Concerning the Dissolution and Changes of the World.* London: Samuel Smith, 1692.

Raymond, Daniel. *Thoughts on Political Economy.* Baltimore: Fielding Lucas, Junior, 1820.

Raynal, Guillaume-Thomas François, abbé de. *Histoire philosophique et politique, des établissements et du commerce des Européens dans les deux Indes.* 6 vols. Amsterdam: s.n., 1770.

Réaumur, René-Antoine Ferchault de. *The Art of Hatching and Bringing up Domestic Fowls, by Means of Artificial Heat. . . . Translated from the French.* London: C. Davis, 1750.

Reese, George, ed. *The Official Papers of Francis Fauquier, Lieutenant Governor of Virginia, 1758–1768.* 3 vols. Charlottesville: Published for the Virginia Historical Society by the University of Virginia Press, 1980–83.

Reid, Thomas. *An Inquiry into the Human Mind, on the Principles of Common Sense.* Edinburgh: A. Millar, 1764.

Reid-Maroney, Nina. *Philadelphia's Enlightenment, 1740–1800: Kingdom of Christ, Empire of Reason.* Westport, Conn.: Greenwood, 2001.

Rice, Howard. "Jefferson's Gift of Fossils to the Museum of Natural History in Paris." *American Philosophical Society Proceedings* 95 (1951): 597–627.

Rice, Howard. *The Rittenhouse Orrery: Princeton's Eighteenth-Century Planetarium, 1767–1954; A Commentary on an Exhibition Held in the Princeton University Library.* Princeton: Princeton University Library, 1954.

Richard, Carl. *The Founders and the Classics: Greece, Rome, and the American Enlightenment.* Cambridge: Harvard University Press, 1994.

Richardson, Robert D., Jr. "Introduction." In Charles-François Dupuis, *The Origins of All Religious Worship.* New York: Garland, 1984. v–vii.

Rigal, Laura. *The American Manufactory: Art, Labor, and the World of Things in the Early Republic.* Princeton: Princeton University Press, 1998.

Rigal, Laura. "Peale's Mammoth." In *American Iconology: New Approaches to Nineteenth-Century Art and Literature*, ed. David C. Miller. New Haven: Yale University Press, 1993. 18–38.

Ring, Betty. *Girlhood Embroidery: American Samplers and Pictorial Needlework, 1650–1850.* 2 vols. New York: Knopf, 1993.

Robbins, Caroline. *The Eighteenth-Century Commonwealthman: Studies in the Transmission, Development and Circumstance of English Liberal Thought from the Restoration of Charles II until the War with the Thirteen Colonies.* Cambridge: Harvard University Press, 1959.

Roberts, Jane. *Royal Landscape: The Gardens and Parks of Windsor.* New Haven: Yale University Press, 1997.

Roberts, Jane, ed. *George III and Queen Charlotte: Patronage, Collecting, and Court Taste.* London: Royal Collection Publications, 2006.

Roberts, Justin. *Slavery and the Enlightenment in the British Atlantic, 1750–1807.* Cambridge: Cambridge University Press, 2013.

Robertson, Donald. *Mexican Manuscript Painting of the Early Colonial Period: The Metropolitan Schools.* New Haven: Yale University Press, 1959.

Robertson, John. *The Case for the Enlightenment: Scotland and Naples, 1680–1760.* Cambridge: Cambridge University Press, 2005.

Robertson, William. *The History of America.* 2 vols. London: W. Strahan and T. Cadell, 1777.

Robson, David. *Educating Republicans: The College in the Era of the American Revolution, 1750–1800.* Westport, Conn.: Greenwood, 1985.

Rochefoucauld-Liancourt, François Alexandre Frédéric, duc de la. *Travels Through the United States of North America, the Country of the Iroquois, and*

Upper Canada, in the Years 1795, 1796, and 1797; with an Authentic Account of Lower Canada. 2 vols. London: R. Phillips, 1799.

Rogers, Robert. *A Concise Account of North America.* London: Printed for the author and sold by J. Millan, 1765.

Romans, Bernard. *A Concise Natural History of East and West Florida.* New York: Printed for the author, 1775.

Ronda, James P. "Lewis and Clark and Enlightenment Ethnography." In *Enlightenment Science in the Pacific Northwest: The Lewis and Clark Expedition,* ed. William F. Willingham and Leonoor Swets Ingraham. Portland, Ore.: Dynagraphics, Inc., for Lewis and Clark College, 1984. 5–17.

Ross, Earle D. "Benjamin Franklin as an Eighteenth-Century Agricultural Leader." *Journal of Political Economy* 37, no. 1 (February 1929): 57–72.

Ross, Ian Simpson. *Lord Kames and the Scotland of His Day.* Oxford: Clarendon, 1972.

Rossi, Paolo. *The Dark Abyss of Time: The History of Earth and the History of Nations from Hooke to Vico.* Trans. Lydia G. Cochrane. Chicago: University of Chicago Press, 1984.

Rothschild, Emma. *The Inner Life of Empires: An Eighteenth-Century History.* Princeton: Princeton University Press, 2011.

Rudwick, Martin. *Bursting the Limits of Time: The Reconstruction of Geohistory in the Age of Revolution.* Chicago: University of Chicago Press, 2005.

Rudwick, Martin. "Geohistory and the Historicity of Genesis." In *Jean-André Deluc: Historian of Earth and Man,* ed. J. L. Heilbron and René Sigrist. Geneva: Slatkine Érudition, 2011. 242–60.

Rudwick, Martin. *The Meaning of Fossils: Episodes in the History of Palaeontology.* London: Macdonald, 1972.

Rumford, Benjamin, Graf von. *The Complete Works of Count Rumford.* 5 vols. London: Macmillan, 1875–76.

Rush, Benjamin. *An Address to the Inhabitants of the British Settlements in America, upon Slave-Keeping.* Boston: John Boyles, for John Langdon, 1773.

Ryan, Michael. "Assimilating New Worlds in the Sixteenth and Seventeenth Centuries." *Comparative Studies in Society and History* 23, no. 4 (October 1981): 519–38.

Safier, Neil. *Measuring the New World: Enlightenment Science and South America.* Chicago: University of Chicago Press, 2008.

Sala-Molins, Louis. *Les Misères des lumières: sous la raison, l'outrage.* Paris: R. Laffont, 1992.

Sanders, Daniel Clarke. *A History of the Indian Wars with the First Settlers of the United States to the Commencement of the Late War.* Rochester, N.Y.: Edwin Scrantom, 1828.

Saugera, Éric. *Bordeaux, Port Négrier: chronologie, économie, idéologie, XVIIe–XIXe siècles.* Biarritz: J & D éditions; Paris: Karthala, 1995.

Sauvagère, Felix-François de la. *Recueil de dissertations … avec de nouvelles assertions sur la végétation spontanée des coquilles du Château des Places, des dessins d'une collection de coquilles fossiles de la Touraine et de l'Anjou; de nouvelles idées sur la Falunière de Touraine, et plusieurs lettres de M. de Voltaire, relatives à ces différents objets.* Paris: Vve Duschesne, Vve Tilliard, 1776.

Say, Jean-Baptiste. *Traité d'économie politique; ou, Simple exposition de la manière dont se forment, se distribuent, et se consomment les richesses.* 2 vols. Paris: De L'Imprimerie de Crapelet, 1803.

Sayre, Gordon. "The Mound Builders and the Imagination of American Antiquity in Jefferson, Bartram, and Chateaubriand." *Early American Literature* 33 (1998): 225–49.

Schiebinger, Londa. *Plants and Empire: Colonial Bioprospecting in the Atlantic World.* Cambridge: Harvard University Press, 2004.

Schmidt, James. "Inventing the Enlightenment: Anti-Jacobins, British Hegelians, and the *Oxford English Dictionary*." *Journal of the History of Ideas* 64, no. 3 (July 2003): 421–43.

Schmidt, James. "The Question of Enlightenment: Kant, Mendelssohn, and the *Mittwochsgesellschaft*." *Journal of the History of Ideas* 50, no. 2 (April–June 1989): 269–91.

Schmidt, Leigh Eric. *Hearing Things: Religion, Illusion, and the American Enlightenment.* Cambridge: Harvard University Press, 2000.

Schoolcraft, Henry Rowe. *Travels in the Central Portions of the Mississippi Valley: Comprising Observations on Its Mineral Geography, Internal Resources, and Aboriginal Population.* New York: Collins and Hannay, 1825.

Scott, Hamish M., ed. *Enlightened Absolutism: Reform and Reformers in Later Eighteenth-Century Europe.* Basingstoke, Hampshire, UK: Macmillan, 1990.

Sebastiani, Silvia. *The Scottish Enlightenment: Race, Gender, and the Limits of Progress.* Trans. Jeremy Carden. New York: Palgrave Macmillan, 2013.

Sedgwick, Romney, ed. *Letters from George III to Lord Bute, 1756–1766.* London: Macmillan, 1939.

Seeber, Edward Derbyshire. *Anti-Slavery Opinion in France During the Second Half of the Eighteenth Century.* 1937; repr. New York: Burt Franklin, 1971.

Segal, Sam. *A Prosperous Past: The Sumptuous Still Life in the Netherlands, 1600–1700.* Ed. William B. Jordan. The Hague: SDU Publishers, 1988.

Sellers, Charles Coleman. *Mr. Peale's Museum: Charles Willson Peale and the First Popular Museum of Natural Science and Art.* New York: Norton, 1980.

Semonin, Paul. *American Monster: How the Nation's First Prehistoric Creature Became a Symbol of National Identity.* New York: New York University Press, 2000.

Sewall, Samuel. *The Selling of Joseph: A Memorial.* Ed. Sidney Kaplan. Northampton: University of Massachusetts Press, 1969.

Shaw, Helen Louise. *British Administration of the Southern Indians, 1756–1783.* Lancaster, Pa.: Lancaster Press, 1931.

Sheehan, Jonathan. "Sacred and Profane: Idolatry, Antiquarianism and the Polemics of Distinction in the Seventeenth Century." *Past and Present* 192 (August 2006): 35–66.

Shelford, April. *Transforming the Republic of Letters: Pierre-Daniel Huet and European Intellectual Life, 1650–1720.* Rochester, N.Y.: University of Rochester Press, 2007.

Sher, Richard. *The Enlightenment and the Book: Scottish Authors and Their Publishers in Eighteenth-Century Britain, Ireland, and America.* Chicago: University of Chicago Press, 2006.

Shields, David S. *Civil Tongues and Polite Letters in British America.* Chapel Hill: Published for the Omohundro Institute of Early American History and Culture, Williamsburg, Virginia, by the University of North Carolina Press, 1997.

Shields, David S. "The Manuscript in the British American World of Print." *Proceedings of the American Antiquarian Society* 102, no. 2 (1993): 403–16.

Short, Thomas. *A Comparative History of the Increase and Decrease of Mankind in England, and Several Countries Abroad, According to the Different Soils, Situations, Business of Life, Use of the Non-Naturals, &c. Faithfully Collected from, and Attested by, Above Three Hundred Vouchers, and Many of Them for a Long Course of Years, in Two Different Periods.* London: W. Nicoll, 1767.

Silverberg, Robert. *Mound Builders of Ancient America: The Archaeology of a Myth.* Greenwich, Conn.: New York Graphic Society, 1968.

Silverman, Kenneth, comp. *Selected Letters of Cotton Mather.* Baton Rouge: Louisiana State University Press, 1971.

Simms, Brendan, and Torsten Riotte, eds. *The Hanoverian Dimension in British History, 1714–1837.* Cambridge: Cambridge University Press, 2007.

Simpson, George. "The Beginnings of Vertebrate Paleontology in North America." *Proceedings of the American Philosophical Society* 86 (1942): 130–88.

Sinclair, John. *The Statistical Account of Scotland.* 21 vols. Edinburgh: William Creech, 1791–99.

Skinner, Andrew. "James Steuart: Aspects of Economic Policy." In *The Economics of James Steuart*, ed. Ramón Tortajada. London: Routledge, 1999. 139–50.

Skinner, Quentin. *The Foundations of Modern Political Thought.* 2 vols. Cambridge: Cambridge University Press, 1978.

Sklansky, Jeffrey. *The Soul's Economy: Market Society and Selfhood in American Thought, 1820–1920.* Chapel Hill: University of North Carolina Press, 2002.

Sloan, Douglas. *The Scottish Enlightenment and the American College Ideal.* New York: Teachers College Press of Columbia University, 1971.

Sloan, Kim. *A New World: England's First View of America.* Chapel Hill: University of North Carolina Press, 2007.

Sloane, Hans. *A Voyage to the Islands Madera, Barbados, Nieves, S. Christophers and Jamaica, with the Natural History of the Herbs and Trees, Four-footed Beasts, Fishes, Birds, Insects, Reptiles, &c.* 2 vols. London: B. M., 1707.

Slotkin, Richard. *Regeneration Through Violence: The Mythology of the American Frontier, 1600–1860.* Middletown, Conn.: Wesleyan University Press, 1973.

Smith, Adam. *The Glasgow Edition of the Works and Correspondence of Adam Smith: Adam Smith's Library, a Catalogue.* Electronic Edition. Ed. Hiroshi Mizuta. Charlottesville, Va.: InteLex Corporation, 2002.

Smith, Adam. *An Inquiry into the Nature and Causes of the Wealth of Nations.* 2 vols. London: W. Strahan and T. Cadell, 1776.

Smith, Adam. *An Inquiry into the Nature and Causes of the Wealth of Nations.* 3 vols. Dublin: Whitestone, et al., 1776.

Smith, Adam. *The Theory of Moral Sentiments. To Which Is Added a Dissertation on the Origin of Languages.* 1759; repr. London: A. Millar, A. Kincaid and J. Bell in Edinburgh, 1767.

Smith, John. *A Map of Virginia.* Oxford: Joseph Barnes, 1612.

Smith, Pamela, and Paula Findlen, eds. *Merchants and Marvels: Commerce, Science, and Art in Early Modern Europe.* New York: Routledge, 2002.

Smith, Samuel Stanhope. *An Essay on the Causes of the Variety of Complexion and Figure in the Human Species. To Which Are Added, Strictures on Lord Kaims's Discourse on the Original Diversity of Mankind.* Philadelphia: Robert Aitken, 1787.

Smith, Samuel Stanhope. *The Lectures, Corrected and Improved, Which Have Been Delivered for a Series of Years, in the College of New Jersey; On the Subjects of Moral and Political Philosophy.* 2 vols. Trenton, N.J.: Daniel Fenton, 1812.

Smith, Sydney. "[Review of] *Statistical Annals of the United States of America,* by Adam Seybert." *Edinburgh Review* 33 (January 1820): 69–80.

Smith, William. *The History of the Province of New-York, from the First Discovery to the Year M.DCC.XXXII.* London: Thomas Wilcox, 1757.

Smith, William. *Some Thoughts on Education: With Reasons for Erecting a College in this Province, and Fixing the Same at the City of New-York.* New York: James Parker, 1752.

Smolinski, Reiner, and Jan Stievermann, eds. *Cotton Mather and "Biblia Americana": America's First Bible Commentary.* 4 vols. to date. Tübingen: Mohr Siebeck, 2010–.

Solberg, Winton U., ed. *The Christian Philosopher / Cotton Mather.* Urbana: University of Illinois Press, 1994.

Soulavie, Jean-Marie Giraud. *Histoire naturelle de la France méridionale.* 7 vols. Paris: J. F. Quillau, 1780–84.

Souligné, de. *A Comparison Between Old Rome in Its Glory, as to the Extent and Populousness, and London as It Is at Present.* London: John Nutt, 1706.

Speeches on the Passage of the Bill for the Removal of the Indians, Delivered in the Congress of the United States, April and May, 1830. Boston: Perkins and Marvin, 1830.

Spencer, Mark G., ed. *The Bloomsbury Encyclopedia of the American Enlightenment.* 2 vols. New York: Bloomsbury, 2015.

Spengler, J. J. "Malthusianism in Late Eighteenth Century America." *American Economic Review* 25, no. 4 (December 1935): 691–707.

Squier, Ephraim G., and Edwin H. Davis. *Ancient Monuments of the Mississippi Valley.* New York: Bartlett and Welford, 1848.

Stabile, Susan. *Memory's Daughters: The Material Culture of Remembrance in Eighteenth-Century America.* Ithaca: Cornell University Press, 2004.

Staloff, Darren. *Hamilton, Adams, Jefferson: The Politics of Enlightenment and the American Founding.* New York: Hill and Wang, 2005.

Stanford, Donald E. "The Giant Bones of Claverack, New York, 1705." *New York History* 40, no. 1 (January 1959): 47–61.

Stanton, Lucia. *Free Some Day: The African-American Families of Monticello.* Charlottesville: Thomas Jefferson Foundation, 2000.

Stanwood, Owen. "Catholics, Protestants, and the Clash of Civilizations in Early America." In *The First Prejudice: Religious Tolerance and Intolerance in Early America*, ed. Chris Beneke and Christopher S. Grenda. Philadelphia: University of Pennsylvania Press, 2011. 218–40.

Stanwood, Owen. "The Protestant Moment: Antipopery, the Revolution of 1688–1689, and the Making of an Anglo-American Empire." *Journal of British Studies* 46, no. 3 (July 2007): 481–508.

Stapelbroek, Koen, and Jani Marjanen, eds. *The Rise of Economic Societies in the Eighteenth Century: Patriotic Reform in Europe and North America.* Houndmills, Basingstoke, UK: Palgrave Macmillan, 2012.

Stearns, Raymond Phineas. *Science in the British Colonies of America.* Urbana: University of Illinois Press, 1970.

Stein, Robert L. *The French Sugar Business in the Eighteenth Century.* Baton Rouge: Louisiana State University Press, 1988.

Steiner, Bill. *Audubon Art Prints: A Collector's Guide to Every Edition.* Columbia: University of South Carolina Press, 2003.

Steuart, James. *An Inquiry into the Principles of Political Oeconomy; Being an Essay on the Science of Domestic Policy in Free Nations.* 2 vols. London: A Millar and T. Cadell, 1767.

Stiles, Ezra. *A Discourse on the Christian Union: The Substance of Which Was Delivered Before the Reverend Convention of the Congregational Clergy in the Colony of Rhode-Island; Assembled at Bristol April 23, 1760.* Boston: Edes and Gill, 1761.

Stiles, Ezra. *The United States Elevated to Glory and Honor.* 1783; Worcester, Mass.: Isaiah Thomas, 1785.

Stone, Lawrence, ed. *The University in Society.* 2 vols. Princeton: Princeton University Press, 1974.

Styles, John, and Amanda Vickery, eds. *Gender, Taste, and Material Culture in Britain and North America, 1700–1830.* New Haven: Yale University Press, 2006.

Sullivan, James, ed. *The Papers of Sir William Johnson*. 14 vols. Albany: University of the State of New York, 1921–65.

Taylor, John ["A Citizen of Virginia"]. *Arator; Being a Series of Agricultural Essays, Practical & Political: In Sixty One Numbers*. Georgetown [Washington, D.C.]: J. M. and J. B. Carter, 1813.

Taylor, John. *An Inquiry into the Principles and Policy of the Government of the United States*. Fredericksburg, Va.: Green and Cady, 1814.

Taylor, Stephen, Richard Connors, and Clyve Jones, eds. *Hanoverian Britain and Empire: Essays in Memory of Philip Lawson*. Woodbridge, Suffolk, UK: Boydell Press, 1998.

Thomson, Keith S. *The Legacy of the Mastodon: The Golden Age of Fossils in America*. New Haven: Yale University Press, 2008.

Thompson, Andrew C. *George II: King and Elector*. New Haven: Yale University Press, 2011.

Thornton, Russell. *American Indian Holocaust and Survival: A Population History Since 1492*. Norman: University of Oklahoma Press, 1987.

Thornton, Tamara Plakins. *Handwriting in America: A Cultural History*. New Haven: Yale University Press, 1996.

Thuesen, Peter J., ed. *Catalogues of Books*. Vol. 26 of *The Works of Jonathan Edwards*. New Haven: Yale University Press, 2008.

Thwaites, Reuben Gold, ed. *The Jesuit Relations and Allied Documents*. 73 vols. Cleveland, Ohio: Burrows Brothers, 1896–1901.

Tillotson, John. *Sermons Preach'd upon Several Occasions*. London: A. M. for Sa. Gellibrand, 1671.

Tinling, Marion, ed. *The Correspondence of the Three William Byrds of Westover, Virginia, 1684–1776*. 2 vols. Charlottesville: Published for the Virginia Historical Society by the University Press of Virginia, 1977.

Tolles, Frederick B. *George Logan of Philadelphia*. New York: Oxford University Press, 1953.

Tolles, Frederick B. "Unofficial Ambassador: George Logan's Mission to France, 1798." *William and Mary Quarterly* 7, no. 1 (January 1950): 1–25.

Torre, Jose R. *The Political Economy of Sentiment: Paper Credit and the Scottish Enlightenment in Early Republic Boston, 1780–1820*. London: Pickering and Chatto, 2006.

Towner, Lawrence W. "The Sewall-Saffin Dialogue on Slavery." *William and Mary Quarterly* 21, no. 1 (January 1964): 40–52.

Trumbull, Benjamin. *A Complete History of Connecticut, Civil and Ecclesiastical, from the Emigration of Its First Planters from England, in MDCXXX, to MDCCXIII*. Hartford: Hudson and Goodwin, 1797.

Tucker, St. George. *Blackstone's Commentaries: With Notes of Reference, to the Constitution and Laws, of the Federal Government of the United States; and of the Commonwealth of Virginia*. 5 vols. Philadelphia: William Young Birch and Abraham Small, 1803.

Tucker, St. George. *A Dissertation on Slavery: With a Proposal for the Gradual Abolition of It, in the State of Virginia.* Philadelphia: M. Carey, 1796.

Tucker, St. George. "Queries Respecting the Slavery and Emancipation of Negroes in Massachusetts, Proposed by the Hon. Judge Tucker of Virginia, and Answered by Dr. Belknap." *Massachusetts Historical Society Collections* ser. 1, 4 (1795): 191–211.

Tufte, Edward. *The Visual Display of Quantitative Information.* 1983; repr. Cheshire, Conn.: Graphics Press, 2001.

Turnbull, Gordon. *Letters to a Young Planter; or, Observations on the Management of a Sugar-Plantation.* London: Stuart and Stevenson, 1785.

Turner, Charles. *A Sermon Preached Before His Excellency Thomas Hutchinson, Esq; Governor: The Honorable His Majesty's Council, and the Honorable House of Representatives, of the Province of the Massachusetts-Bay in New-England, May 26. 1773.* Boston: Richard Draper, 1773.

Turner, James. *Religion Enters the Academy: The Origins of the Scholarly Study of Religion in America.* Athens: University of Georgia Press, 2011.

Turner, James. *Without God, Without Creed: The Origins of Unbelief in America.* Baltimore: Johns Hopkins University Press, 1985.

Tylor, Edward Burnet. *Anahuac; or, Mexico and the Mexicans, Ancient and Modern.* London: Longman, Green, Longman, and Roberts, 1861.

Ulloa, Antonio de. *Noticias americanas.* Madrid: Don Francisco Manuel de Mena, 1772.

Vardi, Liana. *The Physiocrats and the World of the Enlightenment.* Cambridge: Cambridge University Press, 2012.

View of Exertions Lately Made for the Purpose of Colonizing the Free People of Colour, in the United States, in Africa, or Elsewhere, A. Washington, D.C.: Jonathan Elliot, 1817.

Villela, Khristaan D., and Mary Ellen Miller, eds. *The Aztec Calendar Stone.* Los Angeles: Getty Research Institute, 2010.

Volney, Constantin-François de Chasseboeuf, comte de. *Les Ruines; ou, Méditation sur les révolutions des empires.* Paris: Desenne, 1791.

Volney, Constantin-François de Chasseboeuf, comte de. *The Ruins; or, A Survey of the Revolutions of Empires.* New York: William A. Davis, 1796.

Volney, Constantin-François de Chasseboeuf, comte de. *Tableau du climat et du sol des Etats-Unis d'Amérique.* Paris: Chez Courcier, 1803.

Volney, Constantin François de Chasseboeuf, comte de. *View of the Climate and Soil of the United States of America* London: J. Johnson, 1804.

Voltaire, "Des coquilles et des systêmes batis sur des coquilles." In *Quéstions sur l'encyclopédie.* Vol. 4: *CIC.-DAV.* London: s.n., 1771. 114–30.

Voltaire. *An Essay on Universal History.* 4 vols. 1756; repr. London: J. Nourse, 1759.

Voltaire. *Letters Concerning the English Nation.* London: C. Davis and A. Lyon, 1733.

Wainwright, Nicholas B., ed. "George Croghan's Journal April 3, 1759–April [30], 1763." *Pennsylvania Magazine of History and Biography* 71, no. 4 (October 1947): 313–444.

Walch, Timothy, ed. *Early American Catholicism, 1634–1820: Selected Historical Essays*. New York: Garland, 1988.

Walker, Thomas D. "The State of Libraries in Eighteenth-Century Europe: Adalbert Blumenschein's 'Beschreibung Verschiedener Bibliotheken in Europa.' " *Library Quarterly* 65, no. 3 (July 1995): 269–94.

Wallace, Anthony F. *Jefferson and the Indians: The Tragic Fate of the First Americans*. Cambridge, Mass.: Belknap, 1999.

Wallace, Robert. *A Dissertation on the Numbers of Mankind in Antient and Modern Times: In Which the Superior Populousness of Antiquity Is Maintained*. Edinburgh: G. Hamilton and J. Balfour, 1753.

Warburton, William. *The Divine Legation of Moses Demonstrated*. 2 vols. London: Fletcher Gyles, 1738–41.

Warner, Michael. *The Letters of the Republic: Publication and the Public Sphere in Eighteenth-Century America*. Cambridge: Harvard University Press, 1990.

Waterman, Bryan. *Republic of Intellect: The Friendly Club of New York City and the Making of American Literature*. Baltimore: Johns Hopkins University Press, 2007.

Weber, David. *Bárbaros: Spaniards and Their Savages in the Age of Enlightenment*. New Haven: Yale University Press, 2005.

Weems, Mason Locke. *A History of the Life and Death, Virtues and Exploits, of General George Washington*. 3rd ed. Philadelphia: John Bioren, 1800.

Wells, Robert V. *The Population of the British Colonies in America Before 1776: A Survey of Census Data*. Princeton: Princeton University Press, 1975.

Wertenbaker, Thomas Jefferson. *Princeton, 1746–1896*. 1946; repr. Princeton: Princeton University Press, 1996.

Whatley, George. *Principles of Trade*. London: Brotherton and Sewell, 1774.

Whelan, Frederick G. "Population and Ideology in the Enlightenment." *History of Political Thought* 12, no. 1 (1991): 35–72.

Whiston, William. *A New Theory of the Earth, from Its Original, to the Consummation of All Things*. London: R. Roberts, for Benjamin Tooke, 1696.

Whitefield, George. *A Select Collection of Letters of the Late Reverend George Whitefield, M. A.* 3 vols. London: Edward and Charles Dilly, 1772.

Whitehead, James L., ed. "Notes and Documents. The Autobiography of Peter Stephen Du Ponceau. V." *Pennsylvania Magazine of History and Biography* 64, no. 2 (April 1940): 243–69.

Whiteman, Anne, John Selwyn Bromley, and Peter George Muir Dickson, eds. *Statesmen, Scholars and Merchants: Essays in Eighteenth-Century History Presented to Dame Lucy Sutherland*. Oxford: Clarendon, 1973.

Wills, Garry. *Cincinnatus: George Washington and the Enlightenment*. Garden City, N.Y.: Doubleday, 1984.

Wilson, Douglas L. "Thomas Jefferson's Early Notebooks." *William and Mary Quarterly* 3rd ser., 42, no. 4 (October 1985): 433–52.

Winch, Donald. *Riches and Poverty: An Intellectual History of Political Economy in Britain, 1750–1834.* Cambridge: Cambridge University Press, 1996.

Winchester, Elhanan. *Ten Letters Addressed to Mr. Paine, in Answer to His Pamphlet, Entitled The Age of Reason: Containing Some Clear and Satisfying Evidences of the Truth of Divine Revelation; and Especially of the Resurrection and Ascension of Jesus.* 1794; repr. New York: Samuel Campbell, 1795.

Winterer, Caroline. *The Culture of Classicism: Ancient Greece and Rome in American Intellectual Life, 1780–1910.* Baltimore: Johns Hopkins University Press, 2002.

Winterer, Caroline. "Is There an Intellectual History of Early American Women?" *Modern Intellectual History* 4, no. 1 (April 2007): 173–90.

Winterer, Caroline. *The Mirror of Antiquity: American Women and the Classical Tradition, 1750–1900.* Ithaca: Cornell University Press, 2007.

Winterer, Caroline. "Model Empire, Lost City: Ancient Carthage and the Science of Politics in Revolutionary America." *William and Mary Quarterly* 67, no. 1 (January 2010): 3–30.

Winterer, Caroline. "What Was the American Enlightenment?" In *The Worlds of American Intellectual History,* ed. Joel Isaac, James Kloppenberg, Michael O'Brien, and Jennifer Ratner-Rosenhagen. New York: Oxford University Press, 2016.

Winterer, Caroline. "Where Is America in the Republic of Letters?" *Modern Intellectual History* 9, no. 3 (November 2012): 597–623.

Winthrop, John. *Two Lectures on the Parallax and Distance of the Sun, as Deducible from the Transit of Venus.* Boston: Edes and Gill, 1769.

"Winthrop Papers, The." *Massachusetts Historical Society Collections,* 6th ser., 5 (1892): 5–511.

Withers, Charles W. J. *Placing the Enlightenment: Thinking Geographically About the Age of Reason.* Chicago: University of Chicago Press, 2007.

Withey, Lynne. *Dearest Friend: A Life of Abigail Adams.* New York: Free Press, 1981.

Wolf, Edwin, 2d. "The Dispersal of the Library of William Byrd of Westover." *Proceedings of the American Antiquarian Society* 68 (April 1958): 19–106.

Wolf, Edwin, 2d. *James Logan, 1674–1751: Bookman Extraordinary; An Exhibition of Books and Manuscripts from the Library of James Logan, Supplemented by His Writings and Documents Relating to the History of the Bibliotheca Loganiana.* Philadelphia: Library Company of Philadelphia, 1971.

Wolf, Edwin, 2d. *The Library of James Logan of Philadelphia, 1674–1751.* Philadelphia: Library Company of Philadelphia, 1974.

Wolf, Edwin, 2d, and Kevin J. Hayes. *The Library of Benjamin Franklin.* Philadelphia: American Philosophical Society and Library Company of Philadelphia, 2006.

Wolf, Eva Sheppard. *Race and Liberty in the New Nation: Emancipation in Virginia from the Revolution to Nat Turner's Rebellion.* Baton Rouge: Louisiana State University Press, 2006.

Wollstonecraft, Mary. *A Vindication of the Rights of Woman: With Strictures on Political and Moral Subjects.* London: J. Johnson, 1792.

Wood, Gordon S. "The American Enlightenment." In Gary L. McDowell and Johnathan O'Neill, eds., *America and Enlightenment Constitutionalism.* New York: Palgrave Macmillan, 2006. 159–75.

Wood, Peter. *Black Majority: Negroes in Colonial South Carolina from 1670 Through the Stono Rebellion.* New York: Knopf, 1974.

Woodward, John. *An Essay Toward a Natural History of the Earth: And Terrestrial Bodies, Especially Minerals.* 1695; London: T. W. for Richard Wilkin, 1702.

Woodward, Walter W. *Prospero's America: John Winthrop, Jr., Alchemy, and the Creation of New England Culture, 1606–1676.* Chapel Hill: Published for the Omohundro Institute of Early American History and Culture, Williamsburg, Virginia, by the University of North Carolina Press, 2010.

Young, Alfred F. *Liberty Tree: Ordinary People and the American Revolution.* New York: New York University Press, 2006.

Young, Arthur. *The Farmer's Letters to the People of England.* London: W. Nicoll, 1767.

Young, Arthur. *Political Arithmetic.* London: W. Nicoll, 1774.

Zagarri, Rosemarie. *Revolutionary Backlash: Women and Politics in the Early American Republic.* Philadelphia: University of Pennsylvania Press, 2007.

Zakai, Avihu. *Jonathan Edwards's Philosophy of History: The Re-Enchantment of the World in the Age of Enlightenment.* Princeton: Princeton University Press, 2003.

Zakai, Avihu. *Jonathan Edwards's Philosophy of Nature: The Re-Enchantment of the World in the Age of Scientific Reasoning.* London: T. and T. Clark, 2010.

Ziesche, Phillip. "Thomas Paine and Benjamin Franklin's French Circle." In *Paine and Jefferson in the Age of Revolutions,* ed. Simon P. Newman and Peter S. Onuf. Charlottesville: University of Virginia Press, 2013. 121–36.

Index

Page numbers in *italic* type indicate illustrations.